1990

Dante and the Medieval Other World

A major new study of the *Divine Comedy*, this book offers an original perspective on Dante's representation of the afterlife. Dr Morgan departs from the conventional critical emphasis on Dante's place in relation to the learned tradition of such representations by undertaking the first thorough examination of the poem in the context of popular beliefs. Her principal sources are thus not the highly literary texts (such as Virgil's *Aeneid* or Thomas Aquinas's *Summa Theologiae*) which have become a familiar context for the poem, but rather the visions of the other world found in popular writings, painting and sculpture from the centuries leading up to its composition. The view of Dante which emerges from this investigation calls for a radical revision of modern critical opinion concerning the nature of his originality.

The book will be of interest to non-specialists as well as to scholars of Dante, since it offers a clear preliminary account of the other world tradition, supported by appendices giving a chronology of its principal representations and summaries of the major texts. Fully illustrated throughout, it integrates with the literary and theological aspects of Dante's heritage the important but hitherto neglected dimension of art history.

CAMBRIDGE STUDIES IN MEDIEVAL LITERATURE

General Editor: Professor Alastair Minnis, Professor of Medieval
Literature, University of York

Editorial Board
Professor Piero Boitani (Professor of English, Rome)
Professor Patrick Boyde (Serena Professor of Italian, Cambridge)
Professor John Burrow, FBA (Winterstoke Professor of English, Bristol)
Peter Dronke, FBA (Reader in Medieval Latin Literature, Cambridge)
Professor John Freccero (Rosina Pierotti Professor of Italian, Stanford)
Tony Hunt (Reader in French, St Andrew's)
Dr Nigel Palmer (Lecturer in Medieval German, Oxford)
Professor Winthrop Wetherbee (Professor of English, Cornell)

This series of critical books seeks to cover the whole area of literature written
in the major medieval languages – the main European vernaculars, and
Medieval Latin and Greek – during the period *c.* 1100–*c.* 1500. Its chief aim is
to publish and stimulate fresh scholarship and criticism on medieval literature,
special emphasis being placed on understanding major works of poetry, prose
and drama in relation to the contemporary cultures and learning which
fostered them.

Dante and the
Medieval Other World

ALISON MORGAN

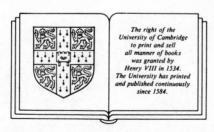

The right of the
University of Cambridge
to print and sell
all manner of books
was granted by
Henry VIII in 1534.
The University has printed
and published continuously
since 1584.

CAMBRIDGE UNIVERSITY PRESS

Cambridge

New York   Port Chester   Melbourne   Sydney

Published by the Press Syndicate of the University of Cambridge
The Pitt Building, Trumpington Street, Cambridge CB2 1RP
40 West 20th Street, New York, NY 10011, USA
10 Stamford Road, Oakleigh, Melbourne 3166, Australia

First published 1990

Printed in Great Britain at the University Press, Cambridge

British Library cataloguing in publication data
Morgan, Alison
Dante and the medieval other world. – (Cambridge studies in medieval literature; 8)
1. Poetry in Italian. Dante Alighieri, 1265–1321.
Critical studies
1. Title
851'.1

Library of Congress cataloguing in publication data applied for

ISBN 0 521 36069 2

Contents

Illustrations

Preface

This book has grown out of the dissertation submitted for the degree of Doctor of Philosophy and accepted by the University of Cambridge in 1986 under the title 'The Popular Representation of the Afterlife before Dante and its Relationship to the *Comedy*'. It is the fruit of a number of years' work, during which time I have become indebted to many people. In particular I would like to thank Patrick Boyde, who has been the source of unfailing stimulation, help and encouragement to me throughout that period. I am also most grateful to Robin Kirkpatrick and Philip McNair for their advice and comments, and to the students of the Italian departments in both Cambridge and Birmingham who have listened to, and commented upon, some of the ideas presented in this book in the form of lectures. My thanks must also go to Nicola Vollkommer, who assisted me with her fluent German; to my mother, Faith Keymer, who first taught me Italian; to my father, William Keymer, who made many detailed comments and compiled the index; and, last but not least, to my husband Roger for his consistent support.

The book is written for all those interested in Dante and in the medieval period, and I have therefore not assumed fluency in either Italian or Latin. Quotations from the *Comedy* are taken from the edition by Petrocchi, and biblical references from the Knox translation of the Vulgate. Translations from the *Comedy* and from those texts where no English translation is available are my own.

Introduction

The notion that man in some way survives death is found in all societies and civilisations from the earliest times up to the present day.[1] Although some of the beliefs of these societies are relevant to an understanding of Dante's *Comedy*, his poem is founded upon specifically Christian tenets regarding life after death, and it is therefore with these that we are primarily concerned. More particularly, this book explores the relationship between the poem and previous 'popular' Christian belief concerning the afterlife, as manifested in both written and visual representations of the other world between the third century and the year 1321, the date of Dante's death.[2] This 'popular' Christian tradition is defined in such a way as to exclude non-Christian, highly literary and learned works such as Virgil's *Aeneid*, Alan of Lille's *Anticlaudianus*, or the *Summa Theologiae* of Thomas Aquinas, although these may be discussed as background material.

The book is therefore based on the study of the hundred or so surviving non-learned texts purporting to describe the other world, and on significant works from the visual arts. For the reader's convenience these are set out in chronological order in Appendix I and alphabetically in Appendix II. Each entry in Appendix II gives a summary of the text together with information on its length and distribution and a short bibliography. The appendix is divided into two sections, the first of which deals with classical, apocryphal and early Christian representations of the other world, and the second of which is devoted to the medieval accounts. It is assumed that the reader will refer to these entries where necessary, and the information contained within them is therefore not repeated in the discussion itself. Unless otherwise stated, the short references given in the text and notes refer to the first edition cited in the appropriate entry of Appendix II (or, in the case of translations, to the first English edition). Full publication details for other works referred to in the notes are given in the main bibliography.

Written representations of the other world

The Christian accounts and visions of the other world with which this study is concerned fall within a period which stretches from the third century, when the *Apocalypse of Paul* is believed to have been written, to the fourteenth, when the *Comedy* was completed. They have their roots in both the classical and the biblical traditions, and ultimately therefore in the Eastern beliefs which influenced the formation of these.

Dante and the Medieval Other World

The classical tradition offers two very different models for the representation of the afterlife: the older consists of a shadowy underworld, first depicted by Homer and taken over by Virgil, Ovid and Statius; the other offers a description of the heavenly spheres, and forms the context for Plato's four myths of the other world and for two visions related by Plutarch.[3]

The biblical tradition spans over a thousand years, and shows a gradual evolution in belief. The Old Testament picture is of an underworld, Sheol, similar to that described by Homer: a land of darkness, gloom and oblivion, in which there is neither hope nor torment.[4] Later in the Old Testament the concept of resurrection is found,[5] and this is succeeded by the idea of a judgment following immediately on death; Sheol becomes an intermediate waiting place in which the good are separated from the bad. This concept is illustrated most fully in the intertestamental literature of the Hellenistic Age of Judaism,[6] and notably in the apocryphal *Book of Enoch*. In later works, such as *II Enoch*, the *Apocalypse of Baruch* and *IV Esdras*, Sheol becomes a place for the damned alone, while the good are admitted upon death to the heavens, thus foreshadowing the Christian distinction between heaven and hell.

The emphasis placed by the New Testament on the individual, rather than on the nation as in the Old Testament, leads to a greater preoccupation with his eternal destiny. It offers no systematic discussion of the nature of salvation or damnation, but the concept of judgment, whether on death or on an appointed day at the end of time, is firmly established.[7]

The apocrypha of the New Testament seek to supply the details lacking in the biblical texts.[8] In so doing they draw particularly on classical Greek works. The earliest of these books to survive is the *Apocalypse of Peter*; the most influential was the *Apocalypse of Paul*. They form the basis of the medieval representations of heaven and hell.

The early Christian literature concerning the other world is varied in nature but predominantly optimistic. Martyrs such as Perpetua and Saturus gave accounts of the visions they received before they died; other texts such as the visions of Carpus and Pachomius and the *Shepherd of Hermas* urge repentance of sin as the necessary precondition for salvation.

Although there are many earlier descriptions of the other world in literary, philosophical and religious works, it is not until the late sixth century that the vision of the other world becomes established as a genre. This is in large measure due to Gregory the Great, who includes several accounts of the afterlife in his *Dialogues*, and to his contemporary Gregory of Tours, who relates four visions in his *History of the Franks*. The *Dialogues* in particular served to confer the stamp of papal authority on visions of the other world, and are frequently cited by later visionaries.[9] Other visions of the period are recounted in the works of authoritative Churchmen, most important among these being Bede, whose *Ecclesiastical History* contains the visions of Furseus and Drythelm. These three writers gave a great impetus to the vision genre, at once giving respectability to the recording of visions of the other world and causing a number of visions to become widely known and eventually to serve as models for others. Their primary purpose seems to have been to use such accounts as a means of instructing the faithful and encouraging them to choose the way of salvation.

In the Carolingian era the character of the visions undergoes an abrupt change, becoming political and satirical in nature rather than didactic. The visionaries of this period are almost always monks, and the redactors usually bishops or archbishops – this contrasts with the preceding period, in which the visionaries include a soldier, a householder and a layman whose status is not specified.[10] The vision of the other world, in short, becomes a political weapon in the hands of the Church. The clearest example of this is the vision of Wetti, longer than any of its predecessors; the vision of Charles the Fat, of unknown authorship, is also political in its aims. Other texts aim to strengthen the power of the Church in other ways, notably by insisting on the necessity for prayers and masses to be purchased on behalf of the dead.

The tenth and eleventh centuries form an intermediate period in which there is no clearly discernible trend in the otherworld literature. This is not to say that the works produced are without importance. Two Irish texts were to become widely known on the Continent, the *Vision of Adamnan*, based on the apocrypha, and the *Voyage of Brendan*, based on Celtic legend and aptly described as 'a sort of monkish Odyssey'.[11] And at Ratisbon the first collection of visions of the other world was compiled by the monk Othlo.

The climax of the vision tradition, in terms both of the number of visions produced and of their amplitude, occurs in the twelfth century. The vision becomes not primarily didactic or political but literary in character. There is a complete change in the source of the visions: although they are still written by ecclesiastical figures, the majority of the visionaries are no longer clerics. Of the eight major visions of the twelfth century, only two are experienced by monks; of the others, two are related by peasants, two by children and two by knights. The redactors themselves are no longer powerful figures but humble monks or, occasionally, abbots.

The earliest of the major visions is that of Alberic, and the latest that of Thurkill, dated 1206 but belonging in its character to the twelfth-century visions. The most widely known was the *Vision of Tundale*, of which there are over 200 extant manuscripts. This period also saw the composition and diffusion of the many redactions and translations of the *Vision of Paul*, the fourth- or fifth-century Latin version of the original Greek apocalypse.

The twelfth-century texts are much longer and more complex than any of their predecessors, and begin to reflect the social and intellectual changes with which they are contemporary. But at the same time the vision of the other world began to die as a genre. This may have been due to the changing structure of society, in particular the shift from the monasteries as the primary centres of learning to the cathedral schools and subsequently to the universities; or to the increasing complexity of the subject matter in the light of the many new ideas which gained ground during the century. No new visions are recorded after that of Thurkill in 1206, although old ones continue to be copied and included in histories and encyclopaedias with a wide circulation throughout Christian Europe, indicating that the tradition itself remained alive. The next complete representation of the other world after the *Vision of Thurkill* is the *Comedy*.

The visions of previous centuries are included in five major works of the thirteenth century, in which they would have been readily accessible to the educated reader. Earliest among these is the *Flowers of History* of Roger of Wendover, which gives an account of the visions of Drythelm, the Monk of Eynsham, and Thurkill, as well as the story of St Patrick's Purgatory; the latter three are repeated by Matthew Paris, whose *Great Chronicle* completes the *Flowers of History*. The chronicle of Helinand of Froidmont relates the visions of Charles the Fat, Gunthelm, Drythelm and Tundale; the *Golden Legend* includes *St Patrick's Purgatory* and the visions of Furseus, Josaphat and Perpetua. Finally, the historical section of Vincent of Beauvais's encyclopaedia gives an account of thirteen visions, together with those found in Gregory's *Dialogues*.[12] Additionally, brief and partial accounts of the other world are included in thirteenth-century collections of *exempla*, notably those of Caesarius of Heisterbach and Etienne of Bourbon.

It is not known to what extent Dante was acquainted with any one of the visions discussed above; it is clear, however, that the tradition was widespread during his lifetime. In addition to the works mentioned here, there were many vernacular translations made, particularly of *St Patrick's Purgatory* and the visions of Tundale and Paul; the French *trouvères* composed a number of light-hearted poems on the subject of the afterlife; and in Italy Bonvesin da Riva and Giacomino da Verona wrote didactic poems describing the celestial Jerusalem and the infernal Babylon. It was also in this century that the legend of Mohammed's journey to the other world reached Christian Europe from Spain. The vision tradition was known to Albert the Great, whose discussion of the other world refers to Gregory the Great and *St Patrick's Purgatory*; to Bonaventure, who considers *St Patrick's Purgatory*; and to Aquinas, who mentions the tradition in general.[13]

Visual representations of the other world

In addition to these translations and collections, many visual representations of the afterlife testify to the continued presence of the popular otherworld tradition during the thirteenth century. The Last Judgment was commonly represented on the cathedral tympana of twelfth- and thirteenth-century France, and many mosaics and paintings of the other world survive in churches all over Europe. The purpose of those who commissioned such works was to keep the question of their eternal destiny at the forefront of the minds of the faithful.[14] The words attributed by Villon to his mother are well known:

> Femme je suis povrecte et ancïenne,
> Qui riens ne sçay, onques lettres ne leuz.
> Au moustier voy, dont suis paroïssienne,
> Paradiz paint, ou sont harpes et leuz,
> Et ung enffer, ou dampnez sont bouluz;
> L'un me fait paour, l'autre joye et liesse.[15]

4

Introduction

[I am a poor and elderly woman, ignorant and unable to read. In my parish church I see paradise painted, with harps and lutes, and hell too, where the damned boil. The painting of hell frightens me, but that of paradise fills me with joy and happiness.]

Dante was familiar with such representations, and explains that his *Comedy* is written with the same purpose in mind:

> Cosí parlar conviensi al vostro ingegno,
> però che solo da sensato apprende
> ciò che fa poscia d'intelletto degno.
>   Per questo la Scrittura condescende
> a vostra facultate, e piedi e mano
> attribuisce a Dio e altro intende;
>   e Santa Chiesa con aspetto umano
> Gabriel e Michel vi rappresenta,
> e l'altro che Tobia rifece sano.
>
> (Par IV 40–8)

[It is necessary to speak in this way to your understanding, since only through the senses can it grasp that which it then makes fit for the intellect. For this reason Scripture condescends to your capacity and attributes hands and feet to God, but meaning something else, and the Holy Church represents in human form Gabriel and Michael and the other who made Tobit whole again.]

The Last Judgment is the form most commonly chosen for the illustration of the other world. Its iconography is Eastern in origin, and many of the Western frescoes show traces of Byzantine influence. It first appears in the West in the Carolingian era, in the schools of St Gall and Reichenau, but becomes widespread only in the twelfth century, particularly in England. The earliest representation in Italy is that painted in the late eleventh century at S. Angelo in Formis, a dependency of Montecassino; this was imitated throughout southern Italy and the Abruzzi. In the twelfth century the Last Judgment was represented in mosaic in the cathedral of Torcello, and by the thirteenth century the practice was firmly established; frescoes predating 1321 survive, in addition to the mosaic in the Florentine baptistry, in S. Cecilia in Trastevere, the Scrovegni Chapel in Padua, S. Maria Maggiore in Tuscania, S. Maria in Piano near Loreto Aprutino, and the church of Donnaregina, Naples. Derivatives of these continued to be painted throughout the fourteenth century.[16]

Critical approaches

The earliest reference to the medieval visions of the other world in relation to the *Comedy* is made in the commentary by Jacopo di Dante, who interprets the line 'Andovvi poi lo Vas d'elezïone' (Inf II 28) in the light of the *Vision of Paul*, 'il quale poi (. . .) pelinferno si misse'. Jacopo is followed by both the Anonimo fiorentino and Francesco da Buti.[17] This is the only line in the poem which could be interpreted as a clear reference to the vision literature, and has been accepted as such by a number of modern critics.[18]

Until the sixteenth century, the *Aeneid* was regarded as the only model for Dante's depiction of the afterlife. In 1587, attention was drawn to the popular tradition by Mazzoni; but it was not until the discovery of the *Vision of Alberic* that the vision literature began to receive serious critical attention. In 1752 Mazocchi became the first to suggest that *Alberic* was a direct source for the *Comedy*.[19] The 'Alberic debate' began in earnest the following year, and continued until the beginning of the present century, effectively setting the pattern for all discussion of the role of the vision literature in the formation of the *Comedy*. The debate focussed round one question: to what extent does the recurrence of common motifs in particular visions and in the *Comedy* suggest that Dante was imitating particular texts?[20] Other visions were soon claimed as sources for the *Comedy*. The *Vision of Tundale* received considerable attention, but *Furseus* and *St Patrick's Purgatory* were also suggested as models. In this century, *Adamnan*, *Charles the Fat*, *Ansellus* and *Drythelm* have been put forward as visions known to Dante.[21]

As more and more manuscripts of particular visions were discovered during the nineteenth century, a second critical approach arose: the visions were seen as members of a continuous tradition. This tradition was first outlined in 1844 by Wright, who emphasised its importance for Dante studies:

The *Divina Commedia* (. . .) has transmitted to modern ages the popular belief and knowledge of a period which has hitherto been very little understood by modern readers; who have therefore set down to his inventive imagination pictures and notions which were familiar to his contemporaries. Commentators have laboured to discover hidden meanings and allegorical descriptions, where an acquaintance with the popular science of the age of Dante would have shown nothing but literal description.[22]

Ozanam wrote along similar lines in 1839 and 1855, and Labitte in 1842. Ozanam regards the *Comedy* as the climax of a long, uninterrupted tradition and suggests that Dante's accomplishment is to have imposed order on a subject which had been developing over the previous six thousand years.[23] He sees the visions as the raw materials from which the poem is formed: 'either I am very much mistaken, or the framework of a great epic is forming, its outlines being drawn, its images taking on colour; but like the images of gothic stained glass windows, fire was needed to fuse them together'.[24]

Between 1865 and 1915 in Italy there prevailed a school of criticism known as the 'scuola storica'; this provided the context for the first Italian research into early representations of the afterlife and their relation to the *Comedy*.[25] In 1865 Villari published a number of vernacular translations of the otherworld legends, prefaced by an essay which sought to define them as precursors to the *Comedy*.[26] The studies of D'Ancona and Rajna in 1874 and 1908 reveal their closeness to the position of Ozanam and Labitte in their titles, respectively *I precursori di Dante* and *La genesi della 'Divina Commedia'*. D'Ancona defines the tradition thus: 'all these visions are links in a long chain which goes back to the earliest times'.[27]

The approach of these scholars has been followed by later critics. Dods in 1903 wrote on the *Forerunners of Dante*, remarking that 'the present research is not conducted from Dante backwards, but from the infancy of the idea forwards to the master interpreter as a convenient stopping place and climax'.[28] In 1922 Diels wrote an essay entitled 'Himmels- und Höllenfahrten von Homer bis Dante',[29] and Zabughin in his outline of the vision tradition remarked that 'Dante builds with a free and steady hand, but his materials are all taken from tradition'.[30] Zingarelli and Vossler include a discussion of the vision tradition in their examination of the sources of the *Comedy*.[31]

The excessive claims made for these early descriptions of the other world as sources for the *Comedy* led some critics to deny that there was any relation whatsoever between the visions and the poem,[32] and by the 1930s the popular tradition had been virtually abandoned in favour of an analysis of Dante's learned sources. The vision literature thus ceased to form the subject of study, on the grounds that

the smallest contribution – if indeed there was any at all – came from the legendary otherworld – visions of popular religious stamp which circulated so widely in Latin and the vernaculars during the Middle Ages. Dante stands within the learned tradition of the Middle Ages.[33]

It is clear from a reading of the previous accounts and visions of the other world that there *is* a relationship between these and the *Comedy* in a number of important respects. This relationship is, however, to be found in the study of broad aspects of the otherworld tradition and not in individual texts as the early critics claimed. In their search to establish links between the poem and this or that particular vision, lamenting Dante's silence with regard to these texts, and exaggerating the extent to which they can be seen as direct sources of the poem, they misunderstood the nature of the otherworld tradition. It is not primarily a textual tradition made up of a number of recognised works. The texts do not themselves constitute the tradition; they, along with the visual representations of the other world, reflect what Gurevič describes as

a complex and contradictory confusion of popular beliefs and Christian doctrine, a peculiar product of the prolonged process of mutual activity and interaction between two forces, a product which can be designated as 'popular Christianity' or 'parish catholicism', professed by the great mass of the population of medieval Europe.[34]

It is with the relationship between the *Comedy* and this product that this book is concerned, and not with the debt Dante may or may not have owed to particular visionaries. To this end the book is divided into six chapters, each of which takes as its subject a different aspect of the representation of the other world as manifested throughout the written and, where appropriate, the visual traditions.

If there is an argument beyond this, it is not that the *Comedy* is the last and best in an uninterrupted and continuous line of works purporting to describe the other world, but rather that the poem stands apart from the popular tradition in a particularly significant way. Firstly, it must be noted that the vision genre does not show a continuous but a discontinuous development: it consists of a number of different phases with different aims, influenced by different cultural conditions and using the description of the other world for different purposes.[35] And, significantly, it is interrupted at the beginning of the thirteenth century. After 1206 and the *Vision of Thurkill*, no new visions of the other world were recorded. The *Comedy* follows a century of silence.

Secondly, we must remember that this century of silence was preceded by a period of great intellectual and social change stimulated by renewed contact with the cultures of Byzantium and the Arab world. Between 1099 and 1221 there were five crusades to Jerusalem and Constantinople; at the same time, inroads were made into Arab Sicily and Spain, and Christian kingdoms established there. Trade routes with the East sprang up, and spices, cloth, and artefacts were imported into Europe.[36] These routes facilitated a new exchange in ideas. The Arabs had translated the scientific writings of the Greeks and composed their own commentaries on them, and during the late twelfth century much of this body of learning was translated into Latin and spread to all the intellectual centres of Europe. The result was a revolution in physics, astronomy, astrology, mathematics, medicine, alchemy and philosophy.[37]

The twelfth century was an age not only of discovery but also of revival. The classical Latin authors were widely read and studied; commentaries were written, and a large body of Latin prose and verse composed. The full corpus of Roman law was recovered for the first time since the fall of the Empire; Bologna became established as the legal centre of Europe, and a new civil and canon law developed.[38]

After all these changes, the thirteenth century was destined to be a century of assimilation. Encyclopaedias were written, and the first universities were established. Theological debate raged as the church sought to sort and absorb the new learning. In the space of two hundred years, the intellectual map of Europe was transformed. And these are the two hundred years which immediately preceded the writing of the *Comedy*.

It was perhaps the difficulty of assimilating these new ideas into the framework of the popular vision of the other world which caused its demise. It is certainly the case that in writing the *Comedy* Dante took full account of the intellectual developments of the preceding two centuries. He is the first Christian writer to combine the popular material with the theological and philosophical systems of his day, selecting, adapting, and reinterpreting the traditional images in a new way. The relationship between the *Comedy* and the previous medieval accounts of the other world is therefore one of both similarity and difference.

The only full study of the relationship between the popular tradition of the other world and the *Comedy* was written in 1945 by August Rüegg. It aimed to re-evaluate the relationship between the poem and particular texts. One of the two volumes is concerned with classical sources for figures such as Geryon, Minos, and Cato. The other gives a chronological outline of the major descriptions of the other world from Homer onwards. This approach limits the author to a series of summaries of the primary texts, together with a text-by-text discussion of those motifs which recur from one to the other and are found in Dante. Such an approach has been avoided in the present work in order to concentrate on those wider aspects of the representation of the other world which span the entire tradition, and which have never been examined in detail. The only significant study since Rüegg is an article published in 1984 by Cesare Segre,[39] which gives a brief survey of texts prior to Dante describing journeys into or visions of the other world, and offers a brief reconstruction of Dante's three realms using material from individual visions. He concludes that 'whether he wished it or not, Dante could not be unaware of all this visionary material'.[40]

The aim of this book is to examine the *Comedy* and its relationship to the popular material in the light of all these factors. Much of it is based on the wealth of research done since the writing of Rüegg's study, both in the area of the vision literature in particular[41] and in that of the many changes which occurred in the twelfth century in general. I have endeavoured to acknowledge the many debts I owe to the work of others in fields in which I am not a specialist both in the notes and in the general bibliography.

Notes

1 Helpful outlines are given by L. Moraldi, *L'aldilà dell'uomo nelle civiltà babilonese, egizia, greca, latina, ebraica, cristiana e musulmana*, 1985; and in *An Illustrated History of the World's Religions*, edited by G. Parrinder, 1983.

2 It is not my intention to enter into the debate concerning the precise relationship between 'popular' and 'learned' works. The medieval visions of the other world obviously cannot be said to stem entirely from the populace, as many of them were recorded by ecclesiastics, and as indeed the beliefs which they express stem in part from the teachings of the Church. But they are nonetheless quite distinct from the writing of contemporary theologians and poets in style, register, genesis, content and relationship to one another, and it is to these differences that I refer.

3 For details of these and subsequent works cited see entries in Appendices.

4 See e.g. Job 3.11–19; 10.20–2; Psalms 87.2–17.

5 E.g. Isaiah 26.19.

6 Discussed by N. De Lange, *Apocrypha: Jewish Literature of the Hellenistic Age*, 1978.

7 Biblical sources for the concept of judgment at death are Luke 16.9–31 (the story of Lazarus) and 23.42–3 (the Good Thief). The main source for the concept of judgment at the end of time is Matthew 25.31–46.

8 They are published in M.R. James, *The Apocryphal New Testament*, 1924, and in *Excluded Books of the New Testament*, edited by J. B. Lightfoot *et al.*, 1927.

9 Most strikingly by Wetti, who calls for a copy of the *Dialogues* as he lies on his sick bed, and later by Thurkill, the last visionary, who names Bede and the major visions of the twelfth century as his authorities and guarantors.

10 The vision of the soldier is found in Gregory's *Dialogues*, as is that of Stephen, the layman. Drythelm is described by Bede as a Northumbrian householder, 'paterfamilias'. For detailed references see the appropriate entries in Appendix II.

11 A. F. Ozanam, 'Du cycle poétique et légendaire auquel appartient la "Divine Comédie"', 1893, p. 334.

12 Vincent's visions are those of the Cistercian novice, Josaphat, Pachomius, *St Patrick's Purgatory*, the *Voyage of Brendan*, Mohammed, Furseus, Salvius, Charles the Fat, the Boy William, Tundale, Gunthelm and Ansellus.

13 Albert: *De Resurrectione*, edited by W. Kubel in *Alberti Magni Opera Omnia*, XXVI, 1958, q. 9 'De loci poenarum simul', pp. 320–1. Bonaventure: 'Commentary on the *Sententiae* of Peter Lombard', edited by Quaracchi, IV, p. 526. Aquinas: *Summa Theologiae* Ia q. lxxxix a. 8 and in the *Supplement* q. lxix a. 3. These passages are discussed by J. Le Goff, *La Naissance du Purgatoire*, 1981, pp. 271, 345, 361 and 371.

14 The major representations of the Last Judgment are listed in Appendix I. For the French cathedral sculpture see the studies by E. Mâle and W. Sauerländer listed in the bibliography. For the frescoes see R. Hughes, *Heaven and Hell in Western Art*, 1968, and R. Cavendish, *Visions of Heaven and Hell*, 1977.

15 *Le Testament Villon*, quoted in R. Manselli, *La Religion populaire au moyen âge*, 1975, p. 117.

16 Fourteenth-century frescoes survive at Viboldone, Pomposa, San Gimignano, and in S. Maria Novella, Florence, the only one directly modelled on the *Comedy*.

17 *Chiose alla Cantica dell'Inferno di Dante Allighieri attribuite a Jacopo suo figlio ora per la prima volta date in luce*, 1848, pp. 8–9. See also the *Commento alla Cantica dell'Inferno di Dante Allighieri di autore Anonimo ora per la prima volta dato in luce*, 1848, p. 29; and the *Commento di Francesco da Buti sopra la Divina Commedia di Dante Allighieri pubblicato per cura di Crescentino Giannini*, 1858, I, p. 63. All are quoted by G. Ricciotti, *L'Apocalisse di Paolo siriaca*, 1932, I, pp. 28–29.

18 Zabughin (*Dante e l'iconografia dell'oltretomba*, 1921, p. 519), Ricciotti (*L'Apocalisse di Paolo siriaca*, I, pp. 27–31), and Silverstein ('Dante and the "Visio Pauli"', 1932, p. 399) are all in favour of a direct knowledge on Dante's part of the *Vision of Paul*.

19 The early history of this criticism is outlined by U. Cosmo, 'Le prime ricerche intorno all'originalità dantesca e due letterati padovani del secolo passato', 1891, 33–43 and 65–74.

20 Critics claiming Alberic as a source for Dante were Bottari (1753), Di Costanzo (1800), Cancellieri (1814), De Romanis (1822), Vitti (1890) and De Vivo (1899). See main bibliography.

21 *Furseus*: see M. Mulhall, 'The Celtic Sources of the "Divina Commedia"', 1896. *Patrick*: see F. Vinton, 'St. Patrick's Purgatory, and the "Inferno" of Dante', 1873, pp. 275–86. *Adamnan*: see C. S. Boswell, *An Irish Precursor of Dante*, 1908. *Charles the Fat*: see T. Silverstein, '"Inferno"', XII, 100–26, and the "Visio Karoli Crassi"', 1936, pp. 449–52. *Ansellus*: see F. Ermini, 'La "Visio Anselli" e l'imitazione nella "Divina Commedia"', 1938, pp. 309–15. *Drythelm*: see G. Musca, 'Dante e Beda', 1972, pp. 497–524.

22 *St Patrick's Purgatory: An Essay on the Legends of Purgatory, Hell, and Paradise*, 1844, p. 117.

23 See A. F. Ozanam, 'Du cycle poétique', p. 341; 'Des sources poétiques de la "Divine Comédie"', 1855, p. 415; C. Labitte, 'La "Divine Comédie" avant Dante', 1842.

24 Ozanam, 'Des sources poétiques', p. 362.

25 For an outline of the school see C. Dionisotti, 'La scuola storica', pp. 339–55.

26 *Antiche leggende e tradizioni che illustrano la 'Divina Commedia', precedute da alcune osservazioni di P. Villari*, 1865.

27 *I precursori di Dante*, 1874, reprinted 1912–13, p. 65.

28 *Forerunners of Dante*, 1903, p. 3.

29 In *Neue Jahrbucher für das klassische Altertum, Geschichte und deutsche Literatur*, 49 (1922), pp. 239–53.

30 *L'oltretomba classico, medievale, dantesco nel Rinascimento*, 1922, p. 19.

31 N. Zingarelli, *Dante* [undated]; K. Vossler, *La fonte della 'Divina Commedia' studiata nella sua genesi e interpretata*, 1927.

32 Principally Torraca (1906), Guercio (1909) and Zanfrognini (1911).

33 E. R. Curtius, *European Literature and the Latin Middle Ages*, 1953, p. 362.

34 A. J. Gurevič, 'Popular and Scholarly Medieval Cultural Traditions: Notes in the Margin of Jacques Le Goff's Book', 1983, p. 80.

35 For an exploration of the different phases and purposes of the otherworld visions see C. Zaleski, *Otherworld Journeys*, 1987, chapter 2.

36 An account of the crusades and their effects is given by R. W. Southern, *The Making of the Middle Ages*, 1967, pp. 49–62. For the courts of Sicily and Spain and trade routes see C. H. Haskins, *The Renaissance of the Twelfth Century*, 1927, ch. 1, 'Intellectual centres'.

37 The standard text for all these aspects is Haskins, *ibid*. Also important are Southern, *The Making of the Middle Ages*, especially ch. 4; G. Leff, *Medieval Thought*, 1958, Part II; and R. Bolgar, *The Classical Heritage and its Beneficiaries*, 1954, chs. 4 and 5.

38 See Haskins, *The Renaissance of the Twelfth Century*, ch. 7, 'The revival of jurisprudence'.

39 A. Rüegg, *Die Jenseitsvorstellungen vor Dante und die übringen literarischen Voraussetzungen der 'Divina Commedia'*, 2 vols., 1945; C. Segre, 'L'itinerarium animae nel Duecento e Dante', 1984.

40 *Ibid.*, p. 25.

41 Particularly the work of A. Gurevič, P. Dinzelbacher, J. Le Goff and C. Carozzi.

Topographical motifs of the other world

Discussion of the relation between the *Comedy* and previous representations of the afterlife has hitherto been centred around the question of the motifs of the other world – features of landscape or of narrative which recur from vision to vision, fresco to fresco, and which are also found in the *Comedy*. Some are topographical: rivers, ladders, bridges, lakes, pits, mountains. Some are moral: punishment by burning, by freezing, by disfigurement. Others reflect particular moments in the narrative: the battle between angels and devils for possession of a soul, the moment of admission to Paradise, the precise timing of the journey. These motifs recur throughout the popular tradition, particularly in the depiction of Hell, reaching a peak in the graphic representations of the twelfth century – so that by the beginning of the thirteenth the visionary had at his disposal what has been

Plate 1 Fresco in the church of St Peter and St Paul, Chaldon, Surrey, *c.* AD 1200, showing the weighing of souls, the Harrowing of Hell, the cauldron, the bridge and the ladder of salvation

variously termed 'a popular language of the other world', and an 'eschatological encyclopaedia'.[1]

Now it may be said that the very existence of these motifs raises a number of questions concerning the nature of the vision tradition itself – questions which indeed one might repeat with regard to the *Comedy*. Is the vision properly to be thought of as a work of fiction which merely imitates its predecessors? Or is it the report of an authentic and individual experience? The existence of recurring motifs would seem to support the former hypothesis; and yet visionaries and redactors are united in their insistence on the latter.

Critics studying the vision literature have reacted variously to this problem. Owen suggests that the development of a pool of infernal motifs would seem to be attributable to a simple process of accumulation: 'as each new treatment of the theme appeared, the collection of infernal lore was increased, so that it became a well from which any one might draw'.[2] Carrouges postulates a more complex situation, rejecting the idea of a linear development: 'all the representations of Hell born of the human imagination intercommunicate by means of an inextricably tangled web of influences, conscious or unconscious'.[3] And there is the rub – was the borrowing conscious or unconscious? Traill remarks that 'one of the hardest problems in dealing with the history of vision literature, and possibly the most futile, is to attempt to determine in any given vision the extent of conscious borrowing of elements from earlier visions'.[4] He suggests that the borrowing of established motifs was indirect and unconscious, fostered by the familiarity of Gregory's *Dialogues* and of the *Vision of Paul*. Gurevič, on the other hand, suggests that the borrowing was conscious, and yet maintains that the visions were nonetheless authentic; the adoption of standard motifs is evidence not so much of an unreal literary genre as of the need to express experiences in an acceptable way:

Medieval man, whose dreams and nightmares were full of the other world, endeavoured to describe his visions and impressions, turning in his attempt to express them to the only language accessible to him: that of the traditional images and symbols which gave deep meaning to visions.[5]

The recurrence of a number of motifs would thus be due to this need to conform to tradition:

In order to evaluate individual experience, practical or religious, it was necessary to relate it to tradition – or at least to understand and perceive that experience according to the categories of the collective consciousness.[6]

This is also the settled view of the most recent critics, and I think the correct one. Zaleski sees the medieval vision as a work built up of a number of layers, pointing out that the visionary's experience will have been shaped by his conscious and unconscious expectations, and that in his turn the redactor will also seek to bring the written text into conformity with existing models. She too reminds us that

whereas modern readers might doubt the veracity of a narrative filled with easily recognized conventions, medieval readers believed that after all the proofs have been tallied, there is no better index of an account's validity than its edifying qualities and its conformity to tradition.[7]

It seems wise therefore to reject the traditional diachronic analysis which views the vision literature as a succession of written texts each of which imitates its predecessors, and instead to adopt a synchronic approach which, bearing in mind the 'popular' nature of the tradition, and passing no comment on the question of imitation versus authenticity, interprets not a chronological succession of visions but a horizontal panorama of motifs. We shall then be able to look diachronically at the relation between this panorama of motifs and the *Comedy*, considering as we do so the intellectual developments of the twelfth century which lie between them, and the difference these make to the way in which Dante uses the traditional material. Those motifs have been selected which best illustrate the heterogeneity of the popular concept of the afterlife: some motifs spring from the existence of an archetypal image, some from the literal interpretation of a metaphor; others arise in the attempt to create a topography of Hell which would run parallel to that of Paradise; some derive from the Bible or from the doctrines of Eastern religion, others from classical literature; some are products of the imagination, and others extensions of earthly tortures and punishments. It thus becomes clear that the development of the motifs is not merely cumulative, each successive visionary adding his own new motif; and yet neither is it the 'inextricably tangled web of influences' which permits no clear understanding of the formation of the popular tradition.

THE CAULDRON

Inferno XXI–XXIII

There are two episodes in the *Inferno* which are especially reminiscent in tone of the popular representations of previous centuries, and which consequently have often been thought to be out of keeping with the rest of the poem. The first of these is Dante's description of the fifth *bolgia* of Hell, in which those guilty of barratry, corruption in public office, are confined.

Dante and Virgil have descended through the first seven circles of Hell and reached the eighth, in which fraud is punished. The circle is divided into ten concentric ditches or *bolge*, crossed by a series of arched bridges, each ditch being lower in level than its predecessor; it is surrounded on the outside by a high cliff, and encloses in its middle the pit in which Satan and the treacherous are imprisoned. The opening of canto XXI finds Dante and Virgil pausing halfway across the bridge which traverses the fifth of these ditches. Looking down into it, they see that it is exceedingly dark, and appears to be filled with a boiling black pitch which Dante-poet likens to that prepared in the Venetian Arsenal for the repairing of ships. Large bubbles rise slowly to the surface and burst silently; there is no sign of life.

Suddenly Virgil sees a black devil running along the bank, a man slung over his shoulder as a butcher might carry a carcass. The man is flung down on the bank; his identity is announced – he was a member of the government of Lucca – and the devil shoots off to collect his next victim. At this point the drama begins. The miserable soul leaps into the pitch in the nick of time as other devils rush up, armed with hooks, and warn him that should he surface he will be pounced upon. The poet compares them to scullery boys cooking meat in a giant cauldron, pushing each lump down beneath the surface with forks:

> Non altrimenti i cuochi a' lor vassalli
> fanno attuffare in mezzo la caldaia
> la carne con li uncin, perché non galli.
> (Inf XXI 55–7)

At this point Virgil instructs Dante to squat in safety behind a rock, and leaves the bridge for the embankment dividing the fifth and sixth ditches in order to negotiate a safe passage with the devils. This accomplished, Dante joins him. The devil Malacoda explains (truthfully) that the bridge over the next *bolgia* is broken, but (untruthfully) that there is another further on. He appoints ten devils to escort the poets to this non-existent bridge – devils whose names are curiously reminiscent of the names of certain Florentine officials of Dante's time.[8]

The drama continues in canto XXII. Barrators plunge in terror into the depths of the pitch as the devils approach; but one, Ciampolo, is too slow, and is hooked by Graffiacane. Ciampolo promises to give a safety signal, thus attracting other Tuscan and Lombard barrators onto the bank, if the devils will withdraw a little. They argue; then agree. Instantly Ciampolo leaps back into the pitch, hotly pursued by Alichino. Meanwhile Calcabrino flings himself upon Alichino, whom he holds to blame for the escape; both devils fall struggling into the pitch, and are cooked just like their victims, 'cotti dentro dalla crosta' (XXII 150). As the others haul them out, Dante and Virgil continue along the bank. The devils realise that their prey is escaping and engage in hot pursuit; Virgil is forced to grab Dante and scramble down the cliff into the sixth *bolgia*, leaving their pursuers to gaze furiously down on them from the top of the cliff.

·Now the whole of this episode recalls several others recounted in previous descriptions of Hell. Drythelm and Tundale, for example, are both threatened by packs of devils, and rescued only in the nick of time by their guides.[9] But more particularly, a number of the earlier representations of the other world make use, like Dante in this episode, of imagery or actual hell-torment modelled on the contemporary kitchen.

The cauldron: sources

One of the most common motifs of Hell is that of the cauldron. Although it owes its later development to the popular imagination of the twelfth century, it is in fact one of the few motifs which ultimately derive from the scriptures. Sheol is several times in the Old Testament personified as an insatiable demon with wide-open jaws, and from the sixth century onwards the monster Leviathan which is described by Job had been regarded as a figure for Satan.[10] From the earliest centuries of the Christian era, the metaphor used to represent the place in which the souls of the elect awaited the Day of Judgment was that of Abraham's bosom, and although the concept of an intermediate waiting place was rejected by theologians

Plate 2 Illumination from the Psalter of St Louis, 1223–30, showing Hell, represented as a cauldron in the jaws of Leviathan, and Paradise, represented as Abraham's bosom

Plate 3 Leviathan and the cauldron of Hell, detail from Last Judgment Portal, Ferrara Cathedral, *c.* 1300

from the fifth century onwards, it survived as a popular picture of the place to which the souls of the blessed went after death.[11] Leviathan became accepted as a parallel image for the place to which the damned were sent, and Hell was conceived in terms of Job chapter 41:

flames come from his jaws, bright as a burning torch, smoke from his nostrils, thick as the fumes of a seething pot; his very breath will set coals aflame, such fire issues from that mouth. (Job 41.19–21)

Plate 2 shows a typical representation of Heaven and Hell according to this tradition. Abraham's bosom and the cauldron are also depicted on many of the Last Judgment portals of the French gothic cathedrals, the first example being that at Conques, carved at the end of the twelfth century. In Italy there is a particularly fine representation at Ferrara (Plate 3).

The cauldron in the vision literature

In the early visions of the other world, the cauldron is not common; it becomes widely used only after the beginning of the twelfth century. The twelfth-century visions contain a wealth of descriptive detail not found in the short accounts which precede them, and the motif is expanded and altered; spits, ovens and frying pans all contribute to the creation of a new infernal topos. With the popularisation of the iconography of the devil as a small black creature with bat wings and a long fork, ready to attack the souls of the damned, the scope of the cookery motif as a dramatic infernal torment is greatly increased.[12]

At its simplest the cauldron is, as in art, the sole motif representing Hell. Guntram's vision of Chilperic, recorded by Gregory of Tours, is of this kind:

Et cum diu multumque quasi altercantes haec inter se verba proferrent, conspicio eminus aeneum super ignem positum fervere vehementer. Tunc me flente, adpraehensum infilicem Chilpericum, confractis membris, proiciunt in aeneum. (p. 166)

[And while the three bishops exchanged words, almost as if they were quarrelling, I saw from a distance a cauldron placed over a fire and burning fiercely. Then I watched in tears as they seized the unhappy Chilperic, broke his limbs and threw him into the cauldron.]

A similar episode is described much later by Etienne de Bourbon as a punishment for adultery:

Duxit eum ad domum teterrimam, in qua vidit demones horribiles apportantes cuveam igneam, in qua projecerunt unum burgensum mortuum de villa sua et uxorem alterius; et ibi comburebantur et balniabantur tanquam in metallo bullienti. (*Tractatus*, p. 24)

[They led him into a dark building. Here he saw horrible devils bringing a copper cauldron, into which they threw a deceased burgess from his town together with another man's wife. Here they burned and melted as if boiling in metal.][13]

Of the two accounts, that in Gregory is much closer to the description of Leviathan, with the essential elements of cauldron, fire and burning, whereas Etienne has introduced a specification of sin and the detail of molten metals, and replaced the three bishops who throw Chilperic into the cauldron by a troupe of devils. His description is well illustrated by the contemporary sculpture at Rheims shown in Plate 4. But although the two visions are seven centuries apart, the same motif is used in fundamentally the same way.

The twelfth-century visions develop the motif in greater detail. Its transformation is particularly striking in the *Vision of the Boy William*, where the devils are described as infernal cooks and their victims as pieces of meat, thus foreshadowing Inf xxi 55–7:

Vidit a daemonibus carnes, quae perfecti hominis formam habere videbantur, in caldaria proiici, & sub momento quasi mox nati infantes apparebant. Hae fuscinulis ignitis a caldariis erectae statim in priorem aetatem transformari videbantur, & sic saepius in caldariis retorquebantur.

[He saw the devils throw into the cauldrons pieces of meat in the shape of human bodies. Immediately, newborn infants appeared. The fire was lit under the cauldrons, and as they came to the surface they were transformed back into adults. They were often tormented in this way in the cauldrons.]

The liquid in the cauldron is of various kinds; Alberic like Etienne describes boiling metals, together with sulphur and resin:

Vidi et aliud subplicium (. . .) quod ad instar cuiusdam vasis immense longitudinis atque vastitatis videbatur esse. Plenum quoque erat here, stagno, plumbo, sulphure et resina, ita omnibus liquescentibus et ferventibus, ac si oleum in frixorio super ignem bulliens.

(p. 89, repunctuated)

Plate 4 Detail from the Last Judgment Portal, Rheims Cathedral, *c.* 1230, showing the resurrection of the dead, the elect and the damned, Abraham's bosom and the gates of Paradise, and the cauldron of Hell

[I saw another torment (. . .) which was like a pot of immense size. It was full of bronze, tin, lead, sulphur and resin, all molten and burning, just as oil boils in a frying pan over the fire.]

An early extension of the cauldron motif was that of the spit. It is first described in the Long Latin version of the *Vision of Paul*, and is represented among the torments of Hell in the Florentine Baptistry and in the Scrovegni chapel, and illustrated in psalters such as the one shown in Plate 5. But in the most elaborate of the twelfth-century visions, the motif is developed even further: the knight Owen, the Monk of Eynsham and Tundale all see the damned being tormented in an infernal frying pan.[14]

To this increasing realism of description, the *Vision of Thurkill* brings the urgency of drama. The souls of the damned are tormented in turn in a theatre built specially for the purpose and manned by devils. It is the turn of a man whose sin was pride:

demones vero ira excandescentes tridentibus et uncis igneis miserum coram eis paulo ante ludentem membratim discerpserunt. unus autem ex eis adipem cum pice et aliis liquaminibus in sartagine ferventi torrens singula membra discerpta cum quodam instrumento respersit illo bullienti unguine; et ad singulas demonis respersiones membra stridorem magnum emittebant, velut cum aqua frigida in bullienti sagimine inicitur.   (p. 21)

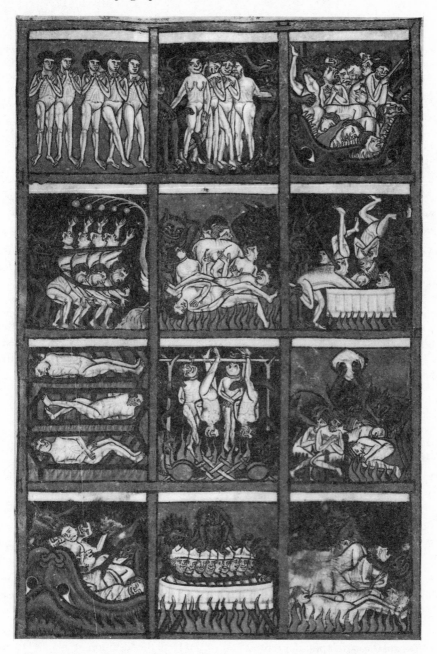

Plate 5 The torments of Hell, including the spit, the cauldron and the jaws of
Leviathan, Gloucester Psalter, thirteenth century

[before the drama the devils, burning with anger, tore the wretch limb from limb with prongs and fiery iron hooks. But one of them put fat with pitch and other greasy substances in a burning pan, and fried each limb as it was torn away with that boiling grease; and each time the devil sprinkled them with the grease, the limbs sent forth a great hissing, like that caused by pouring cold water on boiling blood.]

The man is restored to one piece and sent back to his seat while another sinner is hauled out onto the stage.

In this episode the devil-play of the *Comedy* is foreshadowed. The pleasure of Thurkill's demons is equalled by that of Dante's, and hooks are similarly to the fore:

> . . . preseli 'l braccio col runciglio,
> sí che, stracciando, ne portò un lacerto.
> (Inf XXII 71–2)

[he took him by the arm with his hook in such a way that in tearing it he ripped off a muscle.]

Action in both is swift, the intention malicious and sadistic, the episode in its entirety threatening to the protagonist; Thurkill, like Dante, is placed by his guide behind a protective obstacle – a rock in the *Comedy*, a wall in the vision.[15]

In only one text, however, is the irony which dominates *Inferno* XXI–XXII employed. This is in Giacomino da Verona's description of the city of Babylon, where the principal torment outlined is the roasting of the sinner on a spit by Bacabu, the infernal cook, who serves the dish up to Satan only to have it rejected as underdone. But a new arrival is expected, and the devils eagerly pick up their hooks and prepare the fire. They rush towards their victim,

> Criando cascaun: 'Amaça, amaça, amaça!
> Ca no gne po scanpar quel fel lar, falsa capa'.
> (ll. 179–80)

[each shouting 'kill him, kill him, kill him; he mustn't get away, the wicked sinner, false cleric!']

Like Ciampolo, the sinner nonetheless tries to escape, but is hooked by the devils, who set upon him with sadistic glee:

> Altri ge da per braci, altri ge da per gambe,
> Altri ge speca li ossi cun baston e cun stange,
> Cun cape e cun baili, cun manare e cun vange,
> Lo corpo g'emplo tuto de plage molto grande.
> (ll. 213–16)

[Some set upon his arms, some upon his legs; others broke his bones with sticks and rods, with clubs [?] and shovels, with hatchets and spades. They filled his whole body with great wounds.]

There is therefore a certain similarity between Dante's description of the fifth *bolgia* and the earlier popular representations of Hell: the adoption of imagery from the kitchen – boiling oil, the cooking of meat, the use of forks; and the devil-play, drama and irony which accompanies the cookery motif in some of the twelfth- and thirteenth-century texts.

Inferno XXI–XXII are often regarded as something of a peculiarity, as differing both in tone and fictional approach from the rest of the *cantica*. This is perhaps deliberate on the part of the poet, and for a specific reason. In these cantos, which together form the longest single episode in the *Inferno*, Dante is dealing with the sin of which he himself had been publicly accused, for which he stood exiled from Florence, and concerning which he must have found it hard to be dispassionate. In his description of the fifth *bolgia* we see fraud in action, with both the devils – whose names resemble those of high-ranking Florentine officials – and Ciampolo spinning webs of malicious deceit beneath dignified offers of service. And we see the two innocent poets, Dante and Virgil, threatened and nearly seriously harmed by these deceits. Dante consistently protested that he was innocent of the charge of barratry; and his choice of this most naive topos when treating the sin of which he sought to exonerate himself, using it to expose and ridicule the sin and those guilty of it, must be deliberate.

THE PRESENTATION OF SATAN

The second episode in the *Inferno* which is particularly reminiscent in tone of the twelfth-century representations comes at the very bottom of the pit of Cocytus: Dante's encounter with Satan.

To the modern reader of the *Comedy*, the representation of Satan seems somewhat incongruous. We have heeded Virgil's warning to Dante to take courage: 'convien che di fortezza t'armi' (XXXIV 21), and are prepared to meet the incarnation of evil, the 'imperador del doloroso regno' (XXXIV 28). We have travelled through the realm of eternal torment, encountering figures of the dramatic stature of Farinata and Ugolino, and figures with the emotional impact of Francesca and Brunetto. And at the climax of the cantica, at the lowest point of Hell, we find, to our 'gran maraviglia' (XXXIV 37), a gigantic, three-headed, helpless, tearful, hairy Satan, flapping his six bat-like wings, down whose furry body Dante and Virgil scramble:

> e quando l'ali fuoro aperte assai,
>   appigliò sé alle vellute coste:
> di vello in vello giú discese poscia
>   tra 'l folto pelo e le gelate croste.
>   (Inf XXXIV 72–5)

[and when the wings were wide open, (Virgil) caught hold of the furry flanks, then descended from tuft to tuft between the thick hair and the frozen crust.]

All these elements are present in the previous representations of Satan. Dante says that he himself 'compares better with a giant than do giants with his arms' (XXXIV 30–1). In the popular tradition Satan is also oversized: in the Latin *Vision of Esdras* the author explains 'I could not specify exactly how long and tall he was, but it was about seventy cubits' (about 117 feet) (p. 54). Esdras goes on to explain, understandably, that by comparison with Satan the souls of the damned seem like flies.

Dante and the Medieval Other World

Dante's Satan has human arms and legs but the black wings of a bat; Tundale describes him as having a human shape from the feet to the head, except that he had many hands and a tail, and compares his blackness not to that of a bat but to that of a crow: 'erat namque prefata bestia nigerrima sicut corvus, habens formam humani corporis a pedibus usque ad caput, excepto, quod illa plurimas habebat manus et caudam' (p. 36). He adds that each hand was a hundred cubits long and ten cubits wide, which makes even Esdras's Devil seem small.

Dante's Satan is helpless, unable to move and with no power over the demons who populate Hell; in redaction IX of the *Vision of Paul* Belzebut is chained and immobile, and Tundale's Satan is chained to an iron grid. Like us, Tundale finds this surprising:

Vellem, inquit, scire, quam ob causam illud monstrum princeps vocatur tenebrarum, cum neminem possit defendere nec semet ipsum valeat liberare?

[I would like to know, he said, for what reason this monster is called the prince of darkness, when he can defend nobody and hasn't even got what it takes to free himself?]

The answer comes: 'Princeps (. . .) non propter potentiam ipse vocatur, set propter primatum, quem tenet in tenebris' [he is called Prince not because of the power, but because of the primacy which he holds in the underworld] (p. 39).

Dante's Satan has three heads, and in each mouth chews a sinner; six of the redactions of the *Vision of Paul* represent an infernal monster or demon with a number of heads. He is named in the various redactions as Belzebut, Parthemon, Bachimach, Pahtmot, Parphimon and Patinut. His heads vary from three (Bachimach) to a thousand (Pahtmot and Patinut), the most common number being a hundred. In each mouth a sinner is chewed. In all these texts, and in the *Vision of the Boy William*, Satan is located, as in the *Inferno*, in the lowest depths of Hell.

These characteristics are repeated in the visual representations of Satan. In the Florentine Baptistry he is gigantic, and his head has three mouths; another two are found lower down the body (see Plate 6). In the Scrovegni chapel he is large and black, of human form, and apparently seated on a dragon, as described in the redactions of the *Vision of Paul*.

There are of course differences between Dante's treatment of Satan and that of the previous representations; Dante is a learned poet, not an uneducated visionary. Satan's three heads are of different colours, and from the time of the early commentators they have been regarded as symbols of the three attributes contrary to those of the Trinity – impotence, ignorance and hate. Satan, located in the depths of Hell, is thus placed in clear spiritual antithesis to the Trinity, which Dante sees in his final vision in the *Paradiso*. He also has a topographical significance: he is the worm at the exact centre of the rotten apple which is Earth, at the furthest remove possible from God. And he has a moral significance: it is the icy draught from his flapping wings which creates the breeze which blows in Cocytus and freezes the lake, representing the cold-blooded acts of the traitors who are confined there; and it is in his treacherous mouths that the greatest traitors of all time, Judas, Brutus and Cassius, suffer eternal torment. But despite these

Plate 6 Satan and the damned, detail of the ceiling mosaic in the Florence Baptistry, thirteenth century

differences, the appearance of Dante's Satan is essentially that of the twelfth- and thirteenth-century representations, both written and visual, of the Devil. This is perhaps for a specific reason. Like that of the barrators, this whole episode stands at the furthest possible remove from the *Aeneid*, and seems strangely out of keeping with the rest of Dante's poem. Farinata is allowed to preserve a certain dignity; Satan, the prince of evil, is not. Francesca can command a certain pity; Satan, the defeated enemy of God, cannot. Made ridiculous by the naivety of popular representation, this Satan does not, like that of Milton, offer an admirable or tempting alternative to the perfection of the final vision of God; the 'state of happiness' which Dante describes in the *Paradiso* will offer us something incomparably more awe-inspiring and attractive than the 'state of misery' represented by this giant, furry bat.

USURY

Above the cliff which marks the beginning of the eighth circle of Hell lies an area of burning sand upon which fall flakes of fire. Beyond that is a wood, surrounded in its turn by the Phlegethon, a boiling river of blood. These together constitute the seventh circle, the circle of the violent. Immersed in the river are those guilty of violence against others. Imprisoned in the wood are those who committed acts of violence against themselves – suicides and profligates. And scorched on the burning sand are those who were violent towards God: blasphemers, homosexuals and money-lenders or usurers.

In canto XI of the *Inferno* Virgil explains the reasoning behind this threefold division: 'it is also possible to act with violence towards God, denying and cursing him (blasphemy), and despising nature and its goodness (homosexuality and money-lending)' (XI 46–51). It is reasonably clear how homosexuality can be said to despise the natural order, and therefore its creator; but Dante is moved to ask how the practice of money-lending can be said to do the same. Virgil reminds him that man is meant to work for his living, according to the example set by God in creation and followed by the natural world, and not to live off the fruits of other men's work by lending them money at interest:

> 'Da queste due, se tu ti rechi a mente
> lo Genesí dal principio, convene
> prender sua vita e avanzar la gente;
> e perché l'usuriere altra via tene,
> per sé natura e per la sua seguace
> dispregia, poi ch'in altro pon la spene.'
> (XI 106–11)

Usury is expressly forbidden in the Bible, and was condemned by the medieval Church.[16] It was also a subject close to Dante's heart. Florence underwent rapid economic expansion in the second half of the thirteenth century, and this increased wealth affected the city profoundly.[17] Dante has just spoken with three Florentines who lived in the middle of the century and thus represent the old generation, and has told them that the *nouveaux riches* in the city are responsible for its moral decline:

> 'La gente nuova e i súbiti guadagni,
> orgoglio e dismisura han generata,
> Fiorenza, in te, sí che tu già ten piagni.'
> (XVI 73–5)

He will take up the theme again when he describes his encounter with his ancestor Cacciaguida in the Heaven of Mars. And it is important to realise that the economic expansion which had brought about these changes was itself built on a foundation of usury.[18] And so in the seventeenth canto of the *Inferno* Dante describes the eternal condition of some of the usurers responsible. They sit huddled on the burning sand, alternately shielding themselves with their arms from the fireflakes and lifting themselves up onto their hands in order to relieve the pain of their burning bottoms. Each usurer is identifiable only by the family crest portrayed on the money bag which hangs around his neck, and on which his eyes are firmly fixed:

> . . . dal collo a ciascun pendea una tasca
> ch'avea certo colore e certo segno,
> e quindi par che 'l loro occhio si pasca.
> (XVII 55–7)

One bag has a lion, azure on or, the crest of the Florentine Gianfigliazzi family. One has a goose, argent on gules, the crest of the Florentine Obriachi family. A

Plate 7 Dante meets the usurers in Hell; *Inferno* XVII 58–66; illumination from a
Ferrara MS of the *Comedy*, 1474–82

third has a sow, azure on argent, the crest of the Paduan Scrovegni family. Plate
7 shows a fifteenth-century illustration of their plight. The arrival of a third
Florentine, from the Becchi family, is predicted.

The popular tradition offers two related punishments for those guilty of sins
concerning money. Avarice, fraud and the taking of bribes are punished in the
visions of William, the Monk of Eynsham and Thurkill by the enforced
swallowing of burning coins; this torment is illustrated in the fresco of Hell in the
Collegiate church of San Gimignano painted in 1396. In the other form, usurers
wear a heavy money bag round their necks, exactly as in the *Inferno*. The sculpture
of the Last Judgment at Ferrara shows, among the damned being escorted from
the scales of judgment to the cauldron of Hell, a figure with a purse hanging round
his throat (Plate 8); similar figures are depicted in the fresco of the Last Judgment
painted by Giotto in the chapel built by Enrico Scrovegni. Enrico was the son of
the usurer Reginaldo Scrovegni, who is probably the member of the Scrovegni
family seated on the burning sand with the Florentines. Several of the sinners

Plate 8 Detail of the damned, Last Judgment Portal, Ferrara Cathedral, *c.* 1300

depicted in Hell in the Scrovegni chapel are identified by the presence of moneybags as usurers: one is lending to a king, three hang by nooses made from the strings of their purses, and one even re-enacts a financial transaction under the close supervision of two devils and a toothed reptile (Plate 9). In building the chapel and commissioning this fresco, Enrico is thought to have been asking divine forgiveness for his father's usury and his own inherited fortune.

It seems therefore that in his use of this motif Dante has deviated little from tradition.

THE RIVERS OF HELL

When the poets reach the desert of burning sand, they come to a narrow red stream which trickles out of the wood of the suicides and runs across the sand; it is by walking along the high stone embankment of this stream that the two poets cross the desert unscathed. Its presence prompts him to ask Virgil for an explanation, which he receives. An old man, 'un gran veglio' (XIV 103), stands in the depths of Mount Ida, on the island of Crete. His head is of gold, his chest and arms of silver, his body of copper, his legs and left foot of iron, and his right foot, which takes most of his weight, of clay. From the chest downwards runs a deep fissure, with tears streaming down it. The old man represents the successive and degenerative phases of human history, culminating in the separation of the Church and the Empire represented by the clay and iron feet; and his tears drip into the earth and run underground to create the river system of Hell.[19]

26

Plate 9 A usurer and his client in Hell; detail from Giotto's fresco of the Last Judgment in the Scrovegni chapel, Padua, c. 1305

Once the tears reach Hell, they form a river divided into four reaches. The first is the Acheron, which runs round the outer circle, and must be crossed by ferry. Charon is the ferryman. The second is the Styx, which surrounds the city of Dis and forms the sixth circle, in which the wrathful are punished – although it is more a stagnant marsh than a river. Phlegyas is the ferryman. The third is the Phlegethon, the red river which runs within the seventh circle, and in which those who were violent towards others are immersed; a ford crosses it. The fourth is the Cocytus, which forms a frozen lake at the bottom of Hell, and in which the treacherous are immersed. Water flows from each reach of the river down to the next, and the red stream which crosses the desert carries water from the Phlegethon to the Cocytus.

The biblical tradition

The idea that rivers flow through Hell goes back a very long way. The oldest biblical texts envisaged a shadowy, featureless underworld, but during the Graeco-Roman period of Jewish history a more detailed picture emerged. In his vision of the Day of Judgment, Daniel saw a river of fire flowing from the feet of the Ancient of Days, and this river became a standard element in medieval representations of the Last Judgment, where it flows downwards and engulfs the wicked.[20] In the apocryphal *I Enoch* a river of fire forms part of the first hell of torment,[21] and by the time the New Testament was written liquid fire was an established part of Hell. The author of the Apocalypse insists three times that the wicked will be thrown into a lake of fire,[22] and the apocryphal descriptions of the other world adopt and expand the theme.

The second phase in the development of a system of fiery otherworld rivers was the elaboration of the concept of purification by fire, based on such texts as I Corinthians 3.10–15. Early theologians taught that this fire will be in the form of a river in which we shall be purified of our sinful works, and it is on this foundation that the doctrine of Purgatory later began to rise.[23] As the vast majority of the visions of the other world do not distinguish Hell and Purgatory as separate places, this teaching also contributed to the establishment of the motif.

The classical tradition

The classical accounts of the other world also describe infernal rivers, usually four in number. These four rivers were as much commonplaces of the underworld as were Ixion, Tantalus, Sisyphus and Tityos. They occur first in Homer: the sea Oceanus encircles the Earth's surface, and the four rivers of the Underworld are named as the Acheron, the Pyriphlegethon, the Cocytus and the Styx. Plato offers the same; Virgil omits Oceanus but includes the other four, renaming the Pyriphlegethon the Phlegethon, and adding the river Lethe.[24] Some variation occurs within the classical tradition; the Styx becomes a lake in Plato, a swamp in Virgil, and the way in which the various waters connect with one another is not constant.

The early Christian tradition

The early Christian apocrypha sought to fill in the details concerning the other world which were not supplied in the scriptures, and they did this partly by turning to classical literature. The four rivers of the Earthly Paradise were clearly described in Genesis,[25] but for Hell the Bible provided no more than vague suggestions of infernal lakes and rivers of fire. The classical tradition, on the other hand, offered a quadripartite river structure for Hell which seemed to parallel that of the biblical Paradise; and the link was strengthened by the identification of the Phlegethon, a river of fire, with the biblical rivers and lakes of fire. Early theologians such as Claudian and Tertullian discussed the Virgilian rivers, as did the widely known commentaries on the *Aeneid* by Servius and Macròbius.[26]

The first text specifically to make the connection between the rivers of the classical underworld and the Christian Hell was the *Vision of Paul*, composed in the third century probably in Greek but possibly in Syriac.[27] Reissued in the following century, revised and translated into Latin in the sixth, and ultimately producing a network of Latin redactions and vernacular translations, the *Vision of Paul* is the most important single text for the development of the motif of the infernal rivers in the Western tradition.

Early versions of the vision show the influence of Greek cosmography, most especially in the inclusion of Oceanus, which is not found in the classical Latin descriptions. It is present in the three extant manuscripts of the early Latin text, and in two of the redactions. Of the three early manuscripts, the first describes Oceanus and two rivers of fire; the second substitutes an 'Acherusius lacus' for one of these rivers; and the third has the Oceanus and two rivers of pitch and sulphur. Redactions II and VIII are similar.[28]

Another three of the redactions are clearly influenced less by Greek ideas than by the *Aeneid*. Redaction I adds to Oceanus the Styx, Phlegethon, Acheron and Cochiton (but the latter is an area of Hell). The Pyriphlegethon appears in redaction III, and redaction VII adds to Oceanus the Cocciton, the Flegeton, and a mysterious Rapion. In these texts linguistic similarities with the *Aeneid* remove any doubt as to its use as a source.[29]

The later redactions, namely IV, V, IX and Br, take the infernal rivers a step further away from Virgil, retaining the Phlegethon as the river of fire, but eliminating the other three rivers. Instead, further characteristics are added: monsters lurk in the river of IV, and sinners are immersed to varying degrees in that of V. Redaction VI describes areas of liquid pitch and molten metals but no rivers; X includes three rivers, one of which is named Cocitus.

Other early visions describe infernal rivers, but they are never named: Sunniulf, the Monk of Wenlock, Wetti and Charles the Fat all describe rivers of fire, adding bridges, whirlpools and molten metals.

The major twelfth-century visions adapt the motif further. Tundale describes a sulphurous and stinking river at the bottom of a dark valley; Godeschalc, retaining like Dante the Virgilian concept of a river as the boundary of the Underworld, describes a river filled with knives which must be crossed by all souls on their way to their eternal destiny – the souls of the just are provided with planks which act as rafts to carry them across. *St Patrick's Purgatory* is the first to give any detailed description of an icy river; souls are chased into it by demons.[30]

None of the twelfth-century visions, other than the redactions of the *Vision of Paul*, mention the Virgilian rivers by name. But in the thirteenth century, the semi-popular poem *Anticerberus* includes in its description of the infernal city Babylon the following waters: 'Styx, Lethes, Flegeton, Acheron, cochitia septa' (l. 153).

So Dante is not the first to name the infernal rivers after those of the classical tradition in general and Virgil in particular. He adds other details from the *Aeneid*: Virgil's Charon ferries the newly arrived souls over the Acheron in the *Inferno* as in the *Aeneid*, and the Styx is a marsh rather than a river. Dante also appoints the Virgilian Phlegyas boatman of the Styx, and includes the Lethe, which in the *Aeneid* runs through the Elysian Fields, in his Earthly Paradise.[31]

The motif of gradated immersion

But there is one aspect of Dante's rivers which suggests more strongly that he was influenced by the popular tradition as well as by the *Aeneid*. This is his use of the motif of gradated immersion, whereby souls are immersed to varying degrees in an infernal river according to the gravity of the sin they have committed. Immersion of this kind occurs in two of the rivers of the *Inferno*, the Phlegethon and the Cocytus.

Dante's Phlegethon is a river not of fire but of boiling blood, and it is not just a river of Hell but also an instrument of torment for the first category of the violent, those who were violent towards others and who now bathe in the blood of their victims. It runs like a moat between the cliff the poets have just descended from the city of Dis and the wood of the suicides, thus forming a circle. The river is deeper on one side than the other; Dante starts from the deepest point, and so as he walks round along the outer bank he sees people immersed in it to ever decreasing degrees, until the shallowest point is reached and he is able to cross. Nessus, the Centaur who is his escort, identifies the various categories.

First they come to the tyrants, immersed up to the eyebrows, identified by Nessus as those who gave themselves to bloodshed and plunder:

> Io vidi gente sotto infino al ciglio;
> e 'l gran centauro disse: 'E' son tiranni
> che dier nel sangue e ne l'aver di piglio.'
>
> (XII 103–5)

Then on to the murderers, visible only from the throat upwards:

> Poco piú oltre il centauro s'affisse
> sovr'una gente che 'nfino a la gola
> parea che di quel bulicame uscisse.
>
> (115–17)

They continue along the bank, and come to those whose heads and trunks emerge from the river; Dante recognises many of these:

> Poi vidi gente che di fuor del rio
> tenean la testa e ancor tutto 'l casso
> e di costoro assai riconobb'io.
>
> (121–3)

Finally Dante sees those who have only their feet immersed in the river, and at this point crosses to the wood:

> Cosí a piú a piú si facea basso
> quel sangue, sí che cocea pur li piedi;
> e quindi fu del fosso il nostro passo.
>
> (124–6)

From the outline of the sins of violence which Virgil gave Dante in canto XI, we assume that these last two categories must be those who inflicted 'ferute dogliose' [painful wounds] on others and the 'guastatori e predon' [pillagers and plunderers].[32]

The immersion motif occurs again in the frozen lake at the base of Hell, where the position of the sinners frozen into the ice becomes progressively more uncomfortable. The betrayers of kin in Caina are frozen in the ice at the edge of the lake, immersed to the chin, 'insin al dove appar vergogna' (XXXII 34), each facing downwards. The betrayers of country are in the same position, further towards the centre of the lake, in the area known as Antenora. The betrayers of guests, in Tolomea, still nearer the centre, are positioned face upwards, 'non volta in giú, ma tutta riversata' (XXXIII 93), so that they cannot clear the ice from their faces. Finally, the betrayers of benefactors, in Giudecca, are completely immersed:

> Già era, e con paura il metto in metro,
> là dove l'ombre tutte eran coperte,
> e trasparien come festuca in vetro.
> Altre sono a giacere; altre stanno erte,
> quella col capo e quella con le piante;
> altra, com'arco, il volto a piè rinverte.
>
> (XXXIV 10–15)

[I was already – and with fear I put it into verse – where the shades were completely covered and showed through like straws in glass. Some were lying horizontally; others were upright, one on his head, one on his soles, another like a bow, bent face to feet.]

The immersion motif occurs in most versions of the *Vision of Paul* and in seven of the popular visions from the sixth to the thirteenth centuries.[33] It is based on the biblical warning that 'therewithal a man sinneth, by the same also shall he be punished' (*Wisdom* 11.16). Sinners are therefore often immersed to parts of the body appropriate to their crimes – fornicators to the navel, slanderers to the lips, murderers completely. The motif is both a means of *contrapasso* and of classification.

The most detailed description of the immersion of sinners in a river occurs in the oldest manuscript of the *Vision of Paul*, where the category of the indifferent ('neither hot nor cold') who are the subjects of the punishment (modelled on the description of the church of the Laodiceans in Apocalypse 3.15–16), reminds us strongly of the souls confined to the vestibule of Dante's Hell, 'coloro/ che visser sanza 'nfamia e sanza lodo' [those who lived without disgrace and without praise] (Inf III 36):

Et uidi illic fluuium ignis feruentem, et ingressus multitudo uirorum et mulierum dimersus usque ad ienua et alios uiros usque ad umbiculum, alios enim usque ad labia, alios autem usque ad capillos; et interrogaui angelum et dixi: Domine, qui sunt isti in flumine igneo? Et respondit angelus et dixit mihi: Neque calidi neque frigidi sunt, quia neque in numero iustorum inuenti sunt neque in numero impiorum. Isti enim inpenderunt tempus uite suae in terris dies aliquos facientes in oracionibus, alios uero dies in peccatis et fornicacionibus usque ad mortem. Et interrogaui et dixi: Qui sunt hii, domine, dimersi usque ad ienua in igne? Respondens dixit mihi: Hi sunt qui cum exierint de aecclesia inmitunt se in sermonibus alienis disceptare. Histi uero qui dimersi sunt usque ad umbiculum, hi sunt qui cum sumpserunt corpus et sanguinem Christi eunt et fornicant et non cessauerunt a peccatis suis usque quo morerentur. Dimersi autem usque ad labia hi sunt detractores alterutrum conuenientes in aecclesiam dei; usque ad superlicia uero dimersi hii sunt qui innuunt sibi, malignitatem insidiantur proximo suo. (Paris MS pp. 28–9)

[And there I saw a burning river of fire, and in it a multitude of men and women immersed up to the knees, and others up the the navel, others up to the lips, and yet others up to the hair; and I asked the angel 'who are these in the fiery river?' And the angel replied 'they are those who were neither hot nor cold, who are therefore included neither among the just nor among the wicked. For they spent their lives gossiping, or sinning and fornicating until their death'. And I asked 'who are those, master, immersed up to the knees in the fire?' He answered 'they are those who as soon as they came out of church began to argue about unrelated matters. Those immersed to the navel took communion and then fornicated, and did not cease to sin until their deaths. Those immersed to the lips slandered others in church; and those immersed to the eyebrows are those who harmed others, or plotted maliciously against their neighbour.']

The four categories described here are retained, with variations of detail, until the twelfth century, when many more degrees of immersion are present. The greatest number, eleven, occurs in *St Patrick's Purgatory*, where sinners are immersed in individual pits of boiling metals up to their eyebrows, eyes, lips, necks, chest, waist, thighs, knees, calves, one foot and one hand.[34]

There has been considerable critical discussion of Dante's use of the immersion motif. Three visions in particular have been put forward as specific sources: *Paul*, *Charles the Fat*, and *Alberic*.[35] But in none of these texts is the motif used exactly as in the *Inferno*. Firstly, both the *Vision of Paul* and the *Comedy* depict the immersion of sinners in blood; but there is little correspondence between the sins for which this is said to be the torment. The immersion in *Paul* indeed seems closest not to that in Dante's Phlegethon but to that in his Cocytus in which, as in the vision, the greatest degree of immersion is suffered by those who most gravely betrayed trust. And in redactions II and VIII, the rivers of fire in which the sinners are punished are called 'Cogiton' and 'Cociton' respectively.

Secondly, both the *Vision of Alberic* and the *Comedy* describe immersion in ice – Alberic reports as follows:

Hec dicens apostolus ostendit michi vallem terribilem in qua innumeros quasi congelate glaciei acervos conspexi tante nimirum altitudinis, ut vix eorum cacumina oculis aspicerem.
(p. 87, repunctuated)

[Saying this, the apostle showed me a terrible valley in which I saw innumerable frozen souls piled together in the ice so deep down that I could scarcely make out the tops of their heads.]

But immersion in ice is also described by Thurkill, who sees sinners completing their purgation in an icy lake:

quarum quedam usque ad verticem, quedam usque ad collum, nonnulle usque ad pectus et brachia, alie ad umbilicum et renes, quedam usque ad genua et nonnulle vix usque ad cavillam pedem immersae fuerunt.
(p. 16)

[some of whom were immersed to the crown, some to the neck, some to the chest and arms, others to the waist and back, some to the knees and some only up to the heel.]

Alberic goes on to describe the varying degrees of immersion, but again the sins punished are unrelated to those in either the circle of the violent or the circle of the treacherous; they are adultery (immersed to the heels), incest (immersed to the knees), debauchery (to the thighs), lust or *luxuria* (to the chest) and fornication (to the crown).

Thirdly, Charles the Fat describes immersion as a punishment for homicide and robbery, as does Dante; but the immersion is described as taking place in burning rivers and boiling metals. And again, he is not alone: Alberic sees homicides plunged in a lake of 'blood', the waves of which are in fact flames, and Godeschalc describes three types of murderer immersed to varying degrees in fire.[36]

So although the close correspondence between Dante's use of the motif of gradated immersion and its description in earlier texts such as the visions of Paul, Charles the Fat and Alberic does indicate strongly that the poet was familiar with popular beliefs concerning the other world (and may indeed have been familiar with one or more of these texts), it cannot be said, given the differences between the use of the motif in the *Comedy* and individual visions, that he was imitating any one of them. The motif of gradated immersion bears witness to the way in which no one particular text but rather the whole tradition of the popular representation of the afterlife lies behind the *Comedy*.

<h3 style="text-align:center">THE BRIDGE</h3>

Intimately connected with the motifs of rivers and immersion is that of the bridge. It first occurs in Western visions of the other world in the sixth century, and is particularly widespread in the twelfth; it is illustrated in both illumination and fresco. It is the most common motif in the twelfth-century representations of the afterlife, and yet it is the only one not found in recognisable form in the *Comedy*. It is nonetheless important because an examination of its role in the popular tradition helps us to understand the way in which the intellectual changes of the twelfth century come between the previous representations of the other world and the *Comedy*.

The bridge is first described in the visions related by Gregory the Great and his contemporary Gregory of Tours.[37] The account in the *Dialogues* is fuller than the bare outline given in the *History of the Franks*, and contains all the essential elements of the motif as it developed later: a soldier dies of plague, is transported to the other world and sees a dark, smelly river crossed by a bridge. Beyond the bridge are flowery, scented meadows. Every soul must cross the bridge to reach the meadows beyond and, while the just find the crossing easy, the unjust fall into the river below.[38] Those who fall from such a bridge are often immersed to varying degrees in accordance with the gravity of their sins, as illustrated in Plate 10, which is taken from a manuscript of a French version of the *Vision of Paul*. The motif occurs in texts of all periods up to the thirteenth century,[39] and its sources have been analysed in detail by Dinzelbacher and by Culianu, who found it to derive on the one hand from early Irish myth, and on the other from Persian belief.[40]

The only form of bridge in the *Comedy* is the series of 'ponticelli' which link the separate areas of the *Malebolge*, and the question naturally arises: is there any relationship between these and the bridge motif?[41] In order to answer this question we must look more closely at the bridge in the visions, concentrating particularly on its function. The bridge as a motif is exceptional in that it does not constitute merely another topographical detail within the geography of Hell; it itself forms part of that geography, serving as a link between two realms, and therefore has a much wider significance than the majority of motifs.

Plate 10 The bridge of Hell, the river of torment and the gates of Paradise;
illumination from a French manuscript of the *Vision of Paul*,
thirteenth–fourteenth centuries

The bridge is used in the visions in four different ways. Firstly, it is a torment like any other, and merely an instrument of punishment. This is the case in the *Vision of Tundale*, where the bridge is a punishment for theft. Paved with nails, it stretches long, high and narrow over a lake in which lurk hungry monsters. Tundale, who once stole a cow, is told that he must cross this bridge, taking the cow with him. In horror he protests that he returned it, but his angel guide unrelentingly points out that he did so only when it could no longer be concealed. Tundale begins his painful journey. Every time he takes a step forward, the cow nearly falls off, and every time he gets the cow to take a step forward, he himself nearly loses his balance: 'cum stabat anima, cadebat vacca, et cum vacca stabat, cadebat anima' (p. 21). Eventually he reaches the half-way point, only to find the path blocked by a soul carrying a sheaf of wheat and coming in the opposite direction. Fortunately his guide relents, and Tundale is transported to the other side.[42]

A second group of texts describes the bridge as an instrument of judgment, serving to separate the sheep from the goats.[43] Adamnan divides those who cross into three categories: those who lived a life of religious zeal find the bridge wide, and cross easily; those who were initially reluctant but later became zealous find it narrow at first, but later broad; they too cross. And those who refused to live a Christian life find that the bridge is broad at the beginning, but narrows; they fall into the fire below.[44]

Topographical motifs of the other world

The use of the bridge motif in *St Patrick's Purgatory*, in which it separates those destined for Hell from those on their way to Paradise, is the most reminiscent of Dante's 'ponticelli' of all the popular texts. As Owen approaches the end of Purgatory, he comes to a pit, where he is greeted by a troop of devils. They tell him that the pit is the entrance to Hell, that he who enters never returns, but that they will show him round and restore him unharmed to the entrance. Owen, undeceived, refuses, but is dragged in and released only when he invokes the name of Christ. A second troop of devils appears, explaining that

'socii nostri tibi dixerunt, quod hic sit infernus: mentiti sunt; non ita fore scias; nam consuetudinis nostrae semper est mentiri, ut quos per verum decipere non possumus, decipiamus per mendacium; hic non est infernus, sed nunc ad infernum te ducemus.'

(col. 995)

['our colleagues told you that this was Hell; they lied, and it is not so. For it is our custom to lie always, so that we might deceive with falsehood those whom we cannot deceive with the truth. This is not Hell, but now we will lead you there.']

They lead him to a river crossed by a bridge, and make the same promise of safe conduct. As Owen crosses, the bridge widens; the infuriated devils, waiting below 'come cani arrabbiati' [like enraged dogs] in the Italian version, shake it and surround it with tempestuous winds, lunging towards Owen with their hooks but failing to dislodge him. He reaches the Earthly Paradise on the other side, and leaves them beside themselves with rage.

This whole episode foreshadows Dante's encounter with the demons in the fifth *bolgia*: the promise of safety (*Inferno* XXI 115–26), the attempt to capture by force (XXI 67–71), the attempt to deceive with a mixture of true and false statements (XXI 106–14), the comparison of the devils to famished dogs (XXIII 16–18) and the enraged pursuit as the prey escapes (XXIII 34–54).

In the eleventh and twelfth centuries a third function of the bridge develops: it becomes part of the mechanism of purgation. The Monk of Wenlock records that the sinners who fall from the bridge undergo not eternal torment but purgation; once purged, they succeed in crossing.[45] Alberic gives the most complete description:

vidi flumen magnum de inferno procedere, ardens, atque piceum, in cuius medio pons erat ferreus multam habens latitudinem, per quem pontem iustorum anime tam facilius tamque velocius transeunt, quam immunes inveniuntur a delictis. Peccatorum autem ponderibus gravati cum ad medium eius venerint, tam efficitur subtilis, ut ad fili quantitatem eius latitudo videatur redigi. Qua illi difficultate prepediti, in eundem flumen corruunt; rursumque assurgentes ac denuo recidentes, tandiu ibidem cruciantur, donec in morem carnium excocti e purgati, liberam habeant transeundi pontis facultatem. (p. 93)

[I saw a great black burning river flowing out of Hell, crossed by a very wide iron bridge, over which the souls of the just passed easily and quickly, arriving unharmed in Paradise. But when the souls of the sinful reached the middle, the bridge suddenly became very narrow, as narrow as a hair, and overcome by this difficulty they fell into the river. They climbed out but fell off again, and were tormented there until eventually they were boiled and purged, and were able to cross the bridge freely.]

Plate 11 The bridge of trial and the weighing of souls, detail from fresco in S. Maria in Piano, Loreto Aprutino, fourteenth century

The final use of the bridge occurs in the last of the visions, that of Thurkill, where it forms not just one element of the mechanism of purgation but part of the structure of Purgatory itself. Purgatory consists of three areas, clearly separated and differentiated from Hell for the first time in the popular tradition. These are a fire, a lake and a bridge covered in nails, 'pons magnus aculeis et sudibus per totum affixus' (p. 12). Purgation begins in the fire and continues in the lake and on the bridge, being finally completed only on the slopes of the mountain of joy to which the bridge leads. As souls near the end of their purgation in the lake, they move gradually closer to the bridge, until at the edge of the lake they reach the series of steps which lead up to it. The immersion motif is thus also adapted, varying degrees of immersion corresponding not to particular sins but to the amount of purgation still to be undergone. A third phase of purgation begins on the bridge, where souls cross at different rates according to their moral state, and purgation is finally completed on the mountain of joy to which the bridge gives access.[46] With the exception of the nails, the essential elements of this description are illustrated in the fresco at S. Maria in Piano, Loreto Aprutino, which is thought to date from the thirteenth or fourteenth century (see Plate 11). The presence of Michael with the

36

scales of judgment on the bank suggests that some purgation is still to be undergone after successful negotiation of the bridge, as in *Thurkill*.

The *Vision of Thurkill* thus represents the climax of a gradual development in the use of the bridge motif. From its earlier functions as a form of punishment or means of judgment, the bridge becomes firstly an instrument of purgation in a Hell which provides both eternal and purgative torment and finally, with the *Vision of Thurkill*, part of the structure of Purgatory itself. Now, as we shall see when we come to look at the representation of Purgatory, the idea that the purgation of sins occurs in a third realm of the other world separate from the other two became fully accepted only during the second half of the twelfth century.[47] Thurkill, who experienced his vision in 1206, saw a bridge as part of that realm – a very natural choice because of its suitability both to constitute part of the structure of the middle realm and also to form a topographical link between the other two realms. Dante chose not a bridge but a mountain, likewise suitable both to be a realm in its own right and to link the other two, in this case an underground Hell and a celestial Paradise. And so the bridge as it had been used in the twelfth-century visions became redundant. The 'ponticelli' of *Malebolge*, which form part of an episode which echoes the one in *St Patrick's Purgatory*, are not therefore themselves connected directly to the traditional use of the bridge motif, in any of its four forms, except in so far as Dante's elimination of its purgative function freed the motif for other purposes.

THE LADDER

So far we have looked at two topographical motifs: the rivers, relevant to the *Inferno*; and the bridge, relevant to the *Inferno* and *Purgatorio*. There is another major topographical motif which occurs throughout the popular tradition, and which is of particular relevance to the *Purgatorio* and *Paradiso*: the motif of the ladder.

Dante uses the ladder in two different ways. Firstly, the ladder is the last of the four great visual images seen by the poet in the course of his ascent to the Empyrean. The souls of the Heaven of the Sun appear to him in the form of three revolving crowns, symbolising the Trinity, source of the wisdom which they possessed. Those in Mars move against the background of a gigantic cross, symbol of the faith for which they fought. Those in Jupiter assume the shape of an eagle's head, symbol of the Roman Empire and of the Justice which they upheld. And in the Heaven of Saturn the souls of the contemplatives appear to Dante on a golden ladder.

Secondly, Dante presents the ascent up the mountain of Purgatory as the climbing of a long and winding staircase leading from terrace to terrace (it is important to remember that the word 'scala' signifies both ladder and stairs). And his journey in its entirety is described as the ascent of a 'lunga scala' (Par XXVI 111) from Earth to Heaven.

Both these uses of the ladder are found in the previous visions of the other world.

The ladder as link

The concept of the ascent to heaven is a universal and archetypal one, occurring in many different religious traditions.[48] The first important vision of the afterlife in the Christian tradition, the *Vision of Paul*, is built around the biblical verses which describe Paul being caught up into the third heaven, and the majority of its successors, including the *Comedy*, are likewise built on a framework of ascent into heaven and descent into Hell. The vehicle most commonly used in all such texts to represent or embody this ascent, and on occasion descent, is that of the *scala*, ladder or stairs.

In the Western tradition, the key text is the biblical account of the ladder seen in a dream by Jacob:

he dreamed that he saw a ladder standing on the earth, with its top reaching up into heaven; a stairway for the angels of God to go up and come down. Over this ladder the Lord himself leaned down, and spoke to Jacob (. . .). When he awoke from his dream, Jacob (. . .) shuddered; What a fearsome place is this! said he. This can be nothing other than the house of God; this is the gate of Heaven. (Genesis 28. 12–27)

This scene is represented in art as early as the fourth century, when it appears in the Roman catacombs.[49] In the twelfth and thirteenth centuries it was commonly depicted in psalters and Bibles, like the one shown in Plate 12.

Jacob's ladder soon became the subject of an apocryphal text of uncertain date devoted entirely to the dream,[50] and it passed into a number of visions of the other world. The presence of the motif in Raoul de Houdenc's satirical description of the other world indicates that it was a commonly accepted ingredient of the afterlife by the thirteenth century.

The first function of the ladder in the vision literature is to act as a link between Heaven and Earth. In the *Liber de Scalis* or *Book of the Ladder*, Mohammed begins his journey by ascending to the first heaven on a ladder of precious metals:

Gabriel (. . .) ostendit mihi quamdam scalam que durabat a primo celo usque ad terram ubi stabam (. . .). Gabriel quoque me per manum accepit et elevans a terra posuit me super primum scale gradum et dixit mihi: 'Ascende, Machomete!' Et ascendi, et Gabriel mecum similiter. Angeli vero cuncti associabant me qui erant ad scale custodiam deputati. (p. 49)

[Gabriel showed me a certain ladder which stretched from the first heaven to the earth on which I was standing. He took me by the hand and, lifting me up from the ground, put me on the first rung of the ladder and said to me: 'Climb, Mohammed!' And I climbed, and Gabriel likewise with me. And many angels accompanied me, the appointed custodians of the ladder.]

The Monk of Eynsham likewise finds that, once having reached the wall which encloses Paradise, a stairway is the only way forward:

Erant quoque ab imo usque ad summitatem eius gradus mira pulchritudine dispositi per quos ascendebant agmina laetantium, mox ut fuissent per ianuam introgressi. Nullus fuit ascendentium labor, difficultas nulla, non quelibet in ascendendo mora, superior semper alacrius quam inferior scandebatur gradus (. . .). Ad altiora vero oculos defigens conspexi in throno glorie residentem Dominum et Salvatorem nostrum in specie humana. (p. 315)

Plate 12 Jacob's ladder; illustration to Genesis 28.12–17, Lambeth Bible, twelfth century

Plate 13 Detail of ladder linking the Earthly and Heavenly Paradises, St Nicholas, Matrei, Austria, 1260–70

[Steps of great beauty stretched from the base to the top of the wall, which the rejoicing souls ascended as soon as they came in through the door. Climbing them required no effort, and there was no difficulty or delay, for each step was ascended more quickly than the last. At the top I saw our Lord and Saviour in human form, sitting in a throne of glory.]

The role of the ladder as a link is illustrated in the thirteenth-century frescoes of St Nicholas in Matrei, Austria (plate 13). Both the Earthly and the Heavenly Paradises are depicted, and the ladder joins the one to the other.

Part of Dante's ascent from the Earthly Paradise to the eternal dwelling of God is likewise accomplished by means of Jacob's ladder. In the seventh heaven Dante sees a golden ladder rising up before him, with the souls of the contemplatives moving down it to greet him:

> di color d'oro in che raggio traluce
> vid'io uno scaleo eretto in suso
> tanto, che nol seguiva la mia luce.
>   Vidi anche per li gradi scender giuso
> tanti splendor, ch'io pensai ch'ogne lume
> che par nel ciel, quindi fosse diffuso.
> (Par XXI 28–33)

[Of the colour of gold flashing in the sun, I saw a ladder which rose so high that my sight could not follow it. I saw, too, coming down the steps, so many splendours that I thought every light in heaven was shining there.]

One of the lights, Benedict, explains that the ladder goes up to the eternal dwelling of God, and that it is identical to the one seen by Jacob in his dream (XXII 61–72). At the end of the encounter, the souls ascend back up the ladder, and Beatrice and Dante follow them on the next stage of their journey (XXII 97–105). The scene is illustrated in the miniature shown in Plate 14.

We saw earlier that the word *scala* has two meanings, ladder and stairs. And while a ladder appears to Dante in the Heaven of Saturn, it occurs under its other meaning, flight of stairs, throughout the *Purgatorio*. In order to climb from one terrace to another on the mountain of Purgatory, Dante and Virgil must seek out the narrow stairway which leads upwards through crevices in the rock. On every terrace they ask the way to these steps, and every time, like the Monk of Eynsham, Dante finds the ascent easier.[51] And once we have grown accustomed to the idea of this gradual, literal climbing of a series of flights of steps, Dante begins to use the 'scala' metaphorically. His whole spiritual journey becomes the ascent of a ladder which will be climbed again by anyone who reaches its summit, 'quella scala/u senza risalir nessun discende' (Par x 86–7), a spiritual ladder which leads the soul back to God.[52]

The ladder as test

A second group of visions employs the motif of the ladder at a greater level of complexity. No longer is it seen merely as a link between heaven and earth; a new element, that of testing or trial, is added. The first visionary to use the ladder in this way was Perpetua, martyred in the third century:

Plate 14 *Paradiso* XXII: the Heaven of Saturn; illumination from a manuscript of the
Comedy with the commentary of Francesco da Buti, showing the ladder of the
contemplatives

video scalam aeream mirae magnitudinis pertingentem usque ad caelum, et angustam, per quam nonnisi singuli ascendere possent: et in lateribus scalae omne genus ferramentorum infixum. Erant ibi gladii, lanceae, hami, macherae, veruta ut si quis neglegenter aut non sursum adtendens ascenderet, laniaretur et carnes eius inhaererent ferramentis. Et erat sub ipsa scala draco cubans mirae magnitudinis, qui ascendentibus insidias praestabat, et exterrebat ne ascenderent. (p. 180)

[I saw a golden ladder of great height stretching right up to heaven. It was narrow, so that only one person could ascend at a time. To the sides of the ladder were fixed all kinds of iron weapons – swords, javelins, hooks, nails: so that if anyone ascending was not very careful he would be torn to pieces. And at the bottom of the ladder I saw an enormous dragon plotting how to trap those who would ascend it.]

At the summit is an Earthly Paradise to which Perpetua and her companions ascend, and in which they are greeted by a white-haired shepherd. Witness to the independent survival of the motif is the illustration in a twelfth-century *Speculum virginum* (Plate 15) which includes all the elements of Perpetua's vision; the additional figure near the top of the ladder is an Ethiopian, similar to the Egyptian who is defeated by Perpetua in a later vision, and who represents the devil.

The ladder was made familiar as a symbol of trial by the *Scala celestis* of St John Climacus (he is named after the work) in the seventh century; it was influential in later centuries in both East and West. John described a ladder, identified with that of Jacob, which joined the earth to heaven. The souls of the dead mount this ladder, of which each rung signifies a particular virtue, and during the ascent many fall back to earth under the assault of demons representing particular vices.

John's representation of the ladder is reflected in the *Vision of Gunthelm*. Gunthelm's journey begins with an ascent to the chapel of the Virgin Mary, and his experiences are those described in the *Scala celestis*. He starts at the base of the ladder:

In singulis uero gradibus demones bini et bini residebant, qui quos poterant omnes ad superiora conscendere nitentes terribiliter infestabant. Quos ut uidit nouicius, ualde nimirum expauit, attamen a beati Benedicti uestigiis non recessit. Ascendentibus itaque sancto et nouicio, nequam spiritus sancto nocere non apposuerunt, sed subsequentem discipulum per gradus singulos grauiter afflixerunt. Alius eum soffocabat, alius uehementer impellebat, alius pugno eum in dorso percutiebat, alius illum colaphizabat, alius eum frendens dentibus subsannabat, et alius illum calumpniis et exprobationibus deterrebat.

(pp. 106–7)

[On each rung there were pairs of demons, who attacked all those who would ascend to the rung above. When the novice monk saw them, he was petrified, but he did not cease to follow in the footsteps of saint Benedict. So as the novice and the saint climbed up, the evil spirits did not oppose the saint, but on every step they sorely afflicted the novice. One suffocated him, another pushed him violently, another hit him in the back with his fist, another struck him, another sank his teeth into him, and another tried to deter him with slander and abuse.]

Upheld by Benedict, Gunthelm succeeds in reaching his destination. It is noticeable that in the *Paradiso*, the ladder is also associated particularly with Benedict, and that it leads Dante, as it does Gunthelm, straight to a vision of Mary and the Church Triumphant.

Plate 15 Nuns ascending the ladder of virtue, from a *Speculum Virginum* of the late twelfth century

These experiences foreshadow that of Dante as he climbs up from terrace to terrace in the *Purgatorio* and through the spheres of the *Paradiso*. On one level, the mountain is a stairway linking Earth to Heaven. But it is also an instrument of trial or testing. As he ascends the ladder which leads to the chapel of Mary, Gunthelm is attacked by devils representing his vices. And as he ascends the stairs of the mountain, Dante is also confronted by the vices which held sway over him: he bends double on the terrace of pride, staggers through the mist on the terrace of the angry, and experiences the most excruciating pain as he crosses the wall of fire on the terrace of the lustful.

The ladder as tool

It will by now have become clear that there is considerable precedent in the popular tradition for Dante's adoption of the ladder motif in both the *Purgatorio* and the *Paradiso*. But in order to understand precisely why the ladder is appropriate as a symbol in the Heaven of Saturn, and why it is used as a metaphor for Dante's entire spiritual journey, we must turn to the mystic writings of the twelfth century which lie behind the motif in both the contemporary visions and the *Comedy*.

In *Paradiso* XXII Benedict describes the contemplative life embraced by his Order as the ascent of a ladder, and laments that few now climb it. And if we look at the spiritual writings of the twelfth century we find that Jacob's ladder was often taken as a figure for the ascent of the contemplative to an understanding of divine reality. In the *Scala paradisi* of Guigo, the rungs of the ladder are identified with the four mystic stages of *lectio*, *meditatio*, *oratio*, and *contemplatio*.[53] The *Scala coeli major* and the *Scala coeli minor* of Honorius of Autun[54] conceive of the ladder as a symbol of the virtues which lead the soul from its state of sinfulness to God: 'in valle lacrymarum, imo in lacu miseriae sumus constituti; de qua ad altum supernae patriae montem per quamdam scalam sumus ascensuri' [we live in a valley of tears, indeed in a lake of misery, from which we are created to ascend to the mountain of the celestial paradise by means of a ladder] (col. 1230). The ladder reaches from Earth to the first, second and third heavens, and each rung represents a particular virtue.

The divisions of Honorius's ladder are interesting. In the first heaven of 'corporeal' vision, the soul contemplates the Ladder or Scale of Being, on which all forms of existence from primary matter to the first Intelligence were thought to have a place, arranged in ascending order according to the degree in which they partake of divine perfection.[55] By contemplating the various levels of the visible world, the soul begins its itinerary to God, their Creator.

The second heaven, according to Honorius, is the place in which corporeal vision is succeeded by the acquisition of spiritual vision, in which the imagination takes over from the eye, and the contemplative experiences dreams and visions. Twelve steps are involved.

In the third heaven, intellectual vision is reached. There are three major steps. 'First we consider the virtues of the soul, second the orders of angels, third the universe in the mind of God' (col. 1235). And at this point, Honorius tells us, Paradise has been reached.

Texts like the *Scala coeli major* explain why the ladder is appropriate to the contemplatives in the Heaven of Saturn, and why the twelfth-century visions often describe the ascent to heaven in terms of the ascent of a ladder. But the parallel is closer than that. Honorius tells us how to ascend by a process of careful contemplation from this world to an understanding of God; Dante actually does it before our very eyes, and invites us to join him – 'the aim (. . .) is to remove the living in this life from their state of misery, and to lead them to a state of happiness'.[56] Dante, like Honorius, intends to achieve by this the gradual re-education of the reader. Honorius begins with the Scale of Being, a concept with which Dante was familiar.[57] And the poet too makes us contemplate the material world – plants and their growth, the development of the human embryo, the phenomenon of light and its properties. Sometimes this is in simile, sometimes Dante actually breaks off from the narrative to explain it. In reading the book of Dante, we are to learn as he did to read the book of the universe; and by reading that we shall approach the thoughts of God. Then Honorius urges us to move on to a second level, that of spiritual experience, in which we see visions and dream dreams. Dante dreams about Rachel and Leah, and sees a vision of Mary and the Church Triumphant. His whole ascent is a spiritual journey, and with each encounter he learns a further truth – to recognise, and not excuse, his own sin in the figures of Paolo and Francesca; to understand the folly of Ulysses' search for a knowledge which is beyond the limits God has set for man; to acknowledge and repent of his own pride; to grasp the essence of faith, hope and love. Then the intellectual section, in which Honorius urges us to think about the virtues of the soul, the angelic orders, and finally the universe itself as it seems in the mind of God. This is the subject of the *Paradiso*. Dante ascends through the celestial spheres, in which the souls of the blessed appear to him, specially arranged virtue by virtue. Here he sees the nine angelic orders. And there he finally penetrates the truth, understanding the central paradoxes of the Christian faith, and momentarily penetrating the mind of God – in other words, he reaches the end point anticipated by Honorius. And the poem in its entirety is presented as a recollecting of the gradual process by which he came to reach that point.

So while it is true that Dante uses the ladder motif in a way which is superficially similar to its use in the popular tradition, it is dependent also on the mystical writings of the twelfth century. The result is that the ladder is not only a topographical motif; it reflects and embodies the spiritual movement of the whole poem, and thus provides an excellent clue to the understanding of the relation between the *Comedy* and the popular representations of the other world.

CONCLUSION

There are many motifs of the other world recurring throughout the popular tradition and resurfacing in the *Comedy*, and it would be possible to examine others. Dante's journey occurs at Easter; so does that of the Monk of Eynsham.[58] The admission of Statius to Paradise is accompanied by an earthquake and much joyful and noisy celebration; the entry of a righteous man to Paradise is described in similar terms in the *Vision of Paul*.[59] And six of the popular texts tell of a contest between angels and devils for the custody of a recently deceased soul, similar to that outlined in *Inferno* xxii with regard to Guido da Montefeltro.[60] But what is significant about Dante's use of these motifs, as of those we have examined in detail, is that they always form part of an integrated whole, an other world which is governed by consistent laws. They do not stand on their own as in the visions, each of which includes one or more motifs linked neither to one another nor to any overall pattern of meaning; they are part of a consistent philosophical and theological system. Until the twelfth century, the motifs of the other world had accumulated from a variety of sources, not necessarily Western or even Christian. But the intellectual developments of that century meant that description of the other world by the simple accumulation of a number of well-known motifs was no longer possible. Dante was able, as the visionaries and their redactors were not, to reinterpret the popular tradition in the light of these developments, discarding, adapting or occasionally retaining. So, for example, his souls are no longer subjected to the ancient Egyptian practice of being weighed to measure their merit. Other motifs, most especially the bridge and the ladder, are modified in the light of the writings of twelfth-century theologians. And those that are preserved unchanged – the cauldron, the presentation of Satan – are preserved for a particular purpose.

Notes

1 C. Segre, '*L'itinerarium animae* nel Duecento e Dante', 1984, p. 19; R. Palgen, *Mittelalterliche Eschatologie in Dantes 'Komodie'*, 1975, p. 22.

2 D. D. R. Owen, *The Vision of Hell: Infernal Journeys in Medieval French Literature*, 1970, p. 262.

3 M. Carrouges, 'Immagini dell'inferno nella letteratura', 1953, p. 27.

4 D. A. Traill, *Walahfrid Strabo's 'Visio Wettini': text, translation and commentary*, 1974, p. 12.

5 'Au Moyen Age: conscience individuelle et image de l'au-delà', 1982, p. 260.

6 'Per un'antropologia delle visioni ultraterrene nella cultura occidentale del Medioevo', 1977, p. 450.

7 *Otherworld Journeys*, 1987, p. 85.

8 For example, Ruffiacani (who becomes Graffiacane), Aliotto (Alichino), and Jacopo Ricci (Barbariccia).

9 See chapter 3, p. 97.

10 See L. Réau, *Iconographie de l'art chrétien*, 1955–9, vol. ii, pp. 751–3.

11 See P. Ariès, *The Hour of Our Death*, 1983, pp. 153–4 *et passim*.

12 The iconography of the devil is discussed by E. Mâle in *Religious Art in France. The Twelfth Century*, 1978 (first edition 1922), pp. 364–72.

13 Similar imagery is used by Dante in Purg. xxiv 136–8: 'drizzai la testa per veder che fossi;/e già mai non si videro in fornace/vetri o metalli sí lucenti e rossi'.

14 Described in the fullest detail by Tundale, p. 13.

15 Inf xxi 58–60; *Vision of Thurkill*, p. 20.

16 'do not charge interest to thy fellow Israelite when thou lendest him money or grain or anything else of thine', Deuteronomy 23. 19.

17 For the economic development of Florence see G. Luzzatto, *Storia economica d'Italia*, i, 1949.

18 Because of the increase in trade and expanding population, many small-scale banking and money-lending operations grew up alongside the international banking families. Florence became an 'enterprise culture' in which small businesses were launched on borrowed capital.

19 Inf XIV 94–120. The symbolism derives from two sources. The first is the Book of Daniel, chapter 2, where Nebuchadnezzar's dream of such a figure is interpreted by Daniel, who says that the different parts of his body symbolised Nebuchadnezzar's empire (the gold) and those which would follow. The other source is classical legend. Crete was the cradle of the Trojan race, and therefore of the Roman race which sprang from it, and the centre of the Golden Age under the reign of Saturn. The Golden Age was followed by the Silver, Bronze and Iron Ages. See Ovid's *Metamorphoses*, I, 90. In Purg XXVIII 139–41 Dante identifies the classical Golden Age with the time when man still lived in the Garden of Eden.

20 Daniel 7. 10. The river of fire is illustrated in the twelfth-century mosaic of the Last Judgment at Torcello and in the thirteenth-century frescoes in the Scrovegni chapel and in S. Maria Maggiore, Tuscania.

21 *I Enoch* 18. 11–16. According to T. H. Gaster the biblical rivers of fire derive from the East: 'the concept was doubtless influenced by the infiltration of Iranian ideas, for the articulation of it is clearly patterned on the Avestan doctrine of the ultimate judgment of the wicked in a stream of molten metal', 'Gehenna', *Interpreter's Dictionary of the Bible*, II, 1962, p. 351.

22 19. 20, 20.14, 21.8.

23 For example Cyrillus of Jerusalem; see A. Michel, 'Purgatoire', *Dictionnaire de Théologie Catholique*, XIII, col. 1198. For a discussion of 1 Cor 3.10–15 and an analysis of later exegesis see also J. Le Goff, *La Naissance du Purgatoire*, 1981, p. 66 *et passim*.

24 *Odyssey*, XI, pp. 172–3; *Phaedo*, pp. 112–13 – for Plato's sources see R. Hackforth, *Plato's Phaedo*, 1955, p. 185, and C. Pascal, *Le credenze d'oltretomba nelle opere letterarie dell'antichità classica*, 1924, vol. II, pp. 95–6. Virgil describes the infernal rivers in Aen VI 131–2 (Cocytus), 295–330 (Acheron, Cocytus and Styx), 384–440 (Styx), 548–56 (Phlegethon), and 703–15 (Lethe).

25 Genesis 2.10–14.

26 For Tertullian and Claudian see P. Courcelle, 'Les Pères de l'Eglise devant les enfers virgiliens', 1955, p. 25.

27 The argument for a Greek original is given by T. Silverstein, *Visio Sancti Pauli*, 1935, p. 3; the argument for a Syrian original is propounded by G. Ricciotti, *L'Apocalisse di Paolo siriaca*, 1932, I, p. 21.

28 The relationships between the various MSS of the *Vision of Paul* are as follows (amended from T. Silverstein, '*Visio Sancti Pauli*', p. 61, to include MSS discovered since 1935 and described in his 'The Vision of Paul: New Links and Patterns in the Western Tradition', 1959).

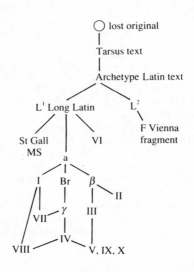

29 Analysed by Silverstein, *Visio Sancti Pauli*, pp. 65–6.

30 *Vision of Tundale*, pp. 14–15; *Vision of Godeschalc*, p. 96; *St Patrick's Purgatory*, cols. 994–5.

31 Charon: Inf III 82–99, Aen VI 298–304; Phlegyas: Inf VIII 13–24, Aen VI 618–20; Styx: Inf VII 106–11, Aen VI 323; Lethe: Purg XXXI 94–105; XXXIII 94–6, 121–3; Aen VI 705, 749.

32 'Morte per forza e ferute dogliose/ nel prossimo si danno, e nel suo avere/ ruine, incendi e tollette dannose;/ onde omicide e ciascun che mal fiere,/ guastatori e predon, tutti tormenta/ lo giron primo per diverse schiere.' (Inf XI 34–9) Dante divides violence against others into three types: violence causing death (later subdivided into tyranny, which causes the death of many, and murder, which causes the death of individuals), violence causing injury, and violence against property.

33 It is present in all redactions of the *Vision of Paul* except VI and VIII; in the derivative ninth-century *Apocalypse of the Virgin*; in the visions of Sunniulf (sixth century), the Monk of Wenlock, and the woman whose vision was recorded by the bishop of Lull (eighth century); in the *Vision of Charles the Fat* (ninth century); and in *Alberic, St Patrick's Purgatory* and the *Vision of Thurkill* (twelfth and thirteenth centuries).

34 'Quorum alii erant omnino immersi, alii usque ad supercilia, alii ad oculos, alii ad labia, alii ad colla, alii ad pectus, alii ad umbilicum, alii ad femora, alii ad genua, alii ad tibias, alii uno pede tantum, alii utraque manu' (col. 994).

35 The first critic to point out the existence of the immersion motif in the popular tradition and to suggest that Dante was imitating a particular text was Di Costanzo, in his discussion of the *Vision of Alberic*: 'riferendo questo tormento di sommersione di diversi gradi, pose Dante il sommergimento dei peccatori nel lago di sangue, che Alberico posto avea nella ghiacciaia, diversità che nullo toglie al parallelo che andiamo facendo' ('Di un antico testo a penna della "Divina Commedia"', 1800, p. 176). D'Ovidio regarded the use of the motif as the strongest indication of Dante's use of the *Vision of Paul*: 'il tratto piú caratteristico d'affinità con Paolo sarebbe veramente la gradualità dell'immersione di certe anime in un fiume, in misura proporzionata alla gravita dei loro peccati' (*Studii sulla 'Divina Commedia'*, 1901, p. 351). Most recently, the *Vision of Charles the Fat* has been postulated by Silverstein as Dante's source in *Inferno* XII, on the grounds that it alone among the visions uses the motif of gradated immersion for the punishment of bloodshed: 'only in the *Vision of Charles the Fat* is it true that the sinners plunged to varying depths into the boiling stream are, as in *Inferno*, XII, those who, out of their greed for earthly things, were guilty of bloodshed and rapine' ('"Inferno", XII, 100–26, and the "Visio Karoli Crassi"', 1936, p. 451).

36 *Vision of Alberic*, p. 89, *Vision of Godeschalc*, pp. 111–12.

37 Visions of Stephen, *Dialogues*, IV, 37 (pp. 286–7), and Sunniulf, *History of the Franks*, IV, 33 (p. 240).

38 The description is as follows: 'pons erat, sub quo niger adque caligosus foetoris intolerabilis nebulam exhalans fluvius decurrebat. transacto autem ponte, amoena erant prata, adque virentia odiferis herbarum floribus exornata (. . .). haec viro erat in praedicto ponte probatio, ut quisquis per eum iniustorum vellit transire, in tenebroso foetentique fluvio laberetur; iusti viro, quibus culpa non obsisterit, securo per eum gressu ac libero ad loca amoena pervenirent' (pp. 287–8).

39 It occurs in the later redactions of the *Vision of Paul* (VI, V, VIII, IX, X) and in the Italian and French versions; also in the *Vision of the Monk of Wenlock*, the *Fís Adamnáin*, the twelfth-century *Vision of Esdras*, *St Patrick's Purgatory*, and the visions of Alberic, Tundale (twice) and Thurkill. It is also found in the *Tractatus* of Etienne de Bourbon, in the *Liber de Scalis*, and in Celtic literature, particularly Arthurian romance.

40 See P. Dinzelbacher, *Die Jenseitsbrucke im Mittelalter*, Vienna, 1973, and L. Culianu, '"Pons subtilis": storia e significato di un simbolo', 1979, pp. 301–12. Culianu summarises the history of the motif as follows: 'Di origine indo-europea, esso appare nelle fonti indiane antiche sotto la forma di un "sentiero stretto". Cosí lo incontriamo ancora nell'apocrifo 4 Esdra. Negli scritti in lingua medio-persiana, il ponte Cinvat diventa largo per lasciar passare le anime dei Giusti o affilato per far precipitare nell'Inferno le anime dei peccatori. Questo motivo penetra nel cristianesimo già nel VI secolo e lo ritroviamo nelle leggende islamiche del mi'rag di Mohammed a partire dall'VIII secolo: sia attraverso un influsso iranico diretto, come crede Asin Palacios, sia attraverso un influsso cristiano. Infine, una tradizione sul ponte pericoloso esiste già in Irlanda: essa viene "riattivata"

dalla penetrazione di elementi orientali. È importante notare che la rappresentazione celtica viene completamente sostituita da quella araba', p. 310–11.

41 Critics have reacted variously to these bridges. Rüegg identifies them with the traditional bridge motif (*Die Jenseitvorstellungen vor Dante*, 1945, I, pp. 363–4, 419 (but see also p. 346); D'Ancona and Guercio deny any connection (*I precursori di Dante*, 1874, p. 42, and *Di alcuni rapporti tra le visioni medievali e la 'Divina Commedia'*, 1909, p. 74); and Becker remarks on the singularity of the omission (*A Contribution to the Comparative Study of the Medieval Visions of Heaven and Hell*, 1899, p. 37). But none has studied the motif in detail.

42 The episode is described on pp. 19–23.

43 This is the case in the majority of the early texts and in some later ones: Gregory the Great and Gregory of Tours, the *Vision of Paul* (with the exception of redaction IX), the *Fís Adamnáin*, the Latin *Vision of Esdras*, and *St Patrick's Purgatory*.

44 pp. 38–9.

45 p. 254.

46 p. 16.

47 See chapter 5. The most recent study on the development of the concept of Purgatory is that by J. Le Goff, *La Naissance du Purgatoire*.

48 It occurs in ancient Egypt, in Islam, in the Mithraic mysteries, in Japan and in Judaism. See M. Eliade, *Shamanism: Archaic Techniques of Ecstasy*, 1964, pp. 487–93.

49 See A. Grabar, *Christian Iconography: A Study of its Origins*, 1969, plate 243.

50 For translation and comment see M. R. James, *The Lost Apocrypha of the Old Testament, their Titles and Fragments*, 1920, pp. 96–103.

51 References to the stairs in the *Purgatorio*: III 46–51; XI 39–40; XII 115–17; XIII 1–3; XV 34–6; XVII 64–9; XVII 76–8; XXV 7–9.

52 Purg XXI 19–21; Par X 82–7; XXI 64–6; XXVI 109–11.

53 *Patrologia Latina*, CLXXXIV, cols. 475–84, where it is given its alternative title *Scala claustralium*. Discussed by G. Lodolo, 'Il tema simbolico del Paradiso nella tradizione monastica dell'Occidente latino (secoli VI–XII): lo spazio del simbolo', 1977, p. 273.

54 *Patrologia Latina*, CLXXII, cols. 1229–42.

55 The standard authority is A. O. Lovejoy, *The Great Chain of Being: A Study in the History of an Idea*, 1936.

56 *Epistola*, XIII, 39.

57 *Convivio*, III, vii.

58 The Monk goes into a trance on the evening of Maundy Thursday, and his vision is completed at midnight between Easter Saturday and Easter Sunday. Compare Dante, whose experience begins at the same time, but ends later; by midnight he has reached the bottom of Hell but not yet visited Purgatory and Paradise. See U. Foscolo's review of Cancellieri's study of the *Vision of Alberic* in *Edinburgh Review*, September 1818, p. 319, and H. Thurston, 'Visio monachi de Eynsham', *Analecta Bollandiana*, 22 (1903), p. 232.

59 *Vision of Paul*, Paris MS, p. 17. The motif is also present in the redactions.

60 Inf XXVII 112–20. The six texts are Barontus, the *Monk of Wenlock*, Tundale, Paul, the soldier whose vision is described by Gregory the Great, and the *Monk of Eynsham*.

2

The inhabitants of the other world

The aim of this chapter is to examine the inhabitants of Dante's other world in relation to those in the popular representations of the afterlife, concentrating particularly on the identities of the persons included. It is not intended to discuss the relationship between the individual and the area of Hell, Purgatory or Paradise in which he is found, or the nature of his torment, suffering or reward; the emphasis will be on the choice and presentation of individuals.

It has generally been assumed that one of the major achievements of the *Comedy* was the introduction into the poem of contemporary figures and obscure persons of the poet's acquaintance – an assumption which remained unchanged after the discovery of the previous medieval representations of the afterlife. This view is summarised by Curtius:

> The great number and variety of persons in the *Commedia* is explained by the most impressive and most fertile innovation which Dante's genius incorporated into the antique and medieval heritage: his drawing upon contemporary history. Dante summons popes and emperors of his own times to judgment; kings and prelates; statesmen, tyrants, generals; men and women from the nobility and the bourgeoisie, from guild and school.[1]

Curtius adds in a footnote that 'such a precedent as Walafrid's putting Charlemagne in Hell (. . .) stands quite alone'.

Other critics have carried this a stage further, and stated that Dante's originality lies not only in the inclusion of contemporary characters in his other world but also in his portrayal of them as lifelike individuals. Auerbach writes that the poet

> was the first to configure what antiquity had configured very differently and the Middle Ages not at all: man not as a remote legendary hero, not as an abstract or anecdotal representation of an ethical type, but man as we know him in historical reality, the concrete individual in his unity and wholeness.[2]

The aim of this chapter is to re-examine these views on Dante's choice and presentation of characters in the light of the popular descriptions of the other world, looking in particular at the inclusion of contemporary characters and at the depiction of the individual.

INHABITANTS OF THE OTHER WORLD: A BRIEF OUTLINE
Choice of characters

The characters present in the vision literature vary in type from period to period. In the classical representations we are shown warriors, great rulers and their wives and daughters and, exceptionally, a group such as that described in the *Aeneid* of those who met their deaths through love. Homer offers us figures such as Leda, Ariadne, Agamemnon and Achilles; Virgil presents Phaedra, Dido, Theseus and Orpheus; and Statius includes Minos, Manto, Cadmus and Actaeon. This is the period in which the greatest variety is offered; from these few examples it can be seen that the afterlife characters include the historical and the legendary, the famous and the fictitious, the poet, the warrior and the ruler.

In the apocryphal descriptions of Heaven and Hell, the inhabitants of the other world are exclusively biblical, and generally confined to Paradise. They consist typically of patriarchs, prophets and the four evangelists. *IV Esdras* offers the widest mixture of specifically named characters: Enoch, Elijah, Moses, Peter, Paul, Luke, Matthew and, exceptionally, Herod in Hell. The *Vision of Paul* and the early Christian visions follow, in the main, the apocryphal descriptions, although Saturus sees in Paradise Bishop Optatus and the presbyter Aspasius, bishop and priest to the martyrs – the first examples of the inclusion of characters known to the visionary.

From the fifth century, on the authority of Augustine and Chrysostom, Hell became generally accepted as the place to which not only infidels but sinful believers would be consigned after death.[3] As a result of this change, the emphasis in the visions shifts from Paradise to Hell, and the genre begins to be used as a vehicle for political comment. The earliest example of this occurs in a vision recorded by Gregory of Tours at the end of the sixth century, in which Chilperic, King of Neustria from 561 to his assassination in 584, is said to be in Hell; his eternal destination would seem to confirm the justice of his murder.

In the Carolingian era representations of the other world become almost exclusively political in their aims. Curtius refers to Walafrid's depiction of Charlemagne as wholly exceptional; and yet the emperor is shown in two other ninth-century compositions: in the vision of Rotcharius he is represented in Paradise, and in that of the Poor Woman also in Hell. Satire extends to Church leaders; Bernoldus records the presence in Hell of no fewer than forty-one bishops, of whom he names three, and Walafrid describes Bishop Adalhelm[4] suffering alongside Charlemagne.

The eleventh century saw another change in the kind of characters depicted: instead of meeting well-known figures in the other world, we are introduced predominantly to obscure individuals. The *Vision of Walkelin* is the most significant in this respect, offering a range of local villagers, all of whom had died recently. Walkelin sees Hugh, the recent bishop of Lisieux, and two local abbots, Mainer of St Evroul and Gerbert of Saint-Wandrille; the two sons of a local count, Richard and Baldwin; and a justiciary who had died during the last twelve months, Landricus of Orbec.[5] Landricus is followed by William of Glos, a usurer, who gives an account of his sins and begs Walkelin to take a message to his wife, in the same way that many of the characters Dante meets entreat him to pass on their words to the living.[6] The procession is concluded with an encounter between Walkelin and his brother Robert, the story of whose life is given in the same way.

It is only, however, in the twelfth century that all these different types come together, and we find patriarchs and prophets, prominent figures and obscure ones, saints and monks, lists of names and, for the first time, portraits of individuals. It is here that the ground is prepared for the *Comedy*: no longer are characters included because it is traditional to do so, or because the visionary or his redactor is seeking to make some political point; they are included for their own sakes, as familiar but unimportant individuals with their own stories and personalities.

The fullest vision, in terms of the variety of contemporary figures presented, is that of the monk of Eynsham. The monk sees two historical characters (the saints Nicholas and Margaret), and twenty-seven of his contemporaries. These include Henry II; Baldwin the archbishop of Canterbury, who died in 1191; three other bishops, one of whom has been tentatively identified as Hugo Puiset, bishop of Durham;[7] Richard Palmer, who had died while bishop of Messina; an abbot and two abbesses, all recently deceased; three knights of the monk's acquaintance; the village goldsmith and lawyer; two local women; and a selection of nuns, monks, priests and priors together with a sacristan and a 'clericus scholasticus'. Digressions lasting for several chapters relate the personal stories of the characters – the goldsmith, for example, occupies no fewer than five, and the surrounding rigours of Hell recede temporarily into the background.

The characters of the *Comedy* are chosen in accordance with many of the same criteria as those in previous representations of the afterlife. Biblical characters are named as in the early visions; political figures are prominent as in the Carolingian texts; obscure individuals known to the poet are depicted as in the popular representations of the twelfth century – although Dante explains through Cacciaguida that by and large the famous and notorious have been chosen as examples (Par XVII 135–42). Surprisingly few of the characters named in the *Comedy* have already been included in previous visions of the other world. Five of these are taken from classical representations: Tiresias and Achilles from Homer (of whom of course Dante had no direct knowledge), Aeneas and Dido from Virgil, and Manto (with Tiresias again) from Statius. Orpheus, present in Limbo, is also associated with the underworld in accounts such as those in the *Metamorphoses* and Virgil's *Georgics*.[8] From the Old Testament Dante includes Abel, Abraham, Jacob, Isaac, Moses, David, Noah, Adam and the twelve sons of Jacob; from the New Testament Peter, Mary, John the Baptist, Caiaphas, Judas, Annas and John the Evangelist. All these occur in previous texts; the remaining eighteen biblical characters in the *Comedy* do not. Among the historical characters of the poem only two have figured in previous representations: Charlemagne and Benedict.

Like the visionaries of the twelfth century, Dante is perhaps the most striking for the inclusion of his contemporaries, ranging from kings and emperors to shoemakers and manuscript illuminators. There are theologians such as Thomas Aquinas and Bonaventure; musicians and instrument-makers such as Belacqua and Casella; poets like Sordello, Guido Cavalcanti, Guido Guinizzelli; artisans such as Asdente the shoemaker, Guglielmo Borsiere the pursemaker, Maestro Adamo the mint-master; noblewomen such as Francesca da Rimini, Cunizza da Romano, Pia de' Tolomei; political leaders such as Buonconte da Montefeltro, Farinata degli

Uberti, Corso Donati; rulers like Obizzo II d'Este, Guido da Montefeltro, Currado Malaspina; and clerics such as Ruggieri degli Ubaldini, archbishop of Pisa, and five popes including Boniface VIII. And although not the most numerous group, it is these characters who occupy the most space in the *Comedy*, and therefore to which most critical attention has been paid.

Presentation of characters

Not only the choice of inhabitants of the other world but also the way in which they are presented changes from century to century. Initially, and to some extent throughout the tradition, characters in Hell are grouped according to sin and are frequently nameless and faceless. In Paradise, individuals and groups of individuals such as the twelve apostles are named in a haphazard way. This is the case in the *Vision of Paul*. Later, in texts such as the *Vision of Barontus*, the inhabitants of Hell are grouped by sin as before, but some of them are named; and this grouping is now echoed in Paradise, so that at the first gate Barontus sees the deceased monks of his monastery, at the second children and virgins, and at the third saints and martyrs. When they are named, inhabitants are merely listed, and no attempt is made to portray character. This remains the pattern until the late twelfth century, when Godeschalc, the Monk of Eynsham and Thurkill abandon all forms of classification in groups according to sin in favour of the presentation of successive individuals with case histories, often in such detail that the vision reads more like a document of social history than an account of the other world.

The chosen grouping of the characters in the *Comedy* is essentially the same as the grouping in the visions. In Hell they are arranged by sin, as is traditional in all but the later visions. The practice of division according to role in society persists in the *Comedy* to some extent, both where profession is a sin – as in the case of the usurers – and in the Heaven of Saturn, where Benedict reveals that other Benedictines are here with him (Par XXII 50–1).

The later visions had abandoned the traditional practice whereby individuals appeared within determined categories of sin or beatitude, in favour of the presentation of a succession of individuals with no classificatory scheme. This gave more flexibility in the portrayal of rounded characters, but excluded the possibility of any systematic framework. Dante is the first to combine the two approaches by introducing the reader to a convincing character who incarnates the sin of which he is suffering the consequences. The startling discrepancy which occurs at times between the treatment of the individual sinner and the area to which he is allocated – Brunetto does not appear, poetically, to be guilty of the sin for which he was condemned – is without precedent in the popular tradition.

CHOICE OF CHARACTERS IN THE VISION LITERATURE AND THE *COMEDY*

There has been surprisingly little critical analysis of the demography of Dante's other world. A few studies have attempted to number and categorise the inhabitants of Hell, Purgatory and Paradise, but none is in agreement either with regard to the method used or to the totals obtained, and none is conducted in such a way as to facilitate comparison with previous accounts of the afterlife.[9] For this reason the characters identified in both the *Comedy* and the visions are listed in the tables at the end of this chapter.

There are, in the *Comedy*, approximately 600 characters. The total must remain approximate because some characters have not been identified, and because of an inevitable uncertainty as to where to draw the line – there are grounds for including or excluding the 'staff' of Hell, or the symbolic figures in the Earthly Paradise, for example. Of these 600, about half are mentioned in simile only, and are not said to be resident in the other world. Discounting these, it proves to be the case that exactly 300 people, excluding 'staff' and symbolic figures, are said to inhabit Hell, Purgatory and Paradise. Of these 300, 299 are already dead, and one, Branca d'Oria, is still alive, his spirit having preceded his body to eternal damnation (Inf XXXIII 135–47). Despite Dante's astonishment at seeing him there, Branca's case is not without precedent. A number of the earlier visionaries came across individuals in the other world who were still alive: the monk of Wenlock found Ceolred, king of Mercia, whom his abbot and redactor states to have been alive at the time; and Charles the Fat saw his heir Ludovic.[10]

In addition to the 300 already in eternity, Dante mentions just three who although still alive are destined for particular areas of the other world. These are the Popes Boniface VIII (died 1303) and Clement V (died 1314), and Corso Donati, leader of the Black Guelphs in Florence (died 1308). For this too there is precedent in the vision tradition: the beggar whose vision is recorded by Othlo saw the places prepared for Henry III and Gebehard, bishop of Ratisbon, and Tundale saw the seat made ready for a contemporary Irish bishop.[11]

In order to compare the characters chosen by Dante with those seen by earlier visionaries, it seems best to divide them into categories, and it is in terms of these categories that they are listed in the tables at the end of the chapter. They fall into four groups: classical characters, biblical characters, historical characters and contemporary characters. Contemporary characters are taken to be those alive during the visionary's lifetime, in Dante's case after 1265. Contemporary characters have been further divided into six social groupings; this enables exploration of the relationship between the identity of the visionary and the type of characters he sees in the other world, and facilitates comparison between the breadth of selection of poet and visionaries of different periods.

At this point a warning must be sounded. The disadvantage of this numerical approach is that it does not measure the amount of space which each character receives, and therefore his importance. This varies more in the *Comedy* than in previous representations of the other world. The total numbers of classical and contemporary characters in Dante's other world are similar; but the majority of classical figures are dismissed in a mere line, whereas few of the contemporaries receive so little attention. Conversely, only five classical characters occupy more than fifty lines, compared with twenty-two contemporaries.[12] These differences are illustrated in Figure 1, which shows how much weight, in terms of numbers of

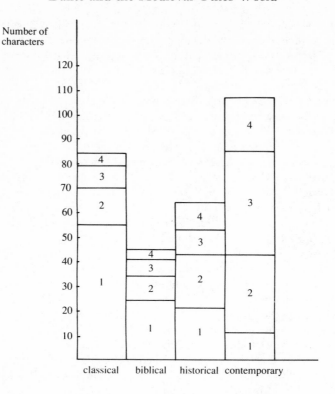

Number of characters

Key: 1 = 1 line allocated
       2 = 2–10 lines
       3 = 11–50 lines
       4 = 50+ lines

1 Graph illustrating the differing weight attached to classical, biblical, historical and contemporary characters in the *Comedy*

lines, is given to each of the four categories of individuals in the *Comedy*, and in what proportions.

The first major difference between the *Comedy* and any previous description of the other world is one of scale. Three hundred people are said by Dante to inhabit his eternity; the Monk of Eynsham sees twenty-nine characters, and Godeschalc twenty-three. All the other visions contain fewer individuals. Indeed, the cumulative total for all the (extant) previous descriptions of the other world is virtually the same as the total for the *Comedy* – 294 counting each named individual once irrespective of how many texts mention him, and including fifty-four unnamed characters for whom it seems likely that a specific identity was intended. The closeness between totals makes comparison of the various categories straightforward.

The inhabitants of the other world

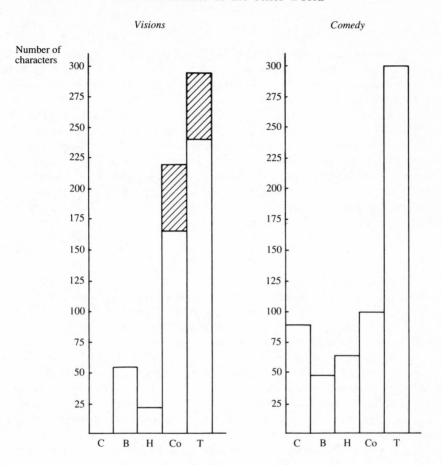

Visions   *Comedy*

Number of characters

Key: C = classical characters
B = biblical characters
H = historical characters
Co = contemporary characters
T = total
Shaded area = ambiguous individuals

2 Graph comparing the choice of characters from different periods in the visions and the *Comedy*

As will be seen from Figure 2, the proportions of characters from the classics, the Bible, history and the visionary's own time differ greatly in the *Comedy* and the vision literature. It is immediately apparent that the *Comedy* contains a lesser, not greater, proportion of contemporary characters than the visions, and that Dante's originality lies not here but rather in the inclusion of classical figures, who are totally unrepresented in the earlier medieval texts.

Classical characters

The absence of classical figures in the vision literature is not unexpected; the works are essentially popular in nature, whereas the *Comedy* is a conscious attempt to create something of the scale and grandeur of a classical epic, and thus to unite the learned and the popular traditions. The classical figures who do occur in the vision literature – for example, Vulcan in the *Vision of Tundale* – have been excluded because of their popular transformation into hybrid monsters retaining little of their classical identities; they are the equivalent of those who have become part of the 'staff' of Hell in the *Comedy*, also losing their classical dignity and becoming medieval in nature.[13] Most of Dante's eighty-four true classical inhabitants of the other world are located in Limbo (fifty-one); twenty-nine suffer torment in the rest of Hell, and of the remaining four, Cato and Statius are seen in Purgatory, Trajan and Ripheus in Paradise.

Biblical characters

The proportions of biblical characters present in the other world are roughly similar in the *Comedy* and in the visions, and many of those included by Dante are also present in the tradition. Of Dante's forty-six characters, five suffer torment in Hell (Judas among the traitors, Caiaphas and Annas among the hypocrites, Potiphar's wife among the falsifiers, and Nimrod chained in Cocytus), and the remaining forty-one are said to be in Paradise; they are either listed as having been released from Hell by Christ, or stated to be among the blessed by Beatrice, or met with during the journey up through the heavens, or seen by Dante in the celestial amphitheatre.[14] There is a certain amount of repetition; Moses, for example, is mentioned in all three discussions of biblical figures residing in Paradise, although we do not meet him.

What is most striking about the treatment of the biblical characters in the visions and in the *Comedy*, however, is not their inclusion but their location. In the vision tradition, these biblical characters conventionally inhabit the Earthly Paradise, to such a degree that a description of the garden is incomplete without a presentation of the accompanying patriarchs, prophets and New Testament characters. Thus the account of the city of Christ in the *Vision of Paul* is centred around the four rivers and a collection of biblical characters, mostly prophets and patriarchs; Anskar's vision of Paradise reveals Peter, John the Baptist, the twenty-four seniors of the Apocalypse, and Christ; Alberic sees Abel, Abraham, Lazarus, the Good Thief and unnamed patriarchs, prophets and apostles; and Giacomino da Verona and the *Liber de Scalis* alike include prophets, patriarchs and apostles as an essential part of their description of Paradise. Dante, however, excludes the majority of these from his Earthly Paradise, their place being taken by symbolic figures, and they themselves being assigned to the celestial Paradise. And the measure of his originality lies not only in the transference of the biblical characters to the heavens – this depends more on a change in belief, whereby men are no longer held to await the Second Coming in a place such as the Earthly Paradise, but are admitted directly to the celestial Paradise on death, than on innovation on the part of the poet[15] – but in the transformation of this, the most conventional part of the other world throughout the tradition, into the setting for a personal drama, the meeting with Beatrice. Biblical characters are removed to the *Paradiso*, symbolic figures representing the books of the Bible replace them; and the entire procession of which they form part has as its climax a Florentine girl with no particular claim to fame.

Historical characters

The historical characters included by Dante in his poem are sixty-three in number, and are drawn from a wide range of eras. In this analysis, the category 'historical' excludes, as we have seen, classical and biblical characters, and includes those thirteenth-century individuals who died before the year of Dante's birth. It is not intended to comment on whether characters presented as historical did in fact exist. Thus Lucan and David, who evidently did exist, are excluded as being classical and biblical respectively, whereas Tristan, who probably did not, is included because treated by Dante as a true historical character. By this method, 21 per cent of the characters of the *Comedy* can be said to be historical, compared with only 7 per cent of characters in the visions. This suggests that Dante was original not in the inclusion of figures from contemporary history, as stated by Curtius, and not only in the inclusion of classical figures, as has been demonstrated, but also in the extent of his inclusion of individuals from earlier centuries.

The visions provide us with twenty-one historical figures in all, of whom three (Benedict, Margaret and Nicholas) occur twice. Five of these come from the *Vision of Wetti*: the saints Dionysus, Hilary, Sebastian, Valentine and Martin. Othlo offers three: Theophano, wife of Otto II, who died in the century preceding the vision; and the saints Adelpertus and Mauricius. Gunthelm is guided by Benedict; the Boy William sees a William crucified by the Jews but otherwise unidentified; Tundale meets the Irish confessor Ruadanus, saint Patrick and the legendary figures Fergusius and Conallus; Godeschalc encounters saint Andrew and the Monk of Eynsham saint Margaret; and finally Thurkill comes across the saints Dominicus,[16] Katherine, Margaret again, and Ositha. Eynsham is guided by Nicholas, Thurkill by Julian.

It is obvious that most of these historical figures are in fact saints, and probably the patron saints of the parish in which the visionary resided. Dionysus, Hilary and Martin would have been well known to any Carolingian, each being associated with an important religious centre – St Denis, Poitiers and Tours.[17] Benedict was the founder of the order to which Alberic belonged, and Patrick is an equally obvious choice for an Irish visionary to make.

The historical figures of the *Comedy* are rather different. Canonised saints are present among them, but constitute a minority (Lucy, Francis and Dominic). The most notable group among these characters, and one which is not paralleled anywhere in the previous tradition, is that which includes intellectuals such as Donatus, Priscian, Avicenna, Michael Scot and Arnaut Daniel. Another group with no precedent contains figures from French epic, including Ganelon, Renouart and Godfrey of Bouillon, or romance, such as Tristan and Mordrec. Various rulers also appear in Dante's other world: Charlemagne has already been noted, but also present are Constantine, Attila, Justinian and Saladin. Finally there is one historical Pope, Anastasius II, and a wealth of other ecclesiasts and theologians, among whom are numbered St John Chrysostom, Isidore, Anselm, Joachim, and an abbot of S. Zeno in Verona. It is interesting to note that the majority of these historical figures (59 per cent) are said to be in Paradise, compared with 30 per cent in Hell. The opposite is true for the contemporary characters, the majority of whom (53 per cent) are in Hell, compared with 8 per cent in Paradise. Dante seems to have found it easier to put historical characters whom he had never met in Paradise than he did his contemporaries with whom perhaps he was only too familiar.

Contemporary characters

The most striking category of otherworld inhabitants both in the *Comedy* and, contrary to received views, in the previous representations of the afterlife, is the last – that which contains contemporary figures. These figures are more, not less, common in the vision literature than in the *Comedy*: they make up 69 per cent of the total number of identified characters in the popular texts, as opposed to only 36 per cent in the poem.

In order to compare the contemporary figures present in the *Comedy* with those in the visions, it is necessary to look more closely at their identities. Figure 3 shows the inhabitants of the other world separated into six groups according to social rank. The first three groups are ecclesiastical, the second three secular.

It is immediately apparent that Dante is the first writer to dare place popes in Hell. In his lifetime there had been six popes, of whom only one, Giovanni XII, is allocated to Paradise. Adrian V is undergoing purgation, whilst Celestine V and Nicholas III suffer in Hell for simony. Boniface VIII and Clement V were to die in 1303 and 1314 respectively, after the fictional date of the poem; they are destined to join Celestine and Nicholas.

After popes come clerics of middle rank – abbots, bishops, archbishops, and theologians. In the *Comedy* these fare little better than the popes. Dante includes seven of this group in his other world, of whom three suffer in Hell – Ruggieri degli Ubaldini, archbishop of Pisa, Ottaviano his uncle, bishop of Bologna, and Andrea de' Mozzi, bishop of Florence. Bonifazio de' Fieschi, archbishop of Ravenna, undergoes purgation for gluttony, and three theologians, Bonaventure, Albert the Great and Thomas Aquinas, rejoice in Paradise.

As one would expect from Cacciaguida's statement that the well-known are shown to Dante as they offer a better example, the *Comedy* includes few simple monks and friars. Indeed, if one discounts the lay Frati Godenti who walk with the hypocrites in *Inferno* XXIII, there is only Frate Gomita, the Sardinian friar who acted as secretary to Nino Visconti, judge of Gallura, and who now suffers among the barrators.

The inhabitants of the other world

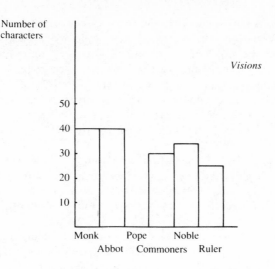

Number of characters

Visions

50
40
30
20
10

Monk   Pope   Noble
   Abbot   Commoners   Ruler

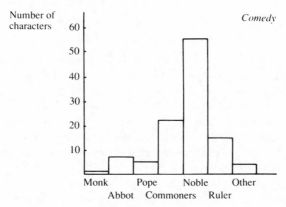

Number of characters

Comedy

60
50
40
30
20
10

Monk   Pope   Noble   Other
   Abbot   Commoners   Ruler

3 Graph comparing the social class of contemporary characters in the visions with those in the *Comedy*

At the top of the secular hierarchy are rulers, kings and emperors. Most of the fifteen seen by Dante reside in the Valley of Princes on the lower slopes of Purgatory, but two, Guy de Montfort and Obizzo II d'Este, guilty of murder and tyranny respectively, are immersed in the Phlegethon, and two, Charles Martel and Henry VII of Luxembourg, are located, or due to be located, in Paradise.

The biggest category in Dante's other world is made up of the nobility, many of whom were actively involved in politics and government. No fewer than fifty-five of them are present, of whom thirty-five are allocated to Hell, seventeen to Purgatory and only three – Beatrice, Cunizza da Romano and Piccarda Donati – to Paradise.

Dante and the Medieval Other World

The lowest ranks of the secular world are much better represented in the *Comedy* than those of the ecclesiastical world. Dante includes twenty-one individuals who are either commoners or sufficiently obscure for us to know little about them. Among them are Asdente, a shoemaker and soothsayer from Parma, Belacqua, a Florentine lute-maker, Capocchio, an alchemist, Casella, a musician, Guglielmo Borsiere, a pursemaker, Guido Bonatti, a tiler and astrologer, Oderisi da Gubbio, a manuscript illuminator, Maestro Adamo, a counterfeiter, Rinier da Corneto, a highwayman, and Sordello, a troubadour. Most are found in Hell, and the rest in Purgatory.

Finally, there are four 'professionals' who do not fit readily into any of the six categories. They are Bonagiunta, a lawyer and lyric poet, Brunetto Latini, a notary, Francesco d'Accorso, another lawyer, and Siger of Brabant, a university lecturer at Paris. Bonagiunta is in Purgatory, Brunetto and Francesco in Hell, Siger in Paradise.

Representatives from five of these six categories of contemporary characters are also found in the vision tradition, and are listed in the tables given at the end of the chapter. Instead of looking at whole groups, however, a better idea of the inclusion of contemporaries can perhaps be had by looking in detail at one representative of each group.

King Cormachus

Cormac was the king of Cork and Cashel in Ireland; he was murdered in 1138. He was involved during his rule in several wars, including one against Donachus in which his ally was Conchobar; both these figures are represented with him in the same vision, that of Tundale (pp. 42–5). They are seen not in Hell, but immediately within the enclosure of the Earthly Paradise, where they spend part of the time in rejoicing, and part undergoing torment for their late-repented sins. They therefore correspond closely to those rulers confined to the valley of the late repentant on Dante's mountain of Purgatory.

Tundale and his guide approach a magnificent house of gold, studded with precious stones, and round in shape. Inside they see a golden throne; Cormac is seated upon it, clothed in garments such as no earthly king has ever worn. As they watch, spirits arrive bearing joyful gifts which they offer to him: 'venerunt plurimi in illam domum cum muneribus ad regem et offerebant illi singuli cum gaudio munera sua'. They are followed by richly dressed ministers of the Church: 'venerunt multi sacerdotes et levite vestiti sollempniter sicut ad missam cum sericis casulis et ceteris ornatibus valde bonis'. Tundale wonders at their arrival, protesting that he does not recognise them from among those who ministered to Cormac during his lifetime; the angel explains that these are the spirits of the poor whom the king helped. Tundale asks a further question: 'Vellem (. . .) scire, si iste dominus meus rex passus est umquam tormenta, postquam relicto corpore venit ad requiem?' [I would like to know if my king has undergone any torment since he left the body and came to eternal rest?] Not only has he suffered, but he suffers still, and will continue to suffer, is the answer: 'Passus est (. . .) et cotidie patitur et adhuc patietur.' As they watch, the ministers leave Cormac, and the gifts and rich clothes are replaced by encasement in fire from the waist downwards, and a hairshirt from the waist upwards. These are the torments for those of his sins which are yet to be purged, and he must endure them for three hours in every twenty-four. The nature of these sins – for which, as is often the case in the *Comedy*, there is no historical record – is then explained:

Ideo ignem patitur usque ad umbilicum, quia legitimi conjugii maculavit sacramentum, et ab umbilico sursum patitur cilicium, quia jussit interficere comitem juxta sanctum Patricium et prevaricatus est jusjurandum. Exceptis his duobus cuncta sunt ejus crimina remissa.

[He suffers burning up to the waist, because he stained the sacrament of legitimate marriage, and he suffers the hairshirt from the waist upwards because he ordered someone to be killed on saint Patrick's day, and told a lie on oath. Except for these two, all his sins are forgiven.]

An English noble

A representative of the class of nobles is provided by the early thirteenth-century *Vision of Thurkill* (pp. 17–19). As Thurkill watches the judgment of a newly arrived soul, he sees a devil coming headlong towards him, driving the black horse which is his mount with great glee and as much cruelty. Thurkill's guide asks the devil whose soul the horse represents, and learns that it is a nobleman of the king of England, who is unnamed but about whom enough details, including the precise day of his death, are provided to make identification by a contemporary likely:

At ille ait hunc fuisse ex proceribus regis Anglie, qui nocte precedenti subito absque confessione et dominici corporis viatico obierat multaque flagitia commiserat, precipue erga homines suos durus et crudelis existens multosque ad extremam inopiam redigens per indebitas exactiones atque iniustas calumpnias. quod maxime fecerat instigatione pessime uxoris sue, que eum semper ad crudelitatis rapacitatem instigavit.

[He said that it was one of the nobles of the kingdom of England, who had died unexpectedly on the preceding night without confession or taking communion. Amongst the many other faults which he had committed, his principal crime was his cruelty towards his own men, many of whom he had brought to extreme want, which he had done mostly at the instigation of his wife, who always urged him on to deeds of cruelty.]

The devil adds that he and his colleagues have the power to transform their victims into the shape of their choice; he is riding this particular soul to the devils' theatre, in which he will undergo torment. This episode is perhaps the most reminiscent of the devils' treatment of Ciampolo Navarrese in the *Comedy* (Inf XXII 31–123).

Godeschalcus Dasonide

Godeschalc, like Thurkill, was a peasant, and his other world is peopled by the members of the village in which he lived. One of these is his namesake Godeschalc, son of Daso the elder, said to be contemporary to the visionary, 'contemporaneus nobis existens', whose story is told in a digression which lasts for five chapters (pp. 101–7). Godeschalc, like Dante's Vanni Fucci, is undergoing punishment for theft from a church, that of St Martin. The principal ingredient of his torment is fire; he is enclosed in a glass vase, with only his face protruding, and immersed in flames. His suffering is described in a passage whose syntax mirrors his restless tossing:

impacienter exulceratus, pede terens, pugnum contorquens, cervice rigens, buccas inflatus, genas inflammatus, oculis ardens, visu jaculans, signisque aliis evidentibus internum animi sui motum minaciter forinsecus terribiliterque manifestet.

[covered with unbearable sores, twisting his foot, clenching his fist, stiffening his neck, his cheeks swollen, his jaws inflamed, his eyes burning, his face sticking out, and with other clear signs revealing on the outside the inner turmoil of his soul.]

One of Godeschalc's guides explains the circumstances of the crime, in a long and complicated story which involves another local family, the Bakarides, of Slavonic origin. Godeschalc (henceforth called Dasonides to avoid confusion with the visionary) and Tributus, father of this family, laid their plans and together executed the theft:

Nam nocte quadam, (. . .) ecclesiam in Northorpe in honore beati Martini constructam, et ad titulum ejus dedicatam, per fenestram humiliorem irrepentes, ecclesie suppellectilem totam cum scrinio, reliquias beati Martini continente, diripientes, asportaverunt.

[For on a certain night, they climbed into the church built in honour of St Martin in Northorpe by a lower window, and hurriedly carried away the whole chest which held the reliquary containing the remains of the blessed Martin.]

Suspicion falls; the crime is denied; public debate begins. Prominent figures in both villages, that of Dasonides and that of Tributus where the crime was committed, become involved; the Bakarides are forced to flee to their own country, taking the booty with them, and Dasonides escapes blame – while he remains alive.

Baldwin, archbishop of Canterbury

The archbishop seen by the Monk of Eynsham (pp. 290–2) is the ecclesiastical figure of highest rank found in any of the visions. He is not directly named – as is the case with all the characters in this text – but is identifiable from the year of death, rank, and from the details of his life, which accord with those attributed in contemporary annals to Baldwin, archbishop of Canterbury, who died in 1190. The encounter occupies a whole chapter of the narrative.

The archbishop is introduced with a summary of his life. At the outset of his career he lived with religious devotion in a simple monastery, fervent in his faith and disciplined with his body, 'in religione fervens, in corporis maceratione rigidus'. He was strong in meditation, and blessed with many spiritual gifts, 'strenuus in sacris meditacionibus, in multarum carismatibus virtutum prestantissimus', and as a result was made first bishop and then archbishop. However, there were other aspects to his character, and the monk proceeds to outline Baldwin's shortcomings, explaining that he gave office to the unworthy, refused to do anything which might give displeasure to the king to whom he owed his office, and failed to be effective in his duty to promote Christianity and uproot sin. On the other hand, he had founded a hospital dedicated to Thomas à Becket for the benefit of pilgrims; 'xenodochium instituit nomine eius intitulatum ad magnum refrigerium peregrinorum'. And he had also undertaken a pilgrimage to Jerusalem. For his sins he undergoes torment, but by reason of his good actions he, like all the others seen in this purgative hell, cannot be said to be eternally damned – the monk explains: 'ego autem in tota visione ista neminem conspexi qui spem funditus amisisset indulgencie et sub certitudine estuaret perdicionis eterne' ['in the whole vision I saw nobody who was without hope of mercy and certain of eternal perdition']. Dante too insists on the unpredictability of damnation: in *Inferno* XVII we meet Guido da Montefeltro who died a Franciscan under the full absolution of the Pope, but who nonetheless is confined in the valley of the fraudulent counsellors for his failure to repent; and in *Purgatorio* III we meet the excommunicates, whom one would have naturally assumed to be in Hell. One of them, Manfred, the son of Frederick II of Sicily, explains that they are in Antepurgatory because they repented at the moment of death.

A prior

The last example, from the category of the lower ranks of the clergy, also comes from the *Vision of the Monk of Eynsham*; the encounter is a direct and personal one, presented to us not in a passage of description as above, but in a lengthy monologue on the part of the prior himself (pp. 279–82). The monk introduces the character, whom he scarcely recognised due to the deformity caused to him by the baths of fire and sulphur in which he is tormented, explaining that he was the local priest and had died that very same year. They greet one another, and a long conversation follows. The prior explains that he suffers not only for his own sins, but also for those which he failed to correct in his flock; even those he helped have now forgotten him in consequence of this failing, and he is deprived of their prayers. His torment increases in proportion to the number of his parishioners who die in a state of sin, with the result that he is dreading the death of certain homosexuals, for their punishment is the worst. The monk protests that the monastery underwent great reforms during the prior's lifetime; he receives the answer that this was in no wise due to the prior himself:

Verum ipsa tantum mala ad penam me respiciunt; de melioratione nullus michi fructus, merces nulla ascribitur; immo et augetur cruciatus. Nimis enim infestus obstiti correctionibus eorum.

[In truth many evils cause me this torment; the improvements were in no way the fruits of my labours, and are not to be attributed to me; on the contrary, they increase my suffering. For I was strongly opposed to the reforms.]

The atmosphere throughout the encounter is one of surprise on the part of the visionary; he recognises, despite the torment and the state of deformity of the sinners in this area of punishment, a man whom he knew well, and whom he respected as virtuous and successful. These aspects of the encounter foreshadow Dante's meeting with Brunetto. He learns from that man's own lips the reasons for which he now endures correction. At the same time, comment is implicitly passed, as in the case of many of the ecclesiastical figures encountered in the afterlife, on the correct conduct of a pastor: not just to attend to the state of his own soul, not just to correct the errors of his flock, but also to encourage the virtuous and take full responsibility for the spiritual welfare of the entire community. This prior, like Dante's Abbot of S. Zeno who purges his sins on the terrace of the slothful, failed to do that.

Summary

In so far as contemporary characters are concerned, therefore, the only innovation made by Dante seems to have been the inclusion of popes among the inhabitants of the other world. Despite Curtius's assertion to the contrary, virtually all the categories he mentions as innovatory in the *Comedy* are found in the previous representations of the afterlife: there are emperors such as Charlemagne, Ludovic and Lotharius (visions of Wetti, Rotcharius, Charles the Fat); kings such as Henry II of England, Chilperic of Neustria, and Ceolred of Mercia (Eynsham, Guntram and Wenlock); prelates such as Baldwin, archbishop of Canterbury, Reginald Fitzjocelin, bishop of Bath, and Nemias, bishop of Cluny (Eynsham, Tundale); statesmen such as Count Otharius, Guncelinus and the nobles of the court of Ludovic (Bernoldus, Godeschalc); tyrants such as Bertolph, duke of Zähringen and Ludovic the Landgrave (Caesarius of Heisterbach); no generals but many knights; members of the nobility such as count Gerold, the unnamed English nobleman and Adtholfus (Wetti, Thurkill, Godeschalc); members of the bourgeoisie such as Evrardus, Daso and the local man and his wife seen by Godeschalc (Guibert, Godeschalc); and members of the guilds such as the goldsmith (Eynsham).

Although it is clearly not true to say that the 'most impressive and fertile innovation' of Dante in the creation of the *Comedy* is 'his drawing upon contemporary history', Dante does give us a breadth of vision in his choice of contemporary characters which is found in no single preceding work. The differences between the *Comedy* and the previous tradition taken as a whole are summarised in Figure 3. There are also differences between one vision and another; in every account of the afterlife, the characters chosen are indicative of the narrowness or breadth of the world of the visionary.

These differences are explicable in terms of two related factors: the identities of the visionaries and the poet, and the consequent breadth or narrowness of the social world of which they form part; and the aims and motivation which lie behind the visions and the accounts given of them, and behind the *Comedy*. Barontus, a provincial monk, sees the members of his monastery in Paradise – the presbyters Corbolenus and Fraudolenus, the deacon Austrulfus, the readers Leodaldus and Ebbo, and the monks Baudolenus and Framnoaldus; his Hell contains the bishops Vulfredus and Dido. The *Vision of Wetti*, recorded by Walafrid Strabo who moved in court circles and was not confined to a monastery, has as its otherworld inhabitants members of the secular and ecclesiastical ruling classes, and as its motivation the expression of political sympathies. An earlier vision, that of a woman described by Lull, bishop of Mentz, records the presence in Hell of

Cuthberga, wife of Alfred king of Northumberland who had died probably within the lifetime of the visionary, another court figure named Wialan, the recently dead tyrant Aethilbealdus, king of Mercia, and a local count named Ceolla Snoding. The vision of the ruler Charles the Fat is exclusively concerned with other rulers; he describes his father, King Ludovic, together with his bishops and nobles; his uncle Lotharius and his own ultimate successor, the child Ludovic. In the twelfth century Tundale, an Irish knight moving in a secular world, sees three recent Irish kings, Donachus, Conchobar and Cormachus, as well as four powerful bishops. In this text there are no obscure figures at all, the vision having been written down not in Ireland but in Ratisbon, where only the prominent would have been recognised. And at the opposite end of the scale there is Thurkill, an Essex peasant, who saw many familiar faces – 'conspexit (. . .) multos (. . .) quos in seculo viventes cognoverat' (p. 32) – some of whom are named and all of whom are local and of relatively lowly station.

Dante too includes in his other world a large number of people of his own social group. As a Florentine of noble family, he includes others of similar extraction in his poem, and these constitute the largest group of characters. There are Florentines such as Forese and Piccarda Donati, and Camicion de' Pazzi; Tuscans such as Foccaccia, Guccio de' Tarlati di Pietramala, Pia de' Tolomei; nobles from other parts of Italy such as Rinaldo degli Scrovigni, Paolo Malatesta, Tebaldello de' Zambrasi. As a political leader, he includes rulers and prominent politicians, such as Buonconte da Montefeltro, Provenzan Salvani and Farinata degli Uberti; as a man with strong views on the corruption of the Church, he portrays ecclesiastical leaders – popes such as Nicholas III, Adrian V and John XXI, bishops and archbishops such as Andrea de' Mozzi, Ruggieri degli Ubaldini and Bonifazio de' Fieschi, and theologians such as Aquinas and Albert the Great. And as an ordinary man he includes other ordinary men, such as the lute-maker Belacqua, the shoemaker-soothsayer Asdente, and the tiler-astrologer Guido Bonatti. If it is true to say that each previous visionary wrote with one aim, or at least with one set of experiences, then it must be concluded that the difference between their works and the *Comedy* is in this respect one of degree rather than of kind; Dante's vision is vastly more complex and comprehensive, and his characters proportionately greater in number. He, like each separate visionary, includes a majority of the class to which he belongs; beyond that he gives us a panorama of contemporary society which is rivalled by all the visions taken together, but by none of them considered separately.

PRESENTATION OF CHARACTERS IN THE VISION LITERATURE AND THE *COMEDY*

Although named individuals are portrayed in all periods of the Christian representation of the afterlife, the way in which they are presented develops gradually from century to century. The early texts merely list the characters said to be in the other world, whereas at the other extreme the twelfth- and thirteenth-century visions offer long biographical digressions in which particular characters are introduced.

This development is made possible by the intellectual and social changes which occurred in the twelfth century, and in particular by the so-called 'discovery of the individual'. This is manifested in literature and art, which prior to the twelfth century is often anonymous, whereas after the twelfth century it becomes named and individual, and new genres arise which presuppose an interest in the personal rather than the collective – such as romance and lyric poetry. Greater emphasis also begins to be placed on the judgment of the individual at death, and the weight of the visions shifts from salvation to purgation.[18] The change is summarised by Colin Morris as follows:

> The men of the [twelfth century] were not only interested in their own reactions ('the discovery of the self') but also in those of other people whom they knew ('the discovery of the individual') (. . .). There are signs that writers were attempting not only to describe types of men, but to present the character, and occasionally even the appearance, of the person of whom they were writing.[19]

The vision literature and the *Comedy* show that there are essentially four stages in the presentation of the individual, each more complex than the last.

1 The inclusion of the individual

From earliest times, the description of the other world has included the names of a number of known individuals. In the first few centuries of the Christian era, most are biblical characters, although persons known to the visionary are listed from the third century onwards. By the Carolingian period, an increasingly wide selection of characters is said to be present, including obscure contemporaries and historical characters. But in none of the early texts is there any attempt to describe or characterise the individual mentioned.

2 The description of appearance

In the ninth century a change occurs. The earlier visionaries enter into detailed descriptions of the landscape and torments of the other world, but remain silent concerning the individuals they see there. Now for the first time we find a description of the physical appearance of two inhabitants of the other world. This is how Anskar describes Peter and John, influenced perhaps by the tradition of the visual arts:

> Quorum unus erat senior, cano capite, capillo plano et spisso, facie rubenti, vultu subtristi, veste candida et colorata, statura brevi; quem ipse sanctum Petrum esse nemine narrante statim agnovit. Alius vero iuvenis erat, statura procerior, barbam emittens, capite subfusco atque subcrispo, facie macilenta, vultu iocundo, in veste serica; quem ille sanctum Iohannem esse omnino credidit. (p. 22)

> [One of them was an old man with thick, straight white hair and a reddish face. He was short, with rather a sad expression, and was wearing a brightly coloured robe. [Anskar] immediately recognised him as St Peter without being told. The other was a young man, taller, bearded, with brown curly hair. He had a thin, cheerful face, and was wearing a silken robe, and [Anskar] knew him to be St John.]

The inhabitants of the other world

And this is how in the twelfth century Alberic describes St Peter:

Ipsius autem beati petri statura quantum ego cognovi nec longa multum nec brevis, set media et iusta erat. corpore compressior, vultus grossior, canis habens aspersum caput, indutus erat tunica candidissima, quam circa pectus et collum torques aurea decorabat. Auream in capite gestabat coronam, claves quoque magnas manibus tenebat, in quibus omnium pretiosiorum gemme inserte videbantur. Claves autem cuius essent speciei, cuiusque metalli cognoscere non potui. (p. 102, repunctuated)

[St Peter, as far as I could see, was neither particularly tall nor particularly short, but of a pleasant medium height. His body was stocky, his features large. His head was covered in white hair. He was dressed in a very bright tunic, which was decorated with gold around the chest and neck. He wore a golden crown on his head, and held large keys in his hand, which were studded with every kind of precious stone. I was not able to see of what kind of metal the keys were made.]

The twelfth century saw the composition of a number of rhetorical manuals for the guidance of writers, and these too begin to stress the importance of physical description. One of the most widely used was the *Poetria Nova* of Geoffrey of Vinsauf, written in about 1200. Geoffrey devotes a section of his work to the *descriptio personarum*, and offers an example of the description of a lady's beauty, followed by an example of the description of her attire.[20] So this is the second stage of the presentation of the individual: we are told what the person looks like – although such descriptions in the vision literature fall a long way short of Geoffrey's ideals, written as they are by simple monks and not learned poets.

3 The description of circumstances

The third stage of the presentation of the individual in the other world develops during the twelfth and early thirteenth centuries, when for the first time we are given detailed descriptions of the person's earthly circumstances.

We have already looked at five contemporary characters presented in the twelfth- and thirteenth-century visions. But there is one outstanding example of an ordinary man with whom we may empathise; it occurs in the vision of the Monk of Eynsham. As the monk and his guide walk through the second area of torment, they meet the local goldsmith, an alcoholic who had recently died as a result of a bout of excessive drinking, and who offers the story of his life in a digression which takes us completely away from the horrors of Hell and introduces us to a true individual, a man with his own set of circumstances, his own struggles against them and his own thoughts and feelings. He launches into an eloquent account of his battle against the alcoholism which gripped him:

'Although I devoted myself to those evils which appear to be sinful, particularly to drunkenness, I did not consent to this with my will. Indeed, it displeased me greatly, and I was very sorry that I could not rid myself of this destructive vice. I frequently confronted myself, firmly resolving to throw off the yoke of this vile slavery in which I saw myself caught. But soon the desire to drink, and for the company of my drinking companions, compelled me to give in, and I was drawn once more a captive into the kingdom of sin which lived in my throat and jaws.'[21]

He goes on to explain that God's grace did allow him to persevere in the devotion he had to St Nicholas. However much he had drunk the night before, he would be found early the following morning in the church, where he kept a candle constantly burning to the saint. Such indeed was his loyalty to the church that he would take it upon himself to rebuke those who gave less in tithes than their due. And twice a year, at Christmas and Easter, he would confess his sins and carry out the penance given.

Nonetheless, it was the goldsmith's inability to conquer his habit which eventually caused his death. Having tasted wine at communion, he began to drink again:

'On Christmas Day (. . .) I participated in holy communion, as was my custom. When I got home – and I cannot think of it without great horror – I fell by excessive drinking into a state of inebriation, dishonouring both my body and my mind, and suffering greatly. The next morning before dawn I went, as usual, to the church where I had been the previous day, crying and seeking to escape damnation. But to no purpose. (. . .) I had firmly resolved to stay sober, but when the opportunity to drink came the enemy pressed me and, bereft of the power of perseverance, I succumbed, without eating, to the enticing base vice, just as I had the day before. (. . .) On the following day also I did not stop drinking until I completely destroyed the home of my senses and lost all control. And so, seeking my own bed in my own home in the middle of the night, dressed as I was and without even unlacing my shoes, I slept fitfully.'[22]

Eventually he fell into a deep sleep, and death came upon him. A devil came to collect him, but he was rescued by Nicholas, in whom he had placed his trust while alive. He now undergoes purgative torment not for his alcoholism, for which he has obtained pardon, but because of the fraud he practised in the exercise of his trade.

The struggle between an angel or saint and a devil for the possession of a newly dead soul is a theme which occurs elsewhere in the tradition. It is recalled in *Inferno* XXVII, where Guido da Montefeltro describes the contest which took place between Francis, come to lead a Franciscan to Paradise, and a devil, come to point out that absolution without repentance is invalid. In the earlier texts, 'Paul' witnesses angels coming to possess a virtuous soul and devils a wicked one, and a similar contest occurs over the souls of the monk of Wenlock and Tundale. Devotion to a particular saint or angel who then acts on behalf of the devotee, usually as his guide through the other world, is also a theme in the visions; this is discussed in the next chapter. Dante is described as devoted to the saint Lucy, and she both sends Beatrice to help him and intervenes directly on his behalf by lifting him as he sleeps from the lower slopes of the mountain to the gate of Purgatory itself.[23]

4 The description of character

There is one further stage to go in the presentation of a character. We have met with the individual in so far as his appearance distinguishes him from others, and with the individual in so far as his life circumstances distinguish him from others;

but we have not yet met with the essence of the person, with what it is at the core of his being which distinguishes him from others. This is how Alain Robbe-Grillet defines the character of a novel:

a character must have his own name, name and surname if possible. He must have parents and an inheritance. He must have an occupation (. . .). Finally, he must have a 'personality', a face which reflects it, a past which modelled this and that. His personality will dictate his actions and will cause him to react in a particular way to each event. His personality allows the reader to judge him, to love him, to hate him. It is thanks to this personality that one day he will bequeath his name to a human type which was waiting, we shall say, to receive its official baptism. And so it is essential that the character should both be unique and able to rise to the height of a category. He needs enough particularity to be irreplaceable and yet enough generality to become universal.[24]

So if a character is to be fully convincing, we need more than physical description and biographical detail. He must have a character which is reflected by his appearance and formed by his past. This character will determine his actions, so that if we have understood his character we should be able to say how he will behave in any given situation. And yet he must at the same time be recognisable to others; he must have a universal quality. Now some of these things we may pick up if given a fairly full account of a person's life. As the goldsmith relates his story we identify, interpret, conjecture, and build up a picture of his character. But the goldsmith occupies five chapters of the monk's account, many times more space than Dante has available for any one of his 300 otherworld inhabitants. We cannot possibly absorb all this information in the *Comedy* unless Dante finds some way of feeding it to us artificially.

This he does in a number of different ways. One is the use of language: each individual speaks in a register which reflects his background and reveals the misbeliefs which determined his eternal destiny. Francesca uses the smooth language of romance, using a false syllogism replete with emotive vocabulary to minimise the responsibility she carries for the sin of deliberate adultery: 'Amor, ch'al cor gentil ratto s'apprende'; 'Amor, ch'a nullo amato amar perdona'; 'Amor condusse noi ad una morte' ['Love, which is quickly kindled in the noble heart'; 'Love, which absolves no one who is loved from loving'; 'Love brought us to one death']. Pier speaks in the convoluted language of a rhetorician, his tangled words reflecting his tangled reasoning as he likewise gives an account of the crucial moment of his life:

> 'L'animo mio, per disdegnoso gusto,
> credendo col morir fuggir disdegno,
> ingiusto fece me contra me giusto.'
> (Inf XIII 70–2)

['My mind, in disdain thinking I would flee from disdain in death, made me, just, unjust to myself.']

Ulysses too tells of the moment in which the essence of his character was revealed, as he substituted the pursuit of knowledge for the pursuit of God, and persuaded his men to do likewise:

'Considerate la vostra semenza:
fatti non foste a viver come bruti,
ma per seguir virtute e canoscenza.'
(Inf xxvi 118–20)

['Consider the seed from which you spring. You were not born to live as brutes, but to follow virtue and knowledge.']

Another way in which Dante portrays the essence of a character is through the use of drama. Francesca, Pier and Ulysses reveal what lies in their hearts by the language they use in the account of the moment which encapsulated their entire destinies, and exposed what lay at the heart of their being. Another way in which the exposure may occur is by introducing into their fixed eternity an event in time – the appearance of Dante himself in Hell – and showing their reactions.[25] Farinata and Cavalcante show their pride and their pusillanimity as they surge and crawl respectively out of their tombs to speak to the poet, the one obsessed with Florentine politics, the other consumed with anxiety about his son.

Dante's achievement in the presentation of character lies therefore in his capacity to expose what lies at the centre of the personality. For Bernard, as he leads Dante in prayer in the Empyrean, it was God. For Francesca, it was earthly passion; for Ulysses, knowledge; for Pier, honour; for Farinata, Florence; for Cavalcante, his son – all things which in themselves are good, but which, in terms of *Purgatorio* xvii, can become an end in themselves rather than a means of finding the supreme good which is God. In Hell, we meet the souls of those who clearly substituted an earthly and illegitimate goal for the search for God. In Purgatory, we meet the souls of those who are still learning to find the correct balance, and it is that struggle which lies at the core of their being. Oderisi is still torn between pride in his success and reputation as an artist, and the knowledge that art is not what matters, and that tension dominates our encounter with him. Casella, admitted to Antepurgatory because of his pilgrimage to Rome in Jubilee year, is still paying more attention to his music than to his maker. At the other end of the mountain is the love poet Arnaut Daniel, who addresses Dante in dignified Provençal verse, weighed down with sadness for his misunderstanding of love, and disappears into the fire which is helping him to gain the proper perspective.

CONCLUSIONS

Several general conclusions may be drawn from this brief analysis of the inhabitants of the other world. Firstly, it is clear that of the four main groups into which the characters of the visions and the *Comedy* may be divided (classical, biblical, historical and contemporary), all but the first are found both in the previous representations of the afterlife and in the poem. Dante's introduction of classical figures is innovatory, and consonant with the aim of writing a work which would rival the classical epic as well as take account of the classical revival of the twelfth century. The widespread use of historical characters is also largely without precedent; most are intellectuals, and most are placed in Paradise. Contemporary characters, on the other hand, make up a greater proportion, numerically, of the inhabitants of the other world in previous representations than in the *Comedy*; in this respect Dante's originality has hitherto been greatly overestimated. Indeed, his only innovation in this respect is the inclusion for the first time of popes amongst the inhabitants of the other world.

In so far as the presentation of the characters is concerned, there is a gradual development in the visions from mere listing to the description of appearance, and finally to a twelfth-century rambling digression in which the story and circumstances of specific individuals known to the visionary are told. This is superseded in the *Comedy* by a combination of listing and presentation of the individual in an essential, concise manner with the simultaneous making of the political, ecclesiastical or social point. In this sense the presentation of character reaches a climax in the *Comedy*. Only in the *Comedy* do we meet with 'man not as a remote legendary hero, not as an abstract or anecdotal representation of an ethical type, but man as we know him in historical reality, the concrete individual in his unity and wholeness'.

However, although Auerbach is undoubtedly correct in suggesting that true portrayal of character is found for the first time in the *Comedy*, the way is paved in the late twelfth- and early thirteenth-century visions. The prior encountered by the Monk of Eynsham is a real man, beset by fears and anguish, and the meeting between them is a personal one. The goldsmith from the same village, who tells the story of his struggles on earth against the alcoholism which finally caused his death, and of his devotion throughout that time to St Nicholas, is not legendary but of flesh and blood, not an anecdotal representation of an ethical type but an individual who is not fitted into any ethical system; he suffers in Hell not for drunkenness but for fraud. Indeed, both the Monk of Eynsham and Thurkill abandon any attempt to make one character represent one sin; classification is subordinate to the complexities of individual circumstance, and each figure circulates in the area of torment until all his sins have been purged. The way in which Dante dealt with the classification of sin, while retaining the complexities of character and circumstance introduced by Eynsham and Thurkill, is the subject of chapter 4 of this study.

SUPPLEMENTARY TABLES

There are various problems which arise in any attempt to identify individual characters in the legends of the other world. It is at times impossible to determine whether an unnamed character is intended to be representative and fictitious, or whether he is a person whom the visionary would expect a local, contemporary audience to recognise. When Bernoldus describes forty-one bishops, of whom he names three, it is not clear whether these are specific bishops or not; when Peter describes to Alberic the life of a particular rich man, and of a particular hermit, we do not know whether these are representative lives or real ones; and when in the *Vision of Thurkill* we witness the devils' theatre in which a priest, a knight, a lawyer, a miller and others in turn are dragged into the arena, we cannot establish with certainty whether these are men from the village or merely representatives of social classes. These ambiguous cases have generally been excluded from this analysis.[26]

Dante and the Medieval Other World

A Biblical inhabitants of the popular other world

Vision of Paul
Enoch, Elijah, Isaiah, Jeremiah, Ezekiel, Amos, Micah, Zachariah, Abraham, Isaac, Jacob, Lot, Job, David, Mary, 12 sons of Jacob, Moses, Noah, Elisha

Barontus
Peter, Abraham

Anskar
Mary, Peter, John the Baptist

Bernoldus
Jesse

Brendan
Judas, Herod, Pilate, Annas, Caiaphas

Heriger
John the Baptist, Peter

Adamnan
12 apostles, Mary, 12 sons of Jacob, Elijah

Alberic
Peter, Judas, Annas, Caiaphas, Herod, Abel, Abraham, Lazarus, Good Thief, 12 sons of Jacob, 12 apostles

Orm
Mary, 12 apostles

Gunthelm
Mary, Adam, Judas

Godeschalc
John

Thurkill
Peter, Paul, Adam

Total = 54 individuals

B Historical inhabitants of the popular other world

Wetti
St Martin, St Hilary, St Dionysus, St Sebastian, St Valentine

Othlo
Theophano, wife of Otto II, d. 983; St Mauricius; St Adelpertus

Alberic
Benedict

74

Boy William
William

Tundale
Fergusius, Conallus, St Patrick, Ruadanus

Gunthelm
Benedict

Godeschalc
St Andrew

Eynsham
St Nicholas, St Margaret

Thurkill
St Julian the Hospitaler, St Nicholas, St Dominicus, St Katharine, St Ositha, St Margaret

Total = 21 individuals

C Contemporary inhabitants of the popular other world

Category 1: monks, priors, priests, nuns, etc.
Category 2: bishops, abbots, abbesses
Category 3: popes
Category 4: commoners
Category 5: nobles, politicians
Category 6: emperors, kings, other rulers

Carpus
4: two members

Perpetua
4: Dinocrates

Saturus
1: Aspasius
2: Optatus

Guntram
2: Tetricus, Agroecula, Nicetius
6: Chilperic

Soldier
4: Peter

Bonellus
4: a pauper

Barontus

1: Baudolenus, Ebbo, Framnoaldus, Corbolenus, Fraudolenus, Austrulfus, Leodaldus

2: Dido, Vulfredus

Monk of Wenlock

2: an abbot

4: miller girl and her brother; a man he had wounded

6: Ceolred, king of Mercia (d. 716)

A Woman

2: abbot

5: Count Ceolla Snoding

6: Cuthberga, wife of Alfred king of Northumberland; Wialan; Aethilbealdus, king of Mercia

Wetti

2: an abbot Waldo, a bishop Adalhelm, Benedict of Aniane

5: Count Gerold

6: Charlemagne

Anskar

2: an abbot Adalhard

Charles the Fat

6: Ludovic, father to the visionary; Lotharius, uncle to the visionary; Ludovic, son of Lotharius; Ludovic, unborn descendent of Lotharius

Bernoldus

2: Bishops Ebo, Leopardellus, Aeneas, Hincmar + 38 unnamed bishops

5: Count Otharius and his adviser

6: Charles the Bald

Rotcharius

6: Charlemagne

Poor Woman

5: Picho, friend of Ludovic

6: Charlemagne, Irmingard, Bernard, Ludovic

Othlo

1: Gunther

2: Bishops of Ratisbon and Prague (still alive; seats are reserved for them in Hell); Gebehard bishop of Ratisbon, also alive

5: Ruotpoldus and his wife

6: Henry III, alive at the time of the vision

Walkelin

1: a monk

2: Hugh, bishop of Lisieux; Mainer, abbot of St Evroul; Gerbert, abbot of Saint-Wandrille

5: Richard and Baldwin, sons of Count Gilbert; knight William, of Glos, steward to the Earl of Hereford; Robert Blondus, son of Ralph; Landricus of Orbec

Mother of Guibert of Nogent
4: her husband Evrardus and her son; Evrardus's illegitimate son; an old woman
5: Rainaldus

Orm
5: daughter of knight Stephen

Tundale
2: Celestine, archbishop of Arthmachanus; Malachius, his successor; Christianus, bishop of Lyons; Nemias, bishop of Cluanens; a living colleague
6: Kings Donachus, Conchobar, and Cormachus

Gunthelm
4: a pauper
5: two powerful men

Godeschalc
1: Gripo, Gerhardus, canon Thancmarus, brother Godefridus, canon Eppo, canon Herioldus, Volquardus (all from local monastery); parish priest Unno
4: Daso, Daso, a boy, Godeschalcus son of Daso the elder; the lawyer Reinmarus; a man and his wife; Godeschalc's first wife
5: Count Guncelinus of Schwerin, Marcradus senior prefect of Holstein, Marcradus junior prefect of Holstein, Count Adtholfus, Tymmo son of Marcradus senior

Monk of Eynsham (no character is identified by name)
1: a clerk, a prior, a monk, a priest, a prior, a nun, a monk, two nuns, a sacristan
2: an abbess, an abbess, an abbot, Richard Palmer archbishop of Messina, Baldwin archbishop of Canterbury, Reginald Fitzjocelin bishop of Bath, three bishops (one is perhaps Hugo Puiset, bishop of Durham, d. 1195)
4: a lawyer, a goldsmith, two women
5: three knights
6: Henry II of England

Thurkill
1: a monk
4: his father
5: Roger Picoth his landlord; an English nobleman; Robert of Cleveland

Caesarius of Heisterbach
1: a priest, Christina, Elizabeth, Margaret, William, a monk, a priest, a nun, a nun Mary, a prior of Clairvaux, sacristan John
2: Cardinal Jordan, an abbot, the abbot of Corvey, Ermentrude
4: a steward, a steward, Everwach, a usurer
5: Frederick, a Bavarian official, a knight's wife, Rudinger, count William of Julich, Bruno and son
6: Ludwig the Landgrave, Bertolph duke of Zähringen, Herman the Landgrave

Total = 165 individuals

Dante and the Medieval Other World

D Inhabitants of Dante's other world

It is not always apparent which characters of the *Comedy* are to be included as actually present in the other world, as opposed to destined for a particular area, and the determination of their precise identities is often difficult. It is generally clear when a character is said to be present and when he is only mentioned: many of the classical figures are merely listed as occupants of Limbo, and are either recognised by Dante as he passes by or listed by Virgil to Statius, but nonetheless they are distinguishable from those who are used in simile or included among the examples on the terraces of Purgatory. Those characters who are still alive in 1300, but for whom a special place is reserved in the other world, are included, as are their counterparts in the vision literature; the symbolic figures in the procession of the Earthly Paradise are not. Likewise Minos and Phlegyas are discounted, as being to some extent symbolic, and present not as their historical selves but as part of the 'staff' of Hell, a staff which includes the Centaurs, Harpies, and the company of devils headed by Malacoda. Identification of the unnamed characters is easier than in the vision literature, thanks largely to the attention paid by early commentators to the poem; even so, little is known about some figures (for example, Maestro Adamo is of uncertain provenance), and the identity of others is a mystery (for example, the Florentine suicide in the circle of the violent). These are included where a specific identity seems intended.

Classical characters

Achilles, Aeneas, Agathon, Alexander the Great, Amphiaraus, Anaxagoras, Antaeus, Antigone, Antiphon, Argia, Aristotle, Aruns, Brutus, Brutus (Lucius Junius), Cacus, Caecilius, Caesar (Gaius Julius), Camilla, Capaneus, Cassius, Cato, Cicero, Cleopatra, Cornelia, Curio, Deidamia, Deiphyle, Democritus, Dido, Diogenes, Dionysus of Syracuse, Diomedes, Dioscorides, Electra, Empedocles, Ephialtes, Epicurus, Euclid, Euripedes, Euripyle, Galen, Hector, Helen, Heraclitus, Hippocrates, Homer, Horace, Ismene, Jason, Julia, Latinus, Lavinia, Linus, Lucan, Lucretia, Manto, Marcia, Myrrha, Orpheus, Ovid, Paris, Penthesilea, Persius, Plato, Plautus, Ptolemy, Pyrrhus, Ripheus, Semiramis, Seneca, Sextus, Simonides, Sinon, Socrates, Statius, Thais, Thales, Thetis, Tiresias, Trajan, Ulysses, Varro, Virgil, Zeno.

Biblical characters

Abel, Abraham, Adam, Annas, Anne, Caiaphas, David, Dionysus the Areopagite, Eve, Hezekiah, Isaac, James, Jacob, 12 sons of Jacob, John the Baptist, John the Evangelist, Joshua, Judas, Judas Maccabeus, Judith, Leah, Mary, Moses, Nathan, Nimrod, Noah, Peter, Potiphar's wife, Rachel, Rahab, Rebecca, Ruth, Samuel, Sarah, Solomon.

The inhabitants of the other world

Historical characters (chronological order)

Lucy, John Chrysostom, Macarius, Augustine, Donatus, Constantine, Orosius, Attila, Anastasius II, Benedict, Boethius, Justinian, Priscian, Isidore, Mahomet, Ali, Charlemagne, Roland, Ganelon, Bede, Rabanus Maurus, William of Orange, Renouart, Hugh Capet, Romoaldo degli Onesti, Anselm, Godfrey of Bouillon, Robert Guiscard, Peter Damian, Avicenna, Saladin, Bertran de Born, Tristan, Mordrec, Averroes, Arnaut Daniel, Abbot of S. Zeno, Guglielmo II of Sicily, Gratian, Constance, Richard of St Victor, Peter Lombard, Cacciaguida, Peter Comestor, Bernard, Hugh of St Victor, Joachim, Folquet de Marseilles, Dominic, Michael Scot, Giacomo da Sant'Andrea, Tesauro dei Beccheria, Federigo II, Pier della Vigna, Ezzolino III da Romano, Mosca de' Lamberti, Manfredi, Guido del Duca, Omberto Aldobrandesco, Illuminato da Rieti, Augustino da Assisi, Francis, Romeo di Villanova.

Contemporary characters

(i) Monks, friars (excluding the lay Frati Godenti)

    Frate Gomita

(ii) Archbishops, bishops, theologians

    Ruggieri degli Ubaldini
    Bonifazio dei Fieschi
    Ottaviano degli Ubaldini
    Andrea de' Mozzi
    Bonaventure
    Albert the Great
    Aquinas

(iii) Popes

    Adrian V
    Boniface VIII (place prepared)
    Celestine V
    Giovanni XXI
    Nicholas III

(iv) Commoners

    Agnolo (Brunelleschi)
    Alessio Interminei
    Asdente
    Belacqua
    Bonturo Dati (place prepared)
    Buoso
    Capocchio

Casella
Ciacco
Ciampolo Navarrese
Guglielmo Borsiere
Guido Bonatti
Griffolino d'Arezzo
Iacopo Rusticucci
Oderisi da Gubbio
Maestro Adamo
Marco Lombardo
Michel Zanche
Pier da Medicina
Rinier da Corneto
Sordello
Suicida fiorentino

(v) Nobles

Alessandro degli Alberti
Beatrice
Benincasa da Laterina
Bocca degli Abati
Buonconte da Montefeltro
Branca d'Oria (alive)
Buoso da Duera
Camicion de' Pazzi
Carlino de' Pazzi
Catalano dei Catalani
Cavalcante
Cianfa dei Donati
Corso Donati (place prepared)
Cunizza da Romano
Farinata degli Scornigliani
Farinata degli Uberti
Federigo Novello
Filippo Argenti
Forese Donati
Francesca da Rimini
Francesco dei Cavalcanti
Alberigo di Ugolino dei Manfredi
Geri del Bello
Gianni Buiamonte
Gianni Schicchi
Gianni de' Soldanier
Guccio dei Tarlati de Pietramala

Guido Guinizzelli
Guido Guerra
Iacopo del Cassero
Lano de' Maconi
Loderingo degli Andalò
Marchese degli Argogliosi
Napoleone degli Alberti
Nino de' Visconti
Orso degli Alberti
Paolo Malatesta
Pia de' Tolomei
Piccarda Donati
Pierre de la Brosse
Provenzan Salvani
Puccio Sciancato
Rinaldo degli Scrovigni
Rinieri da Calboli
Rinier de' Pazzi
Sapia
Sassol Mascheroni
Tebaldello de' Zambrasi
Tegghiaio Aldobrandi
Ubaldin della Pila
Ugolino della Gherardesca
Vanni de' Cancellieri (Vanni Fucci)
Venedico Caccianemico
Vitaliano de Padova

(vi) Rulers

Charles I of Anjou
Charles Martel
Currado Malaspina
Guglielmo VII of Monferrato
Guido da Montefeltro
Guy de Montfort
Henry I of Navarre
Henry III of England
Henry VII of Luxembourg
Obizzo II d'Este
Ottokar II of Bohemia
Peter III of Aragona
Peter his son
Philip III of France
Rudolph of Hapsburg

(vii) Others

Bonagiunta da Lucca
Brunetto Latini
Francesco d'Accorso
Siger of Brabant

Notes

1 E. R. Curtius, *European Literature and the Latin Middle Ages*, 1953, p. 365.

2 E. Auerbach, *Dante, Poet of the Secular World*, 1961, p. 171.

3 See G. Bardy, 'I Padri della Chiesa di fronte ai problemi posti dall'inferno', 1953, pp. 140–6.

4 'son nom figure le 23 janvier [824?] dans la Nécrologie d'Augsbourg', A. Thérive, 'L'Ancêtre de la "Divine Comédie"', 1921, p. 701.

5 'Hic Orbecci uicecomes et causidicus fuerat et ultra natales suos ingenio et probitate admodum excreuerat. In negociis et placitis ad libitum iudicabat, et pro acceptione munerum iudicia peruertebat, magisque cupiditati et falsitati quam rectitudini seruiebat' (p. 242).

6 'Ego sum Guillelmus de Glotis filius Barnonis qui famosus fuit quondam dapifer Guillelmi Bretoliensis et patris eius Guillelmi Herfordensis comitis. Praeiudiciis et rapinis inter mortales anhelaui multisque facinoribus plus quam referri potest peccaui. Ceterum super omnia me cruciat usura. Nam indigenti cuidam pecuniam meam erogaui, et quaddam molendinum eius pro pignore recepi, ipsoque censum reddere non valente tota uita mea pignus retinui, et legitimo herede exheredato heredibus meis reliqui (. . .). Dic ergo Beatrici uxori meae et Rogerio filio meo ut michi subueniant et uadimonium unde multo plus receperunt quam dedi uelociter heredi restituant' (p. 244).

7 Characters identified by H. Thurston in the footnotes to his edition of the vision.

8 *Metamorphoses* XI; *Georgics* IV.

9 The first to address the question was E. R. Curtius, who discusses 'The personnel of the *Commedia*' in his chapter on Dante in *European Literature and the Latin Middle Ages*, first published in 1948. He offers a 'summary classification' and calls for further study. He was followed in 1964 and 1967 by T. G. Bergin, 'Hell: Topography and Demography' in *Essays on Dante*, and 'On the *Personae* of the *Comedy*' in *American Critical Essays on the 'Divine Comedy'*, edited by R. J. Clements. Bergin divides the characters of the *Comedy* into three categories: those met or seen by Dante in the narrative, those mentioned by Dante-character or other characters in the narrative, and those referred to by Dante-poet. He offers a total of 408 characters in the first category (although the figures given for the separate *cantiche* add up to only 311), 426 (or 360) in the second, and 112 in the third. No details are given concerning who belongs in which category. The third critic to study the inhabitants of Dante's other world is Bernard Delmay, whose *I personaggi della 'Divina Commedia'*, published in 1986, offers a complete census of the poem. 364 characters are listed as actually present in the other world, including 31 non-human figures and a number of unidentified individuals. They are subdivided in various ways.

10 *Vision of the Monk of Wenlock*, p. 256; *Vision of Charles the Fat*, p. 115.

11 Inf XIX 52–81; 82–7; Purg XXIV 82–90; *Liber visionum*, cols. 365–6; *Vison of Tundale*, p. 54.

12 The classical characters are Ulysses and Diomedes, Cato, Statius and Virgil; the contemporaries are Farinata, Brunetto, Forese, Piccarda, Beatrice, Ugolino, Vanni Fucci, Sapia, Nicholas III, Guido da Montefeltro, Paolo and Francesca, Maestro Adamo, Adrian V, Sordello, Marco Lombardo, Guido Guinizzelli, Oderisi, Aquinas, Bonaventure, Ciampolo and Charles Martel.

13 An exception is found in the thirteenth-century *Anticerberus*, written by the Franciscan Bongiovanni da Cavriana. It belongs to the class of work often entitled 'De Contemptu mundi', is later than the last visions, and includes a description of Babylon based on the *Aeneid*. In Babylon Bongiovanni includes Gorgons, Harpies, Centaurs, Cerberus and Minos, who preside over the inhabitants – Tityus, Tantalus, Sisyphus, Ixion, Deiphobus and others.

14 Inf iv 52–63; Par iv 28–36; Par xxxii. The only figure not included in one of these lists is Leah.
15 See P. Ariès, *The Hour of Our Death*, 1983, pp. 147–8, for a discussion of the concept of a period of waiting. From the twelfth century, visions begin to admit contemporary characters to Paradise, the only exception before this being the *Vision of Barontus*.
16 Dominicus, or Dompninus, is identified by Ward as the Spanish saint Dominic who died in 1109 and gave his name to the town Santo Domingo de la Calzada, lying on one of the roads to Compostela. Ositha was a virgin martyr of Essex. See H. L. D. Ward, 'The Vision of Thurkill', 1875, p. 430.
17 See D. A. Traill, *Walahfrid Strabo's 'Visio Wettini': Text, Translation and Commentary*, 1974, p. 158.
18 These changes are discussed by historians such as C. Morris, *The Discovery of the Individual: 1050–1200*, 1972, and W. Ullmann, *The Individual and Society in the Middle Ages*, 1966; see also C. W. Bynum, 'Did the xiith Century Discover the Individual?', 1980; E. R. Curtius, 'Mention of the author's name in medieval literature' in *European Literature and the Latin Middle Ages*, pp. 515–18; and R. Southern, 'From epic to romance' in *The Making of the Middle Ages*, 1953, pp. 211–44.
19 'Individualism in Twelfth-Century Religion', 1980, p. 202.
20 *Poetria Nova of Geoffrey of Vinsauf*, translated by Margaret F. Nims, Toronto, 1967, pp. 36–8. See also V. Russo, *Il romanzo teologico: sondaggi sulla 'Commedia' di Dante*, 1984, of which the third chapter draws attention to the increased emphasis placed by the rhetorical manuals of the twelfth and thirteenth centuries on the *descriptio personarum*.
21 'quantum ad ea que in prospectu intuentibus patent crimini maximo ebrietatis mala devinctus consuetudine finetenus deservivi, non tamen volens quantum ad interioris hominis votum, multum enim michi displicebat multumque dolebam quod vitium hoc pestiferum deserere non potui. Frequenter etiam erexi me contra me quasi firmiter proponens quod iugum turpissime servitutis huius qua detentum me vidi abicerem, sed mox bibendi voluptate et combibentium importunitate quibus ex equo inique compotare urgebar devictus, trahebar denuo captivus in peccati regnum quod erat in gula et faucibus meis' (pp. 264–5).
22 'de more siquidem, ut prelibavi, Natalis Domini die, (. . .) cum essem vivifica mense celestis participatione refectus, quod meminisse sine ingenti horrore non valeo, nimia potatione in ebrietatem traductus sum non sine iniuria et dolenda inhonoratione tanti hospitis quem mentis habitaculo susceperam. In crastino ad ecclesiam ut moris michi fuit ante lucem processi, quod pridie feceram lugens et dampnans ac de cetero dampnare proponens. At id frustra. (. . .) Sic, sic nimirum, virile sobrietatis propositum quod mente conceperam, occasione potandi ingesta, instigante adversario et virtutis instancia destitutus, in facto non edidi, sed turpiter sicut heri, sic et hodie vitio blandiente succubui. (. . .) Die postera quoque non ante a sobrietatis hostili infestatione destiti quam funditus ipsam a sensuum meorum inhabitatione bibendo profligavi. Itaque nocte profunda de loco potationis lares proprios propriumque cubile repetens, sicut eram vestitus, calceis etiam non solutis, modice dormivi' (pp. 266–7).
23 Inf xxvii 112–20; *Vision of Paul*, pp. 16–19; *Vision of the Monk of Wenlock*, p. 253–4; *Vision of Tundale*, pp. 9–12; Inf ii 94–105; Purg ix 52–63. For a discussion of devotion to a saint and the use of the word 'fedele' in Inf ii 98 see E. Moore, 'Sta Lucia in the "Divina Commedia"', *Studies in Dante, Fourth Series*, 1917, p. 319.
24 A. Robbe-Grillet, *Pour un nouveau roman*, Paris 1963, p. 31.
25 See E. Auerbach's essay 'Farinata and Cavalcante', *Mimesis*, 1946.
26 The complete list of ambiguous figures in the visions is as follows: *Vision of Bernoldus*, 38 bishops; *Vision of Alberic*, a rich man and a hermit; *Vision of Tundale*, a monk and a thief; *St Patrick's Purgatory*, two archbishops; *Vision of Thurkill*, a proud man, a priest, a knight, a lawyer, two adulterers, a farmer, a ploughman, a miller and a merchant. They are excluded except where stated otherwise.

The guide

From the time of the earliest commentators onwards, critics of the *Comedy* have sought to interpret the figures chosen by Dante to act as guides during his journey through the other world. Attention has been paid only to certain aspects of these guides, and most particularly to their role within the allegory of the poem. If we take the *Enciclopedia Dantesca* as a guide to received opinion in the early 1970s, the three figures of Virgil, Beatrice and Bernard are interpreted as follows. Regarding Virgil,

the main exegetical poles are still those of Virgil–reason and Virgil–pagan wisdom, Virgil–natural intelligence and Virgil–philosophy, *documentum* of imperial authority.[1]

Beatrice, on the other hand, is usually said to represent 'theology or divine knowledge'; she is 'the light of an idea, image or spiritual representation, which Dante calls Beatrice and which acts in him as a final cause'.[2] Finally, Bernard is the expression of Contemplation or 'mystic theology' – although Botterill in his recent study argues persuasively that Bernard does not fulfil the function of a true guide and should not be regarded as such.[3] Each of these three figures has been held to be particularly suited to guide Dante through a different stage of his journey:

the rational philosophical phase in which Virgil was guide is followed by the theological phase in which Beatrice is guide; finally Bernard accompanies Dante through the intuitive and mystic phase which leads to union with God.[4]

Secondly, modern criticism in particular has concentrated on the personal nature of the choice of guides, and on the resultant relationship between Dante-character and each one. Thus of Virgil it has been said that

seldom in literature has the filial sentiment, blending reverence and affection, been so finely expressed as in this relationship which carries the central narrative line through so much of the great poem.[5]

And of Beatrice:

both for Virgil and above all for Beatrice, the role of guide is valid and authoritative not only from the point of view of reason, but also from that of sentiment, through which the act of the teacher evokes a warm and lively participation in the pupil.[6]

This well-established critical tradition has, however, ignored the possibility that the popular legends of the afterlife may contain material which could profitably be studied in relation to the *Comedy*. Such critical comment as there has been –

virtually all in relation to the *Vision of Alberic* and written almost two centuries ago – has fallen into one of two extreme positions. One group of critics maintained that as a guide is present in both the vision and the *Comedy*, Dante must have been writing in imitation of the earlier text.[7] A second group of critics went to the opposite extreme, denying that the guide was anything other than an absolute necessity to any journey, and stating that there could consequently be no possible relation in this respect between the *Comedy* and previous journeys into the afterlife.[8]

Analysis of the choice and role of the guide in the popular descriptions of the other world shows, however, that whereas the claims that there is a direct link between the visions and the *Comedy* are undoubtedly exaggerated, the fundamental aspects of Dante's representation of his guides are already present in the popular tradition. A personal choice of guide is often made, so that the visionary is led on his journey by a figure known to him or in some way appropriate to his particular circumstances; the relationship between guide and guided is sometimes formal, as with Bernard, sometimes a mixture of formality and informality, as with Virgil and Beatrice. A succession of guides often lead the visionary to his destination, as in the *Comedy*; and the guides frequently state that they are sent to intervene in the visionary's life, rebuking him for past conduct, and instructing him to communicate what he has seen as a warning to others, in the manner of Dante's guides.

These common elements occur to some degree throughout the popular tradition, and the first part of this chapter will therefore consist of an outline of the role of the guide from the earliest times to the eleventh century. However, it is in the visions of the twelfth and thirteenth centuries that the closest parallels with the *Comedy* are found, and the second part of the chapter will examine in turn the various aspects of the choice and role of the guide throughout the visions of that period.

THE GUIDE: ORIGINS TO THE ELEVENTH CENTURY

The classical tradition

Most of the classical treatments of the other world do not include a guide. Homer and Statius represent the spirits of the dead leaving the Underworld in response to an invocation; Hesiod and Pindar merely describe the other world; Plato presents it in myth or dream form; Aristophanes and Lucian give a dramatic or satirical treatment.[9]

Three texts do, however, present a guide figure: Cicero's *Somnium Scipionis*, Virgil's *Aeneid*, and Plutarch's *Vision of Thespesius*. The *Somnium Scipionis* is modelled on Plato's myth of Er. Scipio is addressed in a dream by his uncle who, like Cacciaguida in the *Paradiso*, foretells his earthly future and urges him to the fulfilment of his duty and, like Beatrice in *Paradiso* XXII and XXVI, bids him look down through the heavenly spheres to the earth. Thespesius too is guided by 'a kinsman', whose main function is to interpret to him the things which he sees; he provides explanations of such topics as judgment and punishment, of the appearance of the soul after death, of purgation and of reincarnation. He also hurries his charge, who is inclined to linger, and on one occasion abandons him to the threats of 'certain others of frightful aspect' (p. 293). All of these aspects of the guide's role recur in later texts and in the *Comedy*.

The third text, the *Aeneid*, is the first and only work of classical literature in which the protagonist, Aeneas, undertakes a literal journey into the other world in the company of a guide, the Sibyl. She gives him the initial directions and instructions, and is present throughout his journey, sometimes acting as guide, sometimes standing aside. It is the Sibyl who, like Virgil in the *Inferno*, overcomes the threats of Charon and Cerberus; it is the Sibyl who, like Virgil, explains the divisions of the Underworld, identifies crimes and explains divine judgment.[10] Although she is the main guide, she is not, however, the only guide, being superseded at one point by Hecate, and in Elysium standing aside for Anchises.

The Apocrypha

Almost all apocryphal representations of the other world portray some kind of guide figure, although generally impersonal: the typical guide is an angel of whom few details are given. Among the Old Testament apocrypha we find the archangels, especially Michael (*I Enoch*, *Apocalypse of Esdras*, *Testament of Abraham*), as well as the generic 'an angel', and this pattern is repeated in the New Testament apocrypha, where the guide is Michael in the *Apocalypse of the Virgin*, and an angel in most of the others.[11]

The main role of the guide in these texts is to interpret what is seen: explanations are offered for the divisions of the other world and the coming of divine judgment (*I Enoch* I xxi–xxxvi and II xxviii, *Testament of Abraham* xi–xii, *Apocalypse of Paul* 11 *et passim*), for the Flood, for the sun and its necessity to life on Earth, for the moon and why it is of lesser brightness than the sun (*Apocalypse of Baruch*, 5, 6, 9), as well as for the nature and variety of sin (*Apocalypse of Esdras* pp. 472–3, *Apocalypse of Paul* 11 *et passim*). This is the explanation offered to Baruch for the cause of rainfall:

And again the angel took me forcibly and shewed me a very great lake and said to me: This is the lake whence the clouds draw water and send rain upon the earth. And I, Baruch, said to the angel: How do men say that the clouds go out of the sea, draw up the water of the sea, and rain on the earth? And the angel said to me: The race of man is deceived, knowing nothing. All the water of the sea is salt, for if the rain came from the sea, no fruit would grow on the earth. (p. 100)

Baruch's guide also shows him those who built the tower of Babel, explaining that from the time of Adam until the construction of the tower all nations had spoken Syrian (p. 99) – an issue which Adam himself discusses with Dante in *Paradiso* xxvi, with the difference that the original language is said to have been Hebrew.

Passages such as these foreshadow the scientific and doctrinal explanations given by Dante's guides, dealing with subjects such as the nature of the spots on the moon (Par ii), the divisions of the other world (Inf xi, Purg xvii, Par iv), the doctrine of redemption (Par vii), the influence of the stars on men (Par viii), the Creation (Par xxix), and many others.

A second aspect of the role of the guide is seen in the *Narrative of Zosimus* in which, for the first time in the Judaeo-Christian tradition, a series of guides is provided for the various stages of the journey. An 'angel of the Lord' (p. 220) appears to Zosimus and announces his journey to the land of the blessed. On arrival in this land, a second angel leads him from the bank of the Eumeles to the place where the elders are seated. There he is given a third guide, who remains with him for the rest of his stay.

A further element of the function of the guide as it develops in later works is found in the *Shepherd of Hermas*. Hermas falls into a spiritual crisis, the exact nature of which is not specified, and receives a series of dream visions in which first Rhoda, a woman with whom he had fallen in love while still a slave in Rome, and subsequently Ecclesia, rebuke and instruct him, thereby leading him back to a state of spiritual wholeness. In his recent article on the importance of Hermas in the development of medieval visionary allegory, Bogdanos links these two figures together and compares them to Beatrice. Rhoda is 'the first Beatrice of Western civilisation', and is to be identified with Ecclesia, of whom Bogdanos remarks:

in her fusion with the historical beloved – emerging here as a literary figure for the first time – Ecclesia serves also as a prototype to later, typological practice, as in Dante, where certain historical personalities achieve an anagogical dimension without losing their human identity and, hence, meaningful proximity to us.[12]

Historical personalities serve as spiritual guides to the visionaries of the other world from this point onwards.

The early Christian tradition

The role of the guide continues to develop throughout the period which extends from the beginning of the Christian era to the close of the seventh century. In some texts we still find the generic and impersonal angel figure (visions of Saturus, Peter and Salvius); the angel receives the soul as it leaves the body, conducts it to Heaven, and plays relatively little part in the rest of the vision. In three texts, however, the role of the guide is of particular importance.

The first of these is the *Vision of Maximus*, reported by Valerius, a contemporary of Isidore of Seville. The journey itself is not especially innovative; Maximus dies, and is led by his guide – an 'angel of light' (col. 431) – to Paradise where, like Dante, he is made to drink of the waters of a river; he is given a glimpse of Hell, and sent back to his monastery with instructions to live virtuously. What is particularly significant in this short vision is the nature of the relationship between Maximus and his guide: for the first time we find a personal, paternal and colloquial slant to the interaction between guide and guided. The guide gives instructions in a familiar and straightforward manner: ' "gusta de hac aqua" ', ' "taste this water" '; ' "inclina modo aurem tuam in hoc praecipitio" ', ' "bend over this pit and listen" ' (col. 432). He reassures Maximus who cries out ' "Domine, tene me, ne cadam" ' ['master, hold me, in case I fall'] with the words ' "Ne timeas, quia non cadis modo"' ['don't worry, you won't'], and encourages him: ' "Surge nunc" ', ['stand up now'] (col. 432). As between Virgil and Dante, the relationship is simultaneously one of father to son and master to pupil; it is affectionate but uncompromising. The angel, on making his charge drink from the river of Paradise, enquires in a kindly manner whether the earth has such water, ' "habet terra tua talem aquam?" ' On hearing that it does not, he prods again: ' "placet tibi locus iste? Aut si habet terra tua talem amoenitatem, vel si vis hic habitare?" ' ['do you like this place? Is your earth as beautiful as this, or would you like to live here?']. Maximus shyly answers that he would, and is asked which he prefers, the Hell he has just seen, or the pleasant land he saw before: ' "quid tibi magis placet ex his? Illa amoenitas quam prius vidisti, an iste infernus quem novissime intuitus es?" ' (col. 432). And then comes the crunch; the seemingly innocent questions lead to the severe instruction: ' "Bene. Vadens modo revertere in domum tuam, et si bene egeris, beneque poenitueris, mox iterum [cum] reversus fueris in isto amoenitatis loco te suscipiam, et meque permanebis usque in aeternum" ' ['Good. Go back home now and, if you behave well, and do proper penance, then soon I will bring you back to this beautiful place, and you will stay with me for all eternity'] (col. 433).

The second of the three visions is also reported by Valerius, and is ascribed to Bonellus. As in the *Narrative of Zosimus*, Bonellus is guided in the successive stages of his journey by a number of different figures. The journey is one of spiritual instruction, the aim of which appears to be that of the *Comedy*: to show Bonellus the damned and the saved, and thereby to encourage him to reform his sinful life. He is taken first of all by an angel to Paradise, which is represented as a golden, gem-encrusted cell. Here he is told that perseverance will earn him a place there: 'si perseveraveris usque in finem, in hac te habitatione suscipiam' (col. 434). He is then seized by a wicked angel, an 'angelus malignus' and thrust into the depths of Hell, where he meets a pauper whom he had assisted in life:

ibi inveni quemdam pauperem, quem statim cognovi, quia dudum venerat ad praedictam retrusionem meam infirmus atque mendicans. Et tenui eum apud me multis diebus. (col. 434)

[here I found a certain pauper, whom I once knew, because he had once come to my home, ill and begging. And I looked after him for many days.]

The pauper now seeks unsuccessfully to secure Bonellus's release. Bonellus is taken before Satan, and then conducted by three more renegade angels, 'angeli iniquissimi', to a sea of fire. Here he makes the sign of the cross, and a further guide appears to release him from the bad angels and restore him to the light of the world: 'venit qui me abstulit de iniqua eorum dominatione, et huic supernae luci restituit' (col. 435). Having thus received, in his experience of Paradise, a positive example accompanied by encouragement and, in his experience of Hell, where he finds the pauper whom he had helped but not restored, a negative example, Bonellus returns to earth with the conclusion that only perseverance brings beatitude: 'scriptum est enim: Potius est bonum non inchoare propositum, quam eum perducere ad detestabilem terminum' (col. 435). [For it is written: better never to begin a good resolution, than to pursue it to a bad end]. His spiritual journey is complete.

The third vision is that of Barontus, a hermit of Pistoia in the seventh century. Barontus is given three guides in the course of his journey, two of whom are selected for personal reasons. His first guide is Raphael, who rescues him from the onslaught of two demons and conducts him through Paradise. At the fourth gate the demons return, and press their claim for the possession of his soul, accusing Barontus principally of sexual sin. Raphael calls upon St Peter, to whom Barontus's monastery church is dedicated, to deal with the matter. Peter questions the hapless Barontus: ' "Est veritas, frater?" ' (p. 572) ['is this the truth, brother?'] Barontus admits that it is. Peter dismisses the demons' claim on the grounds that the sin has been confessed and expiated by the giving of alms, and when the demons refuse to accept this verdict he threatens to smite them with his keys; 'voluit eos ex ipsis clauibus in capite percutere'. He then turns to Barontus with the dignity and severity later shown by Beatrice towards Dante, and warns: 'Redime te frater' ['reform yourself, brother']. When Barontus asks, 'cum grandi tremore', how he is to achieve this, Peter issues him with detailed instructions. Having thus, as does Beatrice, exacted confession and issued a rebuke, Peter summons two boys and tells them that Barontus is, like Dante (see Purg xxx 136–8), to be shown the damned as a further warning:

iussit S. Petrus duobus puerulis (. . .) ut me usque ad primam portam Paradisi deducerent (. . .) & inde me ipsi per infernum deducerent, ut omnia tormenta pecatorum inspicerem, & scirem quid apud alios Fratres deberem dicere. (p. 572)

[St Peter ordered two boys to take me to the first gate of Paradise, and then to take me through Hell, so that I would see every kind of torment, and would know what I was later to say to the other brothers.]

The two boys lead Barontus to the first gate of Paradise, where they appoint a new guide to conduct him through Hell:

Rogauerunt unum ex Fratribus, nomine Framnoaldum, qui in isto monasterio nostro, quod illi pietas diuina concessit, in puerili aetate a corpore migrauit. (p. 573)

[They asked one of the brothers, Framnoaldus, who by divine grace passed from his body while still a boy in this our monastery.]

Framnoaldus takes Barontus safely through Hell and back to the monastery, where he asks him to tend his tomb. He is thus the third of three successive guides. Barontus's journey has been divided into three stages, with one guide for each stage: for Paradise, a remote figure unknown to the visionary, Raphael; for Hell, a colleague and fellow-monk, Framnoaldus; and in between these two the crucial stage in which Barontus is rebuked and instructed by Peter, with whom as patron of the monastery the spiritual responsibility for his soul lies. These three anticipate the guides of the twelfth century, and for the first time clearly foreshadow those given to Dante – Bernard, a remote figure who leads him to the highest point of his journey; Virgil, a fellow-poet who conducts him through Hell; and Beatrice, Dante's patron, who rebukes and instructs him as he passes from the one to the other.

Dante and the Medieval Other World

From the eighth to the eleventh centuries

During the next four centuries the figure of the guide continues to have an increasingly complex role, although an unnamed angel remains the typical choice. Several visions are of particular importance.

First among these is the *Vision of Drythelm*. The visionary is led by a figure of light dressed in a white robe: 'lucidus (. . .) aspectu, et clarus erat indumento qui me ducebat' (p. 254). For the first time in the vision tradition, this guide on several occasions reads the unspoken thoughts of his charge, and corrects them. Thus we are told:

respondit cogitationi meae ductor (. . .) 'Non hoc', inquiens, 'suspiceris; non enim hic infernus est ille quam putas.' (p. 256)

[my leader answered my thoughts, saying 'You are wrong; this is not Hell as you think.']

And again later:

respondit ille cogitatui meo: 'Non', inquiens, 'non hoc est regnum caelorum quod autumas.' (p. 260)

[he answered my thought, saying 'No, this is not the kingdom of heaven as you think.']

Secondly, with the precedent only of the *Vision of Thespesius*, the guide abandons his charge during the journey through Hell to the onslaught of fearful creatures; 'quo cum perductus essem, repente ductor meus disparuit, ac me solum in medio tenebrarum et horridae visionis reliquit' [when I had been led here, my guide suddenly disappeared, and left me alone in the midst of the darkness and the horrible vision] (p. 256). Dark spirits surround Drythelm, and only the timely reappearance of the guide disperses them. The guide explains that this was done as a warning: ' "Namque ego cum ad tempus abscessissem a te, ad hoc feci ut quid de te fieri deberet agnoscerem" ' (p. 264), and gives Drythelm instructions on how to conduct the rest of his life in order to secure salvation. This motif of abandonment becomes common in subsequent texts.

The next text of importance is the *Vision of the Monk of Wenlock*. It is here that, for the first time since the composition of the apocrypha, the role of the guide becomes not just to lead the way, but to interpret what is seen. The Monk is guided by an unspecified number of angels, who take it in turns to explain to him the scenes he is witnessing; at each point in the journey we are told that 'one of the angels said', and given a direct quotation of the explanation offered – concerning, for example, the distinction between upper and lower Hell, or between those who will eventually be granted eternal rest and those who will remain in torment. These explanations tend to be in the form of brief interpretations of what is seen, and from now onwards the guide plays an increasingly important role in the transmission to the reader of the meaning of what is seen, as opposed to the mere external details thereof.

The role of the guide as interpreter is greatly expanded in the *Vision of Wetti*, the first popular medieval representation of the afterlife to be written in verse. As in the apocrypha, the guide is Wetti's guardian angel – the existence of guardian angels being justified by reference to the *Shepherd of Hermas*: 'The Holy Scriptures relate that men have heavenly guardians, and the teaching of our Lord Jesus shows that they stand before the face of the Father and protect the faithful. The Book of the Shepherd tells of the same assistance'.[13] And although the guide remains impersonal in that he is an angel without a name, the relationship between him and Wetti is highly personal – so personal indeed in tone that his role is perhaps the closest to that of Beatrice in any of the texts antecedent to the *Comedy*. He fulfils many functions, explaining the structure and meaning of the afterlife, identifying the individuals seen, answering Wetti's questions, and uttering lengthy diatribes against the sinfulness of the world, concentrating particularly on sins against nature and on the errors of the clergy.

One such diatribe, against adultery and lust, is followed by a warning of eternal torment in fire for those who commit these sins. And just as Dante on the terrace of lust is encouraged by Virgil to test the intensity of the flames through which he must pass on his way to meet Beatrice (Purg XXVII 28–30), so Wetti is now instructed by his guide to test the fire with his finger:

> 'Quaeso probare velis digitum, si ferre per ignem
> Hunc facilem possis; certe sufferre recusas.'
>
> (667–8)

He is also instructed at several points, like Barontus and Drythelm, and as Cacciaguida instructs Dante in *Purgatorio* XVII 127–42, to pass on what he has seen as a warning to others. One such message is this: 'in the name of our Maker I bid you make a public declaration of this, proclaiming in a loud voice, without concealment, how dangerous it is that women should be concubines of several men'.[14] Wetti, like Dante at the beginning of his journey (Inf II 10–48), is reluctant to accept this mission:

> 'Domine, haec proferre pavesco.
> Vilis enim persona mihi est, nec congruit isti
> Indicio quod ad humanas transmittitur aures.'
>
> (672–4)

['Master, I am afraid to deliver this message. I am a lowly person, unfit for this announcement to men's ears.']

And just as Virgil rebukes Dante for his cowardice, so the angel rebukes Wetti:

> 'Quod summa dei sententia iussit,
> Non audes proferre pigro torpore retentus?'
>
> (676–7)

['What the supreme wisdom of God has ordained, you lack the courage to pronounce, held back by dull lethargy?']

He continues in much the tone of Beatrice, explaining that he as Wetti's guardian angel had special responsibility for him from birth: 'I am he who was ordered to watch over you, and remain the guardian angel of your affairs'.[15] Wetti began life well, but turned from good to evil ways:

'Ergo puer bene castus eras; mihi quippe placebas.
Sed postquam propriis coepisti vivere votis,
Displicuit tua vita mihi, nam pravus abisti.'

(690–2)

['As a boy you were quite chaste and I was pleased with you. But after you began to live according to your own desires, your life displeased me, for you resorted to depravity.']

The same was true of Dante:

'Questi fu tal ne la sua vita nova
virtüalmente, ch'ogne abito destro
fatto averebbe in lui mirabil prova.'

(Purg XXX 115–17)

['this man in his early life was potentially one in whom every right inclination could have come to fruition'].

But he too

'volse i passi suoi per via non vera
imagini di ben seguendo false,
che nulla promession rendono intera.'

(Purg XXX 130–2)

['turned his steps away from the true path, following false images of good which fail to fulfil their promise.']

In *Convivio* III xi, Dante presents this deviation as being more doctrinal than emotional; Father Foster summarised it as 'a rationalism content to stay within the limits of human knowledge and regarding with a certain detachment the Christian mysteries formulated by theology'.[16] Wetti's deviation, it seems, was similar but more severe; a voice is heard to proclaim: 'if he calls back to the path again those whom with the gall of sin he has deceived by his evil teaching, lured from the path, and sent careering down the slope of lawlessness, all his transgressions will be freely forgiven' (ll. 580–2). The angel laments the number of those who turn to 'worldly things', 'mundanis rebus' (l. 702), and orders Wetti to reform: 'then the angel gave Wetti full warning to correct his behaviour, and illumine his life with rays of blessedness' (ll. 678–9). Wetti, like Dante (Purg XXXI 85–90), is remorseful; and, like Dante, he is forgiven:

'Nunc iterum placido temet complector amore
Merentem lacrimis et toto corde reversum.'

(693–4)

['Now that you shed tears of sorrow with full repentance in your heart, I embrace you again in tender love.']

The remaining visions of this period are less striking than that of Wetti, but contribute nonetheless in different ways to the further development of the representation of the guide. The *Vita Anskarii* is the first text in the popular tradition of the other world to describe the guides, Peter and John, in terms of their physical appearance.[17] And the eleventh-century vision of the monk Isaac, related

The guide

by Othlo, offers for the figure of guide a certain Gunther, a monk from the same monastery, who welcomes Isaac with the friendly words:

'crede mihi, per multum tempus hoc a Deo petii ut aliquis fratrum nostrorum in saeculo adhuc commorantium huc ad me veniret.' (col. 368)

['believe me, I have been asking God for a long time to allow one of our brothers still in the world to come to me.']

Gunther, as obscure as Framnoaldus, is a purely personal figure of whom neither we nor any reader other than a contemporary member of the same monastery could have any knowledge, and the atmosphere of the vision therefore becomes one in which a familiar earthly relationship is continued into the other world.

THE TWELFTH CENTURY

All the major characteristics of the guide outlined above are present to greater degree in the visions of the twelfth and early thirteenth centuries. In particular, the choice of the guide becomes increasingly personal; his role develops and expands; and his relationship to his ward becomes more similar to that between Virgil, or Beatrice, and Dante.

Choice of guide

Many of the twelfth-century visions still employ an angel as guide – Tundale, like Wetti, is guided by his guardian angel; the Boy William by a 'vir splendidus'; Godeschalc by two angels. In other texts, however, the choice of guide continues to show concern for the particular needs of the visionary as evidenced in some of the earlier visions.

Alberic's guide, like that of Barontus, is Peter, whose physical appearance is described in detail.[18] Gunthelm, a novice monk in the Cistercian order, which followed the Rule of Benedict, presents as his guide the saint himself.

The Monk of Eynsham also presents as his guide a figure who is in some sense his spiritual authority. The vision begins at his request: 'I found myself thinking that I should ask the Lord to show me, in whatever way he pleased, the nature of the other world ('qualis esset futuri seculi status'), and to reveal the condition of souls after death' (que animarum corpore exemptarum post hanc vitam foret conditio') (p. 246). A figure appears, at first unidentified, a white-haired angel-like character dressed in white, of medium height, and says 'follow me' (p. 250). Only when we meet the local goldsmith is the guide named. The goldsmith, like Statius when he sees Virgil, is filled with delight:

Ipse vero intuens in nos et recognoscens, ineffabili gestu leticie applaudebat viro qui ducebat me, expansis manibus crebraque totius corporis inclinatione illum veneratus, atque salutans.
(p. 264)

[Looking at us and recognising us, he greeted the man who led me with a gesture of inexpressible delight, his whole body bowing repeatedly in respect, his hands outstretched in welcome.]

Like Statius, he explains the reason for his pleasure: the guide – now identified as Nicholas, the parish saint – is responsible for his salvation, although at present he is still undergoing purgation. Nicholas is thus the guardian of the spiritual welfare of those, his 'parochiani' (p. 264), who place themselves under his tutelage; he has saved one, the goldsmith, whom he had never met, and one, the monk, whom he guides through the other world as a warning. Likewise Virgil, the poet regarded as their authority by both Statius and Dante, saves one – Statius – through his poetry (Purg xxii 67–81), and one – Dante – by leading him personally through the other world.

The last of the visions, that of Thurkill, also shows a personal choice. Thurkill has two guides: the popular saint Julian the Hospitaler, and another named in different manuscripts as Dompninus, Dominicus or Domnius. Both of these are choices appropriate to an illiterate peasant. Julian is the patron saint of hospitality, and commends Thurkill, who offers him lodging, for his willingness to take him in. He refuses the invitation on the grounds that he is on his way to Denmark, but promises to return.[19] Thurkill is thus to be guided by the saint of hospitality, a virtue in which he and his wife are particularly strong. His second guide is the obscure Dompninus, whom Ward identifies with the Spanish saint Dominic who died in 1109 and gave his name to the town Santo Domingo de la Calzada, which lies on one of the pilgrim routes to the shrine of St James at Compostela.[20] We have already been told that Thurkill was particularly devoted to St James. He was perhaps intending to make a pilgrimage to Compostela, or had recently returned from one, or knew people who had been there.

It would seem therefore that the guides represented in the twelfth- and early thirteenth-century visions are figures appropriate to the individual visionary. As in the earlier tradition as a whole, and particularly as in the case of Barontus, the twelfth-century visions taken together offer precedents for the choice of each of Dante's three principal guides. Virgil has been his 'maestro' and 'autore', the poet on whom his style is modelled, and Virgil is a fitting guide for the first part of his journey (Inf i 79–89). The previous visionaries were not poets but novice monks or ill-educated laymen, led in the other world by their own mentors – the founder of their order or the patron of their church. Dante's second guide is Beatrice, responsible for his spiritual development, who now assists him to turn back from the false path, the 'via non vera' (Purg xxx 130). For previous visionaries this role is fulfilled by their guardian angel, by the saint to whom they were particularly devoted and, in one early case, by an earthly woman. Dante's third guide is Bernard, a man of God whom he has never met in any way other than through the written word; he explains to Dante that he has been sent to fulfil his desire, 'a terminar lo tuo desiro' (Par xxxi 65). Bernard perhaps corresponds most closely to guides such as the apostle Peter or the archangel Raphael. The kinds of choice Dante makes for his guides are not therefore without precedent.

The guide

The function of the guide

Intervention and commission

In many of the visions the guide plays an essential part both at the beginning and at the end. It is the guide who rescues the visionary from the state of sin, often symbolised by illness, into which he has fallen, and it is the guide who commissions him to relate what he has seen as a warning to others. The same is true of the *Comedy*. Virgil's appearance before Dante as he wanders in the dark wood, the 'selva oscura' (Inf 1 2), is accompanied by an offer of help:

> Ond'io per lo tuo me' penso e discerno
> che tu mi segui, e io sarò tua guida,
> e trarrotti di qui per loco etterno.
>> (Inf 1 112–14)

[Therefore, considering what is best for you, I think and discern that you should follow me, and I shall be your guide and lead you out of here through an eternal place.]

And when Beatrice succeeds him she gives Dante clear instructions, later repeated by Cacciaguida, what to do on his return to earth:

> Tu nota; e sí come da me son porte,
> cosí queste parole segna a' vivi
> del viver ch'è un correre a la morte.
>> (Pg XXXIII 52–4)

[Take note, and as these words come from me so teach them to those who live the life that is a race to death.]

These two elements of the role of the guide are foreshadowed not only in the *Vision of Wetti* but throughout the visions of the twelfth and thirteenth centuries. Thurkill's guide announces his mission when he first appears, having left his normal place as guardian of the basilica for the newly dead in order to intervene in the life of the peasant: 'I am Julian the hospitaler, sent on your account, so that you might be shown certain secret things normally hidden from men' (p. 6). The commission is given on the night following the vision, when he reappears to Thurkill, with the instruction that he should declare his vision in church on the next day so that all might hear it clearly.[21]

In other texts, either the intervention or the commission is given greater prominence. We saw in chapter 1 how Gunthelm, having committed many sins, is visited by the devil and falls into a trance in which he is close to death. While he is in this state, Benedict appears to him at the instigation of Mary, and leads him safely through Hell. He alone of the visionaries is explicitly forbidden to reveal what he has seen to any but his abbot.

The commission to relate what has been seen is most striking in the *Vision of Alberic*. Peter does not only tell Alberic to report his experiences; he is so concerned about the exactitude of his charge's eventual account of the journey that he compels him to inwardly digest, in the most literal sense, a detailed record written on a piece of paper folded many times:

95

cartam etiam mire magnitudinis habebat in manibus, que tota erat subtiliter descripta. Et cum hec omnia michi ostendisset, plicavit eam in modum parvissime paginule, misitque in hos meum dicens: 'non habeas licentiam neque potestatem qualicumque modo reiciendi eam'. (p. 102, repunctuated)

[he held an enormous piece of paper, covered in fine writing. And as he showed it to me, he folded it into tiny pages and put it in my mouth, saying: 'you have neither permission nor power to reject it in any way'.]

The scene of intervention by the guide on behalf of the visionary, on the other hand, occurs in most detail in the *Vision of Tundale*. Tundale is, at the time of his vision, a worldly man who takes no thought for his eternal destiny, trusting in body rather than soul and enjoying a secular life. It is decided, as Beatrice decides for Dante (Purg xxx 136–8), that the only possibility for Tundale's salvation lies in showing him the damned. He falls into a state of apparent death; his soul leaves his body; he finds himself in a dark place, surrounded by threatening demons. As he despairs, he sees a light approach like a star in the distance, 'a longe venientem quasi stellam lucidissimam' (p. 11). It is his guardian angel, to be his guide. He announces that Tundale is to receive God's mercy, and after the journey will return to his body.[22] Meanwhile his soul will undergo an experience which will be corrective, although the punishments will be much reduced: 'tantum esto secura et leta, quia patieris pauca de multis, que patereris, nisi tibi subvenisset misericordia nostri redemptoris' (p. 11) [relax and be happy, for you will suffer few among the many torments which you would have suffered had the mercy of our redeemer not intervened.]

The guide as leader

Once the vision has begun, the primary role of every guide is to lead the way. Dante describes Virgil as his faithful and trustworthy escort, 'la scorta mia saputa e fida' (Purg xvi 8), and Beatrice as the woman leading him to God, 'quella donna ch'a Dio mi menava' (Par xviii 4). They determine both the route and the timing throughout.[23]

These are the functions of many of the guides in the twelfth-century visions. Alberic describes his guide as the leader of his journey and the revealer of his vision, 'ductor itineris mei, mearumque visionum ostensor' (p. 87), and the words 'ostendit michi', 'he showed me', recur throughout the text as Peter leads him to each successive scene. The Boy William is likewise dependent on the knowledge of his guide, who tells him to follow, for he will bring him back: 'sequere me, quia illuc te reducam, ubi te caepi iubente Deo'. William follows obediently as he is led from torment to torment, and finally to Paradise, while the guide copes with all threatening situations, instructing him to cross himself when danger arises.

The *Vision of Godeschalc* is more complex. Godeschalc is guided by two angels, each of whom has a different role; an 'angelus affabilis' and an 'angelus officiosus'. The former's function is essentially to console and reassure Godeschalc; the latter is in charge of the actual journey, like Virgil issuing instructions and overcoming difficulties. Thus when they reach the thorny plain over which all the sinful must walk barefoot, the angels provide Godeschalc with a pair of shoes, although strictly speaking he does not qualify to receive them.[24]

Thurkill too receives assistance in the overcoming of obstacles met with on his journey. His guides decide to take him to the devils' theatre in Hell, where they install him in a safe position behind a wall, ensuring that he can see but cannot be seen:

ad hunc igitur murum sancti predicti astabant deforis cernentes et discernentes, quicquid miseri deintus patiebantur. at vir ille adductus stabat inter eos quasi sub muro delitescens, ne a demonibus videretur; multociensque ad nutum sancti Dompnini caput erigebat et omnia, que interius agebantur, clare prospiciebat. (p. 20)

[the saints stood behind the wall, looking at the suffering of the souls inside. And the man they had brought with them stood between them, crouching behind the wall lest he be seen by the devils; often he lifted his head at saint Dompninus's nod and saw clearly everything that was going on inside.]

This episode clearly belongs to the same tradition from which Dante's experience with the Malebranche is drawn.[25]

The *Vision of Tundale* shows a further development in the role of the guide. Tundale is the only visionary in the popular tradition systematically to undergo a number of purgative torments; this happens under the supervision of the guide, who stands by while he participates in all those which correspond to the particular sins he has committed, offering assistance where necessary. The most striking of these torments is that for theft.[26] Likewise Virgil leads his charge to the terrace of pride, where Dante bends double beside the souls undergoing purgation; anger – where he guides him through the smoke; and lust – where he encourages him through the wall of fire.

In the *Vision of Tundale* the guide determines not only the route taken but also the timing throughout the journey. At several points he urges Tundale to hurry, as time is short: 'profiscamur, grandis enim nobis restat via' (p. 13); and because other things must be seen: 'eamus, donec ad alia his incomparabilia perveniamus' (p. 15). These injunctions, like those of Virgil, usually come at the end of an episode.[27]

The abandonment of the visionary

One of the most striking ways in which the role of the guide in the popular tradition foreshadows that of Virgil in the *Comedy* is found in the scenes in which he momentarily leaves the visionary alone in Hell. The abandonment of his charge on the part of the guide is a common topos in visions of the other world. It has already been discussed in connection with the visions of Barontus and Drythelm,[28] and also occurs in those of Charles the Fat and Ansellus.

Among the twelfth-century texts the topos occurs in two forms. Firstly, there are those episodes in which the guide instructs his charge to await his return while he makes arrangements for the next stage of the journey. Secondly, there are those episodes in which he momentarily abandons his charge in order to teach him a lesson, returning only just in time to save him from the onslaught of delighted devils. Both these types are found in the *Comedy*.

Three visions in particular offer examples of the first form of the topos. The earliest of these is the *Vision of the Boy William*. As William and his guide reach the end of Hell, the guide vanishes, leaving William trembling with fear: 'ductore vero ille recedente, puer diu in tenebris stetit tremens' (p. 1125). He reappears as suddenly as he went, and leads William to Paradise.

A similar episode occurs in the *Vision of Tundale*. As Tundale and the angel approach the point where it is necessary to make the abrupt descent to the pit of lower Hell, and before they enter that realm, the angel disappears. Immediately the devils of lower Hell rush forward and threaten Tundale with eternal torment. Just as he is about to abandon hope, the angel returns and reassures him of his salvation:

affuit spiritus lucis et fugatis tenebrarum spiritibus solitis eam consolabatur verbis, dicens: Gaude et letare, filia lucis, quia misericordiam et non judicium consequeris.   (p. 35)

[the spirit of light rushed up and, once the spirits of darkness had fled, consoled Tundale's soul, saying 'Rejoice and be happy, daughter of light, for you will experience mercy and not judgment.']

He then leads Tundale on through the pit.

The third example occurs in the *Vision of Godeschalc*. At a certain point near the end of his journey, Godeschalc is warned by his guides that they must now leave him; 'solusque Godeschalcus, ductoribus quoque suis disparentibus derelictus' (p. 118) [and Godeschalc was alone, his guides having disappeared]. He finds himself outside a city in which he recognises various people of his acquaintance, and his vision ends.

These three examples foreshadow three episodes in the *Comedy* in which Virgil leaves Dante. The earliest occurs in the eighth canto of the *Inferno*, when Virgil leaves his charge outside the city of Dis while he seeks to negotiate entry, reassuring him that he will not leave him in the underworld: ' "i' non ti lascerò nel mondo basso" ' (Inf VIII 108). Later, at the top of the cliff which separates the area of violence from that of fraud, Virgil sends Dante alone to talk to the usurers, while he negotiates a passage with Geryon:

> 'Acciò che tutta piena
> esperïenza d'esto giron porti',
> mi disse, 'va, e vedi la lor mena.
>   Li tuoi ragionamenti sian là corti;
> mentre che torni, parlerò con questa,
> che ne conceda i suoi omeri forti.'
>   (Inf XVII 37–42)

['So that you may carry away full experience of this round', he said, 'go and see their condition. Let your conversation there be brief; while you are away I will ask this creature to lend us his strong shoulders.']

And finally, as in the case of Godeschalc but with considerably more impact, Virgil disappears altogether when his mission as guide is complete:

> Ma Virgilio n'avea lasciati scemi
> di sé, Virgilio dolcissimo padre,
> Virgilio a cui per mia salute die'mi.
>   (Purg XXX 49–51)

[But Virgil had vanished without trace, Virgil sweetest father, Virgil to whom I gave myself for my salvation.]

The second form of the abandonment topos is found in those episodes in which the guide rescues his charge from the devils who wish to take possession of his soul. The earliest twelfth-century vision in which this occurs is that of Alberic. Peter is obliged to leave Alberic for a moment while he goes to unlock the gates of Paradise to admit a newly arrived soul. Alberic is terrified, with cause, as the demons rush towards him; Peter returns in the nick of time and seizes his charge:

Cumque ego cum angelis relictus starem pavidus, unus ex illis tartareis ministris horridus, hyspidus aspectuque procerus festinus adveniens, me impellere vel quomodocumque nocere conabatur. Cum ecce apostolus velocius accurrens, meque subito arripiens, in quendam locum gloriose proiecit visionis.   (p. 92, repunctuated)

[As I stood abandoned and fearful amongst the angels of Hell, one of the frightful ministers of Tartarus, tall and prickly, rushed up hastily to seize or in some way harm me. Then the apostle ran back quickly, and grabbed me, and my vision continued in a certain place of glory.]

Alberic's fear at the approach of the devils foreshadows that of Dante:

> e vidi dietro a noi un diavol nero
> correndo su per lo scoglio venire.
> Ahi quant'elli era ne l'aspetto fero!
> e quanto mi parea ne l'atto acerbo,
> con l'ali aperte e sovra i piè leggero!
> (Inf xxi 29–33)

[and I saw behind us a black devil come running up the ridge. Ah, how savage he was, and how fiercely he moved, with open wings and light on his feet!]

Tundale undergoes a similar experience, although forewarned by his guide as he leaves that it is for his own good. The devils arrive, and torment him until the angel returns:

So, when the devils saw that I was all alone, they surrounded me with great fury and rage, reminding me of all my sins (. . .). And then they attacked me with all those iron instruments; each rushed up with his own, and eventually they tore me into little pieces; and when I was pulled apart and ruined in this way, they threw me into the fire in this house (. . .). And then, still in the darkness and in the shadow of death, I saw the light of my guide approach.[29]

Episodes such as these, together with those discussed in chapter 1 in connection with the motifs of the cauldron and the bridge, clearly lie behind Dante's presentation of the demons who torment the barrators. As with Alberic and Tundale, these demons make every attempt to gain possession of Dante. The episode ends, as it does twice for Tundale and once for Alberic, with the protagonist being rescued by his guide:

> io li vidi venir con l'ali tese
> non molto lungi, per volerne prendere.
> Lo duca mio di súbito mi prese,
> (. . .)

e giú dal collo de la ripa dura
supin si diede a la pendente roccia,
che l'un de' lati a l'altra bolgia tura.
(Inf xxiii 35–45)

[I saw them coming with outstretched wings, not far off, meaning to take us. My leader caught me instantly (. . .) and down from the ridge of the stony bank, lying on his back, he let himself go on the sloping rock that encloses the next ditch on one side.]

Neither this episode nor those discussed above are, however, ends in themselves; they have to do with the wider issue of Virgil's limited knowledge due to his paganism. The episode outside the city of Dis is resolved by the intervention of one who is sent from heaven, 'da ciel messo' (Inf ix 85); that in the *bolgia* of the barrators by an undignified scramble occasioned by Virgil's ignorance concerning the state of the bridges of *Malebolge*. Well might Dante ask doubtfully, 'have you been here before?' (Inf ix 16–18). It seems clear that here we have a familiar otherworld topos, being used in an apparently familiar way, but concealing a much more fundamental issue – one which is unprecedented in the popular tradition.

The guide as interpreter

In the twelfth-century visions, more so than in earlier centuries, the guide acts not only as leader but also as the interpreter of what is seen. Godeschalc's angel answers all his questions: 'when Godeschalc asked his interpreter the reason for the differences he saw, he was diligently instructed on all things' (p. 100). He explains, for example, the criteria for the issue of shoes and for the assistance over the river filled with iron spikes; he tells Godeschalc about the persons they meet; and he expounds upon the various categories of sin, concentrating particularly on the distinction between the three types of homicide.[30]

In the *Vision of Alberic* the role of the guide as interpreter is greatly expanded. Peter plays such an important explanatory role that most of the text is in the form of his reported speech. He not only interprets what is seen but also expounds, as do Dante's guides, general principles which it is important that the visionary should understand. Thus we learn the rules governing purgation; we are instructed on the attitude to be adopted by a parishioner to a sinful priest; we receive a sermon on the three root vices of man. He continues in this fashion to the end of the vision, when Alberic writes:

He told and taught me many things about the Old Testament, and also about men still living. He pointed out several sins to me, and instructed me to pass on what I had heard about them.
(p. 102)

The most significant text in this respect is, however, the *Vision of Tundale*. The angel's explanations are as detailed and comprehensive as those of Alberic's guide, with the important difference that they are conveyed to us not in the form of reported speech but, as in the *Comedy*, in that of direct speech. This invariably comes in the form of question and answer, as it does between Dante and his guides.[31] When questioned, the angel identifies the characters met, explains the strucure of the other world and the principles by which it is governed, and deals with such problems as the nature of divine justice:

Question: 'Why, master, have I had to suffer so many great torments? And what is this, when the wise have said to us that the Earth is full of the mercy of God? Where is his mercy and pity?'

Answer: 'Alas, o soul; many less intelligent than you have misunderstood this saying. For God, although merciful, is also just. Justice gives to each person according to their merits, mercy forgives many faults worthy of punishment. But if God forgave everything, how would he be being just towards man? And if he did not detest torment, why would he spare the sinner? And what use would penance be if God were not feared? Therefore God, who distributes all good things, tempers justice with mercy and mercy with justice, so that neither of them might exist without the other.'   (pp. 25–6)

Further questions and answers follow. In the passage quoted above we find, for the first time in the popular tradition, a consciously constructed dialogue: three questions are answered by the angel with a brief statement of the facts, followed by three parallel questions, rhetorical this time, and the formulation of the by now obvious conclusion.

Successive guides for successive stages

Dante's journey through the other world takes place under the tutelage of three successive guides. Virgil, commonly if over-simplistically taken to represent Reason, leads him on the first stage, as far as his 'school' can take him (Purg XXI 33), until he is able to award his charge the crown of self-sufficiency (Purg XXVII 139–42). Beatrice, commonly taken to represent Theology, accompanies him on the second stage; Bernard, whose appearance follows Dante's entry into the Empyrean, leads him by prayer to the experience of the final vision in which his spiritual journey is completed. This division of the journey into successive stages has a precedent in the learned literature of the twelfth century, most especially in the *Anticlaudianus* of Alan of Lille.[32] However, precedents are also found in the popular representations of the other world. In addition to the visions already discussed, three of the twelfth-century texts are of importance in this respect.

The first of these is the *Vision of Gunthelm*. Gunthelm is initially accompanied by Benedict, who with the instruction 'follow me' leads him to a chapel in which he finds the Virgin Mary surrounded by a company of the blessed. Benedict introduces Gunthelm to Mary: 'Lady, here is the novice whom you ordered to be brought' (p. 107). Gunthelm owes his journey, as does Dante, to the Virgin's intercession on his behalf; an intercession which in practice is worked out through a series of intermediate figures.[33] Benedict then escorts Gunthelm to a further place, where the religious dwell, and hands him over to Raphael: 'then saint Raphael took charge of the novice, and led him to paradise' (p. 108).

Thurkill too is led by a succession of figures, each of whom guides him through that area of the other world for which he has special responsibility. Julian and

Dompninus lead him through the purgatorial fire and into the basilica over which they preside, and thence to the devils' theatre; and Michael takes him to the temple of the blessed, before returning him to Julian.

Finally, the *Vision of the Monk of Eynsham* is of interest particularly concerning the relationship between the visionary and his guide as he moves to the next stage of the journey. Throughout Hell and Purgatory the monk's guide has been Nicholas, the parish saint; and throughout this time Nicholas has held his charge reassuringly by the hand. When, however, they reach the entrance to Paradise Nicholas, like Virgil, is forbidden to proceed:

crux ex improviso descendit super manus nostras, meque a ducis mei consectatu arcebat. Quod sentiens ego nimiumque pertimescens, ista piissimi comitis monita audivi: 'Ne paveas', inquit, 'fidem tantum certissimam habeto in Dominum Ihesum Christum, et securus ingredere.' (p. 315)

[the cross suddenly came down over our hands, and separated me from my leader. When I felt that, I was greatly afraid, and heard the pious count say this: 'Don't be afraid; have faith in our Lord Jesus Christ, and enter safely.']

The monk continues, uncertain despite this assurance, and is reunited with Nicholas at the exit to Paradise, only to wake up at the end of his vision and find that he is now, like Dante when left by Virgil, permanently separated from his 'dolcissimo patre': 'a ducis mei dulci comitatu me ex insperato destitutum vidi' [I found myself abandoned by my leader and sweet companion] (p. 317).

In his capacity as leader, therefore, the guide of the vision literature fulfils many of the same functions, and is presented in many of the same ways, as the guides of the *Comedy*. In so far as different guides within one vision lead the visionary through a number of successive stages of his journey, Dante's presentation of his guides seems, as in the case of the various popular motifs, to use traditional material in a way consonant with the learned literature of the twelfth century.

The relationship between guide and visionary

The relationship between the guide and his charge becomes increasingly complex in the visions of the twelfth century. Several aspects in particular foreshadow the relationship between Virgil or Beatrice and Dante in the *Comedy*: the guide reassures the visionary, rebukes him, reads and answers his unspoken thoughts, and treats him as a father would his son, or a master his pupil. In all these areas the twelfth-century visions build on those of earlier centuries.

There are many instances in the popular tradition in which the guide reassures his charge. From the very beginning of his journey, the Boy William is 'comforted' by his guide (p. 1125). Godeschalc is frequently consoled, reassured and comforted by the second of his guides, the 'angelus affabilis', sent precisely for this purpose.[34] The Monk of Eynsham's guide, as we have seen, leads him protectively by the hand throughout the time in which they are together, as does Virgil at the beginning of Dante's journey (Inf III 19–21). Virgil continues to reassure Dante throughout the time in which they are together.[35]

The guide

However, if the twelfth-century guide at one moment comforts his charge, at another he rebukes him severely, as did the guides of both Barontus and Wetti, and as does Beatrice. Thurkill is admonished by his guide not for his sinful deviation from the correct path but for a more mundane sin: ' "It appears", he said, "that you did not pay your tithes in full, and that is why you can smell this stench" ' (p. 12). When Tundale is surrounded by evil spirits, his angel guide points at one of them and says sternly: 'Here is the man whose advice you took, completely neglecting my will' (p. 11). Later in the journey the angel remarks sharply that Tundale must remember how little he hesitated before shedding blood, and that only the merciful intervention of God is rescuing him from his just deserts (p. 22).

In the *Vision of Drythelm* we saw that the guide reads the unspoken thoughts of the visionary. This occurs again only in the twelfth-century texts and in the *Comedy*, where Dante's thoughts are read by Virgil eight times, by Beatrice eight times, and by Bernard once.[36] The same thing happens in the *Vision of Gunthelm*. Raphael repeatedly offers explanations of the things seen; on one occasion, the novice is struck with fear as he espies what he takes to be towers, and Raphael reads his mind and explains that they are in reality the chimneys of Hell:

cernens quasi turrium fusca cacumina ab imo surgentium (. . .) existimauit se inferni loca uidere. Cui haec existimanti angelus inquit: 'Non est infernus quod cernis (. . .), camini sunt infernales per quos ignis aeternus suas euomit flammas.'　　　　　　　　(p. 109)

[seeing what appeared to be like towers with dark tops rising up from the depths, he thought he was looking at Hell. Reading his mind, the angel said: 'This is not Hell you see; these are the infernal chimneys from which the flames of eternal fire are released.']

When Dante similarly assumes he is looking at the towers of Hell, Virgil corrects:

> 'sappi che non son torri, ma giganti,
> e son nel pozzo intorno da la ripa
> da l'umbilico in giuso tutti quanti.'
> (Inf XXXI 31–3)

[know that they are not towers, but giants, and they are all in the pit, round its banks, from the navel downwards.]

We saw in the visions of Maximus and Wetti a certain degree of familiarity in the relationship between the guide and his charge. This reaches a climax in the *Vision of Tundale*, and foreshadows the relationship between Dante and Virgil, which develops during the journey from one between father and son, master and pupil, to one of equality. The angel addresses Tundale's soul as 'filia', 'daughter', on several occasions, just as Virgil addresses Dante as 'figlio', 'figliuol mio', and 'figliuolo'.[37] Tundale is afraid to cross the bridge, just as Dante is afraid to pass through the wall of fire, and the angel encourages him as Virgil encourages Dante, leading him 'with an amused expression', and reminding him: 'don't be afraid, you will be set free from this' (p. 15).

Another characteristic of the relationship between Dante and Virgil is that it changes. Virgil begins by rebuking Dante for his pusillanimity and leading him by the hand through Hell. Gradually, however, his limitations close in, as conversely

Dante's expand; the pagan poet's confident negotiations outside Dis are successful, but not so his equally confident dealings with the Malebranche, whereas his pupil increasingly gets the measure of the situation. Eventually, therefore, Virgil pronounces the pupil to have surpassed the master:

> 'Tratto t'ho qui con ingegno e con arte:
> lo tuo piacer omai prendi per duce;
> fuor se' de l'erte vie, fuor se' de l'arte.
> (. . .)
> Non aspettar mio dir piú né mio cenno;
> libero, dritto e sano è tuo arbitrio,
> e fallo fora non fare a suo senno:
> per ch'io te sovra te corono e mitrio.'
>
> (Purg XXVII 130–42)

['I have brought you here with understanding and art. From now on you may do as you please; you are out of the narrow and difficult paths (. . .). Wait no longer for a word or sign from me. Your will is free, upright and whole, and it would be wrong not to act on its bidding: and so over yourself I crown and mitre you.']

The relationship between Tundale and the angel changes in a way which foreshadows this. As they reach the end of the journey through Hell, in the course of which Tundale has, at the instruction of the angel, undergone the appropriate torments for his sins, the angel announces that his soul has now reached a state of sinlessness, and is free to enjoy its salvation:

Et angelus: Veni, inquit, o felix anima, convertere in requiem tuam, quia dominus benefecit tibi. Non enim patieris neque amplius, nisi iterum promerueris, ista videbis. Huc usque enim inimicorum dei carcerem, amodo autem amicorum ejus videbis gloriam.   (p. 39)

[And the angel said 'Come, happy soul, enter into the rest which the Lord has prepared for you. For unless you deserve it you will suffer no more of the torments you have seen. Let us leave the prison of the enemy of God, and you will see the glory of his friends.']

Tundale is allowed like Dante to proceed to the Earthly Paradise; and from this point onwards his guide becomes more of a companion than a teacher.

CONCLUSION

It would appear from this analysis that many aspects of the choice, role and presentation of the guides in the *Comedy* are foreshadowed in the popular tradition of the other world. The popular guides are commonly chosen for reasons personal to the visionary, and are not merely impersonal figures; different guides lead the visionary on different stages of his journey; the guides rebuke their charges as does Beatrice in the *Comedy*, and instruct them on the publication of their vision once returned to the world of the living; they determine the route and timing of the journey, and deal as does Virgil with the threats of the demons of Hell. They also interpret what is seen throughout the visionary's journey, as do Virgil, Beatrice and Bernard.

   It is clear therefore that in his choice of guides, in the particular role given to the guides and in the kind of relationship the guide has with his charge, Dante is building upon a pre-existent tradition. All the major aspects of the role of Virgil and Beatrice particularly are foreshadowed in the previous popular representations of the other world. And yet Dante's guides are invested with still greater significance than their predecessors. Virgil and Beatrice are fuller characters than any of the previous guides; they each carry their earthly personality into the other world in a way that most of the earlier guides do not, and their relationship with Dante is consequently more complex.[38] The passage from one guide to another in the *Comedy* echoes previous practice, but is also closely linked to theological and philosophical developments in the twelfth and thirteenth centuries.[39] The abandonment topos is common in the popular texts, and yet in the *Comedy* is invested with a whole new meaning: Virgil's failure to deal with the Malebranche reflects his status as an ungraced pagan who died before the birth of Christ. And the ability of the guides to read Dante's thoughts leads to explanations from both Virgil and Beatrice concerning the relationship of the souls in the other world with God.[40] It therefore seems clear that in his treatment of the figure of the guide, as in the other areas examined in this book, Dante does build upon the popular tradition, but adapts and transforms it for his own use, bringing to his portrayal of the guide a familiar realism which he often expresses according to the conventions of the popular visions, and which is in marked contrast to the learned poetry and prose of the period.

Notes

1 D. Consoli: 'Vigilio Marone, Publio', *Enciclopedia Dantesca (ED)*, v, p. 1039.
2 A. Vallone, 'Beatrice', *ED*, i, p. 550; M. Casella, *Le Guide di Dante nella 'Divina Commedia'*, 1944, p. 11.
3 R. Manselli, 'Bernardo di Chiaravalle, santo', *ED*, i, p. 604; S. N. Botterill, 'A Study of the Influence of St Bernard of Clairvaux on the Works of Dante Alighieri', 1984.
4 Manselli, 'Bernardo di Chiaravalle, santo', p. 604.
5 K. Foster, *The Two Dantes and Other Essays*, 1977, p. 156.
6 A. Ciotti, 'Le guide di Dante nel suo viaggio', *ED*, iii, p. 317.
7 Cancellieri, discussing the criticism of Bottari who had first studied the relation between *Alberic* and the *Comedy*, said of the vision: 'incomincia dal pensiere [*sic*] medesimo della guida, con la sola diversità, che con Alberico fu S. Pietro, e Virgilio con Dante' (*Osservazioni intorno alla questione (. . .) sopra l'originalità della 'Divina Commedia' di Dante . . .*, 1814, p. 39). Di Costanzo wrote in similar vein: 'vengo omai ad indicarvi la conformità di moltissimi luoghi della Visione colla divina Commedia. A buon conto io veggo un pensiero medesimo fra il partito preso da Dante di farsi condurre da Virgilio per l'Inferno e pel Purgatorio, e stabilirlo suo monitore per conoscere la qualità delle pene e dei peccatori, con quello che si legge di Alberico, il quale ebbe s. Pietro per compagno del suo viaggio, e per interprete delle cose che vedea' ('Di un antico testo a penna della "Divina Commedia" . . .', 1830, p. 171).
8 Guercio exclaimed: 'in ogni viaggio avventuroso, massime se simbolico e con intento didascalico, sta, elemento prezioso e indispensabile, la guida', and asked: 'chi s'è mai imbattuto in una narrazione di viaggio vero o immaginario dove non abbia avuta la sua parte la guida, sia pure, come ai giorni nostri, "tascabile"?' (*Di alcuni rapporti tra le visioni medievali e la 'Divina Commedia'*, 1909, p. 171.
9 For the classical representation of the other world see F. Cumont, *After Life in Roman Paganism*, 1922; C. Pascal, *Le credenze d'oltretomba nella opere letterarie dell'antichità classica*, 1912; W. F. Jackson Knight, *Elysion: On Ancient Greek and Roman Beliefs Concerning a Life after Death*, 1970; and K. Vossler, *La fonte della 'Divina Commedia' studiata nella sua genesi e interpretata*, 1927.

10 Compare Aen VI 385–410 and 417–25 with Inf III 94–9 and VI 22–33; and Aen VI 540–627 with Inf XI 16–111.

11 See especially *Apocalypse of Zephaniah, Apocalypse of Paul, Narrative of Zosimus*.

12 T. Bogdanos, ' "The Shepherd of Hermas" and the Development of Medieval Visionary Allegory', 1977, p. 46.

13 Lines 695–8. This and all subsequent quotations from Walafrid's *Vision of Wetti* are translated by D. A. Traill.

14 'Unde tibi iubeo auctoris de nomine nostri/Ista palam referens ut clara voce revolvas,/Nec celare velis quantum discrimen adhaeret/Esse subinductas mulieres pluribus aptas.' (656–9).

15 'Ego sum, qui te servare iubebar,/Angelos et custos rerum persisto tuarum' (680–1).

16 K. Foster, *The Two Dantes*, pp. 165–6.

17 See chapter 2, p. 68.

18 See chapter 2, p. 69.

19 'Coniunx tua duas pauperculas mulieres in hospitio tuo iam recepit et ego necdum hospitari queo, quia ad provinciam de Danesei festino, et cum inde hac nocte rediero, ad domum tuam divertam, ut te ad dominum tuum sanctum Iacobum deducam, quem devote iam requisisti' (pp. 5–6). The suggestion made by H. L. D. Ward that Thurkill is a Danish name, and that perhaps having Danish relations in the 'provincia de Danesei' he connected them in his mind with Julian seems less obvious than the possibility that Julian guides Thurkill because Thurkill follows his example of hospitality. See Ward's article 'The Vision of Thurkill', 1875, p. 428.

20 *Ibid.*, p. 430.

21 'ut seriatim et palam cunctis in ecclesia die proxima sollempni publicet visionem' (pp. 8–9).

22 'set quia deus misericordiam semper prefert judicio, tibi etiam non deerit indebita ejus misericordia (. . .). Me igitur sequere et quecunque tibi monstravero, memoriter tene, quia iterum ad corpus tuum debes redire' (p. 11).

23 Route: e.g. Inf VIII 19–27, XII 91–6, XVII 28–36, 79–99; XXXI 133–5, XXXIV 70–5; Purg XVI 10–15; Par XXII 100–5. Timing: e.g. Inf XI 112–15, XIV 139–42, XX 124–9, XXIX 10–12, XXXIV 68–9; Purg IV 137–9, XII 4–6, XII 77–8, XIX 34–6, XXIII 1–6; Par XXXII 139–41.

24 'qua re angelus officiosus, ab altero monitus, ad tiliam redire et inde calciamenta ei afferre, celeriter allatos, ad induendum ei tradidit' (p. 95).

25 Discussed in chapter 1, p. 13–14.

26 Discussed in chapter 1, p. 34.

27 Virgil reminds Dante that time is short: Inf XI 112–15; XIV 139–42; XX 124–9; XXIX 10–12; XXXIV 68–9; Purg IV 137–9; XII 4, 77–8, 85–7; XIX 34–9.

28 See p. 14.

29 'Alora, vedendo li demonii ch'io era cosí sola, con molta furia e grande rabia tuttiquanti mi furono intorno, ricordandomi tutti gli miei peccati (. . .). Et allora mi preseno con tutti quelli instrumenti de ferro; ciascuno con lo suo mi corse adosso, e finalmente tutto me menuciaro in pezzi; e cosí dissipata e guasta, mi gittaro nel fuoco de questa casa (. . .). E stando ancora in tenebre e in umbra de morte, poco stando io viddi la luce da la vita che m'aveva guidato' (pp. 33–4, Italian version).

30 pp. 94, 96 *et passim*, 111–12.

31 Virgil offers many explanations in answer to Dante's questioning: e.g. Inf VII 73–96 (Fortune), XI 16–111 (the moral order of Hell), Purg XV 64–78 (the nature of heavenly love), Purg XVIII 19–75 (the relation between love and the will). Beatrice takes over this role: e.g. Par II 49–148 (the nature of the spots on the moon), Par IV 118–V 84 (free will and broken vows), XXVIII 46–139 (the angelic orders).

32 The precedent offered by the *Anticlaudianus* for the division of the journey through the heavens into stages, each with a separate guide, is discussed by E. R. Curtius, 'Dante und Alanus ab Insulis', 1950, pp. 28–31, and by P. Dronke, 'Boethius, Alanus and Dante', 1966.

33 In Dante's case, Lucy, Beatrice and Virgil (Inf II 94–105).

34 Thus when he is overcome by fear we are told: 'angelus itaque affabilis consolans eum et confortans, equo animo esse premonuit, asserens eum' penam quidem gravissimam visurum, set, a ductoribus suis conservatum, minime passurum' (p. 99).

The guide

35 Virgil reassures Dante on many occasions, e.g. Inf III 19–21, VII 4–6, VIII 103–8, XVII 81–96, Purg III 19–24, IX 46–8. Beatrice has less need to reassure him, most of the dangers of the journey being over, but does so notably in Par XVIII 5–9.

36 Virgil: Inf XIII 25–30, XII 31–6, XVII 90–6, XXIII 25–30; Purg IV 58ss, XIII 73–8, XV 118–38, XXV 10–21. Beatrice: Par I 85–93, IV 1–27, VII 10–24, 52–7 and 121–9; XVII 1–12, XXI 49–51, XXVII 103–5, XXVIII 97–9, XXIX 10–12. Bernard: Par XXXII 49–51.

37 See, for example, pp. 25, 35, 52. Compare Inf III 121, VII 61 and 116, VIII 67 *et passim*. The instances in which Virgil addresses Dante as 'figlio' and Dante addresses Virgil as 'padre' are too numerous to list in full; see Consoli, 'Virgilio Marone, Publio', p. 1038. Three episodes in particular show the filial nature of the relationship: Inf XXIII 37–42 and 50–1 (Virgil carries Dante to safety); Purg XXVII 10–54 (Virgil encourages Dante to enter the wall of fire); and Purg XXX 40–54 (Dante turns to Virgil in fear).

38 See especially Auerbach's essay 'Figura', 1944.

39 Explored by C. S. Singleton, 'The Three Lights', *Journey to Beatrice*, 1958.

40 Purg XVII 55–60; Par XXIX 10–12; see also Par XVII 7–12.

4

The classification of sin

In both the *Inferno* and the *Purgatorio* Dante groups his characters together according to a specified classificatory system. In Purgatory this system is straightforwardly based on the seven capital vices, whereas in Hell we are offered a complex division into sins of incontinence, violence and fraud.

The principles by which sins are classified in Hell are expounded by Virgil in *Inferno* XI. He explains that sins of malice – that is, sins causing direct harm to self, God or others – are punished within the city of Dis, and that these sins fall into two distinct categories: those accomplished by force and those accomplished by fraud (Inf XI 22–4). Sins accomplished by fraud are further subdivided into two main kinds: those where no special relationship of trust existed between the sinner and his victim, and those where such trust did exist (XI 52–4). These categories correspond to the seventh, eighth and ninth circles of Hell, where those guilty of sins of violence, fraud (without trust) and treachery (fraud with trust) are found. In response to a question from Dante, Virgil goes on to explain that the individuals seen in the upper part of the infernal pit, outside the gate of Dis, are those who committed sins of incontinence – that is, sins stemming from lack of self-control rather than from malice – and rebukes Dante for not recalling Aristotle's threefold division of sins into those of incontinence, malice and bestiality (Inf XI 79–84). The detailed outworking of this system is summarised in Table 1 (see p. 134).

The classificatory system which governs the mountain of Purgatory is outlined in *Purgatorio* XVII, again by Virgil, who explains that in each of us there is an inborn love with which we are to seek God, and that we may, through the exercise of our free will, misuse this love (Purg XVII 91–102). Those who directed it towards the harm of others purge their sins on the lowest three terraces. The first is occupied by the proud, who sought to build themselves up at the expense of their neighbours; the second is occupied by the envious, whose fear of losing their power or honour led them to wish for the downfall of rivals; the third is occupied by the wrathful, whose propensity to take offence led them into vindictive thoughts and deeds (XVII 115–26). Others love with insufficient force, and purge their vice, sloth, on the fourth terrace (XVII 125–32). And finally, it is possible to direct one's love towards mistaken goals with excessive force, and this inclination is purged on the upper three terraces, which turn out to be devoted to avarice, gluttony and lust (XVII 133–9).

There are two essential differences between these classificatory systems: firstly that in Hell characters are mostly classified according to their gravest sinful actions

The classification of sin

(with the exception of those guilty of sins of incontinence), whereas in Purgatory they are grouped according to their basic wrong inclination; and secondly that there is no movement in Hell, whereas Purgatory is a transitional realm in which individuals move gradually up the mountain until completely purged of all the capital vices.

Examination of these two systems has given rise to a number of questions and difficulties, particularly with regard to the *Inferno*. In circles two to five sinners are classified according to five of the seven capital vices, this scheme then being abandoned in favour of the distinction between violence and fraud. Certain peculiarities result: for example envy and pride are not categorised in Hell, and prodigality is punished both outside and inside the city of Dis. The same is true of theft, punished both as a sin of violence in circle seven and as a sin of fraud in circle eight. Secondly, Virgil omits to include circles one (lack of faith) and six (heresy and unbelief) in his explanation, and no reason is given for the use of two different schemes in the two *cantiche*. And finally, and perhaps most significantly, there seems to be no clear correspondence between the cited Aristotelian distinctions of malice and bestiality and the Dantean divisions of violence, fraud and treachery.

These difficulties have provoked a certain amount of debate over the last century. Early critics suggested that the inconsistencies were such that the scheme of the *Inferno* cannot have been based on the Aristotelian distinctions;[1] others suggested that it was founded in its totality, like that of the *Purgatorio*, on the seven capital vices.[2] But since the studies of Moore in 1899 and Busnelli in 1905 and 1907, the common view has been that the major divisions of Dante's Hell are derived from the *Ethics* as Virgil implies, and that the detailed breakdown of these major divisions into further categories of sin is Dante's original application of the Aristotelian principles. The question of which sins if any are intended to correspond to the Aristotelian category of bestiality remains open.[3]

The classification of the *Purgatorio* is, in contrast to that of the *Inferno*, clearly and consistently based on the scheme of the seven capital vices. Critics have therefore suggested that the *Purgatorio* takes its structure from conventional Church teaching, and that the capital vices were an obvious system for the poet to choose.[4] But even here there are difficulties. From the third century onwards theologians had proposed a number of different formulations of seven or eight wrong inclinations which give rise to sin, but these had not been officially subsumed into Church doctrine.[5] Still less had they been linked with Purgatory, which was definitively accepted as a third realm of the other world only in the thirteenth century.[6]

Various suggestions have been made but not followed through as to how these difficulties might be resolved. Migliorini Fissi suggests that an understanding of the cultural context might throw some light on Dante's interpretation of the Aristotelian scheme in the *Inferno*.[7] And Moore states that the seven capital vices were identified by theologians 'no doubt for practical reasons which readily suggest themselves in connexion with Penance, Indulgences, and Pardons'.[8] It is the aim of this chapter to explore these suggestions by looking at two groups of texts. The first consists of the popular descriptions of the other world, which reflect an important part of the cultural context underlying the poem, and yet which have been disregarded by all previous discussions of the nature and sources of the classification of sin in the *Comedy*.[9] The second group of texts, dating from the sixth to the fourteenth centuries, consists of the semi-popular confession manuals written for the guidance of priests unable to keep abreast of the latest developments in law and theology; these have been little studied and never compared in any detail with the *Comedy*.[10] The authors and users of the manuals were often also the redactors of the visions, and so it is not surprising to find that the classification of sin in the visions often follows that in the manuals.

It proves to be the case that, although the Aristotelian categories of incontinence, malice and bestiality are not found in either the visions or the manuals, there are close correspondences between the specific sins identified in these texts and in the *Inferno*; and that furthermore there is some relation between the larger divisions of the *cantica* and those of some visions, particularly those of the twelfth century. This would seem to suggest that Dante's classification of sin is in some sense the result of a marriage between a large mass of traditional material and the Aristotelian categories, an explanation which would go some way towards accounting for the inconsistencies discussed above. It also proves to be the case that, although the seven capital vices are nowhere used as a classificatory system for the punishment or purgation of sins in the other world before the *Purgatorio*, and although they did not form part of the official doctrine of the Church, they were commonly taken as a structure for the confession of sins in the twelfth- and thirteenth-century manuals. These manuals must therefore be considered as a possible source for Dante's choice of the capital vices as the classificatory scheme for the purgation of sin in the other world.

THE CLASSIFICATION OF SIN IN THE *VISION OF TUNDALE*

The *Vision of Tundale* shows the most complex approach to the classification of sin among the twelfth-century texts, and will therefore serve to summarise the position reached by the popular representations of the afterlife prior to the *Comedy*. The classification is unsystematic, in the sense that there is no single governing principle which determines the relation of one class of sin to another, and yet the various groups are clearly separated and identified. As in most of the popular texts, Hell and Purgatory are not yet distinguished geographically from one another.

Tundale, like Dante, is told at the outset of the journey that his visit to the infernal regions is to be undertaken with the approval of heaven; and as he proceeds through the various areas of the other world he, like Dante, is corrected for those sins which he has committed in life. In upper Hell he is taken first to a place where murder is punished. His angel guide leads him on to a mountain on which those guilty of ambush and treachery suffer; to a valley in which the proud are confined; past the avaricious to a lake spanned by a bridge over which thieves and robbers must cross; and to the dwellings of gluttons, fornicators and those guilty of sins of the flesh. The last category of sinner found in upper Hell is the category of those who heaped sin upon sin. Virgil's explanation to Dante in *Inferno*

XI of the ethical principles which lie behind the classificatory system of Hell is paralleled by the angel's explanation to Tundale, at an equivalent point shortly after entry into the lower region, that the scheme he is witnessing is arranged according to principles of divine justice. There follows a debate on the nature of divine justice and its relation to divine mercy foreshadowing that in *Paradiso* XIX.

As Tundale proceeds on his journey down into Hell he is constantly warned that crimes gradually increase in gravity and torments worsen; as in the *Comedy*, sins considered relatively minor are punished in these upper regions of Hell, and those which merit greater torment in the lower regions – although in practice the distinction is not always clear.[11] At a certain point his guide tells him: 'you are now about to enter lower Hell' (p. 34). He passes through the gates and, like Dante as he enters the city of Dis, arrives in the place where heretics and unbelievers are punished: 'here are those who neither hoped for the mercy of God nor believed in God' (p. 37). The angel explains the principle which determines which sins are punished here, and lists them:

> Here are those who either wholly denied Christ, or who denied him in their actions, such as adulterers, murderers, thieves, robbers, the proud, and those who did not complete the penances they were given. (p. 38)

It is noticeable that these to some extent duplicate categories found in upper Hell. Beyond these sinners, at the base of lower Hell, Tundale finds, as does Dante, Satan in chains.

There are further similarities between the classification in the vision and that in the *Comedy*. The transition from one class of sinner to another is often marked by the presence of guardians and tormentors: Acherons devours the avaricious, Phristinus guards the gluttons and fornicators, an unnamed monster presides over the lustful, Vulcanus rules over those who committed a multiplicity of sins, devils inhabit the pit of fire at the base of Hell, and Satan occupies the lowest position of all. These figures recall Dante's infernal guardians – Minos, the Centaurs, Geryon, Charon, the devils and likewise Satan.

As Tundale passes from the torments of lower Hell to the purgative area in which the 'not very bad' (p. 40) are confined, his soul, like that of Dante when he reaches the shores of Purgatory, is flooded with relief and light; he turns to his guide for an explanation, in the same way that Dante demands of Virgil an explanation for the changed scenery and the sudden sunlight as they emerge from their passage through the centre of the earth (Inf XXXIV 100–5, Purg I 13–18):

> Conversa ergo anima sequebatur angelum se precedentem et cum non longe pergerent, fetor evanuit et destructis tenebris lux apparuit, fugatoque timore cita securitas rediit, et deposita preterita tristitia anima repleta est gaudio et letitia, ita ut semet ipsam tam cito mutatam miraretur dicens: Domine mi, indica mihi, obsecro, quid est, quod tam cito me mutatam sentio? (pp. 39–40)

> [Tundale followed the angel who walked in front of him, and before very long the stench thinned and the darkness receded. Light appeared, and his fear fled, to be replaced by trust. Laying down its sadness, his soul was filled with joy and happiness; feeling himself to have changed so swiftly he asked in wonder: 'Master, please tell me why is it that I feel so suddenly different?']

It is evident from this account that, although the classification of sin is much less developed in the *Vision of Tundale* than in the *Comedy*, there are nonetheless clear grounds for comparison: the explicit separation of one class of sinner from another; the gradual increase in gravity of sin and corresponding torment as we travel deeper into the pit of Hell; the distinction between sins deserving of punishment in upper Hell and those deserving of punishment in lower Hell, with the offering of a principle according to which the two types are differentiated; the assignment of monsters or guardians to the various classes of sinner, and finally the change in mood as the area of the purgation of minor sins is reached. These correspondences suggest that Dante was perhaps not thinking solely of Aristotle when composing his system of classification, and they invite a more detailed examination of the classification of sin in the popular tradition as manifested in both the vision literature and in the confession manuals which appear to have influenced them.

THE DEVELOPMENT OF THE CLASSIFICATION OF SIN IN THE POPULAR TRADITION

The most straightforward way of examining the classification of sin in the visions and manuals is to undertake a chronological analysis, since classification becomes gradually more complex and shows a number of important changes in emphasis as the centuries progress. This gradual development reaches a climax and crisis point in the twelfth century, during which developments in the disciplines of law and theology begin to exert a profound influence on the concept of sin and its classification. These developments are reflected clearly in the confession manuals, and in a muddled way in the visions. By the end of the twelfth century, a wealth of new distinctions had rendered the whole subject of the classification of sin immensely complicated, and the visions describe a classificatory system which is increasingly full of contradictions. Although the twelfth-century visions were still being copied and translated, no new visions appear to have been recorded after 1206, perhaps in part because of this new complexity. But the confession manuals of the thirteenth century continue to elaborate systems which take account of these theological and legal developments; and at the beginning of the fourteenth Dante once again describes the classification of sin in the context of the other world. He does so in a way which both reflects the previous descriptions, most particularly in the choice of which sins to include in his system, and yet differs markedly from them in the presentation of these sins within an apparently ordered framework. In this respect as in others, the *Comedy* can be said to be a successful response to the intellectual changes which were not assimilated by the popular tradition. It is therefore of considerable importance in this area. Delumeau, in his recent study of the history of the concept and classification of sin, goes so far as to declare that 'it is impossible not to place the *Divine Comedy* at the centre of the history of sin in the West'.[12]

The classification of sin

The classical period

Classical representations of the afterlife base their concept of sin on assumptions not shared by the Judaeo-Christian tradition. In Plato's *Phaedrus* we are told not of categories of misdemeanour but of the degree of wickedness of nine groups of earthly occupations. Virgil's *Aeneid* too mostly classifies the inhabitants of the underworld according to circumstance rather than to individual merit or failure: of the three underground realms, the first houses children, those condemned to death while innocent, guiltless suicides, those whose death was caused by love and those who died in battle; and the third, Elysium, is occupied by heroes and those who will return to life on earth. However, in Tartarus, the second area described by Virgil, individual crimes are punished. These include disloyalty to family, fraud, avarice, adultery, and betrayal of country. The same juxtaposition of two different concepts of the nature of the Underworld is found in Homer.[13] It is this second concept of Tartarus, as a place where specific crimes are punished, which constitutes the classical prehistory of popular Christian belief.[14]

The Bible

The foundational text in the Judaeo-Christian tradition for the classification of sin is the listing of the Ten Commandments in Exodus 20. The majority of statements about categories of sin are, however, found in the New Testament. Two of these occur in the Gospels of Matthew and Mark, and one in the Apocalypse. The gospel passages give an account of Christ teaching the concept that sin arises from within, and does not consist merely of the breaking of external rules:

> For it is from within, from the hearts of men, that their wicked designs come, their sins of adultery, fornication, murder, theft, covetousness, malice, lasciviousness, envy, blasphemy, pride and folly. All these evils come from within, and it is these which make a man unclean.
> (Mark 7.21–23)

Four further lists, suggested by Delumeau to be based on similar lists compiled by the Stoics, are given in Paul's letters to the Romans, Corinthians, Galatians and Ephesians.[15] Of these, the fullest is that given to the Galatians:

> It is easy to see what effects proceed from corrupt nature; they are such things as adultery, impurity, incontinence, luxury, idolatry, withchcraft, feuds, quarrels, jealousies, outbursts of anger, rivalries, dissensions, factions, spite, murder, drunkenness, and debauchery. I warn you, as I have warned you before, that those who live in such a way will not inherit God's kingdom.
> (Galatians 5. 19–21)

These biblical texts form the backbone of the medieval concept of sin as represented in the popular visions of the other world. Of the seven categories of sinner who suffer in Tundale's lower Hell, five have broken one of the commandments – unbelief, adultery, murder, theft and robbery. These and other biblically defined sins recur throughout the tradition: for example, Barontus sees sinners guilty of pride, lust, murder, and envy; Wetti of adultery and avarice; Charles the Fat of robbery and discord; Godeschalc of drunkenness and greed; and the Monk of Eynsham of deceit and sorcery.

The apocrypha

The Old Testament apocrypha offer little of significance in the way of classification of sin, *2 Enoch* being the only work to give any detailed discussion; the New Testament apocrypha, however, offer a wealth of material which remains unsurpassed in complexity until the twelfth century. The *Apocalpyse of Peter*, the *Sibylline Oracles*, the *Apocalypse of Paul* and the *Apocalypse of the Virgin* in particular give lengthy lists of sins. These are based essentially on the Pauline lists, the difference being that whereas *Paul* stressed that these were sins which would earn whoever committed them eternal exclusion from the kingdom of God, the writers of the apocryphal works use them as defining categories for those sinners already in Hell.

The most important of these apocryphal representations of the afterlife is the *Apocalypse of Paul*. The fullest extant manuscript of the early Latin versions presents a motley collection of sins with no apparent principles of classification, but which are echoed many times in later visions.

'Paul' is taken first to see the torment of the negligent, described in the terms of Revelation 3.15 as 'neither hot nor cold', and foreshadowing the inhabitants of the first circle of the *Inferno*, 'those who lived with neither infamy nor praise' (Inf III 36). They are immersed to varying degrees in a fiery river, like the wrathful in Dante's Phlegethon. 'Paul' learns that each degree of immersion corresponds to a particular sin: chatter in church, fornication, slander and deceit. The sinners are not hot because distracted from living according to their faith, and yet not cold because genuine believers. He then sees those who lacked faith in God's saving power – 'hii (. . .) qui non sperauerunt in domino quod possunt abere cum eum adiutorem' (p. 29), perhaps foreshadowing the unbelievers of Dante's sixth circle. These are succeeded by further categories of sinner, many familiar to us from the *Inferno*: various clergymen, usurers, those who mocked the word of God, those who practised magic, adulterers and single women who did not preserve their chastity, persecutors of orphans and widows, those who broke Church fasts, homosexuals, pagans who gave alms, infanticides and procurers of abortion, false ascetics and, finally, those who committed the gravest sin of all and who remain confined in a pit sealed with seven seals:

These are they who did not confess that Christ came to earth as a man, and that he was born of the Virgin Mary, and that the blessed bread and chalice of the eucharist are His body and blood. (p. 34)

The lowest reaches of Hell are thus, as in the *Vision of Tundale*, reserved for those who broke the first commandment.

Many of the sins described here and in other apocryphal texts recur unexpectedly in later centuries. In particular, Alberic describes an outer hell (*Infernus* as opposed to *Tartarus*) in which he locates, among others, women who aborted their unborn offspring – a sin common to all the apocrypha analysed here – women who refused milk to orphans, and married men who failed to observe sexual abstinence on Sundays – both these present in the *Apocalypse of the Virgin*.

The classification of sin

Some of these sins are based on the prohibitions of the Decalogue (unbelief, adultery); others on further biblical prohibitions (usury, sorcery),[16] others on the demands of Church discipline (fast-breaking, chatter in church). They come therefore from a variety of sources, and are not related systematically to one another; they do not become so even in the slightest degree until the twelfth century.

The early Middle Ages

From the sixth to the eleventh centuries a number of visions of the afterlife were recorded. Those of the sixth and early seventh centuries are brief, and make little attempt to distinguish between specific classes of sinner; attention is focussed instead on the infernal scenery and on particular torments.

This situation remained unchanged until the development of a new genre of non-learned religious literature, the penitential books. Composed in response to the change in penitential practice from public to private confession and penance, they took the form of treatises whose aim was to assist the cleric in the giving of suitable penances, and depended in part upon theological developments such as Gregory's reformulation of Cassian's scheme of a number of principal sins.[17] They were further influenced by contemporary legal practice, not only in the selection of sins but also in the manner of satisfaction.[18] These penitentials were the forerunners of the confession manuals, and their existence brought about a sharp change in the way sins were classified in visions contemporary with them.

The earliest penitentials were composed in Ireland, Brittany and Scotland in the sixth century; they were essentially rule-books which listed sins and specified severe remedies. The first penitential of any degree of complexity is that of Cummean, compiled in the seventh century in Scotland or Ireland; it was in circulation in the ninth century in the Frankish Empire, and is based on Cassian's scheme of the eight principal sins.[19] Also from Cassian comes a concept which will become increasingly important: the concept of the pastor as spiritual doctor. The penitential opens with the words: 'different sins call for different penances, just as doctors prescribe different medicines for different illnesses'. Not only the approach but also the aims of the doctor seem to have been emulated; the penances prescribed by these penitentials are intended to assist the confessant in recovering the health which he has lost through sin.[20]

Contemporary with the *Penitential of Cummean*, and equally influential, is the *Penitential of Theodore*, a composite work attributed to the archbishop of Canterbury but in reality drawn up in its fullest version from a number of sources by a 'discipulus umbrensium'.[21] It lists a varied collection of sins: violations of the Decalogue such as heresy, murder and fornication; others such as the thinking of evil thoughts and the eating of impure meat; and some which infringe Church discipline such as fast-breaking and receiving two baptisms. In all cases penance is specified in terms of its duration only. The basic structure of the work is taken from Gregory's formulation of the capital vices.

During the eighth century a number of minor penitentials were produced, such as that of Bede.[22] The great diversity of penitentials provoked a reform in the Carolingian era, the aim of which was to replace anonymous works by collections consisting only of authentic canons. As these omitted the detailed tariffs of previous penitentials, they did not eliminate the need for further compositions. One which became particularly widespread is the *Roman Penitential*, composed by Bishop Halitgar of Cambrai and contained in his *De Poenitentia*; it is a composite work derived from canonical and Celtic penitentials as well as from that of Theodore.[23]

The importance of the penitentials to the study of the classification of sin in the visions of the other world lies in their semi-popular nature, for 'they allow us in their richness and variety to follow the gradual coming together of popular religion, popular Christian morality and the prescriptions of ecclesiastical Christian morality'.[24] Written to be accessible to every priest, however humble and poorly educated – in some areas each priest was obliged by episcopal decree to have a penitential in his possession[25] – and often copied, recopied and amalgamated, they effectively form a compromise between popular belief, on which they were in turn influential, and official doctrine. All of the eighth- and ninth-century visions contemporary with the composition of the penitentials were either experienced or recorded by clerics, ranging from authors of penitentials such as Bede to probable users such as the Monk of Wenlock. And, in contrast to the sixth- and early seventh-century visions, they have two things in common with the penitentials.

Firstly, sins are classified for the first time in the medieval tradition, although less systematically than the use of the capital vices would suggest. It is often the case that a systematic approach, usually based on the capital vices, is announced at the beginning of the work, but that in fact the various sins are discussed completely out of order, so that their relationship to one another and relative gravity cannot be assessed.[26] The same is true of the visions of the period. Barontus, in 684, sees like sinners grouped with like, but does not offer an overall classificatory system: there are those who broke the commandments, guilty of murder, sexual misconduct and envy; those who committed another of the capital vices, pride; and others such as slanderers, perjurers, and the deceitful. Wetti, in 824, offers a mixture of worldly sins and infringements of Church discipline: avarice, adultery, injustice, fornication and the accumulation of worldly possessions in the clergy, and neglect of clerical duty. Charles the Fat describes the sowing of discord, murder, theft, malice, pride, greed and evil counsel.

Secondly, the penance of the penitentials begins to become the punishment of the visions; that is, a correspondence develops between the earthly sin and its purgation or punishment in eternity (Hell and Purgatory, like the penitential aspect of satisfaction and inner healing, are not yet clearly distinguished). Cummean states that 'it is to be noted that a person should do penance for the same length of time as he had persisted in sin' (p. 613). The wealthy man, on the other hand, might make a suitable payment as in contemporary law: 'when the penitent is to live on bread and water for one year, he may instead make a payment of twenty-six shillings' (p. 614).[27] In the visions, the punishment takes the form not of penance of suitable length or payment of a suitable sum but torment of a suitable kind: a monk who accumulated material wealth is imprisoned in a lead casket similar to the wooden one in which he kept his wealth, and adulterers are lashed on the genitals (Wetti); those guilty of *voluptas* are burned in a fire to a degree corresponding with the internal burning of the sin (Furseus); and a usurer who took possession of his debtor's mill has a burning mill-shaft in his mouth (Walkelin).

The twelfth century

With the eleventh century the penitential literature began to change. The nineteenth book of Burchard's *Decretum* is a treatise on penance which the author entitles *Corrector et medicus*. It is essentially a systematisation and updating of previous penitentials, but it points the way forward in one important respect: no longer are fixed penalties prescribed for given sins; for the first time the confessant is treated as an individual with particular circumstances and particular tendencies.[28]

Of the many changes which occurred in the twelfth century, three were especially influential on the development of the concept of sin and the ways in which to classify it: the increased emphasis placed on the individual, and the expansion of the disciplines of law and theology. As a result of these changes, the character of the penitential literature underwent a profound alteration, the changes being in turn closely reflected in the visions of the other world. The difference between the old penitentials and the new works is so great that the latter are known by a different name: the *summae confessorum* or confession manuals.

The importance of the individual

Whereas the old penitentials were impersonal rule-books, the new manuals provide information both on diagnosis and on how to counsel the confessant correctly.[29] And instead of concentrating on sinful actions which could be measured quantitatively as in the penitentials, the manuals additionally deal with wrong attitudes and sins of omission.[30] Both of these developments reflect a new concentration on the individual, his character and his circumstances.

The first of the twelfth-century manuals to fulfil the new requirements is the *Liber Poenitentialis* of Alan of Lille. Written at the end of the century, its sources are Burchard, Gratian, Peter Lombard and Bernard of Pavia.[31] In his prologue Alan, like Burchard, insists that the confessor should regard himself as a spiritual doctor, and stresses the importance of treating the confessant as an individual:

A wise doctor must draw out each thing as best he can, and investigate the distinctions between every case without which a correct judgment cannot be made. For it is written 'be careless in nothing, but always determine what, where, for how long, when and how. And again: who, what, where, with what means, why, how, when. For all actions are not to be weighed with the same scales; people may be gripped by the same vice, and yet there are differences between them – that is, between the free man and the slave, the child, the boy, the adolescent, the old person, the stupid, the knowledgeable, the lay person, the cleric, the monk, the presbyter, the bishop, the deacon, the subdeacon, the reader, the person with rank and the person without rank, the married and the single, the pilgrim, the woman in need, the virgin, the widow, the nun, the weak, the sick, the healthy, the man fornicating with animals and the man fornicating unnaturally with men, the temperate [*continentem*] or intemperate, and between the person acting by choice and the person acting by necessity or by chance, in public or in private. He is to take these differences into account, so that he will be able to set a correct place and duration for the penance.

(*Liber Poenitentialis*, pp. 15–16)

In this passage the influence of both medicine and law, as well as that of rhetoric, is felt. In the rest of the work Alan not only considers the various sins; he also devotes a book to the reception of the penitent and the manner in which the confessor is best advised to conduct the conversation, another to the choice of penance, bearing in mind individual variation and the relation between ecclesiastical and civil punishment, and another to the three steps of confession, contrition and satisfaction.

This emphasis on the individual is clearly present in the twelfth-century visions of Hell. Tundale participates in the torments for some sins but not for others, and the punishments are adjusted to fit the case – for example, Tundale, who once stole a cow, is made to cross an arched, narrow bridge leading the animal with him, whereas a man who had stolen a sheaf of wheat staggers, laden with that sheaf, in the opposite direction. There is a wide variety of different individuals with particular stories to tell and corresponding sufferings to undergo.

These changes pave the way for the *Comedy*, which of course is based on a detailed assessment of the hearts, actions and circumstances of each individual.

Legal developments

The twelfth century also saw the revival of Roman jurisprudence.[32] At its centre was the *Corpus Juris Civilis* of Justinian, which was expounded and glossed at Bologna by Irnerius and his successors. Alongside this state law developed an equally complex Canon law. In 1140 Gratian composed, at Bologna, his *Decretum*,[33] which sought to codify previous canons and decretals. It consists of two parts, the first of which lays down the general principles of law, and the second of which discusses particular cases; and it contains a treatise on penance. The *Decretum* formed the first part of the *Corpus Juris Canonici*; the *Decretals* written by Gregory IX in the following century, together with three later collections, became the second part.

Although in one sense twelfth-century Roman and Canon law, as governing State and Church, were rivals, in practice they were inseparable, developing together from the renewed study of the classical principles laid down by Justinian.[34] Roman lawyers worked alongside Canon lawyers at Bologna and elsewhere, the former producing glosses on Justinian, the latter discussing not specific classifications of sin or catalogues of appropriate punishments as before, but the principles which were being uncovered. By the thirteenth century, the major *summae confessorum* were written by men specifically trained as Roman lawyers, according to the methods and principles of that law.

The close relationship between ecclesiastical and civil law is reflected in the confession manuals and, in turn, in the popular representations of the afterlife. Alan considers the difference between civil punishment and ecclesiastical penance, commenting that the prescriptions of civil law are best described as punishments, and those of ecclesiastical law as penances (pp. 130–1). But in a popular work written in the middle of the twelfth century in France, which has no surviving title but is found in a manuscript known as MS Avranches 136,[35] and which is more closely related to the vision literature than Alan's *Liber Poenitentialis*, penance and punishment are assimilated to one another ('diciturque poenitentia quasi punitentia a puniendo, quia per eam punitur homo', p. 14), and the actual types of punishment in civil and ecclesiastical law are considered, rather than the principles discussed by Alan:

It is to be noted that whenever judgment is to be taken from secular judgments, then there are seven kinds of punishment: a fine (. . .); chains (. . .); floggings (. . .); punishment according to the law 'an eye for an eye, a tooth for a tooth, a bruise for a bruise, a burn for a burn' (Exodus 21.24); public shame (. . .); exile (. . .); servitude (. . .); and lastly death (. . .), which may be executed by strangling, crucifixion, tying to a horse, beheading, decapitation, burning, stoning, and transference from fire to water and back.   (p. 24)

The author then gives examples of particular cases exactly as in the tradition of Roman law, and as given by Burchard and Gratian before him. A typical discussion is that which concerns the various circumstances, calling for varying penances, which may surround the sin of murder. Several examples are given: murder committed in public war; murder resulting from the whipping of a servant, which may be intentional or accidental; murder in self-defence or murder in protection of one's property against a thief; and murder committed when drunk – in which case it is further to be established whether the murderer was unaware of the effects of alcohol, or perpetually drunk, since the two cases must be treated differently (pp. 25–6).

It is therefore in the confession manuals, and not in the legends of the afterlife which do not make the distinction, that the relationship between civil and ecclesiastical punishment and penance is specifically explored. Alan notes the common principles, and observes that in fact punishment is not the same thing as penance (pp. 129–30); but given the identical pattern of action, confession, and retribution, the difference is often forgotten. In the popular visions of the afterlife, no acknowledgment is given to either Roman or Canon law, or to the discussions in the confession manuals; the concepts of earthly punishment, of earthly repentance, of eternal damnation and of the purgation of sin after death all become fused in a common approach to the representation of the other world which could not have developed without them. Gluttony is punished alongside murder, avarice alongside treachery, the breaking of religious vows alongside simony. Only in the thirteenth century is the attempt made to impose coherent principles on this varied material.

Many of the punishments of civil law discussed in texts such as MS Avranches 136 are present as otherworld torments in the twelfth-century visions: chains bind the thieves seen by Alberic, and the principle of 'an eye for an eye' determines the torment of women who refused their milk to orphans, and whose breasts are now sucked by serpents; *St Patrick's Purgatory* describes some sinners being whipped, and others nailed to the ground or to a fiery wheel; Gunthelm sees a thief with his stolen goods suspended round his neck, bound to a burning horse; Tundale watches those guilty of ambush and treachery suffering alternately in fire and ice, and Thurkill describes the passage from fire to icy water of souls undergoing purgation. Godeschalc states the principle of appropriate punishment: 'as the authority of scripture testifies, punishment is given on the particular member guilty of committing the sin' (pp. 100–1). He also, as in MS Avranches 136, carefully distinguishes between various types of murder, according to the circumstances in which they were committed, and differentiating between those which may be purged and that which is punished with the second death, eternal damnation:

He stated that murder may be committed in defence of one's own life, or following the killing of a relation, or thirdly in anger and pride; and that therefore there are three types of murder to be expiated. There is a fourth kind, committed through the desire for power and success, when the murderer swears his loyalty to a person and then breaks that oath and kills him, or betrays him by killing him; this can rarely be expiated, but rather is deserving of eternal damnation. (p. 112)

Godeschalc's fourth category offers the closest parallel in the vision literature to the traitors eternally confined in Dante's Cocytus.

The influence of law is seen particularly clearly in the *Vision of the Monk of Eynsham*. On the one hand, the monk gives a list of fixed otherworld punishments for fixed earthly sins according to the tradition of the old penitentials, the punishments themselves being similar to those listed in MS Avranches 136. Part of this list reads as follows:

For immoderate laughter, floggings; for idle words, strokes in the face; for flippant and wandering thoughts, the breathing of unclean air. Those who sinned in dissolute actions were bound with several rough, burning chains. For committing with others many superfluous actions in sport or idleness, the skinning or crushing of the fingers. (p. 286)

On the other, the bulk of the vision is given to the presentation of 'case' histories such as that of the goldsmith, whose alcoholism is forgiven on the grounds of his perpetual struggle to overcome it and his devotion to St Nicholas. This variation of punishment according to circumstance derives from the new legal principles already manifested in the confession manuals.

There is one secular punishment in particular which often appears in the popular accounts of the other world. Many visions describe sinners bound to a rotating, fiery wheel in Hell.[36] They undergo punishment for a number of crimes, including sorcery, fornication, harming others, adultery, betrayal, theft and arson. They are fastened to the wheel in a variety of ways: by centrifugal force, by hooks, by their genital organs, by stakes and by the attentions of the demons of Hell. The tormented vary in number from one to thousands, the torment being uninterrupted or in alternation with a period of relative rest; and the wheels turn sometimes in a river, like a millwheel, sometimes because rotated by an angel, and sometimes spontaneously.[37]

It is probable that the infernal wheel has its origin in earthly judicial practice –

the wheel has been used as an instrument of torture and punishment since classical times. Death on a wheel was a method of execution for the early Christian martyrs – witness the legend of Catherine of Alexandria – and it continued to be used in the Middle Ages. The *Vision of Godeschalc* describes the agony of a young man guilty of murdering a boy, and whose punishment is to be bound to just such a rotating wheel: 'ad locum penalem trahitur, et, ut in eo genere supplicii fieri solet, menbris singulis singillatim rota confractis' (p. 110). It turns out, however, that Godeschalc is describing not what he saw in Hell but the application of earthly justice in the twelfth-century village of Bunesthorp. The victim had abducted, sexually abused and murdered a nine-year-old boy, and despite his attempts to suggest that the deed had been done by an unknown black man, he was given the usual sentence for murder. The motif perhaps survives, transformed, in the *Comedy*; three Florentine homosexuals form themselves into a wheel rotating over the burning sand in order to speak with Dante (Inf xvi 19–27).

Certain other torments in the *Inferno* have been suggested to derive ultimately from contemporary legal practice. Popes guilty of simony are plunged head downwards into narrow holes in the earth, which the early commentator Francesca da Buti tells us was the standard form of execution for hired cut-throats, the hole being filled in with soil once the assassin had confessed his sins to a priest.[38] And Forese Donati foretells the death of Corso, who will be dragged to Hell tied to the tail of an animal (Purg xxiv 82–7). This recalls the customary Florentine method of execution for traitors, which Corso was held to be; they were dragged through the streets tied to the tail of a horse.[39]

Theological developments

The third main influence on the formation of the twelfth-century approach to sin was the increased activity of theologians. The legal developments so far discussed were most influential on the classification of sin in Hell; the theological developments paved the way for the classification of sin in Purgatory.

It is in the twelfth century that attention was increasingly focussed on the seven capital vices, a development which had a profound impact on learned and popular literature alike. They are widely used as a system of classification in the confession manuals, and on occasion form part of the iconography of Hell on cathedral tympana such as that at Ferrara (Plate 8) – although, significantly, this is more common after the composition of the *Comedy*.[40]

However, the capital vices are nowhere taken as a classificatory scheme for sin in the visions, and are not officially declared in the authoritative version by the Church; nor do they ever appear to have been used in connection with the state or realm of Purgatory. The suggestion that Dante was following a well-established, learned convention in using the seven capital vices for the backbone of his Purgatory must therefore be closely examined.

The history of the seven capital vices was outlined in 1899 by Moore, who came to the conclusion that Dante was free to follow the many theologians who had formulated their own version, but obliged by convention to use one or other form of them; and more recently by Delumeau, who traces their erratic history until the time of Aquinas, when their number was defined as seven.[41] The first recognisable formulation of the capital vices is found in Cassian, who distinguishes eight and gives them a set order: gluttony, fornication, avarice, anger, sadness, sloth, vainglory and pride. [42] This formulation was revised by Gregory, who defined them as pride, vainglory, envy, anger, sadness, avarice, gluttony and lust.[43] Gregory's order was taken up by the authors of the penitentials, and most especially by Theodore and Burchard. The next authoritative discussion occurs in the twelfth century, in the *De Fructibus carnis et spiritu* of Hugh of St Victor; the vices and corresponding virtues are compared to two trees, the respective roots of which are pride and humility; each has seven branches. The seven vices are: vainglory, envy, anger, sadness, avarice, gluttony and lust.[44]

The scheme of the seven capital vices is widely used in the confession manuals, particularly in the thirteenth century but also to some extent in the twelfth. The treatise in MS Avranches 136 lists them on two occasions; Cassian is the source of the first list, Gregory of the second.[45] In the following century, as we shall see, entire manuals are based upon such an enumeration as is here suggested, in conjunction with the ten commandments also cited in the same work.

The twelfth century also saw a great increase in the search for other principles by which sin might be classified. Abelard formulated two new ways of looking at it. The first of these was to separate the actual deed from the underlying intention, a separation which runs directly contrary to the approach adopted by the penitentials. Thus vice is an innate disposition: 'vice is that by which we are made prone to sin' (*Ethics*, p. 5), and sin is consent to this disposition in the form of an evil action: 'this consent we properly call sin'. This, of course, prepares the ground for Dante's distinction between unrepented evil actions (the subject matter of the *Inferno*) and the underlying vices which gave rise to these (the subject matter of the *Purgatorio*). Secondly, carnal sin is to be distinguished from spiritual sin: 'some sins are called spiritual, some carnal, that is, some come from the vices of the soul, some from the weakness of the flesh' (p. 41); this is an expansion of a concept found in Gregory. It is also essentially the same as the Aristotelian distinction revived by Dante between sins of incontinence and sins of malice. Related to this is a third differentiation, between venial and mortal sins: 'some sins are said to be venial and, as it were, light, others damnable or grave' (p. 69). Venial sins are not consented to with the will, but are committed through forgetfulness: 'sins are venial or light when we consent to what we know should not be consented to, but when, however, what we know does not occur to our memory' (pp. 69–71). Mortal sins, on the other hand, are major sins which are committed deliberately, with the consent of the will: 'we do not incur these like the others through forgetfulness, but commit them with assiduity, as it were, and with deliberation' (p. 70).

Contemporary with the development of these distinctions, and in part dependent on them, is the full elaboration of the doctrine of Purgatory, present as a concept for centuries but hitherto ill-defined. On the one hand, individuals are now regarded, as in law, to be deserving of an eternal destiny which precisely matches their conduct on earth, seen in the context of their particular circumstances; they therefore receive, as in the *Vision of the Monk of Eynsham*, a detailed and individual purgation before admission to Paradise. On the other hand, the distinction between venial and mortal sins provides a ready means for the separation of those destined for purgation from those destined for eternal torment: venial sins become the subject of purgation, mortal sins of damnation.

The history of the development of Purgatory as a separate realm of the other world stretches from pre-Christian times to its full manifestation in the *Comedy*.[46] The idea of some form of purgation after death is given its first authoritative expression by Augustine, and its first accepted concrete representation by Gregory.[47] The popular visions of the afterlife gradually develop, in the depiction of many specific examples, the idea of purgation after death; one of the most important of these is Bede's *Vision of Drythelm*. But it is only in the twelfth century that Purgatory is fully accepted as a place which is completely separate from Hell – although the vision literature continues to describe them as one. These visions appear to be founded on the theological position with regard to purgation which prevailed at the beginning of the century: many of the dead will be immediately separated into those destined for Hell and those destined for Paradise, but one or possibly two intermediate categories will undergo some kind of purgation until the Day of Judgment.[48] The precise nature of this purgation remains undefined, except insofar as it involves fire in some way. The majority of visions fail even properly to separate eternal torment in Hell from purgative torment; it is frquently unclear which a particular sinner or group of sinners is undergoing.

By the end of the century, however, legal and theological developments had been assimilated, and Purgatory is represented as the third realm of the other world, with its own *raison d'être* – the bringing to a state of perfection those of the saved whose sins remain unpurged on death, in a way appropriate to the needs of each individual – and its own entrance qualification – the commission of venial, and not mortal, sins. The last two visions, those of the Monk of Eynsham (1196) and of Thurkill (1206), reflect these new concepts in their representation of purgation; but neither yet offers a classification of the sins being purged.

The Vision of the Monk of Eynsham

The *Vision of the Monk of Eynsham* is the longest of the popular visions of the afterlife; in its complexity and level of detail it is unsurpassed. More sins and their derivatives are mentioned than in any other vision, and yet there is no clear system of classification.

The sinners in the joint Hell/Purgatory are distributed in three places of torment. The first contains a variety of sins and professions, although these are not specifically distinguished:

Here there was a numerous crowd of people of both sexes and all conditions, professions and ranks, guilty of all kinds of sin, and condemned to different sorts of torment according to the variety of their offences and the station of their person. (p. 254)

Sinners circulate from torment to torment, purging not merely their gravest sin, but each one in turn. The efficacy of prayer for the dead is stressed.

The second place of torment contains punishments which are all worse than those in the first place, in accordance with the established practice; again it is stressed that souls must purge every sin:

This was the condition of everyone who was tormented in that place, that in order to complete their purgation fully they were obliged to pass right through the place from the beginning to the end. (p. 258)

The third place of torment is reserved for those guilty of homosexuality, and here the monk meets a lawyer who doubts his own salvation. He is undergoing torment until the Day of Judgment, when his fate will be declared – which suggests that purgation occurs in Hell, with eventual release to Paradise.

The monk now proceeds to identify some of the individuals he has met, and to outline their sins. The result is a confused jumble of individuals and categories, with no apparent order or structure. In the first place of torment he meets a negligent prior, a nun, the bishop of Messina, and a woman who used to scold her husband; these are undergoing purgation. In the second place of torment he meets an oppressive bishop, an unchaste bishop, a proud bishop, a weak archbishop. He lists those categories which he will not discuss: murder, adultery, incest, fornication, deceit, perjury, abduction, drunkenness, feasting, treachery, avarice, pride, envy, slander, hatred, vainglory – a mixture of capital vices and biblical prohibitions (p. 293). He describes and identifies yet others: the untimely dead, the repentant, poisoners and women who aborted their children, usurers, deserters of religious orders; an adulterous king, a negligent bishop, a unscrupulous abbot, a nun who neglected an orphan, a knight who sold a church office, an over-economical sacristan, and a harsh clerk – sins deriving from the apocrypha, sins against others, sins which violate Church discipline. He states that of these, none was damned for sure; and explicitly laments the necessity of inventing a classificatory system, since the scriptures say nothing about either the classification or the punishment of sins: 'nullum in scripturis sacris peccati genus describitur, cuius in hiis locis certa non sint auctoribus suis preparata tormenta' (p. 293). And so he pronounces himself to be the first visionary aware of the immensely problematical nature of the classification of sin. He is virtually the last to confront it.

The Vision of Thurkill

The Vision of Thurkill, unlike that of the Monk of Eynsham, pays relatively little attention to the grouping of different classes of sinners. Instead the emphasis is placed on the major topographical divisions of the other world. For the first time in the history of the popular representation of the afterlife, Hell and Purgatory are presented as clearly distinct areas in which different processes occur. Thurkill's other world consists of a basilica, in which the souls of the recently dead are received; a Hell to the north of this, divided into an upper and a lower area; a Purgatory to the east; and beyond that a mountain of joy on which Paradise is situated. Purgatory is divided into three parts: firstly an area of fire in which the

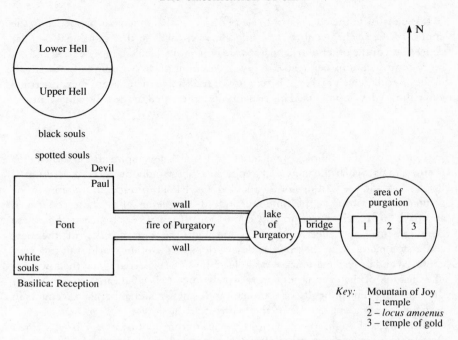

4 Diagram illustrating the topographical structure of the other world as described in the *Vision of Thurkill*

stains of the soul are burnt off – recalling the Platonic concept of the soul as expressed both in Plato's own *Phaedrus* and in Plutarch's *Vision of Thespesius*; secondly a freezing lake in which sinners, as in the *Vision of Paul*, are immersed to varying degrees; thirdly a bridge covered in nails, on which sinners suffer in inverse proportion to the number of prayers said for them by the living and the amount of almsgiving practised by them on earth. The bridge leads to the mountain of joy, on the slopes of which purgation is completed. Sunday is a day of respite, when Uriel drains the lake and extinguishes the fire – a motif which goes back to the early apocryphal representations of the afterlife.

This vision is one which simultaneously adheres firmly to tradition and takes account of the doctrinal developments of the previous century. Purgatory is described in the following words:

In the eastern part of the said basilica there was the fire of Purgatory, contained between two walls. One of these walls faced northwards and the other southwards; there was a wide space between them, which extended sideways towards the East until it reached a certain large, deep lake. In this lake the souls of those who had crossed through the purgatorial fire were immersed. And the water of the lake was incomparably cold and extremely salty, as he was later shown. Then there was a great bridge, covered with nails and stakes which had to be crossed before the Mountain of Joy could be reached. (p. 12)

The geography of Thurkill's other world might be represented diagrammatically as in Figure 4.

It is clear from the analysis of these two visions that much has happened in the course of the twelfth century to bring about changes in the traditional popular conception of the other world; visions are now more detailed, more varied and yet more confused, none being able to give an account of the grouping of individuals in the afterlife which makes coherent use of traditional material and new doctrinal and cultural developments. This situation is aggravated in the following century.

The thirteenth century

It is clear that the complex intellectual and social developments of the twelfth century, in particular the increased importance of the individual, the absorption of Roman law and the writings of the theologians, left a profound impression on the penitential literature of the time and indeed completely altered the traditional approach to the classification and confession of sin. It is also clear that these developments are reflected, perhaps through the intermediacy of the new confession manuals, in the popular descriptions of the other world, but in a very confused and unsystematic way – as indeed might be expected given the low level of education of the visionaries and relatively low intellectual capacity of many of the redactors. The difficulty of assimilating this new material perhaps accounts in part for the apparent demise of the genre after the *Vision of Thurkill*.

However, although no new visions of the afterlife appear to have been written after 1206, there were a number of other important developments which occurred between Thurkill's vision and the writing of the *Comedy*.

The first of these developments was the religious reform instituted by Innocent III, which encouraged and channelled an upsurge in popular religious literature. Innocent's aims were expressed in the Fourth Lateran Council of 1215–16; the correction of vice and ignorance among the faithful; the organisation of a new crusade; and the furthering of the progress of all Christians towards the glory of Heaven.[49] The main measure taken to ensure the accomplishment of the first of these aims was the stipulation that each individual should confess his sins to his priest, and carry out the appropriate penance, at least once a year:

Omnis utriusque sexus fidelis, postquam ad annos discretionis pervenerit, omnia sua solus peccata saltem semel in anno fideliter confiteatur proprio sacerdoti, et injunctam sibi poenitentiam pro viribus studiat adimplere.

This was accompanied by instructions for the priest:

The priest must be discerning and cautious, so that like a skilled doctor he might pour wine and oil over the wound; diligently inquiring about both the sin and the circumstances of the sin, so that with prudence he might understand what advice and remedy to offer, using different means to heal the sick person.

Such a directive placed new demands on the parish priest, who was often ill-fitted by reasons both of training and of intellect to meet them; the result was therefore a vast expansion in the production of the confession manuals which had already begun to appear in the twelfth century.

In England, the most famous of the reformers was Robert Grosseteste, who in

1238 published a reform programme in which he stressed the need for each cleric to master a simple but essential doctrine. This doctrine he centred around the ten commandments, the seven capital vices, and the seven sacraments:

Since therefore without observation of the Decalogue the health of the soul cannot be maintained, we urge in the Lord and firmly charge that every pastor of the soul and every parish priest should know the Decalogue, that is the ten mandates of the law of Moses; and that he should frequently preach and expound it. He should also know which are the seven capital vices, and should likewise exhort the people to flee from them. Beyond that he should know, at least superficially, the seven sacraments of the Church. And those especially who are priests should know which things are to be brought to true confession and to the sacrament of penance.[50]

These three systems, and particularly the first two, became the standard backbone for the expanding *summae confessorum*.

The first confession manuals to use the scheme of the seven capital vices as a systematic approach to the identification, confession and expiation of sin were those of Robert of Flamborough and Thomas of Chabham, written in 1210–15 and 1214–30 respectively.[51] One which was particularly widely used was the Anglo-Norman *Manuel des Péchés*, written at some time between 1250 and 1270, and avowedly intended for use by the laity as well as the clergy: 'pur la laie gent ert fet'.[52] It contains, in its original form, five books. The first deals with the articles of faith; the second with the ten commandments, the third with the capital vices, the fourth with sacrilege, and the fifth with the sacraments. It therefore follows closely the dictates of the reformers. Each commandment, and subsequently each capital vice, is stated, and the different ways in which it may be violated are discussed. Particular case histories are given in illustration of the various sins – such as that of a monk who lusted after a particular woman, and whose struggles against temptation are related in a way which is reminiscent of the account given by the Monk of Eynsham of the goldsmith's struggles against the temptation of drink; and that of a knight who robbed a poor man. These case histories are especially significant not only in that they show the new emphasis on the individual and the precise circumstances of his sin, but also in that they demonstrate the close relationship between these manuals and the popular beliefs concerning the afterlife. Under the fifth commandment, the vision of the soldier recounted in Gregory's *Dialogues* is related, with a full description of the bridge of judgment; under the seventh, we are told of the vision of Furseus and its effect upon his life. Under the vice of pride, we learn of a proud woman and of a backbiting monk who now suffer torment in Hell as a result of their sin: she is fixed to a fiery wheel, and he gnaws his burning tongue.

The capital vices in the *Manuel des Péchés* are as follows: pride, anger, envy, sloth, avarice, gluttony and lust.[53] The order, which is that adopted by Dante, essentially follows Hugh of St Victor. Great detail is entered into concerning the manifestations of each vice; twenty-one are listed under the heading of sloth alone.

During the same period, the theological studies of the previous century continued, leading to the clarification and establishment of a number of doctrines. Thomas Aquinas lists the seven capital vices as follows: pride/vainglory, envy, anger, sadness/sloth, avarice/covetousness, gluttony and lust.[54] This is the order adopted in the *Purgatorio*. He discusses the distinction between vice and sin, defining the former as an evil habit, the latter as an evil action: 'videtur quod vitium idest habitus malus, sit peius quam peccatum, idest actus malus' (*ST* Ia IIae q. 71 a. 3) – essentially the same as Abelard's definition, but this time expressed in Aristotelian terminology. He then turns his attention to the difference between mortal and venial sin, basing his definition on Augustine's distinction between 'crimina levia, quotidiana, veniala' and 'crimina letalia, mortifera', but introducing the new concepts of love and order. A mortal sin, occurring in the rational faculty, is defined thus: 'when the soul is disordered through sin sufficiently to turn it away from its final goal, that is God, to whom we are united by love, that is a mortal sin' ('quando anima deordinatur per peccatum usque ad aversionem ab ultimo fine, scilicet Deo, cui unimur per caritatem, tunc est peccatum mortale') (q. 71 a. 3). A venial sin, occurring in the sensual faculty, is defined: 'when the disorder does not cause a turning away from God, that is a venial sin' ('quando vero fit deordinatio citra aversionem a Deo, tunc est peccatum veniale') (q. 72 a. 5). The concept of ordered and disordered love is of course fundamental to the structure of the *Purgatorio*. A parallel distinction is that now entered into between carnal and spiritual sins. Thomas also differentiates sins in terms of their object, and states that this is the yardstick by which their relative gravity must be measured: 'peccata proprie distinguantur specie secundum obiecta' (q. 72 a. 1). And lastly, he discusses the causes of sin, saying that it may arise from the passions (Dante's sins of incontinence) or, more gravely, from malice (q. 79 a. 1). Distinctions such as these are foreign to the visions but fundamental to the *Comedy*.

Insofar as the development of the doctrine of Purgatory was concerned, great strides were made in the course of the century. Theologians such as Bonaventure and Albert addressed their minds to it; it formed the subject of numerous *exempla*; a Papal definition was issued.[55] By the end of the century the concept of a third realm of the other world was well established, appearing in sermons, wills and vernacular literature; but the iconography of that realm was still to be determined.[56]

One further thirteenth-century development remains to be considered. Beginning in 1220 and writing in the years which immediately followed, Raymond de Penyafort composed his *Summa de casibus poenitentiae*, a work which became the most influential of its kind.[57] Raymond had studied law in Bologna for ten years and, discarding the scheme of the capital vices or ten commandments, he applied the principles of law to the problem of the confession of sin and did so within a structure derived from theological writings. In so doing he further revolutionised the recognised principles by which sins were classified.

The *Summa* is divided into four books, the last of which was perhaps added at a later date. The first treats of sins committed against God, the second of those committed against one's neighbour, the third of the way in which the priest must receive the confessant, and the fourth of marriage. In the first two books, Raymond discusses the various sins not in terms of the capital vices from which they spring, but under the legal headings used by Gratian. For the first time, therefore, sins are arranged, as in the *Inferno*, in a logical structure based on stated rational, secular principles, and not according to the categories of theologians.

CLASSIFICATION IN THE *COMEDY*: A COMPARISON

The intellectual developments of the twelfth and thirteenth centuries, as we have seen, introduced a number of new factors and principles into the traditional conception of the afterlife. Theologians concentrated on the elaboration of the seven capital vices, on the distinction between vice and sin, and on the clarification of the doctrine of Purgatory; lawyers applied the logic of Roman law to the differentiation and punishment of sins; and the rise in the importance of the individual and the discovery of Aristotelian ethics also contributed to the demise of the cultural environment in which the majority of the popular visions of the afterlife had been conceived. In writing the *Comedy*, Dante was able to assimilate these changes and apply them systematically to the classification of sin in the other world, a feat which the visionaries and their redactors had not been able to achieve. He thereby produced a system which was unique in that, for the first time, sins appear to be distinguished and arranged according to two sets of governing principles, an Aristotelian one for Hell and one in which the seven capital vices are subsumed into the principle of ordered and disordered love for Purgatory. And yet, strikingly, the particular sins distinguished in Hell are almost identical to those identified by the visionaries, whilst the vices used for the first time in Purgatory are treated in a way similar to that in which they are used in the confession manuals.

Hell

An analysis of the classification of sin in the visions of the other world from the first to the twelfth centuries reveals a process of gradual change. Greater prominence is given to different sins in different periods: the most frequently cited sins in the New Testament lists are fornication, murder, and evil thoughts or speech. In the apocrypha they become jointly slander, sorcery, persecution, deceit, murder and blasphemy. The early medieval texts stress murder, avarice, deceit, the sowing of discord and theft. In the twelfth century the most common are adultery, lust, theft, and murder.

Further analysis shows that not only do the principal sins change; others are added, or receive greater emphasis. For example, the apocrypha add several sins which are found through to the twelfth-century texts: these are usury, loss of faith or backsliding, loss of chastity in unmarried women, and insincere alms-giving. In the early medieval visions much greater emphasis is placed on theft and the sowing of discord than previously; and in the twelfth century increased prominence is given to treachery, tyranny, pride and gluttony. From the starting point of the ten commandments and the lists given in the New Testament, with the further expansion which occurred initially as the first penitentials were composed and subsequently during the period of the confession manuals, a climax is reached in the twelfth-century visions. At this point the list of sins reaches its greatest length; forty distinct categories occur in the texts analysed.

The degree of similarity between the sins listed in texts of various periods and the *Inferno* becomes apparent when a more detailed comparison is made. Infractions of all ten commandments are punished in Dante's Hell with the sole exception of the fourth, to honour the sabbath.[58] The seven New Testament passages list a total of some thirty-two sins, in order of frequency as follows: fornication, murder, evil thoughts or speech, idolatry, avarice, deceit, impurity, sorcery, foolishness, blasphemy, adultery, theft, pride, quarrelling, envy, drunkenness/gluttony, homosexuality, wickedness, malice and injustice (mentioned in two or more passages), and timidity, unbelief, slander/gossip, evil deeds, disobedience to parents, disorderliness, lust, anger, schism, rivalry, lack of affection and lack of mercy (mentioned only once). These texts make no attempt to classify the sins listed in any way, but it is immediately apparent that the majority of the aims themselves are identical to those represented in the *Inferno*. This suggests that although the New Testament cannot have influenced Dante's classificatory system, his choice of sins to include within that system must have sprung ultimately from the Christian rather than from the Aristotelian tradition.

Such a supposition receives further confirmation if a detailed comparison is made between the sins included in the popular Christian representations of the other world and those of the *Inferno*. The best known of these representations is perhaps the *Vision of Paul*, implied by Dante's son Jacopo to have been known to his father.[59] What is particular about the vision is that, in contrast to the majority of the popular representations of the afterlife, many different redactions and translations were made throughout the medieval period, and taken together these give us a panorama of the various sins punished in the popular other world over a number of centuries. Table 2 (on p. 135) shows the sins represented in the eleven Latin redactions of the vision. In order to bring out the similarity between the sins shown in the vision and those in the *Inferno*, they have been laid out according to the scheme adopted by Dante. All the Dantean sins are represented with the exception of anger and sloth (circle five), suicide, blasphemy and homosexuality (circle seven) and simony (circle eight).

The same pattern emerges if we compare the sins represented in the twelfth-century visions, plus that of Thurkill, with those of the *Inferno*. There are also two texts which do not properly belong to the Western tradition of vision literature, both dating from the thirteenth century: the Eastern *Liber de Scalis* and the verse description of the infernal city of Babylon by Bonvesin da Riva; both these give a classification of sin and have therefore been included. These texts together list a total of some forty-two sins, the most frequent of which are: adultery, lust, murder, theft, robbery, fornication, pride, avarice, gluttony, worldliness, tyranny, divination, abortion, treachery, sacrilege, slander, deceit, hatred, simony, false witness, heresy/unbelief, harm of others, injustice, fraud, indifference, hypocrisy, pandering, sodomy, perjury, envy, usury, idolatry, the sowing of discord, flattery and negligence. As with the *Vision of Paul*, all these are present in the *Inferno* with the exceptions of envy and pride, which are placed by Dante in Purgatory, and abortion, which is usually linked in the visions with divination, punished in the fifth ditch of circle eight in the *Inferno*. The others either have direct equivalents in the *Inferno* or are subsumed into other categories. Table 3 (on p. 136) shows these sins arranged according to Dante's classification.

A similar correspondence can be found between the sins represented in the *Inferno* and those listed in the thirteenth-century confession manuals, although the manuals give a much more detailed breakdown of the forms of each sin than the *Comedy*. The manuals classify sins according to the seven capital vices or the ten commandments, and include almost all those punished in Dante's Hell. Under avarice, for example, the *Summa vitiorum* of Guglielmus Paraldus, written between 1250 and 1260,[60] lists among others usury, robbery, fraud, simony and prodigality, and under lust, seduction, adultery and homosexuality.

The extent to which *Comedy*, visions and manuals correspond to one another in their classification of sin is shown in Table 4 (on p. 137). Each sin represented in the *Inferno* is listed in turn, separated according to Dante's division of Hell into nine circles. The second line of each entry gives an example of the nearest equivalent in the visions, and the third an example from either Guglielmus's *Summa virtutum ac vitiorum* (in Latin) or the *Manuel des Péchés* (in French). The original wording has been preserved wherever possible. It seems from this comparison to be the case that all the sins represented in the *Inferno*, with the single exception of suicide, are also found in the twelfth- and thirteenth-century representations of the other world and in the confession manuals.

In conclusion, then, the thirty-seven sins punished in the *Inferno* are essentially the same sins as those traditionally represented in the popular visions of the other world and listed in the confession manuals of the twelfth and thirteenth centuries. The existence of these correspondences would seem to confirm the suspicion raised by the inconsistencies in Dante's classificatory scheme that the classification of sin in the *Inferno* cannot simply be regarded as an outworking of the broad Aristotelian categories given in *Inferno* XI. Far from constituting surprising enigmas in an original system structured around the distinctions of incontinence, malice and bestiality, the complexities, inconsistencies and ambiguities in the classification of the *Inferno* bear witness to the mass of traditional material which lies behind it and determines its constituent parts. Support is given to this hypothesis by the fact that although taken individually the later visions identify many more sins than the earlier texts, the overall number of sins listed at various periods in the development of the popular Christian tradition and in the *Comedy* remains fairly constant – approximately thirty-two in the New Testament passages taken together, thirty-nine in the medieval redactions of the *Vision of Paul*, forty in the twelfth-century visions and thirty-seven in the *Inferno* (numbers are approximate because of differences in vocabulary and because of the existence of subcategories of sin).

Purgatory

In his classification of sin Dante retained some of the governing principles of the popular representations, including as we have seen the division of Hell itself into upper and lower, with the corresponding allocation of minor and major sins in each. He also, as in the earlier legends, left some of the capital vices in Hell. But, in accordance with the new theological developments, these are removed from the main body of the *Inferno*, and are used instead as a basis for Purgatory, for which no classificatory scheme had ever been suggested.

The doctrine of Purgatory as a place emerged definitively only as the last visions of the afterlife were being composed. Far from adopting the conventional solution as is commonly believed, Dante created his own solution to the problem – there does not seem to have been a convention. All visions up to and including the twelfth-century texts present Hell and Purgatory jumbled together as one realm of the other world; in 1206 Thurkill distinguishes for the first time between them, but suggests no systematic approach to the classification of sin in Purgatory. Taking account of the newly emphasised distinctions between sin and vice, Dante placed sin in Hell and vice in Purgatory, choosing the scheme of the seven capital vices. This choice may well have been influenced not directly by theologians such as Hugh of St Victor, who did not link the capital vices with purgation, but indirectly, through the confession manuals of the thirteenth century. These manuals took the scheme of the seven capital vices as a systematic approach to the confession of sins; Dante took it as a systematic approach to the purgation of those sins. The capital vices appear nowhere, either in legend or in theology, as a purgative scheme; but in confession, as dictated by the manuals, the penitent is taken on a journey through each of the vices in turn, and, like Dante in the journey up the mountain of Purgatory, he confesses and does penance for some of those vices, while remaining silent as others which he has not committed pass before him. Further, in works such as the *Manuel des Péchés*, a link is specifically made between the capital vices, confession of the sins deriving from them, and the eternal consequences in terms of otherworld torment of not doing so.

The second of the thirteenth-century confession manuals quoted in Table 4 is the *Summae virtutum ac vitiorum* of Guglielmus Paraldus, which was one of the most widespread works of its kind. The second volume is dedicated to the confession of sin, and is structured entirely around the seven capital vices, with an additional chapter on the sins of the tongue. Guglielmus goes into great detail under each heading; under the various vices he lists no fewer than 121 different sins, many of which overlap considerably. Like Dante, he thus distinguishes between vice and sin.

Guglielmus is interesting not only in the choice of the capital vices as his scheme for confession, but also in a number of other respects.[61] Biblical examples are given as a warning against each vice, much as in the *Purgatorio*; pride, for example, is illustrated by the last line of Job 41: 'ipse est Rex super omnes filios superbiae' ('he is king over all the sons of pride'), and exemplified by a quote from Isaiah 42: 'gloriam meam alteri non dabo' (I will not give my glory to others). Other quotations are given from the Latin Fathers and from Seneca, thus mingling, as in the *Purgatorio*, pagan and biblical sources. Secondly, Guglielmus, like Dante in the *Purgatorio*, uses the principle of love as a means of determining the relation between one capital vice and another. Thus lust is defined as an excessive love of pleasure by touching – 'inordinatus amor delectationis quae secundum tactum est' – and gluttony as an excessive love of pleasure by tasting – 'inordinatus amor delectationis quae secundum gustum [est]'. Avarice is an 'inordinatus amor pecuniae' (p. 15). And a complex discussion is entered into concerning the difference between ordered and disordered love (p. 163). Both these aspects of the *Purgatorio*, like the whole question of the classification of sin, are generally held to derive from Dante's reading of classical and secular literature; their presence in a semi-popular confession manual is striking and significant.

Guglielmus's *Summa* is far from displaying the coherence later to be shown in the *Comedy*; but it undoubtedly offers an approach to the confession of sin which in many ways foreshadows Dante's description of the process of purgation in the other world. The *Purgatorio* is innovatory in that it creates both a geography for the third realm of the other world and a systematic approach to the purgation of sin, neither of which are fully present in the previous representations of the afterlife; it does so by the assimilation of the twelfth- and thirteenth-century developments in theology which resulted in works such as Guglielmus's *Summa* – works which bridge the gaps on the one hand between the popular and the learned traditions, and on the other between the last visions and the *Comedy*.

Table 1. Classification of sin in the *Inferno*

Vestibule
indifference

Sins of incontinence
1 lack of faith
2 sexual immorality
3 gluttony
4 avarice & prodigality
5 anger & sloth
6 heresy & unbelief

Sins of malice
7 (i) violence against others
    – tyranny
    – murder
    – injury
    – robbery, arson, damage to property
  (ii) violence against self
    – suicide
    – prodigality
  (iii) violence against God
    – blasphemy
    – homosexuality
    – usury

8 Fraud where no special trust exists
  (i) pandering and seduction
  (ii) flattery
  (iii) simony
  (iv) divination and sorcery
  (v) barratry
  (vi) hypocrisy
  (vii) theft
  (viii) evil counsel and slander
  (ix) sowing of discord
  (x) falsification
    – alchemy
    – impersonation
    – forgery
    – deceit

9 Fraud where special trust exists
  (i) betrayal of family
  (ii) betrayal of country or cause
  (iii) betrayal of guests
  (iv) betrayal of lords and benefactors

Table 2. Classification of sin in the redactions of the *Vision of Paul*

Numbering refers to the subdivisions of Dante's *Inferno* detailed in Table 1.

negligentia

1   gentiles qui non sunt baptizati nec crediderunt Christum in carne venientem; qui non speraverunt in dominum
2   adulteria, luxuria, que non servaverunt castitatem usque ad nuptias
3   ebriositas, commessatio
4   avaritia, concupiscentia, qui lucrum quesiuerunt, divites

6   superbia, qui non credunt filium dei Christum venisse in carnem, qui non amant dominum, qui non credunt Christum natum de Maria Virgine, eius resurrectionem non credunt

7   (i)   homicide, qui necaverunt infantes suos
            satrape qui iniquitatem faciunt
            rapina, qui orphanis et viduis nocuerunt
     (iii) feneratores pecuniarum, usura

8   (i)   fornicatio
     (ii)   adolatores
     (iv)   auguria, divinaciones, malefici, incantatrices
     (v)   exactores, mali ministratores
     (vi)   qui fictum animam habent in corde; religiosi ypocrite, falsi Iudei, Cristiani et Sarraceni
     (vii) furtum, qui cavallo/ferramenta inviolaverunt
     (viii) falsi advocati, falsi testes, periuratores
            susurratores, detractores
     (ix)   qui lites faciunt; qui dei ecclesias destruxerunt
            qui seminant discordiam
     (x)   mentientes, fabulationes facere

9   perfidi, qui anuunt mala proximis suis dum fidum habent ad eos, delateres

Other
   iniquos
   qui gaudant de mala proximi sui
   qui solvunt ieiunium ante tempus
   qui frequentes sunt in chorea/tripudio
   qui misericordiam non habuerunt in pauperibus
   invidiosi
   qui pater/mater honores tullerunt
   qui conpatratum fecerunt
   qui non egerunt penitentiam
   maledici
   qui malesides portaverunt
   qui semper cogitaverunt mala facere proximis suis
   toritores

Table 3. Classification of sin in the visions of the twelfth and thirteenth centuries (excluding the redactions of the *Vision of Paul*)

Numbering refers to the subdivisions of Dante's *Inferno* detailed in Table 1.

negligentia, timiditas

1   qui non speraverunt misericordiam a deo, qui de peccatis suis desperaverunt, non sperare in Dio

2   luxuria, adultera, incesti

3   gula, ebriositas, voluptas, commessatio

4   avaritia

5   odiosi, odia proximis, ira

6   superbia, inanis gloria, qui non crediderunt in deum, qui ydola colunt

7   (i)   homicidia, mulieres que suos interficiunt antequam nascantur filios
                tiranni, potens crudelis, oppressores
                percotire altruy
                rapaces, incendiarii, raptus
    (ii)   gesta dissolutiores, peccati del seculare bedescho
    (iii) negare Christum, blasphemia
                vitius sodomiticus
                feneratio

8   (i)   stupratores, fornicatio, meretrix
    (ii)   symonya
    (iv)   veneficia
    (v)   iniustitia
    (vi)   religiosae personae religionis sed sanctimoniae indicia non habentes
    (vii) sacrilegia, fures, latrones
    (viii) falsum testimonium
                detractatio, insidia
    (ix)   seminatores discordiam
    (x)   fraudulentus, qui gentes fraudant
                mendacium, periuratores, sermones impures

9   traditores, perfidia, proditio

Other

   non recte decimare
   fuga de sacris professionibus, votorum infractio, qui ordinem ecclesiasticum reliquerunt
   aborsus
   invidia
   vagatio
   vias ambulando prohibitas
   penitentiam dignam non agentes
   cumulare peccatum super peccatum
   qui prophetis dei credere nolunt
   malitia

Table 4. Classification of sin in the *Comedy* and the visions and manuals of the twelfth and thirteenth centuries

Numbering refers to the subdivisions of Dante's *Inferno* detailed in Table 1. Lettering refers to texts as follows:

a = *Inferno*
b = 12th–13th century visions
c = Confession manuals

1

a coloro che visser sanza infamia e sanza lodo
b negligentia (Paul, Thurkill, Bonvesin)
c tepiditas, ignavia

a non avere battesimo/non adorar debitamente a Dio
b gentiles qui non sunt baptizati (Paul)
c —

2

a peccator carnali/lussuria/libito
b luxuria (Paul, Alberic, Gunthelm, Thurkill), amore carnale (Bonvesin)
c lecherie

   — from passion/adultery
     adulteria (Paul, Alberic, Tundale, Godeschalc, Thurkill)
     adulteriun

   — from lust
     fornicatio (Paul, Alberic, Tundale, Eynsham)
     fornicaciun

3

a gola
b gula (Tundale, Gunthelm, Godeschalc); gola (Bonvesin); commessatio, ebriosus (Eynsham, Paul)
c glotunie

4

a avarizia
b avaritia (Tundale) concupiscentia (Paul)
c coueitise

a guerci che con misura nullo spendio ferci
b seculare bedescho (Bonvesin)
c prodigalitas

5

a ira
b odiosi (Alberic), odia proximis (Eynsham), homicidia in ira sua (Godeschalc)
c ire, hayne auer

a accidia/tristi
b credere in legem Dei et eam derilinquere (Liber de Scalis); qui non speraverunt in deum (Paul)
c desperatio, tristitia; peresce, acidie, negligence

Table 4. *cont.*

6

a   superbia
b   superbia (Paul, Tundale, Eynsham, Thurkill)
c   orgoyl

a   eresiarche/seguaci di Epicureo
b   qui ydola colunt (Liber de Scalis); qui non credunt filium Dei Christum venisse in carnem (Paul)
c   ne crere de ihesu crist

7

(i)   a   omicide
      b   homicidia (Alberic, Tundale, Godeschalc, Eynsham, Thurkill)
      c   oscier; homicidi

      a   tiranni
      b   tiranni (Alberic), potens crudelis (Gunthelm), oppressores (Thurkill), satrape (Paul)
      c   –

      a   dare ferute dogliose
      b   percotire altruy (Bonvesin)
      c   fere tolir a home aucune membre sanz sun pleisir

      a   guastatori
      b   incendiarii (Thurkill), vita guasta (Bonvesin)
      c   de peccato incendiariorum

      a   predoni
      b   rapaces (Alberic), rapina (Paul, Gunthelm, Thurkill)
      c   rober, rapina

(ii) a   privarsi del mondo
      b   –
      c   –

      a   biscazzare
      b   seculare bedescho (Bonvesin)
      c   prodigalitas

(iii) a   negare/bestemmiare la deitade
      b   qui Christum negant (Tundale)
      c   iurere par deu, maudir deu; blasphemia

      a   segno di Soddoma e Caorsa
      b   vitius sodomiticus (Eynsham)
      c   peccatum contra naturam

      a   usura
      b   feneratio (Eynsham, Paul), qui usuras faciunt (Paul)
      c   usurer

Table 4. *cont.*

8

  (i)   a   ruffiani
        b   stupratores (Alberic)
        c   –

        a   ingannatori
        b   inganare (Bonvesin)
        c   (rauir une femme)

  (ii) a   lusinghieri
        b   adolatores (Paul)
        c   losenger, adulationis

 (iii) a   simonia
        b   symonia (Alberic), simonia (Eynsham)
        c   symonie

 (iv) a   indovini/magiche frode/affatturare
        b   veneficia (Eynsham, Thurkill), auguria, divinaciones, malefici (Paul)
        c   nigremancie, enchantement, sorcerie

  (v) a   barattieri
        b   mali ministratores (Paul)
        c   pur auer/pur amur estre faus iuge/aduocat/assessur

 (vi) a   ipocresia, ipocreti
        b   qui fictum animum habent (Paul), religiosi ostendentes custodire legem dei sicut
            ypocrite (Paul)
        c   ypocrisie, hypocrisis

 (vii) a   ladroneccio, ladri
        b   fures (Alberic, Thurkill), furtum (Paul, Tundale, Gunthelm), latrones (Tundale),
            sacrilegia (Tundale)
        c   debruser ad muster, prendre chose a tort.

(viii) a   (falsi consiglieri)
        b   falsum testimonium (Alberic, Liber de Scalis), periuria (Eynsham), falsi advocati (Paul)
        c   mauuais cunseil duner; pravi consilii

        a   (agguatori)
        b   insidia (Tundale)
        c   –

        a   seminator di scandalo
        b   detractatio (Alberic, Eynsham), susurratores (Paul)
        c   detrere

 (ix) a   seminator di scisma
        b   seminatores discordiam (Liber de Scala), qui seminant discordiam (Paul)
        c   de semantibus discordias

Table 4. *cont.*

(x) falsatori
   – a   alchimia
      b   –
      c   –
   – a   falsificarsi in altrui forma
      b   –
      c   –
   – a   falsare fiorini
      b   qui gentes fraudant in ponderibus et mensuris (Liber de Scalis)
          mercator/molendiarius fraudolentus (Thurkill)
          aurifabrus fraudolentus (Eynsham)
      c   estre marchant et deceure la gent per faus peis/mesure
          fauser chartre
          de fraudibus negotiatorum
   – a   dire falso
      b   mendacium (Eynsham), mentientes (Paul)
      c   mentir, fause parole

9
a   traditori
b   traditores (Gunthelm), perfidia (Tundale, Paul), proditio (Eynsham)
c   –

Notes

1 Particularly Ronzoni and Witte; summaries of the arguments of these critics are given in G. Busnelli, 'L'"Etica Nicomachea" e l'ordinamento morale dell'' "Inferno" di Dante', 1905, p. 261 and in E. Moore, 'The Classification of the Sins in the *Inferno* and *Purgatorio*', 1899 (reprinted 1968), pp. 163–7.

2 The first to do so was G. Pascoli, *Minerva oscura*, 1898, followed by F. D'Ovidio, *Studii sulla "Divina Commedia"*, 1901 (reprinted Caserta, 1931), and L. Pietrobono, *Dal centro al cerchio: la struttura morale della 'Divina Commedia'*, [1923]; and more recently by G. Ursino, *La struttura del poema di Dante*, 1959. These studies are, however, mostly forced and unconvincing.

3 This view is summarised by G. Petrocchi, *L'Inferno di Dante*, 1978, pp. 72–3. A complete bibliography of criticism relating to the moral structure of the poem is given in the *Enciclopedia Dantesca*, under the entries 'Inferno' and 'Purgatorio'. For the studies of Moore in 1899 and Busnelli in 1905 see note 1; Busnelli's 1907 study is also entitled *L'"Etica Nicomachea' e l'ordinamento morale dell''Inferno' di Dante*.

4 See E. Moore, 'The Classification of the Sins', 1899, p. 160. Moore is echoed by F. D'Ovidio, 'La topografia morale dell''"Inferno"'', *Studii sulla 'Divina Commedia'*, 1931, pp. 398–9. See also G. Busnelli, *L'ordinamento morale del 'Purgatorio' dantesco*, 1908, in which Gregory's formulation of the capital vices is said to be the source of the scheme in the *Purgatorio*.

5 See E. Moore, 'The Classification of the Sins', p. 183.

6 Purgatory is authoritatively defined for the first time in 1254 in a letter from Innocent IV to the Greeks; it received further official recognition at the Second Council of Lyons in 1274. Both texts are given by J. Le Goff, *La Naissance du Purgatoire*, 1981, pp. 380–3.

7   R. Migliorini Fissi, *Dante*, 1979, p. 112.

8   E. Moore, 'The Classification of the Sins', p. 160.

9   Although their importance was indicated as long ago as 1907 by Busnelli: 'che nell'*Inferno* ci debba essere un ordine traspare da tutte le visioni de' cosi detti precursori di Dante, alcune delle quali non gli dovettero essere ignote, anche nelle particolarità e varietà del diverso modo di esprimerlo e fissarlo', *L'"Etica Nicomachea'*, p. 11.

10 An exploratory article is that by F. Mancini, 'Un *auctoritas* di Dante', 1968, pp. 95–119.

11 Tundale's guide explains that punishments worsen as they come to the areas of homicide (p. 13), avarice (p. 17), gluttons and fornicators (p. 24), immoral clergy (p. 29), and multiple sin (p. 32).

12 J. Delumeau, *Le Péché et la peur: la culpibilisation en Occident, XIIIe–XVIIIe siècles*, 1983, p. 231.

13 See C. Pascal, *Le credenze d'oltretomba nelle opere letterarie dell'antichità classica*, vol. II, 1924, p. 167.

14 This prehistory is outlined by Th. Deman, 'Péché', *Dictionnaire de Théologie Catholique*, XII, (1933), cols. 140–275, and more recently in Delumeau, *Le Péché et la peur*.

15 Delumeau, p. 212. The other lists are in Romans 1.26–31; 1 Corinthians 6.9–10; Galatians 5.19–21; and Ephesians 5.3–5. See also Revelation 21.8.

16 Usury is forbidden in Exodus 22.25 and Deuteronomy 23.19–20; sorcery is forbidden in Deuteronomy 18.10–11.

17 The history of these documents is outlined in Le Bras's article 'Pénitentiels' in the *Dictionnaire de Théologie Catholique*, XII (1933), cols. 1160–79; by J. T. McNeill and H. M. Gamer in *Medieval Handbooks of Penance*, 1938; and most recently and comprehensively by C. Vogel, 'Les "Libri Paenitentiales"', 1978. For the change in the form of penance see McNeill and Gamer, chapter 1: 'Penance in the Ancient Church', and Delumeau, *Le Péché*, pp. 218–19. For the history of the capital vices see Moore, 'The Classification of the Sins', and McNeill and Gamer, pp. 18–19. For Gregory's reformulation see his *Moralia*, Book XXXI, *Patrologia Latina*, LXXVI.

18 Discussed by McNeill and Gamer in *Medieval Handbooks of Penance*, pp. 8 and 35.

19 The *Poenitentiale Cummeani* is edited by H. J. Schmitz in *Die Bussbücher und die Bussdisziplin der Kirche*, Mainz, 1883, (reprinted Graz, 1958), pp. 615–76.

20 See McNeill and Gamer, *Medieval Handbooks of Penance*, pp. 44–5.

21 In Schmitz, *Bussdisziplin*, pp. 524–50. See G. Le Bras, 'Notes pour servir à l'histoire des collections canoniques: v, "Judicia Theodori"', 1931, pp. 95–115; and Vogel, 'Les "Libri Paenitentiales"', pp. 68–9.

22 The minor penitentials are discussed by Vogel, *ibid.*, pp. 70–8.

23 *Patrologia Latina*, CV, cols. 693–710; also in Schmitz, *Bussdisziplin*, pp. 465–89.

24 R. Manselli, *La Religion populaire au moyen âge: problèmes de méthode et d'histoire*, 1975, pp. 181–2.

25 See Le Bras, 'Pénitentials', col 1174.

26 See Vogel, 'Les "Libri Paenitentiales"', p. 104.

27 See McNeill and Gamer, *Medieval Handbooks of Penance*, p. 35.

28 For Burchard see McNeill and Gamer, *ibid.*, p. 321; Le Bras, 'Pénitentials', cols. 1175–6 and Vogel, 'Les "Libri Paenitentiales"', p. 88–90. Text in *Patrologia Latina*, CXL, cols. 949–1018.

29 The most recent authoritative studies of the *summae confessorum* are those by P. Michaud-Quantin: 'À propos des premières "Summae confessorum"', 1959, and *Sommes de casuistique et manuels de confession au moyen âge (XII–XVI siècles)*, 1962.

30 Vogel remarks upon the concentration in the penitentials on external, objectively measurable, sins: 'apparaissent seules les fautes susceptibles d'une évaluation "quantitative". Les fautes contre la justice, la charité, l'amour du prochain, en un mot les "péchés de qualité religieuse et spirituelle", les fautes "intérieures" sont pratiquement absents de nos catalogues', 'Les "Libri Paenitentiales"', p. 105.

31 *Alain de Lille, "Liber Poenitentialis", texte inédit publié et annoté par Jean Longère*, 1965, p. 204.

32 See C. H. Haskins, *The Renaissance of the Twelfth Century*, 1927, chapter 7, 'The revival of jurisprudence'; H. D. Hazeltine, 'Roman and Canon Law in the Middle Ages', 1929, pp. 697–764.

33 *Patrologia Latina*, CLXXXVII.

34 See Hazeltine, 'Roman and Canon Law', p. 705.

35 Edited by P. Michaud-Quantin, *Sacris Erudiri*, XVII (1966), pp. 5–54.

36 The wheel torment is described by Statius (*Thebaid* IV 537–40). Ovid (*Metamorphoses* IV 461), Virgil (*Aeneid* VI 616–17). It occurs in the *Apocalpyse of Peter* (p. 517), the *Sibylline Oracles* (p. 523), the *Acts of Thomas* (p. 419), and two Celtic apocrypha, the *Seven Heavens apocryphon* and the *Reichenau apocryphon*. The medieval visions including the wheel are those of an unnamed woman (p. 404), of 'Paul' (redactions IV, V, VIII, X and the Toulouse and Italian manuscripts), of the Boy William, of Gunthelm (p. 111), of Owen in *St Patrick's Purgatory* (cols. 993–4), and of Thurkill (p. 26).

37 These differences are consonant with a tradition which is essentially oral and in which, with the possible exception of the *Vision of Paul*, beliefs are passed from generation to generation rather than from text to text, changing in response to influences from outside the tradition.

38 *La Divina Commedia: Inferno*, ed. N. Sapegno, 11th reprint from original edition of 1955, Florence, 1978, pp. 213–14.

39 *La Divina Commedia: Purgatorio*, ed. N. Sapegno, 12th reprint, Florence, 1979, p. 268.

40 For the presence of the capital vices on the tympana of the French Gothic cathedrals see E. Mâle, *The Gothic Image*, English edition 1958, pp. 98–105. Other representations are discussed by L. Réau, *Iconographie de l'art chrétien*, III, 1959, p. 752. In particular, the capital vices form the structure of Hell on the (fifteenth-century) Last Judgment tympanum at Berne, and in the (late fourteenth-century) Last Judgment fresco at S. Gimignano.

41 Moore, 'The Classification of the Sins', Delumeau, *Le Péché*.

42 *gola, fornicatio, avaritia, ira, tristitia, accedia, vana gloria, superbia. De Coenobium institutis* I iv, chapter 1, *Patrologia Latina*, XLIX, 202ss.

43 *superbia, inanis gloria, invidia, ira, tristitia, avaritia, ventris ingluvies* and *luxuria. Moralia* XXXI 45; *Patrologia Latina*, LXXVI, 620ss.

44 *vana gloria, invidia, ira, tristitia, avaritia, ventris ingluvies* and *luxuria. Patrologia Latina*, CLXXVI, 997ss.

45 The first list reads 'superbia, scilicet, invidia, ira, acedia, philargyria, gastrimargia, luxuria' (p. 21); the second 'superbia, invidia, ira, tristitia, avaritia, gula, luxuria' (p. 52).

46 This history has been traced most fully by A. Michel, 'Purgatoire', *Dictionnaire de Théologie Catholique*, XIII (1936), cols. 1163–1326, and by J. Le Goff, *La Naissance du Purgatoire*.

47 See Le Goff, *ibid.*, pp. 99ss and 121ss.

48 See *ibid.*, pp. 181–2.

49 The text of the 4th Lateran Council is given by Longère in *Alain de Lille, 'Liber Poenitentialis'*, pp. 225–6. The reforms are also discussed by E. J. Arnould, *Le 'Manuel des Péchés': Étude de littérature religieuse anglo-normande (XIIIme siècle)*, 1940, pp. 1–28.

50 *Ibid.*, p. 20.

51 Discussed by Michaud-Quantin in *Sommes de casuistique*, ch. 1.

52 Line 113. The *Manuel des Péchés* is edited in part by J. F. Furnivall, *Robert of Brunne's 'Handlyng Synne', AD 1303, with those parts of the Anglo-French Treatise on which it was founded, William of Wadington's 'Manuel des Pechiez'*, 1901.

53 *orgoyl, ire, envie, peresce–accidie–negligence, coveitise–avarice, glotunie* and *lecherie.*

54 *superbia/inanis gloria, invidia, ira, tristitia/acedia, avaritia/cupiditas, gula* and *luxuria. Summa Theologiae (ST)*, Ia IIae q. 84 a. 4.

55 'Nos, quia locum purgationis hujus modi dicunt (Graeci) non fuisse sibi ab eorum doctoribus certo et proprio nomine indicatum illum quidem juxta traditiones et auctoritates sanctorum patrum purgatorium nominantes volumus, quod de caetero apud illos isto nomine appeletur.' See Le Goff, *La Naissance du Purgatoire*, p. 380.

56 *Ibid.*, p. 387.

57 Discussed in Michaud-Quantin, *Sommes de casuistique*, pp. 34–40.

58 Violation of the first and second commandments are punished in circle 6 (heresy and unbelief); of the third in circle 7 (blasphemy); of the fifth perhaps most clearly in circle 9 (betrayal of family); of

the sixth in circle 7 (murder); of the seventh in circle 2 (adultery); of the eighth in circle 8 (theft); of the ninth in circle 8 (false words); and of the tenth in circle 4 (avarice).

59 Jacopo is quoted by G. Ricciotti, *L'Apocalisse di Paolo siriaca*, 1932, I, pp. 28–9.

60 *Guillelmus Peraldus: 'Summae virtutum ac vitiorum'*, 2 vols., Moguntiae, 1618, p. 15.

61 See Mancini, 'Un *auctoritas* di Dante'.

The mountain of Purgatory

When Dante reaches the bottom of the pit of Hell, Virgil explains that the topography of the other world is not arbitrary but has a historical cause: it was created by the impact on Earth of the fall of Lucifer, following his expulsion from heaven.[1] At the time of the fall, which occurred in the southern hemisphere, all the land fled to the north and a volume of earth corresponding to that displaced burst through the surface of this new hemisphere of sea, thereby forming a mountain. The summit of this mountain became the site of the Garden of Eden, and its slopes now form the realm of Purgatory.

> 'Da questa parte cadde giú dal cielo;
> e la terra, che pria di qua si sporse,
> per paura di lui fé del mar velo,
>   E venne a l'emisperio nostro; e forse
> per fuggir lui lasciò qui loco vòto
> qualla ch'appar di qua, e sú ricorse.'
>
> Inf XXXIV 121–6

['On this side he fell down from heaven; and the land which before broke the surface of this (southern) hemisphere through fear of him veiled itself with sea, and came to our (northern) hemisphere; and, perhaps to escape from him, the land which now appears here left an empty space and rushed upwards.']

The pit of Hell and the mountain of Purgatory are thus said to have been created by the same disaster which made their very existence necessary: the violent arrival of Satan to lead men astray on Earth.

The mountain of Purgatory is high, reaching above the earth's atmosphere; it is steep and rocky, and into its sides are carved seven concentric terraces on which the seven capital vices are purged in turn. Below these terraces lies the realm of Antepurgatory, where two further categories of souls wait to begin their purgation – the excommunicate and the late repentant. On the summit of the mountain is the Earthly Paradise, separated from the uppermost terrace by a wall of fire, in accordance with the common interpretation of Genesis 3.24.[2] There are therefore ten major areas in the *Purgatorio*, echoing the ten circles of the *Inferno* and foreshadowing the ten heavens of the *Paradiso*.

Dante is indisputably the first writer to offer such a morally coherent, and topographically and historically consistent, scheme for the description of the other world, and it has generally been accepted that his originality extends to the adoption of a mountain on which to locate Purgatory. The *Enciclopedia Dantesca* states that

the imagining of Purgatory as a very high mountain reaching to heaven was born (. . .) in contrast with both the opinion of scholastic theologians and that of popular legend.[3]

This established opinion has recently been challenged by Jacques Le Goff who, in his study of the concept and representation of Purgatory, states that the opposite is true: 'of all the images which the imagination of the other world, after so many centuries, offered to Dante, he chose the only one which expresses the true logic of Purgatory, the one where you climb, the mountain'.[4]

The aim of this chapter is to re-examine Dante's choice of a mountain site for his Purgatory and Earthly Paradise in the light of previous descriptions of the middle realm, and thus to resolve these critical differences.

THE DEVELOPMENT OF THE DOCTRINE OF PURGATORY

Although Dante at the beginning of the fourteenth century divided the other world into three equal realms, and although to the modern Catholic the concept of Purgatory is as familiar and established as are those of Heaven and Hell, nonetheless the history of the middle realm is very different from that of the other two. The essential difficulty is pinpointed by Thomas Aquinas, who states that Purgatory is not mentioned in the scriptures, and that human reasoning alone is inadequate to define it: 'de loco purgatorio non invenitur aliquid expresse determinatum in Scriptura, nec rationes ad hoc possunt efficaces induci' (*IV Sent.*, dist. XXI, q.1 a.1 qu.2). Whereas with the other two realms the apocryphal and vision literature developed and expanded that which was already contained in the scriptures, in the case of Purgatory a lengthy gestation period was necessary while theologians debated first the need for and nature of purgation, and secondly when and where it was to be accomplished. Only in 1274 did the Church issue its first official statement of belief concerning the third realm – well after the date of composition of most of the visions of the other world. The main consequence of this late development of doctrine is that the visions do not offer any consistent precedent for the representation of Purgatory in the way that they do for the other two realms.

Belief in some form of purgation for sin to be undergone after death has its origin in two concepts developed by early theologians from a small number of biblical passages. The first is the concept of prayer for the dead, for which the foundational text is *II Maccabees*, written in the second century BC. Chapter 12 relates how Judeas Maccabees orders money to be sent to Jerusalem so that an offering may be made in intercession for the souls of two soldiers slain in a state of sin.[5]

Equally important for the development of Purgatory is the concept of the remission of sin after death, founded on three New Testament passages. The first is Matthew 5.25–6, where Jesus warns that he who fails to be reconciled to his accuser will be thrown into prison and not released until he has 'paid the last farthing', suggesting to early theologians that there is a term to be served in the other world for the remission of sin.[6] The second is Matthew 12.31–2, where Jesus warns that blasphemy against the Spirit is the only sin which may not be forgiven; this was interpreted by theologians as confirmation that other sins may be remitted after death.[7] The third and most important passage is I Corinthians 3.10–17:

> With what grace God has bestowed on me, I have laid a foundation as a careful architect should; it is left for someone else to build upon it. Only, whoever builds on it must be careful how he builds. The foundation which has been laid is the only one which anybody can lay; I mean Jesus Christ. But on this foundation different men will build in gold, silver, precious stones, wood, grass, or straw, and each man's workmanship will be plainly seen. It is the day of the Lord that will disclose it, since that day is to reveal itself in fire, and fire will test the quality of each man's workmanship. He will receive a reward, if the building he has added on stands firm; if it is burnt up, he will be the loser; and yet he himself will be saved, though only as men are saved by passing through fire.

From earliest times theologians accepted this passage as evidence that each of us will undergo testing by a purgatorial fire after death. Aquinas interprets the fire as both punitive and purgative, and 'the day' as every moment in which judgment is passed on the individual – both in this life, on death, and on the Last Day.[8]

The doctrine of Purgatory began to develop, along the double axis of prayer for the dead and testing by fire, in the writings of the theologians of the early Eastern Church.[9] First among these was Clement of Alexandria, who taught that sins not dealt with in life would have to be purged by fire after death.[10] His contemporary Origen stated that all men will be purified by the baptism of fire promised by John the Baptist (Matthew 3.3). In both cases the fire is the literal fire of the Day of Judgment.[11] These ideas were echoed and developed by others, notably Cyril of Jerusalem, Basil, Gregory of Nazianzus and Gregory of Nyssa.[12]

Early Western theologians also turned their attention to the question of purgation after death. Tertullian taught that on death most people are admitted to Sheol, where the just make payment for their sins prior to the Last Judgment and their admission to Paradise, in accordance with Matthew 5.25–6.[13] Ambrose believed that on the Day of Judgment all men will be tested by fire, which he identified with the baptism of fire and with the burning sword of the cherubim set to guard the Earthly Paradise (Genesis 3.24). Some will be thrown into the lake of burning fire; some will be refreshed and admitted immediately to Paradise; and a third category will be punished and purified before they too are released to Paradise. Both Ambrose and Jerome taught that all ordinary Christians would be saved by this purgation, however sinful they might have been.[14]

By the fourth century, therefore, both Eastern and Western theologians were in agreement that sins may be remitted after death by means of a purifying fire of judgment – a process which may be hastened by the prayers of the living. There was, however, no uniformity of belief concerning the timing and nature of this purgatorial fire or eligibility for it.

A 'definitive synthesis' was reached by Augustine, who has been called 'the true father of Purgatory'.[15] Augustine stated that purification occurs between death and the Last Judgment, and not on the Day of Judgment itself; he reinterpreted 1 Corinthians 3.11–15 in the light of Matthew 25.46 to show that not all Christians will be saved, salvation being dependent on works as well as faith; and taught that purification occurs by a purgatorial fire, *ignis purgatorius*, which may be either real or metaphorical, and which continues until the Day of Judgment. He also distinguished four categories of souls: the wicked, who go straight to Hell; the good, who are admitted immediately to Paradise; the imperfectly good, who are the subject of purgation; and the not excessively bad, also destined for Hell but whose torment may be lessened by intercession.

Augustine's teaching was widely accepted throughout the West, with only some minor modification. In particular, Caesarius of Arles addressed the question of which Christians would be eligible for purgation. To this end he distinguished between minor and capital sins (*minuta* and *capitalia*), the former admitting of purgation but the latter not.[16] And Gregory the Great concluded that the fire of purgation would be real rather than metaphorical.[17]

The views of Augustine were adopted with minor modifications by all the theologians of the following centuries.[18] By the beginning of the twelfth century the common view was as follows: after the Day of Judgment there will be two categories of men, the elect and the damned. On death, each person is judged individually and assigned to one of several possible groups. Martyrs, saints and those unblemished by sin are admitted to Paradise immediately. The wicked are sent forthwith to Hell. Between these groups are one or two intermediate categories, consisting of those who will undergo purgation for their sins and then be admitted to Paradise or, possibly, to a mitigated form of Hell. Purgation is effected by passage through fire and occurs between death and resurrection; where it takes place remains unclear.[19] The resolution of this difficulty was to exercise the minds of theologians for the next two centuries.

In the early twelfth century Honorius of Autun and Bernard of Clairvaux suggested that the purgatorial torment consisted not only of fire but also of ice – as in fact already described by Bede in the vision of Drythelm.[20] Hugh of St Victor stipulated that the fire is real rather than metaphorical, that purgation is for the intermediate category of the imperfectly good (*non valde boni*) and that prayer for the dead is helpful to them; he also suggested that purgation occurs in the place of sin.[21] Peter Lombard stated that venial sins are the objects of purgation, identifying them with the constructions of wood, hay and straw mentioned in 1 Corinthians 3.12, and suggesting that their varying degrees of gravity meet with purification of varying lengths.[22]

The major development concerning the doctrine of Purgatory which occurred during the twelfth century was however the emergence for the first time of the noun *purgatorium* to replace expressions such as *ignis purgatorius, poena purgatoria* and *loca purgatoria*. There has been some disagreement with regard to when exactly the new term Purgatory was coined and also to the implications of its appearance. In his recent study Le Goff draws attention to a number of twelfth-century manuscripts in which the noun is used: a sermon once attributed to Hildebert of Lavardin (d. 1135) but now accepted as written by Peter Comestor (d. 1178 or

1179); a collection of questions recorded from the teaching of Odo of Ourscamp (d. 1171) by his pupils; and two sermons formerly attributed to Peter Damian and Bernard of Clairvaux but assigned by Le Goff to Nicholas of Clairvaux (d. after 1176). In the light of these texts he suggests that the noun *purgatorium* was formed between the years 1170 and 1180, and further that the coining of the noun denotes the invention of the place – for 'an unnamed place does not exist'.[23]

A number of critical objections have been raised to this theory, most importantly that the noun appeared merely for the sake of convenience, to summarise a collection of ideas hitherto expressed by clumsier phrases, and that this process is to be seen in the context of the scholastic practice of coining nouns to replace abstract concepts during the twelfth century.[24] But it remains the case that by the end of the twelfth century 'Purgatory' had appeared as a substantive for the first time and that, if it does not reflect a major development quite so clearly as Le Goff suggests, it must nonetheless both signal the widespread acceptance of the doctrine and pave the way for further discussion.

That discussion took place during the thirteenth century. By this time it seems to have been generally accepted that Purgatory exists, that experience of it is temporary, and that the fire in it is real. Other aspects of purgation, however, continued to be the subject of debate. The distinction was made between mortal sins deserving damnation and venial sins requiring purgation;[25] the state of the soul in Purgatory and the nature of the pain felt was explored;[26] Albert the Great, Alexander of Hales and Thomas Aquinas re-examined the passage in 1 Corinthians 3;[27] Aquinas and Bonaventure emphasized that purgation entailed the dual pain of fire and separation from God;[28] the length of purgation was said to be proportional to the degree of attachment shown by the soul to its sin;[29] and Aquinas suggested that devils have no role in Purgatory and clarified the doctrine concerning prayer for the dead.[30] But no consensus seems to have been reached concerning the location of Purgatory. Aquinas, Bonaventure and others suggested tentatively that it was situated towards the centre of the earth, near Hell; but the relationship and distance between the two realms remained unclear.[31]

By the middle of the thirteenth century the doctrine of Purgatory was sufficiently established, and the differences which had grown up in this respect with the Eastern Church sufficiently great, to necessitate the formulation of an official statement of belief. In 1254 Innocent IV wrote to his legate in Cyprus in the following terms:

Since the Truth of the Gospel affirms that if someone blaspheme against the Holy Spirit he will not be forgiven either in this world or the next, by which it is given to us to understand that some faults are pardonable in this world, others in the other; and since the Apostle declares that the work of each person will be tested by fire and that if it burns the person will suffer loss but be saved himself as by fire (1 Cor 3.15); and since the Greeks themselves believe and profess that the souls of those who die having no time to execute the penance received, or those who die guilty not of mortal but only of venial or minor sins, may be purged after death and can be helped by the suffrage of the Church; then we, aware that the Greeks say they find no proper and certain name in the writings of their doctors to designate the place of this purification, and by the tradition and authority of our Fathers naming this place Purgatory, would like them to receive this word from now onwards.[32]

Negotiations continued and in 1274, on the occasion of the Second Council of Lyons, a more comprehensive statement of belief was prepared, dealing in detail with differences in doctrine between the two Churches, but deliberately omitting to discuss the location of Purgatory – an issue which the visionaries and their redactors were, however, obliged to tackle.

THE DEVELOPMENT OF THE CONCEPT OF PURGATORY IN THE VISIONS

Although there is no direct scriptural authority for either the idea of purgation after death or the existence of a realm called Purgatory, these concepts developed slowly in the vision literature as in the writings of theologians. The emphasis was, however, very different: whereas the theologians were concerned primarily with abstract questions such as the nature of the purgatorial fire and which sins could be purged and which not, the visionaries and their redactors scarcely enter into such matters, preferring instead to concentrate on the description of the state or the realm itself.

Some of the elements of the Christian Purgatory are foreshadowed in the texts of earlier religious systems. The concept of purification by fire was present in the beliefs of both the Persians and the Egyptians.[33] The Greek mystery religions expressed belief in the survival of the dead and conducted various religious rites on their behalf.[34] Plato, perhaps influenced by Orphism, describes in his four eschatological myths how the soul undergoes purificatory punishment and successive reincarnations until it reaches a state of moral perfection and can be admitted to the realm of the blessed;[35] this concept is echoed by Plutarch in the *Vision of Thespesius*.[36] Virgil describes souls waiting on the banks of Lethe, ready to return to Earth after a period of purification in the other world during which 'the stain of guilt is washed away under swirling floods or burned out in fire'. Eventually, 'when the cycle of time is complete', these souls will be restored to the perfection they enjoyed before union with the body (*Aeneid* VI 740–2 and 745). And it was common practice in the classical world to make offerings to and for the dead – a practice continued by many early Christians.[37]

The apocrypha contain nothing specifically concerning Purgatory but in a certain sense prepare the way for its development. *I Enoch* describes an intermediate state between death and judgment, in which the dead are divided into four compartments: the first contains the souls of the righteous, surrounded by light and close to a fountain; the second contains sinners who have received no punishment on Earth and who will be subject to eternal torment; the third contains martyrs; and the fourth contains sinners who will receive neither reward nor punishment (pp. 48–9). All compartments but the first are in darkness. All the other apocrypha envisage a purely binary system of reward and punishment, but the oldest versions of the *Vision of Paul* describe Paul and the angels praying to God on behalf of the souls undergoing torment in Hell – although to secure them temporary respite rather than eventual salvation (Paris MS, pp. 35–6, St Gall MS, pp. 145–6).

The first vision of the other world to give a clear description of a state intermediate between punishment and salvation is recorded by Tertullian in his account of the last days of the third-century martyr Perpetua. In Perpetua's second vision she saw her brother Dinocrates, who had died at the age of seven; the boy was in a place of darkness, suffering from thirst and still bearing the ulcer on his face from which he had died. She prayed on his behalf, and was rewarded with another vision of him, this time healed, wearing clean clothes, drinking from a pool of water and then playing in it.[38]

During the next few centuries theologians – one of whom was of course Tertullian – began to discuss the nature and scope of purification after death; no visions of the other world date from this period. By the time of Gregory the Great there was a well-established doctrine concerning purgation, to which Gregory himself had added. His most significant contribution to the development of the doctrine of Purgatory, however, lay in the use of anecdotes to illustrate his teaching. The stories of a dead priest and monk who communicated with the living to seek intercessory prayer support the practice of prayer for the dead; the tale of Paschasius, who returns to this earth to expiate his sins as a bath attendant, reinforces the idea of purgation between death and the Last Judgment; and the otherworld visions of Stephen, Peter and a soldier established a precedent for the use of such experiences as a didactic tool.[39]

Almost all the visions recorded between the seventh and eleventh centuries describe some form of purgation in the other world, although there is no specific discussion of the concept and no consistency in the way such punishment is said to occur. Barontus in 684 is taken first to Paradise and then to Hell; but between them he comes to a place where an old man is sitting. On enquiring of the identity of this man, he is told 'this is our father Abraham, and you, brother, would be wise to always ask the Lord that when he orders you to leave your body he might allow you to rest in Abraham's bosom' (3.16). The concept of Abraham's bosom as a waiting place between death and resurrection was rejected by theologians at the end of the fifth century, but persisted in the common imagination; Ariès suggests that it was influential in the formation of belief in Purgatory.[40] The relationship between the souls Barontus sees in Abraham's bosom and those in Hell and Paradise is not made clear.

Two visions are recorded by Bede, who like Tertullian and Gregory had contributed to the discussion on the nature and circumstances of purgation after death. Furseus is shown both Heaven and Hell; there is no mention of purgation, but at the end of his vision the guide adds a detail which is perhaps significant: 'he taught him with wise words what would happen to those who repented in the hour of death' (p. 424). This hint of an intermediate state between death and the soul's eternal destiny is expanded in the other vision recorded by Bede, that of Drythelm. This vision is particularly important in that for the first time it distinguishes a separate place of purgation in the other world.[41] This is the valley of ice and fire which Drythelm's guide tells him is not Hell – 'non enim hic infernus est ille quam putas' (p. 256) – and which is then defined as the

place where those souls are examined and punished who delayed the confession and correction of their bad deeds, but who took refuge in repentance at the moment of death.

(p. 262)

The mountain of Purgatory

This place is said to be distinct from the pit of fire which Drythelm also sees, described as the 'mouth of Gehenna, from which anyone who falls there will never be freed in all eternity'.

Drythelm divides the souls of the dead into four categories.[42] The first and second are those of the unrepentant sinners consigned to Hell and the saints rejoicing in the 'heavenly kingdom' (p. 264), as in the *Comedy* and in the majority of the visions. The third consists of souls awaiting the Day of Judgment in a pleasant place; they will eventually enter Paradise, from which they are at present excluded. They are described as the

souls of those who left the body engaged in good works; but they are not of such perfection that they deserve to be admitted immediately to the kingdom of heaven.   (p. 264)

These souls undergo no purgative process other than the pain of separation from God; otherwise they may be compared to those represented in the *Purgatorio*.

The fourth category consists of the late repentant seen by Drythelm in the valley of fire and ice. They too are assured of a place in Paradise. Their release may be hastened by the living: 'the prayers, alms, fasts, and especially masses of the living help to free many even before the Day of Judgment' (p. 262). Meanwhile they are excluded not only from Paradise but also from the area in which the imperfectly good await the Day of Judgment. These three conditions – late repentance, the need for assistance from the living, and exclusion from the realm of the imperfectly good – are precisely the conditions which keep souls in Dante's Antepurgatory. The two terraces below the gate to Purgatory itself confine the excommunicated and the late repentant:

> 'Noi fummo tutti già per forza morti,
> e peccatori infino a l'ultima ora;
> quivi lume del ciel ne fece accorti,
>   sí che, pentendo e perdonando, fora
> di vita uscimmo a Dio pacificati,
> che del disio di sé veder n'accora.'
>
> (Purg v 52–7)

[We all died a violent death, and were sinners right up to our last hour; but then the light of heaven gave us understanding, so that, repenting and forgiving, we came forth from life reconciled to God, who fills our hearts with longing to see him.]

Souls request prayer from Dante or the living to whom he will return throughout the *Purgatorio*, but especially frequently in Antepurgatory[43] and among those in Purgatory itself on the terrace of pride we meet one, Sapia, who has been released from Antepurgatory and allowed to begin her journey to Paradise:

> 'Pace volli con Dio in su lo stremo
> de la mia vita; e ancor non sarebbe
> lo mio dover per penitenza scemo,
>   se ciò non fosse, ch'a memoria m'ebbe
> Pier Pettinaio in sue sante orazioni
> a cui di me per caritate increbbe.'
>
> (Purg XIII 124–9)

[I wanted peace with God at the end of my life; and my debt would still not be reduced by penitence had it not been that Peter the combseller remembered me in his holy prayers, for in his charity he pitied me.]

Drythelm's vision is thus particularly important for an understanding of the area of Dante's other world which is perhaps the least orthodox.

A different treatment is given in the same century by the Monk of Wenlock,[44] who distinguishes between torment in upper Hell, said to be temporal – 'on the Day of Judgment God will give to these souls relief from their torments and eternal rest' – and that in lower Hell, said to be eternal: 'eternal fire will burn them without end' (p. 254). This distinction is continued into later visions, most notably that of Tundale; it clearly foreshadows the distinction between Purgatory and Hell. Also significant is the presence as an instrument of purgation of the bridge, hitherto always of judgment. Souls who fall from this bridge into the river below are immersed to varying degrees and emerge shining and purified of their sins.

The *Vision of Wetti*[45] describes eternal and purgatorial torment as occurring in the same place, and as consisting of similar experiences, but distinguishes clearly between them by specifying when the torment is purgatorial. The necessity of prayer for the dead is stressed.

In the ninth century the missionary Anskar received a vision of his own death and admission to Paradise.[46] But in the vision he is not allowed to proceed immediately from his earthly state to Paradise; he is taken first to a 'certain place which he knew for certain, without being told, to be the purgatorial fire itself' (*ignem purgatorium*) (p. 22) – that is, he knows so clearly that there is a *place* in which the fire of purgation burns that he does not need it to be identified. Like Dante, he is required to suffer in this place before he is fit to continue with his journey; and at the end of this purgation, as with Dante, his memory is taken from him. No mention is made of Hell.

The importance of prayer for the dead is stressed by both Bernoldus and Charles the Fat.[47] Bernoldus is taken to a place of darkness, where souls suffering various torments – extremes of heat and cold, imprisonment in stone, being devoured by worms – ask him to obtain prayer for them from those they helped in life. He does so, and secures their release into Paradise. He also sees a pit in which the souls of those for whom nobody is praying are tortured by demons. The redactor, the archbishop Hincmar, ends his account of the vision with an exhortation that we should pray for one another. Charles the Fat meets his father in the other world, who asks for masses, prayers, psalms, alms and vigils, and explains that his brother and nephew have already been released from torment by the prayers of the saints Peter and Remigius (p. 115). Eternal and purgatorial torment occur in separate places, the former in pits of burning pitch, brimstone, lead, wax and grease, boiling rivers and lakes, the latter in a separate valley part of which is in darkness, part in light. The dark part contains casks of boiling and tepid water, sinners being tormented in one and refreshed in the other; the light part is Paradise.

New ground is broken by the sixth redaction of the *Vision of Paul*,[48] which differs more sharply from the surviving early versions of the original Latin translation than do the other medieval redactions, and in which it seems probable that the entire area of torment is intended to be purgatorial rather than eternal. The pit of lower Hell, reserved in the other texts for unbelievers, is omitted. When 'Paul' asks where his parents are, he is told that they are in Hell – as if this is a separate realm which he does not see. All the torments which he has seen are therefore implied to be, if not purgatorial, at least finite.[49]

In the eleventh century the priest Walkelin encounters an army of the dead as he returns home late one night from visiting a parishioner.[50] He meets his brother, who asks him for prayers and alms, explaining: 'in one year from Palm Sunday I hope to be saved and released from all torments by the mercy of my Creator' (p. 249). It appears that their father was released from torment when Walkelin celebrated his first mass for the dead.

In the same century Othlo records the vision of the monk Isaac, who finds himself in Paradise talking to Gunther, the founder of his monastery. Gunther tells him that all who come there have had to cross the fire of purgatory – *ignem purgatorium* – before being admitted (cols. 368–9). Lastly, the *Vision of Adamnan* divides the souls of the dead into the four categories described by Augustine. The good are admitted on death to the Land of Saints; the imperfectly good will enter this land after the Day of Judgment, but until then they must wander restlessly on the hills outside; the wicked are tormented in Hell for eternity; and the not very wicked are tormented but will be admitted to the 'Haven of Life' after the Day of Judgment (p. 41). But before being placed in one of these categories, the soul must on death travel up through the seven heavens to the throne of God to receive judgment, negotiating obstacles and torments as it ascends. At least some of these are purgatorial; in the second heaven we meet the angel Abersetus, 'who keeps watch over that river [of fire], and purges the souls of the righteous, and washes them in the stream, according to the amount of guilt that cleaves to them, until they become pure and shining as is the radiance of the stars' (p. 36).

During the twelfth century the visions become more and more specific in their description of the area of the other world set aside for purgation, and the purifying process occupies an ever greater proportion of the whole text.

At the beginning of the century the vision of Guibert de Nogent's mother, recorded by him, reaffirms the importance of prayer for the dead.[51] The first major vision of the twelfth century is, however, that of Alberic, recorded between 1127 and 1137.[52] Alberic's other world is divided into four areas. The first of these consists of the 'loca penarum' (p. 87). Alberic is shown children being purged of their sins in fire and smoke. He passes on to witness other torments, none of which are specifically said to be purgative, but some of which have time limits ranging up to eighty years. He then comes to the second area, the pit of Hell proper. He calls it 'loca tartarea' and 'hos infernalis baratri' (pp. 90–1); here sinners are condemned without judgment. He continues in the 'loca penarum', where various sinners are purged in darkness and fire according to the gravity of their sins. Alberic here quotes 1 Corinthians 3.13 and states that each person is tested in the fire and purged like gold, tin, lead and bronze. He continues on his journey and comes to the bridge with a burning river running beneath it; whoever falls into the river below undergoes purgation there. Lastly he comes to a plain of thorns which must be crossed in three days; this too is purgatorial. He then enters the third and fourth realms – a garden Paradise and the celestial spheres – and his vision ends. It would seem that Alberic's 'loca penarum' are intended to represent Purgatory, and the 'loca tartarea' Hell. He thus follows Drythelm, the Monk of Wenlock and the author of the sixth redaction of the *Vision of Paul* in describing purgation as occurring in a place distinct from that of Hell, but surpasses them in the detail and complexity of his description.

One of the most important visions is that of Tundale, who divides the other world into five regions: upper Hell, lower Hell, a rainy enclosure, a beautiful meadow and a walled garden Paradise.[53] In upper Hell certain specified sins are dealt with – murder, ambush and treachery (the punishment for which is alternate immersion by devils in fire and ice), pride, avarice, theft, greed and fornication, and multiple sin. When Tundale reaches lower Hell it is explained that those in the upper region have not yet received judgment, whereas those in the lower have – 'omnes quos vidisti superius, judicium dei expectant, set isti, qui adhuc sunt in inferioribus, jam judicati sunt' (p. 32). The torments of upper Hell are either purgatorial in nature (the word is not used in the text) and are followed by release to the beautiful meadow, or form a prelude to eternal torment in lower Hell, the realm of the wicked. The third region, the rainy enclosure, contains the imperfectly good (*non valde boni*), who must remain here 'for some years' (p. 40) and the fourth, the meadow, contains the not excessively bad (*non valde mali*). Here the purgation begun in upper Hell is completed – King Cormac is immersed in fire from the waist down for three hours a day, all his sins save two having been remitted (pp. 44–5). From here Tundale passes into Paradise, enclosed in successive walls of silver, gold and precious stones, perhaps echoing 1 Corinthians 3.12. This system is the most complex so far described; but the realms of purgation and damnation are still not clearly separated, purgation occurring in three separate places, and the moral progression of the soul is not reflected by any geographical consistency in the way the five realms are linked.[54]

Of the twelfth-century visions that which would seem to be most significant for the development of Purgatory is, by virtue of its title, *St Patrick's Purgatory*, in which Purgatory is named as a place for the first time in the vision literature.[55] The account of Owen's visit to the Purgatory is preceded by a lengthy discussion on the part of the redactor, who explains that the place is named Purgatory because it deals with the purgation of souls ('purgatorium quidem ab effectu animas expiandi, purgandique', col. 977), that the doctrine of Purgatory has already been discussed by Augustine, Gregory and Aquinas, and that purgation may occur in this life and in the next. Once his account of Owen's experiences begins, however, there is little difference between this text and the vision of Drythelm and Alberic. On entering the cave said to purge the sins of whoever spends a night there, Owen finds himself at the entrance to an underground realm of torment. He passes through this realm until he comes to the pit of Hell, crosses a bridge and enters the Earthly Paradise where the just await the Day of Judgment and admittance to the celestial Paradise. The torments he witnesses – four fields containing a great variety of punishments, a fiery wheel, a house of molten metal baths, a wind-whipped mountain and an icy river – are not specifically said to be purgatorial in nature, although they must be assumed to be so because distinguished from the mouth of the pit of Hell. This text still fails to present a neat tripartite division of the other world – and it must be remembered that the noun 'Purgatory' refers to a particular place in Ireland, a cave, in which purgation is believed to be obtainable by the living, and not primarily to a third realm of the other world. Within the account itself, as opposed to the preface, as Carozzi has remarked, the noun *purgatorium* is not used.[56] This text would seem to be less strikingly innovative than has been claimed.

Despite the suggestion made by Le Goff that the increasing awareness of the individual contributes in the twelfth century to the creation of the necessary atmosphere for the development of Purgatory, no critical attention has been paid to the one vision which, as was shown in the analysis of the inhabitants of the other world given in chapter 2, concentrates most fully on the individual: the *Vision of the Monk of Eynsham*.[57] And yet it is in this vision that we are made to face the problem of how the purgation of all one's sins, as opposed to only the most grave, is to occur. The souls circulate in three places of torment, from all of which release may be obtained, until each and every sin is purged. The question of the geography of Purgatory is scarcely considered in this text, but the problem of the nature and extent of purgation for each individual, and how it can be matched to his precise circumstances, is of fundamental importance. The principle of purgation is stated more clearly than in any other vision:

Quam ob causam quicquid spiritibus de hoc mundo migrantium munditie equitatique contrarium inheserit, in illo seculo purgari necesse habet, ut purificatis per supplicia aditus pateat beate quietis, et in quietis loco, peramplius et perfectius ex desiderio divine visionis dignificatis animabus, introitus reseretur glorie celestis.   (p. 285)

[For since impurity clings to the spirits of all those migrating from this world, it is necessary that they be purged after death, so that purified by suffering they may have access to the place of rest of the blessed, in this place be made more perfectly and abundantly worthy by their desire to receive the divine vision, and have opened to them the entrance to celestial glory.]

The monk also specifies that he saw nobody sure to receive eternal damnation (p. 292). Purgation is said to be shortened by the prayers of the living, by good works done while alive, by devotion to a particular saint who may intercede on the sinner's behalf, and by suffering in life.

There is only one representation of the other world before the *Comedy* which offers a clear account of Purgatory as an autonomous realm alongside and equal in importance to Hell and Paradise: the *Vision of Thurkill*, analysed in detail in chapter 4.[58] Souls are purged first in an area of fire and then in a freezing lake before crossing a nailed bridge to the Mountain of Joy. Their suffering on the bridge is in inverse proportion to the prayers said for them and their own almsgiving. Hell is an entirely separate place located in a different part of the other world. Despite the topographical originality of the vision, various elements survive from the earlier tradition: on Sundays Uriel drains the lake and extinguishes the fire to provide a day of respite as in the *Vision of Paul*; purgation is achieved in fire and ice as in

Drythelm; sinners are immersed to varying degrees in the icy lake as in many previous visions, and the souls of the dead are black, white or spotted, the spots representing imperfections to be burnt off as in the Platonic tradition (see especially the *Vision of Thespesius*). These spots provide an interesting precedent for the seven P's, standing for *peccati*, which are erased from Dante's forehead as the ascends from terrace to terrace of the *Purgatorio*. *Thurkill* is also the only vision in which the torments of Purgatory are not the same as those traditionally ascribed to Hell; and the only one to use the noun *purgatorium* within the text itself. This vision offers the most complex and coherent description of the realm and mechanism of purgation before the *Comedy*, and is of the greatest importance in the history of the development of Purgatory. It is also the only full-scale vision of the other world to be recorded in the thirteenth century. Although a number of the anecdotes collected by Caesarius of Heisterbach and Etienne of Bourbon concern Purgatory,[59] there is no new complete representation of the other world until the *Comedy*.

THE ICONOGRAPHY OF PURGATORY IN THE VISIONS
AND THE *COMEDY*

Fire

Most theologians, following 1 Corinthians 3, taught that purgation is effected by fire, and fire plays a part in almost every vision of Purgatory or purgation. Drythelm describes a valley of fire and ice (p. 254); the Monk of Wenlock sees pits of fire and a river of fire (p. 254); Charles the Fat is shown a valley divided into an area of flames containing boiling and cool casks and a pleasant area to which the purged souls are admitted (pp. 114–15). The souls of the blessed seen by Isaac tell him that they have all crossed the fire of Purgatory before being admitted to Paradise ('debes utique aliqua hic considerando discere, qualiter nos primum transeuntes per ignem purgatorium, exinde ducti sumus in istud quod vides refrigerium', cols. 368–9). Adamnan sees the souls of the dead undergoing purgation in a river of fire in the second heaven (p. 36).

In the twelfth century, the fire motif is expanded still further. Alberic describes several forms of purgation in fire and specifically refers to 1 Corinthians 3. Tundale's purgatorial upper Hell contains a number of fiery torments – murderers are fried and sieved over a fire, traitors are forced along a path with fire and ice on each side, gluttons and fornicators are roasted in an oven and tortured, and those guilty of multiple sin are heated and hammered by infernal blacksmiths. Owen sees sinners suspended in fiery chains over flames, fixed to a burning wheel, immersed in molten metal baths and cooked in pans. The Monk of Eynsham describes frying pans, fiery nails driven into the bones, molten metal baths, burning stakes, a mountain of fire and ice, the consumption of burning money, fire-breathing worms in a landscape of pitch-black flames, burning tongues, immersion in red-hot coins, suspension from fiery gibbets and other fire-related torments. Only Thurkill preserves the simplicity of 1 Corinthians 3 and the teaching of the theologians, and represents purgation as occurring in fire alone.

Dante too represents purgation as occurring in part through the medium of fire.

The mountain of Purgatory

A wall of fire separates the seventh terrace from the Earthly Paradise, and in it are purged the lustful. Like Thurkill he reduces the motif to biblical proportions and omits the extravagant elaborations of the twelfth-century visionaries. But the principle of *contrapasso* demands a greater variety of states of purgation than fire alone would permit; though eminently suitable for the purifying of burning lust, and though historically and theologically consistent in its role as the final barrier to the Earthly Paradise,[60] a more complex scheme is needed in the *Purgatorio*.

The bridge

Another common motif used in the vision literature to represent purgation is the bridge, discussed in chapter 1. Occurring in ten major visions, it gradually becomes established as part of the mechanism of purgation and even as a component of the separate realm of Purgatory.[61] Thurkill in particular uses it as the third element of his tripartite Purgatory. But the bridge cannot readily be worked into a topographical scheme governed by the fall of Satan and, like the fire motif, cannot distinguish between different categories of penitents.

The mountain

The view traditionally held by Dante scholarship that the mountain was an entirely original choice for the location of Purgatory in the poem has recently been challenged by Jacques Le Goff, who suggests that there is a strong precedent in the popular tradition for its use.[62] However, Le Goff does not follow up his suggestion in any detail, and gives an account of the *Purgatorio* in which the poem is not compared to the visions. In the course of the book the only mention of a mountain in connection with Purgatory, apart from the summary of the Sicilian legends, comes in the discussion of the *Vision of Wetti*, in which he refers to the 'place held by the mountain as the location of temporary suffering' and remarks 'there will be, at the end of our account, Dante's mountain of Purgatory'.[63]

The question therefore remains: to what extent can the mountain be said to have been offered to Dante as a location for purgatorial torment by the previous popular representations of the other world? Due to the controversial nature of the question, the following discussion is more detailed and refers more closely to the texts than hitherto.

The closest precedent for Dante's mountain in popular legend is found in a series of descriptions of Etna and the volcanic islands off the coast of Sicily. Two such texts are of particular importance.[64]

The first of these is the *Voyage of Saint Brendan*. One of the islands visited by Brendan is a volcano inhabited by demons, described in the Italian redaction as follows:

Having sailed north with the wind, they saw an island covered in enormous rocks. And it was a foul island, without trees, leaves, grass, flowers or fruits, and full of forges and smiths (. . .). And St Brendan comforted all the monks, and said: 'don't be afraid, my sons; the Lord God is and will be our helper. I want you to know that we are near Hell, and this island is part of it.' (pp. 93–4)

In the thirteenth century Caesarius of Heisterbach reports a discussion on Etna:

Novice: What is one to believe concerning these mountains, Stromboli, Etna and Mount Gyber? When souls are sent there, is it to Purgatory or to Hell?
Monk: They are said to be the mouth of Hell, because none of the elect but only the wicked are sent there (. . .). Hell is thought to be in the heart of the Earth.   (p. 326)

Both of these texts represent Hell, and not Purgatory, within the volcano. Only one, recounted by Etienne de Bourbon,[65] describes Etna as the location of Purgatory.

A second group of texts within the vision literature locates some of the torments of Hell on a mountain. The earliest of these is the *Vision of Charles the Fat*,[66] in which part of the geography of Hell is described in the following terms:

ascendimus super montes altissimos igneos, de quibus oriebantur paludes et flumina ferventia, et omnia metallorum genera bullientia, ubi reperi innumeras animas hominum et principum patris mei et fratrum meorum.   (p. 113)

[we climbed high fiery mountains, from which arose lakes and burning rivers and all kinds of boiling metals, where I found immersed innumerable souls of the vassals and princes of my father and brothers.]

Also important is the fourteenth vision described by Othlo,[67] in which the mountain is seen:

repente vecti sunt beatus scilicet Guntharius et monachus in montem excelsum valde, unde pars maxima infernalium poenarum desuper conspici posset.   (col. 369)

[the saint, Gunther, and the monk came swiftly to a very high mountain; the torments of Hell could be discerned on the greater part of its slopes.]

Another such mountain is described in the *Vision of Thurkill*, where the amphitheatre in which the torments of lower Hell occur is presented as if set into its slopes:

perrexerunt ergo ad plagam aquilonarem quasi montem ascendendo, et ecce in descensu montis erat domus amplissima et fuliginosa, muris veternosis circumdata, erantque in ea quasi multe platee.   (p. 19)

[they reached the northern side as if climbing a mountain, and then as they descended again they came to a wide and smoky structure surrounded by ancient walls, in which were many seats.]

The last reference to a mountain in connection with the torments of Hell is found in Bonvesin's account of the twelve eternal torments: 'on both sides of the rivers are dark mountains, remarkably high, fearsome and overgrown, covered in harsh, excessively piercing and poisonous thorns'.

> Da tute doe le parte de li fiumi si è li monti imbrioxi,
> alti ke è maravelia e irti e spaguroxi,
> e sono coperti per tuto pur de spini regoroxi,
> li quali sono oltra modo ponzenti e venenoxi.
>
>   (p. 22)

A final small group of texts represents purgation as in some way connected with a mountain site. The earliest of these, and the only one to pre-date the twelfth

century, is the *Vision of Wetti*.[68] The description of the mountain in the prose
version of the text is as follows:

Ibi etiam ostensa est ei cuiusdam montis altitudo. Et dictum est ab angelo de quodam abbate
ante decennium defuncto, quod in summitate eius esset deputatus ad purgationem suam
(. . .), ibidem eum omnem inclementiam aeris et ventorum incommoditatem imbriumque
pati.   (p. 270)

[There he was shown the height of the mountain. And the angel told him about a certain
abbot who had died a decade earlier, who was assigned to complete his purgation on the
summit (. . .), where he suffered foul air and the discomfort of rainclouds.]

We come now to *St Patrick's Purgatory*. [69] The earliest account of the Purgatory,
composed by Jocelin, a monk at Furness in Lancashire, between 1170 and 1185,
placed it not in a cave but on the mountain Cruachan Aigle, in Connaught. This led
to the practice of individuals spending a night in penance on the mountain:

In hujus igitur montis cacumine jejunare ac vigilare consuescunt plurimi opinantes se postea
nunquam intraturos portas inferni, quia hoc impetratum a Domino existimant meritis et
precibus S. Patricii. Referunt etiam nonnulli, qui pernoctaverunt ibi, se tormenta gravissima
fuisse perpessos, quibus se purgatos a peccatis putant, unde et quidam illorum locum illum
purgatorium S. Patricii vocant.[70]

[On the summit of this mountain many are wont to fast and keep vigil, believing they will
never thereafter enter the gates of Hell, for they hold that by doing so they will obtain favour
from God through the merits and prayers of St Patrick. Some who have spent the night
there report that they endured grave torment, by which they hold themselves to have been
purged of their sins. It is because of this that they call the place St Patrick's Purgatory.]

This is the only text in which a precise parallel is offered to Dante's Purgatory, in
that the mountain represents the whole of the realm, and only purgation occurs on
its slopes. The same reservation applies, however, as to the later version of the
legend: the Purgatory is an earthly phenomenon, and not specifically a realm of the
other world.

The last section of Hugh of Saltrey's account of the Purgatory also describes
purgatorial torment on a mountain. Sinners sit huddled as on Dante's terrace of
envy, afflicted by the torments of demons:

perrexerunt in montem excelsum, et ostenderunt ei utriusque homines, et aetatis diversae
multitudinem copiosam (. . .), omnes nudi sedebant super digitos curvati (. . .). Vix
daemon verba finiebat, et ecce ventus turbinis ab aquilone veniebat, qui et ipsos daemones,
et cum eis militem, totumque populum illum arripuit, et in quoddam flumen fetidum ac
frigidissimum, in aliam montis parten, flentes et miserabiliter ajulantes projecit; in quo
inaestimabili frigore vexabantur.   (cols. 994–5)

[they reached a high mountain, and showed him a great multitude of men and women of all
ages (. . .), all sitting naked and bent over their toes (. . .). Scarcely had the devil finished
speaking when a strong wind came from the north, snatching away the devils themselves,
and with them the knight, and all those who were there, and throwing them into a stinking,
freezing river on another side of the mountain, weeping and howling miserably; and here
they were tormented by unbearable cold.]

A similar scene occurs in the *Vision of the Monk of Eynsham*, in which the second
area of torment is separated from the first by a mountain with fire on one side, ice

on the other; souls are immersed alternately in the one and the other, and the torment is purgatorial. This seems to derive ultimately from the *Vision of Drythelm*.

It must therefore be concluded that there is a considerable amount of precedent in the popular tradition for the location of purgative torment on a mountain.[71]

THE TRADITION OF THE EARTHLY PARADISE

In considering possible precedents for Dante's choice of a mountain site to represent the realm of Purgatory, it has been necessary to look at the concept of a third realm in the writings of theologians and the pronouncements of the Church, and at the representation of purgation and Purgatory and precedents for the choice of a mountain site in the vision literature. But it must not be forgotten that a hundred years separate the *Comedy* from the *Vision of Thurkill*; or that the essential difference between the visions and the poem has been seen in previous chapters to lie in Dante's ability to reinterpret the traditional images in the light of the intellectual developments which were assimilated during those years.[72] It has been generally assumed that Dante located the Earthly Paradise on the summit of the mountain of Purgatory, and his originality in choosing such a mountain for the middle realm has been acclaimed. But there is considerable evidence to suggest that, rather than placing the Earthly Paradise on the summit of the mountain of Purgatory, Dante placed Purgatory on the slopes of the mountain of the Earthly Paradise – that is, that his mountain has its origin not in any traditional iconography for Purgatory, for there was none, but in the learned traditions of Eden and of Jerusalem. These traditions are also reflected in the popular representation of Paradise as manifested in the vision literature.

According to Hebrew cosmology, which has been studied in relation to the *Vision of Paul* by Ricciotti,[73] the earth is tripartite, consisting of an underground Sheol, an earth and a firmament. The earth and the firmament meet at the peaks of mountains, and it is therefore here that the highest destiny of man is accomplished:

In later days, the mountain where the Lord dwells will be lifted high above the mountain-tops, looking down over the hills, and all nations will flock there together. A multitude of people will make their way to it, crying, Come, let us climb up to the Lord's mountain-peak, to the house where the God of Jacob dwells; he shall teach us the right way, we will walk in the paths he has chosen. (Isaiah 2.2–3)

In Ezekiel, Eden is said to be situated on this 'mountain of the Lord' (28.14), and subsequent tradition held that the original Paradise was sited on a mountain. Mountains are represented in the apocrypha; in *I Enoch* we read: 'and they brought me to a place of darkness, and to a mountain the point of whose summit reached to heaven' (p. 44); mountains are the site of the throne of God, and the place in which souls await the Day of Judgment. The Garden of Righteousness is said to lie beyond seven mountains (chapters 18, 22, 23). Baruch is shown a serpent lying on a high mountain, the implication being that this is the site of the original Paradise; 'and I, Baruch, said to the angel: Shew me the tree by which Adam and Eve were seduced and driven out of Paradise' (p. 97). In the Ethiopic text of the *Apocalypse of*

Peter we read 'And my Lord Jesus Christ our king said unto me: Let us go unto the holy mountain.' On it Peter finds the Earthly Paradise, in which dwell Moses, Elias and the righteous; 'and we prayed and went down from the mountain, glorifying God, which hath written the names of the righteous in heaven in the book of life' (p. 519)

From the fifth century onwards, the Earthly Paradise is said to be sited on a mountain, the authoritative formulation being made in the *Glossa ordinaria* of Walafrid Strabo:

Wherever it is, we know it to be earthly, situated in the midst of the Ocean (. . .), remote from our region, on a high site, reaching almost to the circle of the moon; so that the waters of the Flood scarcely touched it.[74]

Nardi has indicated the importance of texts such as this to the *Comedy* in its representation of the Earthly Paradise on the sumit of a mountain.[75] The relationship between Dante and the theologians is summarised by Singleton: 'in his depiction of the terrestrial paradise, its nature and its whereabouts, Dante has paid his respects to an established body of opinion'.[76] And it is from this learned tradition, perhaps more than from the belief that purgation occurs by fire, that Dante takes the wall of fire which surrounds his Eden: Eden was held to be protected by fire originating from the flaming sword set outside it after the Fall.[77] Isidore describes this fire: 'it is surrounded by a sword of flame, that is, girded by a wall of fire'.[78] Nowhere in the vision tradition is the Earthly Paradise linked in this way to Purgatory, or even to an area of purgation – Dante is the first to juxtapose them.

The second learned tradition which provided a precedent for the mountain also stems from Hebrew cosmology, and concerns not the Paradise from which the human race sprang, but that to which it will return: the celestial Jerusalem described in the Apocalypse. It is called the city of Christ, and seen descending 'from heaven' onto 'a great mountain, high up' (Apocalypse 21.10). The exegesis of this passage and its influence on the vision literature is considered in greater detail in chapter 6. It is reflected in many of the popular texts.

The earliest of the visions to represent Paradise in this way is the *Vision of Baldarius*.[79] Baldarius is carried upwards 'above the stars' by three doves:

Ibi, scilicet, induxerunt me in excelsum mirae pulchritudinis montem, qui innumerabilium candidatorum erat coopertus caterva seniorum. Inter quos deducentes perduxerunt me ante conspectum majestatis Domini. (cols. 435–6)

[Here they led me to a high mountain of remarkable beauty, covered with a crowd of innumerable elders dressed in white. Leading me through them they brought me before the sight of the majesty of the Lord.]

Later visions also represent Paradise similarly. The eleventh vision of Othlo describes it as a mountain monastery: 'then he was taken to a high mountain, where he saw an excellent monastery with the trace of many paths leading to it' (col. 366). Alberic describes Paradise as a high plain, 'campus altissimus valde' (p. 98). Thurkill comes closer to Dante; his Paradise is sited on the summit of a mountain, on part of which souls who have successfully crossed the bridge from Purgatory must complete their purgation. Two categories of souls are found in this condition on the slopes of the 'mons gaudii' (p. 13): the first group wait in the atrium to the south of the temple, and the second group wait outside to the north, lying prostrate in the force of an icy wind. Both groups will be allowed to enter when the requisite number of prayers have been uttered on their behalf. The entrance door is guarded by Michael (pp. 29–30). The first group of souls appear to be those who died before they had had time to repent of their sins; they include Thurkill's landlord, Roger Picoth, who died in debt, and a local monk 'qui subito exspiraverat' (p. 30). The second group includes the visionary's father, who needs thirty masses before he can be admitted to the temple. This passage is important not only because the temple of Paradise is situated on a mountain, but also because, like the passage in the *Vision of Drythelm* analysed above, it provides a partial precedent for the souls of Dante's Antepurgatory. In Drythelm the precedent was mainly conceptual – the exclusion from the company of the imperfectly good of those who repented at the last moment. Here it is geographical – these souls, who perhaps are intended to include the late repentant, are made to wait on the lower slopes of a mountain before they may be admitted by the prayer of the living through the gate which bars their progress.

The last text comes from the *Liber Viarum Dei* of Elizabeth of Schönau, who sees in a vision a high mountain with three paths leading to its summit; 'montem excelsum, copioso lumine in summo illustratum, et quasi vias tres, a radice ejus ad cacumen usque porrectas' (col. 164). The paths represent routes through life to eternal beatitude. This text also offers some precedent for a journey up the mountain to Paradise, although Purgatory is not specifically located on its slopes.

It would seem therefore that there is precedent in the popular tradition for the location of some degree of torment, eternal or purgative, on a mountain, and that the first version of *St Patrick's Purgatory* and the *Vision of Thurkill* are particularly important in this respect. The learned traditions of the celestial Jerusalem and the Earthly Paradise also provide a precedent for the location of Eden on a mountain site, as in the *Comedy*, and are echoed to some extent in the visions. Dante's originality thus lies in the putting together of the learned and popular traditions by locating his Purgatory on the slopes of the garden of Eden, thereby creating a geographical link between Hell and Paradise.

Notes

1 For the fall of Lucifer see Isaiah 14.12–20, Luke 10.18, Rev. 12.9.

2 For references see the article 'Purgatorio' by M. Aurigemma in the *Enciclopedia Dantesca*, IV, p. 747.

3 *Ibid.* See also A. Graf, *Miti, leggende e superstizioni del Medio Evo*, 1892, I, p. 5; F. D'Ovidio, *Il Purgatorio*, [1931], p. 270; echoed recently in W. Anderson, *Dante the Maker*, 1980, p. 280.

4 J. Le Goff, *La Naissance du Purgatoire*, 1981, pp. 453–4.

5 *II Maccabees* 12.39–45. Discussed by R. Ombres, 'Images of Healing', 1976, p. 130, and *The Theology of Purgatory*, 1978, pp. 20–1. See also A. Piolanti, 'Il dogma del Purgatorio', 1953, pp. 287–8. For the pagan background see P. Ariès, *The Hour of Our Death*, 1983, pp. 146–7.

6 See A. Piolanti, 'Il dogma del Purgatorio', pp. 288–9.

7 *Ibid.*, p. 289.

8 *Ibid.*, pp. 289–91.

9 The development of the doctrine of Purgatory is summarised by A. Michel, 'Purgatoire', 1936; A. Piolanti, 'Il dogma del Purgatorio'; J. Le Goff, *La Naissance du Purgatoire*; and R. Ombres, 'The Doctrine of Purgatory according to St Thomas Aquinas', 1981; 'Images of Healing', 1976; *The Theology of Purgatory*, 1978. My summary is based on theirs.

10 See Michel, 'Purgatoire', cols. 1192–3, Piolanti, 'Il dogma del Purgatorio', p. 293, Ombres, *The Theology of Purgatory*, p. 34.

11 See Michel, 'Purgatoire', cols. 1193–6, Piolanti, 'Il dogma del Purgatorio', pp. 293–4.

12 See Michel, cols. 1198–1212, Piolanti, pp. 294–5.

13 See Michel, cols. 1213–14, Piolanti, pp. 296–7.

14 See Michel, cols. 1215–18.

15 Quotations from Piolanti, p. 198 and Le Goff, *La Naissance du Purgatoire*, p. 92. Augustine's thought on Purgatory is summarised by Piolanti, pp. 198–9, Michel, cols. 1220–3, Le Goff, pp. 92–118.

16 See Michel, cols. 1224–5.

17 See *ibid.*, cols. 1225–6, Le Goff, pp. 121–31.

18 E.g. Isidore, Bede, Alcuim, Rabanus Maurus, Peter Damian. See Piolanti, p. 300.

19 Summary taken from Le Goff, pp. 181–4.

20 For Bernard and Honorius see Piolanti, p. 300, Le Goff, pp. 185–8 and 197–8. For Bernard see also Michel, col. 1229. For Drythelm's description of the valley of fire and ice see p. 256 of the vision.

21 See Piolanti, p. 300, Michel, col. 1238, Le Goff, pp. 193–6.

22 See Michel, col. 1329, Le Goff, pp. 201–3.

23 See Le Goff., pp. 290–322 and p. 158.

24 See in particular the reviews by R. W. Southern, 'Between Heaven and Hell', 1982, pp. 651–2; A. H. Bredero, 'Le Moyen Age et le Purgatoire', 1983, p. 437; also R. Lerner, 'Jaques Le Goff: "La Naissance du Purgatoire"', 1982, and J. Paul, 'Jacques Le Goff,: "La Naissance du Purgatoire"', 1982.

25 See chapter 4, p. 122.

26 See Michel, 'Purgatoire', cols. 1240–1.

27 *Ibid.*, cols. 1241–2.

28 *Ibid.*, col. 1242.

29 *Ibid.*, col. 1242.

30 *Ibid.*, col. 1243.

31 *Ibid.*, cols. 1242–3. For Aquinas see also Ombres, 'The Doctrine of Purgatory', 1981.

32 Latin text given by Michel, 'Purgatoire', col. 1248.

33 *Ibid.*, cols. 1167–8. The Egyptian *Book of the Dead* shows the weighing of the soul and, immediately afterwards, the purification by fire of the righteous soul. The Persians represented the judgment of the soul by the image of the bridge, but also believed that Hell was purificatory.

34 See P. Ariès, *The Hour of Our Death*, p. 147.

35 For Orphism, see W. F. Jackson Knight, *Elysion*, 1970, p. 76. For Plato see the *Gorgias*, 524a–527a, the *Phaedo*, 113–14, and the *Phaedrus*, 248E–249D.

36 See especially pp. 280–3, where 'purgation' and 'healing' are explained.

37 See P. Ariès, *The Hour of Our Death*, pp. 147–8, and J. Ntedika, *L'Evocation de l'au-delà dans les prières pour les morts*, 1971, pp. 68ff.

38 P. Dronke points out that the thirst of the dead is a common classical motif and recalls the 'special sadness' of those who die young in the *Aeneid* and elsewhere (*Women Writers of the Middle Ages*, 1984, pp. 11–12).

39 *Dialogues* IV 57 (the priest and monk); IV 42 (Paschasius); IV 37 (Stephen, the soldier and Peter).

40 See P. Ariès, *The Hour of Our Death*, pp. 147–8 and 153–4. See also Le Goff, *La Naissance du Purgatoire*, pp. 65–6: 'le sein d'Abraham est la première incarnation chrétienne du Purgatoire'. But Le Goff mentions Barontus only in an appendix, where he omits the reference to Abraham's bosom and states that 'il n'y a pas question du Purgatoire', p. 498.

41 Pointed out by Le Goff in *ibid.*, p. 152. He maintains, however, that this place, 'locus', is not Purgatory since it is unnamed, and 'un lieu innommé n'existe pas', p. 158, and since the souls of the dead are divided into 4 categories and not 3.

42 Le Goff argues that Purgatory is born only when this binary structure is replaced by a ternary structure (p. 158), but in so doing overlooks the one respect in which the vision clearly foreshadows the *Purgatorio*.

43 See Purg IV 133–5; V 67–72; VI 28–42; VIII 67–78.

44 Briefly summarised in Appendix IV by Le Goff, *La Naissance du Purgatoire*, with no reference to the interpretation given in the text of what is seen.

45 *Ibid.*, pp. 159–61.

46 Omitted by Le Goff.

47 The *Vision of Bernoldus* is not discussed by Le Goff, and the *Vision of Charles the Fat* is translated with little comment, pp. 162–6, with the statement that it was 'une des lectures de Dante'. There is no evidence to support this claim, although a case is made on the basis of the similarity of the immersion motif by T. Silverstein in ' "Inferno" XII, 100–26, and the "Visio Karoli Crassi" ', 1936.

48 Ignored by Le Goff.

49 Silverstein suggests that 'in this fashion the redactor made Hell a place distinct from all the preceding regions of pain, which he intended to represent Purgatory, as appears from the occasional references to God's sparing penitent sinners after a specified time of punishment', '*Visio Sancti Pauli*', 1935, p. 88.

50 Omitted by Le Goff.

51 Translated and discussed by Le Goff, pp. 246–50.

52 Discussed by Le Goff, pp. 251–6.

53 Discussed by Le Goff, pp. 256–9.

54 Carozzi distinguishes eight areas of Hell and one of Purgatory, and traces this division to Honorius's *Elucidarium*, 'Structure et fonction de la vision de Tnugdal', 1981, pp. 223–5.

55 Le Goff states that 'the text which holds an essential place in the history of Purgatory, playing an important if not decisive part in its success, is the famous *St Patrick's Purgatory*', p. 259. See also p. 246 where he describes its composition as 'in some way the moment of literary birth of Purgatory'.

56 C. Carozzi, 'La Géographie de l'au-delà et sa signification pendant le haut moyen âge', 1983, p. 485.

57 pp. 311–36. The *Vision of the Monk of Eynsham* is excluded by Le Goff on the grounds that it is 'too close to the *Vision of Drythelm*, and Purgatory is still too fragmented for me to have included it', p. 501.

58 The *Vision of Thurkill* is omitted from the discussion by Le Goff since, in contrast with *St Patrick's Purgatory*, 'it did not bring about the success of Purgatory'; and its representation of the third realm is dismissed as 'confused' and 'archaic', p. 500. The main reason for which Le Goff finds it confused, however, seems to be that he mistakenly believes the devils' theatre, which is a part of the torment of Hell, to be a part of Purgatory.

59 Caesarius of Heisterbach, *Dialogus miraculorum* XII 24–39; Etienne de Bourbon, *Tractatus* I (v).

60 Genesis 3.24 and Matthew 3.3; for learned sources see the article 'Purgatoire', *Enciclopedia Dantesca*, IV, p. 747.

61 The visions in which the bridge occurs are those of the soldier, Sunniulf, Paul (the redactions), the Monk of Wenlock, Adamnan, Alberic, Tundale, *St Patrick's Purgatory*, Thurkill, and the *Liber de Scalis*.

62 See note 4.

63 Le Goff devotes the tenth and final chapter of his study to a discussion of the *Purgatorio*, in which he warns that he is not a Dante specialist, and that he offers only 'une lecture naïve du poème ou [son] guide était le souvenir des nombreaux textes qui avaient précédé la "Divina Commedia" dans la quête du Purgatoire' (p. 449).

64 Le Goff cites a number of legends from the works of such writers as Julien de Vezelay and Gervais of Tilbury, who are, however, in no way connected to the vision tradition, pp. 273–81. He does not discuss the two texts here examined.

65 Quoted by Le Goff, pp. 420–1.

66 Translated with little comment by Le Goff, pp. 162–5.

67 Also omitted by Le Goff.

68 To which Le Goff refers only in the version of Walafrid.

69 Le Goff attaches much importance to H. of Saltrey's version, suggesting that it provided a rival and more congenial image for the depiction of the third realm than that offered by the volcanoes of Sicily, and thus establishing Purgatory as an underground realm. However, the earlier version offers one of the clearest examples of a mountain Purgatory.

70 Chapter 172, quoted by Ph. de Félice, *L'Autre monde*, 1906, p. 20, from the edition of Colgan in *Acta Sanctorum veteris et majoris Scotiae sue hiberniae*, Lovan, 1645–7, vol. II.

71 Le Goff understates the case to be made by ignoring some texts and overstressing others. The Sicilian legends lie outside the main stream of the vision tradition; and if Dante's mountain is to be seen as the natural conclusion to the representation of Purgatory in the visions, then H. of Saltrey's account of *St Patrick's Purgatory* cannot be accorded the importance given to it by Le Goff.

72 Le Goff takes no account of this 150 year gap; he regards the visions as part of a continuous tradition which extends from Bede, 'le "fondateur" des visions mediévales de l'au-delà' (p. 154), to Dante, whose poem is 'une conclusion sublime à la lente genèse du Purgatoire' and constitutes the 'triomphe poétique' (p. 410) of the genre. See Introduction for further discussion of this point of view.

73 *L'Apocalisse di Paolo siriaca, II: La cosmologia della Bibbia e la sua trasmissione fino a Dante*, 1932.

74 Quoted by Ricciotti, *ibid.*, p. 127.

75 'Intorno al sito del Purgatorio e al mito dantesco dell'Eden', 1922, pp. 289–300.

76 C. S. Singleton, *Journey to Beatrice*, 1958, p. 145.

77 See Graf, *Miti, leggende e superstizioni*, 1892, pp. 18–19.

78 *Etymologiae*, quoted by Ricciotti, *L'Apocalisse di Paolo siriaca*, p. 124.

79 Omitted by Le Goff.

6

The representation of Paradise

In the *Comedy* Paradise is represented in three different ways. On the summit of the mountain of Purgatory Dante finds the Garden of Eden, the Earthly Paradise intended by God to be the dwelling place of man, and from which Adam and Eve were expelled as a result of their disobedience. From here he ascends through the celestial spheres – first those of the seven planets, the Moon, Mercury, Venus, the Sun, Mars, Jupiter and Saturn, and then the remaining three spheres, those of the Fixed Stars, the *Primum Mobile* and finally the outer, enclosing Empyrean. In these spheres he meets some of the souls of those who have already been admitted to the eternal Paradise, but who are shown to him in successive heavens, each individual appearing in that which most influenced him (see Par IV 28–63). And finally he reaches the eternal Paradise, located in the Empyrean, at which point he experiences a vision of the Trinity.

These three different models for the representation of Paradise spring from three different traditions; and these traditions are found to varying degrees in the previous, popular representations of Paradise.

The history of the concept of Paradise is a long and complex one which is traced not only in the popular representations of the other world but also in the writings of many theologians and poets. The word 'paradise' derives from the Old Persian word signifying a royal park or enclosure; it passed into Hebrew with the meaning of a garden, and became applied specifically to the Garden of Eden. Later, when the belief arose in the existence of an abode for the righteous dead, the same word paradise was used to refer to that abode. It passed into Greek, and so by New Testament times the word paradise had three distinct meanings: a garden, the Earthly Paradise or Garden of Eden, and the eternal or celestial Paradise or Heaven.[1]

The strictly literary tradition of the Earthly Paradise springs from the etymological union between the original garden in which Adam and Eve were placed and the eternal heaven to which the saved will be admitted. Many of the details of Paradise in the vision literature are influenced by the Earthly Paradise as portrayed in this tradition, and it is this which lies in part behind Dante's representation of the 'divine forest' on the summit of the mountain of Purgatory. But the tradition of the Earthly Paradise became essentially learned and literary rather than popular in nature, and therefore falls outside the scope of this study.[2]

A second tradition, Eastern and classical in origin, located the abode of the righteous dead in the celestial spheres. It influenced Hebrew thought during the

Hellenistic Age of Judaism, and left its mark on the apocrypha in particular.[3] Surviving as an independent tradition in Ireland, it was recovered in the Latin West during the twelfth and thirteenth centuries, and influenced literary works such as the *Cosmographia* of Bernard Silvestris and the *Anticlaudianus* of Alan of Lille.[4] It is this tradition which forms the background to Dante's representation of the ascent through the celestial spheres in the first twenty-nine cantos of the *Paradiso*. It also appears to some extent in the popular tradition, particularly in the later visions, but it is not a defining feature.

The main emphasis of this chapter will therefore lie on the third tradition, which derives from the description of the heavenly Jerusalem in the Apocalypse of John, and dominates the popular representation of Paradise from the fourth century onwards. Many of the details in the popular texts clearly foreshadow Dante's Empyrean vision of the elect in the last four cantos of the *Paradiso*. Previous criticism has, however, dismissed these accounts as unworthy of serious consideration; the general view is summarised in this paragraph by Rajna:

> We come now to Paradise. Whereas in their depiction of the torments (temporary or perpetual) the visionaries who preceded Dante had often demonstrated their ingenuity and powers of invention, when it came to the description of celestial beatitude they struggled so hard to get off the ground that they can only be pitied. Their ostrich wings were really not up to such an arduous flight. And so their paradise was mostly reduced to a mere earthly paradise, or to a poor copy of the heavenly Jerusalem described in the Apocalypse.[5]

It is the aim of the present chapter to give a reappraisal of this view, taking into account not only the vision literature but also the visual arts – which have hitherto been excluded from all serious studies of the relation between the *Comedy* and the previous popular tradition.

THE POPULAR REPRESENTATION OF PARADISE FROM THE FOURTH TO THE THIRTEENTH CENTURIES

Before the fourth century

Before the fourth century Paradise is represented in a number of different ways. Classical texts describe the Elysian Fields or the Isles of the Blessed.[6] The Old Testament apocrypha conceive of a plurality of heavens (see below). The New Testament apocrypha and early Christian texts either adopt one of these two models or, following the pattern of Genesis, describe a garden located in the East.[7]

The Apocalypse

The scriptural tradition of Paradise is entirely different from its rivals. It is securely based on Hebrew cosmology. The universe was believed to have a tripartite structure, consisting of an underground Sheol, a terrestrial region which is the land of the living, and a celestial region which is the abode of God. The terrestrial and celestial regions were linked by mountains, on which the highest destiny of man was to be accomplished (Isaiah 2.2; *Wisdom* 9.8). A city was to be located on such a mountain (Ezekiel 40.2). In John's Apocalypse that city is named 'the holy city Jerusalem' (21.10) and identified as the place in which the elect will dwell with God 'for ever and ever' (22.5).

The process by which the earthly city of Jerusalem first came to be seen as a shadow of this celestial city and eternal abode has been analysed by Ricciotti and, more recently, by Lamirande and by Rosso Ubigli.[8] It begins in the second century BC with the *Book of Enoch*, which declares hope in the restoration of an earthly Jerusalem. Subsequent texts such as *IV Esdras* 10 and *II Baruch* 59 foretell the arrival on earth of a divinely created celestial Jerusalem. Finally this celestial Jerusalem is identified with the eternal abode of the elect, as in *II Baruch* 6.9. The Apocalypse, probably written near the end of the first century, stands at the end of this process.

The city is named early in the book: 'I will write (. . .) the name of the city my God has built, the new Jerusalem which my God is even now sending down from heaven' (3.12). It is seen to descend from the heavens towards the summit of the mountain on which the visionary is standing (21.10); it shines with precious stones and with gold (21.11, 18–21), and is illuminated by the 'glory of God' (21.11, 23). Twelve doors in a wall with twelve foundations lead into the city (21.12–14); the names of the apostles are written on the twelve foundations. The city is square in shape (21.16); and through it flows the river of life (22.1). Chapters 4 and 5, which describe the throne of God, provide further details: 'I (. . .) saw where a throne stood in heaven, and one sat there enthroned (. . .). And now I saw that he who sat on the throne carried in his right hand a scroll' (4.2; 5.1). A rainbow surrounds the throne (4.3); twenty-four elders in white vestments and golden crowns are seated around it in worship (4.4).

The origin, site, shape, materials and inhabitants of the city were to be interpreted in very different ways in subsequent centuries, and the history of the exegesis of the Apocalypse as a whole is complex, and still relatively unexplored. The principal authority remains W. Kamlah's *Apokalypse und Geschichtstheologie* of 1935, which concentrates on those elements in the exegesis which point forward to the thirteenth-century commentary of Joachim, and is avowedly selective in its choice of material. The relationship between the Apocalypse, its exegesis and the visual arts has been the subject of only a few studies;[9] and its impact on the popular visions of the afterlife has never been examined in any detail.

However, a clear preliminary summary of the medieval exegesis of the Apocalypse was provided in 1909 by E. Mangenot's articles in the *Dictionnaire de Théologie Catholique*,[10] and we may follow him in distinguishing three periods: from the first to the fourth centuries, from the fourth to the twelfth, and from the thirteenth onwards (the dividing lines being marked by the commentaries of Ticonius and of Joachim respectively). The majority of the popular representations of Paradise which are dependent to some degree on the Apocalyptic description of the heavenly city fall within the second of these periods.[11]

The representation of Paradise

The first period: the earliest popular vision

The earliest popular vision of the other world to include a description of the heavenly city is the *Vision of Paul*. The text was supposedly discovered some time after the year 388 in the apostle's house at Tarsus, and purports to originate from Paul himself. It is now thought to have been written in the third century, and therefore dates from the first of the exegetical periods defined by Mangenot, in which the Apocalypse was interpreted as a literal account of future events.[12] The Greek archetype of the vision does not survive; the oldest extant manuscript dates from the eighth century and contains a Latin translation composed between the fourth and sixth centuries.[13]

In this text 'Paul' sees the elect in the celestial Jerusalem of the Apocalypse:

ingressus uidi ciuitatem Christi et erat tota aurea, et duodecim muri circuibant eam, et .xii. pirgi interiores (. . .). Et .xii. porte erant in circuitu ciuitatis pulcritudine magna.[14]

[once inside I saw the city of Christ. It was built entirely in gold, and was surrounded by twelve walls with twelve internal towers (. . .). And twelve doors of great beauty led into the city.]

The thrones of the elders described in the fourth chapter of the Apocalypse appear at the gates, and the elders wear golden crowns set with precious stones: 'et conuersus me uidi tronos aureos positos per singulas portas, et super eos uiros habentes diademas aureaus et gemas' (p. 24). Paul meets the psalmist, and an angel hints at the eternal function of the city:

Hic est Dauid: haec est Hierusalem ciuitas: cum autem uenerit Christus rex aeternitatis cum fiducia regni sui, ipse iterum praecedet. (p. 27)

[This is David; this is the city of Jerusalem: and when Christ comes to begin his reign over eternity, David will walk before him.]

It is to be the Land of Promise for all believers; 'when the Christ whom you preach comes to reign, then this earth will be dissolved by the command of God, and the promised land will appear (. . .), and we shall see the Lord Jesus Christ, king of eternity, and with him all the saints who will come to live in the city; and he will reign over them for a thousand years'. (p.22)

The second period: the popular representation of Paradise from the fourth to the twelfth centuries

From the fourth to the twelfth centuries, the second of the periods defined by Mangenot, the Apocalyptic account of the celestial Jerusalem is interpreted not literally, as in the *Vision of Paul*, but allegorically.[15] In his *Dialogues*, for example, Gregory the Great states that his description of the realm of the blessed is to be understood not as literal truth, as a description of events which will actually come to pass, but as an allegory, a way of speaking about eternal truth – although the description itself continues to be based on that of the heavenly Jerusalem of the Apocalypse.[16] He portrays a series of golden buildings grouped together in a garden, where another large house was being built of gold bricks: 'quaedam mira potentiae aedificabatur domus, quae aureis videbatur laterculis construi' (p. 287). Likewise Salvius, in a vision recounted by Gregory of Tours, goes into an indescribably large and brightly lit building with floors shining like silver: 'habitaculum, in quo omne pavimentum erat quasi aurum argentumque renitens, lux ineffabilis, amplitudo inenarrabilis' (p. 92). Here the blessed are found. In the seventh century, Barontus describes a Paradise located in the heavens, in which there are four successive gates, rather than the twelve of the Apocalypse; each encloses a distinct group of the elect, and the third leads to golden buildings like those described by Gregory.

During the Carolingian period the Apocalypse itself was frequently read, and became the object of several important commentaries.[17] The text provided many of the Easter readings in the monasteries, as we know from the Luxueil lectionary, the daily excerpts culminating on the Saturday following Easter with the description of the celestial Jerusalem.[18] Many illustrated manuscripts of the commentaries were produced all over Europe, influencing thought and providing models for the visual arts.[19] It is during this period too that the popular visions of the afterlife place the greatest emphasis on the celestial Jerusalem, often specifically naming it as such. Drythelm depicts Paradise as a walled enclosure in which he sees souls clad in white vestments. The Monk of Wenlock describes a glorious golden city, effulgent with light; it rises up, like the golden buildings described by Gregory the Great, on the far side of a stinking river, and is of stupendous length and immense height: 'et citra illud flumen speculatur muros fulgentes clarissimi splendoris, stupendae longitudinis et altitudinis immensae'. The angels tell him this is the heavenly Jerusalem, in which the souls of the blessed will rejoice forever: 'et sanctos angelos dixisse: "Haec est enim illa sancta et inclita civitas, caelestis Hierusalem, in qua istae perpetualiter sanctae gaudebunt animae"' (p. 255).

The most detailed description, however, is that offered by Wetti. Paradise is described as a heavenly city with walls and arches of silver and gold, containing the blessed arranged in groups, each wearing a crown, all seated around the throne of Christ:

> Hoc opus inmenso nituit splendore coruscans,
> Arcubus effulgens variisque ornatibus aureis,
> Argentique gerens multum structura metallum
> Praebuit arte oculis anaglipha pascere mentem
> Moenia, quae tantum latam longamque tenebant
> Mensuram, pulchrumque statum, mirabile factum,
> Altaque per volucres pandebant culmina ventos,
> Quantum nulla potest intentio mentis in usum
> Claudere tractandi nec quis sermone fateri,
> Aut operi tanto veracem aptare staturam
> Aut decus excellens veris disponere verbis.

(529–39)

[It shone and gleamed with dazzling brilliance, glittering with arches and other ornaments made of gold. The structure was loaded with a great quantity of silver, and presented a feast for the eyes in the contemplation of its skilfully sculptured walls. They were so broad and

Plate 16 Christ in the Heavenly Jerusalem, S. Pietro al Monte, Civate, late eleventh century

stretched so far, so beautiful to behold, so marvellously wrought, and reared so high among the fleeting winds, that no effort of the mind can encompass them within its grasp nor any tongue describe them, whether it be to tell their precise dimensions or truly set forth their magnificent beauty.] (translated by D. A. Traill)

The tenth century has left us no surviving popular representations of the celestial Jerusalem.[20] In the eleventh, the *Vision of Adamnan* describes a city surrounded by crystal walls, in which the Host of Heaven is said to dwell. Of the twelfth-century texts only one, the backward-looking *Vision of the Boy William*, represents Paradise primarily in terms of the heavenly city. In contrast with the biblical text, however, which describes the city as square in shape, William's Jerusalem is circular – which does not prevent him from insisting that three of its twelve gates face the east, three the west and so on:

in patria illa desiderabili apparuit domus rotonda, quae 12. portas habebat, sicut scriptum est: Ab oriente portae tres, &c. (p. 1126)[21]

Throughout this second period the influence of the Apocalypse and its exegesis on the popular concept of Paradise is to be found not only in the vision literature but also in the visual arts.[22]

As in the case of the vision literature, Paradise is represented as the celestial Jerusalem mostly during the second of the three periods defined by Mangenot. The convention can be traced back to the fourth century when the celestial city was commonly depicted on sarcophagi.[23] The fifth century saw the first church mosaic of Jerusalem in S. Maria Maggiore, Rome.[24] Such representations became more common in the sixth,[25] and figure prominently in the magnificent illuminations which ornament the Carolingian commentaries on the Apocalypse mentioned above.[26] Little survives from the tenth century. In the eleventh, it became the practice to decorate churches with frescoes of the celestial city such as the one illustrated in Plate 16, which shows Christ in the centre of a garden enclosed by a square wall with gates and towers. This fresco was studied by Christe in 1979 and Colli in 1982, and is thought to derive from the Ticonian commentaries and the illustrated manuscripts in which they were contained.[27] In the twelfth century Jerusalem was widely represented as the abode of the blessed in both mosaic and fresco.[28]

The third period: the popular representation of Paradise in the twelfth and thirteenth centuries

The twelfth- and thirteenth-century representations of Paradise differ from their predecessors in two main respects. Firstly, a complete change of emphasis occurs. Until the twelfth century, the visionaries concentrated on the description of Paradise at the expense of the description of Hell. Barontus gave 178 lines to the account of his journey through the gates of Paradise, and only 49 to the account of judgment and damnation. Wetti devoted 306 verses to the description of the elect, as opposed to 210 to that of the damned. Adamnan gave 220 lines to Paradise, 120 to Hell. The visions of Drythelm and the Monk of Wenlock devoted equal space to both.

In the twelfth-century texts this emphasis is reversed: the Boy William gives 35 lines to Hell, compared with 23 to Paradise; *St Patrick's Purgatory* devotes four chapters to the description of torment in Purgatory, and only one to the joys of Paradise; and the Monk of Eynsham offers an account of torment in his combined Hell–Purgatory which stretches over thirty-three chapters, confining his description of Paradise to only six. The change in emphasis is seen even more clearly in the various versions of the *Vision of Paul*, which span the entire period from the fourth to the fourteenth centuries.[29] Although it is not possible to date all the medieval versions, it does seem to be the case that those composed in the second of Mangenot's periods represent the condition of the blessed in terms derived from the Apocalypse, whereas the twelfth- and thirteenth-century redactions omit to discuss Paradise altogether in favour of an increased concentration on Hell.[30] Critics have remarked upon this, but rest without a convincing explanation.[31]

The second major change in the description of Paradise in the twelfth- and thirteenth-century visions concerns not the relative importance accorded to Heaven and Hell, but rather the iconography used for the representation of Paradise. In this period there are almost as many different models for Paradise as there are visions, in sharp contrast with the previous centuries in which the heavenly Jerusalem is almost universally adopted as a model. The most common alternative is the model of the celestial spheres (described by Alberic, Orm, Godeshalc, the Monk of Eynsham and *St Patrick's Purgatory*). But Godeschalc and Thurkill also describe Paradise in terms of a temple; William sees it as a city; Tundale, Orm, Gunthelm and the Monk of Eynsham describe a garden Paradise, generally encircled by a wall; and Alberic and *St Patrick's Purgatory* also describe the Earthly Paradise. Most texts include two or more different representations of Paradise, and no single model prevails.

In order to cast some light upon these two major changes and the reasons for them, it is necessary to look beyond the popular tradition to the world of learning on which it ultimately depends, and in particular to the changes which occurred in the twelfth century.

Firstly, the twelfth century saw a radical development in the interpretation of the Apocalypse. Although the twelfth- and thirteenth-century commentaries rely on Carolingian exegesis in the details of their interpretations, their approach is profoundly different from that of their predecessors. The Apocalypse is seen not as the record of the present suffering and eventual salvation of the entire body of believers, as in previous centuries, but as a guide to the spiritual experience of the individual mind as it is illuminated by the Holy Spirit. This new concern, expressed by Rupert of Deutz and Richard of St Victor, is carried to its extreme by Joachim, whose commentary presents itself as a personal experience in which the historical meaning of John's original vision is made clear.[32] The effects of this change on the interpretation of the heavenly Jerusalem are tentatively summarised by Morris:

The field of eschatology is a difficult one which has still not been fully examined, but here too there seems to have been a shift away from the old expectation of a new heaven and a new earth in which the perfection of the Church would be consummated. It is for instance striking that in the symbol of Jerusalem, which was so important for this period, the old meaning was often reversed. In biblical terminology, the new Jerusalem was seen coming down out of heaven from God, and the whole picture was that of the transformation of the human order by divine action. This imagery survived in the hymn *Urbs Beata Jerusalem*, but in the twelfth century the idea was primarily that of a heavenly Jerusalem which each of us must strive to enter (. . .). It is consonant with this change that believers should be urged to meditate on their own personal destiny.[33]

Jerusalem thus persists as a symbol, but loses its previous significance as a model for a future, collective Paradise.

The abandonment of the Apocalypse as the main source for the iconography of Paradise had immediate consequences in the visual arts. Representations of the Second Coming and the heavenly Jerusalem yield at this time to depictions of the Last Judgment as recorded in the Gospel of Matthew. The transition is seen most clearly on the portals of the French cathedrals, where it was first studied by E. Mâle.[34] Until the mid-twelfth century, the portals depict the end of time in imagery derived from the Apocalypse, showing Christ enthroned, holding the book of life and surrounded by the elders and the symbols of the four evangelists. The most influential of these portals was that at Moissac, carved between 1115 and 1136 (Plate 17).

Plate 17 Apocalyptic vision of Christ, South Portal, St Pierre, Moissac, Tarn-et-Garonne, *c.* 1115–36

By 1230, however, which is the *terminus ad quem* for the carving of the widely copied portal at Notre Dame,[35] the iconography of the Last Judgment is dominant. Christ is shown beside the Cross, and displays the *stigmata*; judgment is represented by the presence of Michael holding a pair of scales, while Paradise and Hell are symbolised by the old motifs of Leviathan and Abraham's bosom. This model is imitated at Ferrara (Plate 18).

During the same period, the Last Judgment becomes a common subject for the interior decoration of churches, the heavenly Jerusalem becoming increasingly rare.[36] Ariès comments:

The people of the early Middle Ages awaited the return of Christ without fear of the Last Judgment. Their conception of the end of time was inspired by the Book of Revelation, and passed silently over the dramatic scene of the Resurrection and the Last Judgment recorded in Saint Matthew (. . .). In the thirteenth century the apocalyptic inspiration disappeared (. . .). The idea of judgment was now predominant.[37]

The celestial spheres

The model most commonly taken to replace the heavenly Jerusalem was that of the celestial spheres. This model became available as a result of a second major

174

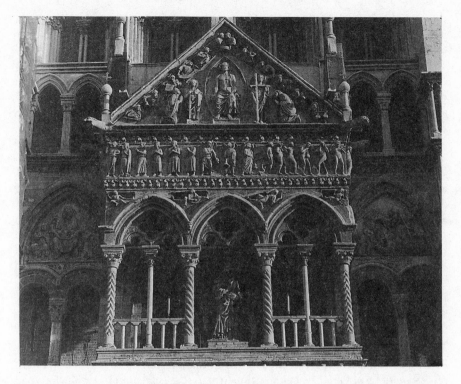

Plate 18 The Last Judgment, West Portal, Ferrara Cathedral, *c.* 1300

development which occurred during the twelfth and thirteenth centuries; it exerted an important influence on the popular representation of Paradise.

Before the adoption of the Apocalypse as the principal authority concerning Paradise, there had been a long-established tradition in both classical and Eastern thought which held that the human soul continued to live after death in the stars or heavens (a belief which is discussed by Dante in *Paradiso* IV). During the Hellenistic Age of Judaism this tradition had in turn influenced Hebrew thought, and by the first century AD, belief in a Paradise in the heavens had become firmly established.[38] It is expressed particularly in the apocrypha. *II Enoch*, written in Greek at Alexandria, describes ten heavens of which six are inhabited, mostly by angels; *3 Baruch* has two, both inhabited, and *IV Esdras* offers a confused cosmology in which Hell is both underground and in the third heaven, and Paradise is 'celestial'. The Christian apocrypha follow suit: the *Apocalypse of Zephaniah* is thought to have contained an account of an ascent through the seven heavens,[39] of which there is a version in the *Ascent of Isaiah*; the *Apocalypse of Paul* locates Paradise in the third heaven. Of these classical representations of the destiny of the soul after death, Plato's accounts (in the *Republic* and the *Phaedrus* in particular) describe an ascent through the heavens; these texts in turn influenced the descriptions of the heavens given by

Plutarch in the *Vision of Thespesius* and by Cicero in the *Somnium Scipionis*. However, in none of these are all the heavens populated by the spirits of the dead.

In the early centuries of the Christian era all these texts were rejected as pagan or uncanonical; and until the twelfth century, as we have seen, the Apocalypse was regarded as the primary eschatological authority. During the twelfth and thirteenth centuries, however, classical and Eastern thought became newly accessible through the manuscripts and translations which penetrated to Western Europe from the East through the courts of Sicily and Spain.[40] This resulted in a new affirmation of the belief that Paradise was located either in or beyond the celestial spheres.

Paradise is situated actually within the celestial spheres in a number of twelfth- and thirteenth-century popular representations of the afterlife. The most striking description occurs in the *Liber de Scalis*, written in thirteenth-century Arab Spain and translated from Arabic into both Latin and French by Bonaventura da Siena in 1264, using an earlier Castilian version.[41] It describes Mohammed's ascent through the heavens, and recapitulates the cosmological beliefs which had been represented in the apocrypha. Each heaven is superior in quality to the previous one, and each bears a different name and has different characteristics:

I saw that the various Paradises were made in different ways, and that each was better than the last. Know that the first is called 'Heden', the second 'Daralgelel', the third 'Daralzelem', the fourth 'Genet halmaulz', the fifth 'Genet halkode', the sixth 'Genet halfardauz', and the seventh 'Genet hanayam'.

The planetary heavens have not altogether disappeared from popular Western representations of Paradise, being maintained to some extent in Ireland, which had kept independent links with the East.[42] They emerge particularly in the *Vision of Adamnan*, written between the ninth and eleventh centuries, in which the characteristics of the seven heavens are described. But it is not until the twelfth century that the spheres begin to appear in the major western visions.

Chief among these is the *Vision of Alberic*, written at Montecassino at the beginning of the twelfth century (Montecassino too having been in close contact with the East).[43] Alberic describes two Paradises: the first is a garden with Eden at its centre, destined to become the abode of the just after the Day of Judgment, and the second is celestial:

I came to the first heaven, that is the heaven of air, and the apostle said to me 'in this first heaven lies the meridian star, and above it is the path of the moon (. . .). The second is called the heaven of aether, and it contains the star of Mars. The third is the sydereal, and contains the star of Mercury. The fourth is called orelon, and the sun runs its path here in three hundred and sixty-five days. The fifth is called iunion, and here is the star of Jupiter. The sixth is venustion, and here is the star of Venus. The seventh is anapecon, and the star of Saturn lies within it (. . .). That is the highest heaven, and the throne of God is there (. . .). Also in the sixth heaven are the choirs of saints, angels, archangels, patriarchs, prophets, apostles, martyrs, confessors and virgins.' (p. 99)

The relation between the two Paradises is unclear. In the following chapter we receive a hint of an eternal city resembling that in the apocalyptic tradition:

after that a dove took me on the orders of the apostle to a place surrounded by a very high wall; and when he stood me on the wall, I saw those who were inside. And I was ordered that I should tell no man.   (p. 100)

It is clear therefore that in the twelfth and thirteenth centuries the Apocalypse ceased to be regarded as the primary eschatological authority, attention being focussed instead on the account of the Last Judgment; that the heavenly Jerusalem was no longer universally accepted as the model for the place in which the blessed dwell for eternity; and that these changes were reflected in the popular representations of the other world by a shift of emphasis from Paradise to Hell and by the introduction of other models for the representation of the eternal dwelling of the elect.

THE POPULAR REPRESENTATION OF PARADISE AND THE *COMEDY*

The Earthly and celestial Paradises

The first twenty-nine cantos of the *Paradiso* describe Dante's ascent from the Earthly Paradise on the summit of the mountain of Purgatory through the celestial spheres to the Empyrean. As has been shown, there are limited precedents for the representation of the celestial spheres in texts such as the *Vision of Alberic* and the *Liber de Scalis*, but Dante's description of the heavens is related essentially to the learned tradition and not to the visions. As he ascends through the spheres, he meets the souls of the blessed who, although they properly dwell in the Empyrean, are shown to him in the various heavens:

> Qui si mostraro, non perché sortita
> sia questa spera lor, ma per far segno
> de la celestïal c'ha men salita.
>   Cosí parlar conviensi al vostro ingegno,
> però che solo da sensato apprende
> ciò che fa poscia d'intelletto degno.
>   (Par IV 37–42)

[They appeared here, not because this sphere is allotted to them, but to show which is the lowest of the celestial states. It is necessary to speak to your mind in this way, since only through the senses does it grasp that which it then makes fit for the intellect.]

There is no precedent in the popular tradition for this device.

There is, however, some precedent for the relationship between the terrestrial and celestial Paradises as presented in the *Comedy*. Most of the twelfth-century visions which mention the existence of a celestial Paradise also describe an Earthly Paradise through which the soul must first pass. The relationship between the two is described most clearly in *St Patrick's Purgatory*. Owen is taken to a walled garden · filled with bright light and sweet scent; many flowers and trees grow there. As he enters he, like Dante in the garden on the summit of Purgatory, sees a solemn procession approaching, in which clergy of all ranks and laity from all walks of life bear crosses and candles. Some wear crowns, some carry palms; some are dressed in purple, others in hyacinth, green or white. The procession comes to a halt, and two archbishops explain to Owen that this is the Earthly Paradise, to which they and the others have been admitted on the completion of their purgation, and from which they will gain access to the celestial Paradise:

Patria ista terrestris est paradisus, de qua propter inobedientiae culpam ejectus est Adam protoplastus (. . .). Omnes enim qui hic sumus ad hanc requiem per illa loca [purgatory] transivimus: et omnes quos in singulis locis poenalibus vidisti, praeter eos qui infra os putei infernalis detinentur, postquam purgati fuerint, ad istam requiem venientes salvi fient (. . .). Ecce, ut vides, a poenis liberi sumus et magna quiete perfruimur, nondum tamen ad supernam sanctorum laetitiam ascendere digni sumus, diemque et terminum nostrae promotionis in melius, nemo nostrum novit: sed post terminum singulis constitutum in majorem requiem transibimus. Quotidie societas nostra quodammodo crescit et decrescit, dum singulis diebus et ad nos a poenis et a nobis in coelestem paradisum quidam ascendunt.

(cols. 998–9)

[This land is the Earthly Paradise, from which our ancestor Adam was expelled on account of his disobedience (. . .). All of us who here enjoy this rest have come through Purgatory; and all those whom you saw in the different areas of torment – except those held within the mouth of the pit of Hell – will come to this place of rest once they have completed their purgation. Here, as you see, we are free from torment, and enjoy great peace, although we are not yet worthy to ascend to be with the saints above. None of us knows the day when we shall pass on to better things; but after that day we shall each cross to a place of even greater rest. Every day our company increases and decreases as people join us from the torments and leave us for the celestial Paradise.]

This episode offers the clearest parallel provided by the popular descriptions of the other world for Dante's representation of the Earthly Paradise, the procession and the meeting with Beatrice which occurs there, and the definition of the relation between this realm and the celestial Paradise. The description of the soul's release from purgative torment to the peace of the Earthly Paradise also provides an interesting precedent for Statius's explanation of his same experience in *Purgatorio* XXI and XXII.

The 'Comedy' and the pre-twelfth-century visions

It is not, however, in Dante's description of the Earthly Paradise, nor in his ascent through the celestial spheres, that the closest links between his poem and the previous popular representations of Paradise are to be found. These come in the closing cantos of the poem, those which describe his vision of the elect in the Empyrean; many of the details here are foreshadowed in the visions of the period which took the Apocalypse as its authority concerning Paradise. Interestingly, the anticipations are often to be found in those texts which adhere least closely to the description of the celestial Jerusalem, while yet remaining within the general tradition.

The images of the Apocalypse are strikingly transformed in the *Vision of Maximus*, in a manner which seems to point the way to the *Comedy*. Maximus, like Dante, is at first overcome by the indescribably bright light: 'nam praeclara lux inenarrabili splendiflui candoris ibidem praefulgurabat claritate' (col. 431).

The representation of Paradise

Cosí mi circunfulse luce viva,
e lasciommi fasciato di tal velo
del suo fulgor, che nulla m'appariva.

(Par xxx 49–51)

[A living light shone around me and left me wrapped in such a veil of brightness that nothing was visible to me.]

Dante sees a river of light with living sparks rising up out of it and dipping into the flowers on its banks, seeming momentarily like rubies set in gold, and returning as if intoxicated by the scent to plunge once again into the river (xxx 61–9):

Di tal fiumana uscian faville vive,
e d'ogne parte si mettien ne' fiori,
quasi rubin che oro circunscrive;
poi, come inebrïate da li odori,
riprofondavan sé nel miro gurge.

(xxx 64–8)

The river becomes circular, and appears now to Dante as a rose. The sparks are identified as angels, and continue to dip into the petals of the rose like bees visiting for nectar:

sí come schiera d'ape che s'infiora
una fïata e una si ritorna
là dove suo laboro s'insapora,
nel gran fior discendeva che s'addorna
di tante foglie.

(xxxi 7–11)

Maximus too describes a wondrous river flowing like honey between its banks: 'mirae pulchritudinis almificus decurrebat rivus' (col. 432). It is fragrant with nectar and gives off a scent of ambrose: 'nectareoque flumine aromatizans fragrabat ambroseus odor'. Neither text makes mention of the precious stones which characterise the city of the Apocalypse; but in both the richness and colour of those stones are present either in metaphor or as attributes of the many coloured flowers which grow on the banks of the river. Dante describes the angels as rubies set in gold (line 66 above), and later as 'topazi' (l. 76); the pearl and quartz, malachite and emerald of the Apocalyptic city are present in the colours of nature – the 'rider de l'erbe' (l. 77), the 'verde' (l. 111), the metaphor of milk (l. 83) and the 'bianche stole' (l. 129). Maximus describes a joyful mass of imperishable flowers growing through the green grass on the river banks: 'diversarum namque herbarum totus ille jucundissimus pagus varia immarcescibilium florum specie erat picturatus' (col. 432). He sees not amethyst but purple crocuses, not pearl but white lilies, not ruby but red roses, not diamond but silver sand. The climax of his Paradise is described with the richness of imagery and in some of the words later knitted together by Dante in his description of the heavenly rose:

rosarum rutilante rubore, liliorum praemicante candore, (. . .) cuncta praefulgebant curusco radiante decore (. . .). vernansque micabat universarum ineffabilis pulchritudo eximiis praemicantibus rutilabat ligustris, atque egregia redolens mulcebat timiama suavitatis.

(col. 432)

179

[glittering with the redness of roses and the gleaming whiteness of lilies (. . .); everything shone brightly with sparkling radiance. An indescribable beauty flourished there, a bush stood out gleaming red, and an exceeding sweetness pervaded the air.]

> Nel giallo de la *rosa* sempiterna,
> che so digrada e dilata e *redole*
> odor di lode al sol che sempre *verna*
> (. . .)
> mi trasse Bëatrice.
>
> (xxx 124-8)

[Beatrice drew me into the yellow of the eternal rose, which expands and dilates and exhales odours of praise to the Sun that makes perpetual spring . . .]

The conclusion to the description of the river comes, as for Dante, with the instruction to taste the water – 'Gusta de hac acqua', and 'di quest'acqua convien che tu bei' (xxx 73) – they, like the blessed of the Apocalypse, must drink of the water. Both authors subsequently describe their experience as beyond their power to understand or communicate: 'dum haec cuncta caeteraque inenarrabilia, quae nec os meum sufficit ad loquendum, nec cor meum cogitationibus queat comprehendere' (col. 432); 'il mio veder fu maggio/che 'l parlar mostra, ch'a tal vista cede' (xxxiii 55-6).

One other text offers a similar precedent for Dante's description of the eternal Paradise, although it differs from the *Vision of Maximus* both in its late date of composition and in its strict adherence to the description of the celestial Jerusalem. This is the poem *De Jerusalem Celesti* written by the thirteenth-century Lombard Giacomino da Verona. Giacomino, like Bonvesin da Riva, follows what has been described as a 'backward theology',[44] both in refusing to acknowledge the by then well-established doctrine of Purgatory and in continuing to adopt the symbol of the heavenly Jerusalem. His poem therefore properly belongs among the early visions rather than with those of the twelfth and thirteenth centuries. Giacomino's account of the celestial city follows the Apocalypse closely: it is a square, walled city, with three gates in each wall, lit by the visible glory of God. A river runs through it, and on the banks grow lilies, roses, grass, violets, and daisies; the waters are sweeter than honey, 'plu (. . .) dulci ke mel' (line 104). The elect contemplate the king of the universe on his throne; his face is full of a light so bright that the sun and moon seem dull in comparison, and from his mouth flows a river

> D'ambro e de moscà, e de balsamo e de menta,
> Ke tuta la cità dentro e de fora s'empla.
>
> (179-80)

[Of ambrose and musk, balsam and mint, which fills the whole city inside and out.]

Next they contemplate Christ, second person of the Trinity. Here the poet strives for harmony of sound and structure, ending consecutive stanzas with the verses

> A contemplar en celo quella faça benegna
> De l'alto Jesù Cristo ke sempro vivo e regna

The representation of Paradise

[Contemplating in the heaven that kindly face of the exalted Jesus Christ, who lives and reigns forever]

and

> Se no a contemplar la faça o lo bel viso
> De Deo omnipotente, ke sempro regna e vivo.
>
> (203–4 and 206–7)

[If not in contemplating the face or the beautiful countenance of omnipotent God, who reigns and lives forever.]

We are reminded of Dante's evocation of the Trinity:

> Quell'uno e due e tre che sempre vive
> e regna sempre in tre e 'n due e 'n uno.
>
> (Par xiv 28–9)

[That one and two and three who ever lives and reigns forever in three and in two and in one.]

From the contemplation of Christ the souls pass to the contemplation of Mary,[45] singing like the inhabitants of Dante's Purgatory 'Salve Regina!/Alma redemptoris! stella matutina!' (239–40) [Hail O queen, redeemer of our souls! morning star!]. Their song is recalled by Dante in his description of Mary, seated in the eternal rose, her beauty reflected by Gabriel as a morning star reflects the light of the sun, 'come del sole stella mattutina' (xxxii 108). Gabriel now sings 'Ave, Maria, gratia plena' (95) [Hail Mary, full of grace]; Giacomino describes the souls of the elect as full of the respect shown by Gabriel when he first greeted Mary, 'quand'el da la Deo parte ge dis: "Ave Maria!"' (236). The poem ends with a prayer to the Virgin:

> Or ne pregemo tuti la Vergene Maria,
> De enanco Jesù Cristo per nui sempro ela sia,
> K'el n'apresto là su celesta albergaria
> Quando la vita nostra quilò serà complia.
>
> (277–80)

[Now we all pray to the Virgin Mary that she will always intercede for us to Jesus Christ that he will open his heavenly home to us when our life here is finished.]

Dante's final vision is foreshadowed to some degree in three of the early texts, all of which are, like the *Vision of Maximus*, influenced but not dominated by the apocalyptic tradition. Baldarius is carried before his Creator. He gazes in amazement at Jesus on the throne of glory and asks who he is. They tell him it is Jesus.

Dum autem insolito stupore mirarem tantam ineffabilis et immensae pulchritudinis gloriam, cujus similitudinem nec possum cogitare, nec valeo enarrare, quia inaestimabilis est.

(col. 436)

[Then I stared with rare stupefaction at his so indescribable and immensely beautiful glory, for which no similitude can be conceived or described, for it is incalculable.]

Jesus orders him to be returned to the body once the sun has risen. As he watches it rise, Baldarius sees a vision of the whole world, its secrets becoming clear to him. As for Dante, such understanding is but momentary, and he is immediately returned to the body.

The second precedent for Dante's final vision occurs in the *Life of Anskar*. In his second vision Anskar is taken to Paradise, where he sees twenty-four seniors as described in the Apocalypse, 'secundum quod in Apocalipsi scriptum est' (p. 24), in adoration of the ineffably bright light which is Christ; we are told that a rainbow surrounds him – 'circa sedentes vero splendor ab ipso procedens, similis arcui nubium tendebatur'. Anskar is told that one day he will return; meanwhile, like Dante, he departs, declaring, with some reminiscence perhaps of Paul's account of his vision of the third heaven in 2 Corinthians 12.1–4:

Et licet aliqua visus sim de tanta dulcedine dulcedinum enarrasse, fateor tamen, quia nequaquam stilus tanta exprimere potuit, quanta animus sentit. Sed nec ipse animus sentit ut fuit, quia illud mihi esse videbatur, quod oculus non vidit, nec auris audivit, nec in cor hominis ascendit. (p. 26)

[And although I seem to have told of such sweetness of sweetnesses, I confess that no pen could express all that my soul felt. But my soul itself did not feel it as it was, for I was shown that which the eye has never seen, nor the ear heard, nor the human heart experienced.]

Finally, in the Irish *Vision of Adamnan* the rainbow recurs: 'over the head of the Glorious One that sitteth upon the royal throne is a great arch (. . .), and the eye which should behold it would forthwith melt away. Three circles are round about it, separating it from the host, and by no explanation may the nature of them be known' (p. 32). God himself is not discernible to the eye, being hidden, as initially to Dante, by the intensity of his own light: 'no human form thereto, with head or foot, may be discerned, but a fiery mass, burning on for ever' (p. 33). Dante, like John (Apocalypse 4.2–3) but in contrast to Adamnan, is able at the climax of his vision to penetrate this light:

> Ne la profonda e chiara sussistenza
> de l'alto lume parvermi tre giri
> di tre colori e d'una contenenza;
> e l'un da l'altro come iri da iri
> parea reflesso, e 'l terzo parea foco
> che quinci e quindi igualmente si spiri.
> (. . .)
> Quella circulazion che sí concetta
> pareva in te come lume reflesso,
> da li occhi miei alquanto circunspetta,
> dentro da sé, del suo colore stesso,
> mi parve pinta de la nostra effige:
> per che 'l mio viso in lei tutto era messo.
> (Par XXXIII 115–20 & 127–32)

[In the deep and clear subsistence of the sublime light appeared to me three circles of three colours and equal circumference, and the first seemed reflected by the second like one rainbow by another, and the third seemed like fire breathed equally from both (. . .). The circle which, described in this way, appeared in you as reflected light, seemed to me, when my eyes dwelt on it for a time, to be painted with our human image within it and in its own colour, and so my sight was wholly given to it.]

The 'Comedy' and the twelfth-century visions

However, it is not only the early texts which offer points of comparison with the *Comedy*. A number of the twelfth-century visions foreshadow Dante's description of the eternal Paradise in different ways.

The *Vision of Gunthelm* describes a double Paradise. Before being admitted to Paradise proper Gunthelm is shown a 'place of great greenness and beauty' (p. 107) containing a chapel in which Mary, dressed in a golden robe, is seated with the elect like a sun amongst stars; 'tanquam regina in uestitu deaurato inter illos uelut sol inter sydera resplendebat'. He is then taken to a walled Paradise described in the traditional way:

vidit quasi ciuitatis deauratos muros, ualde rutilantes et splendidos, et portam quandam inenarrabili pulchritudine decoram, et artificio mirabili compositam, et per totum lapidibus preciosis et gemmis ornatam. (p. 108)

[he saw what seemed to be the golden walls of a city, shining greatly and gleaming, and a door of indescribable beauty, made with wondrous craftsmanship, and studded all over with precious stones and jewels.]

Inside the walls, however, we find not a city but a garden, a paradise with many species of plant and types of tree, where birds sing amongst the many coloured flowers and abundant fruits, and which is filled with a sweet scent:

ostendit ei amenitatem paradysi: herbarum uarietatem, arborum diuersitatem, auium concentus, et uarium florum colorem, fructuum abundantiam, specierum redolentiam, et liquorum omnium uiuificae suauitatis affluentiam. (p. 108–9)

This is the first time in the popular tradition that the vision of Paradise itself has been preceded by a preparatory vision of Mary surrounded by the elect. Gunthelm's experience foreshadows that of Dante, who sees Mary and the elect in the Heaven of the Fixed Stars (Par xxiii), where he describes them, as did Gunthelm in his second vision, in terms of a 'bel giardino' and as 'turbe di splendori', where Mary is a rose among lilies, a 'coronata fiamma'. Dante sees Mary and the elect for the second time in the 'candida rosa', at which point he receives his vision of Christ.

The second major popular text to offer points of comparison with the *Comedy* is that of Tundale. It adopts certain elements from the Jerusalem tradition and others from the literary tradition of the Earthly Paradise. After undergoing purgation, the soul is admitted into a walled garden containing golden buildings and a fountain of life. Within this are a number of further concentric walls enclosing different categories of the elect – the closest precedent in this group of visions to Dante's depiction of the blessed in consecutive heavenly spheres.[46] A silver wall encloses the chaste, a gold wall encircles members of religious orders and martyrs, who sit on golden thrones and are dressed in white and wear crowns. Gold lecterns supporting books stand beside them. Here too is a tree beneath which sit those who established, built up and defended the Church (this is the category of souls seen by Dante in the Heaven of Mars). The tree symbolises the Church; 'hec arbor typus est sancte ecclesie' (p. 51), thus foreshadowing the complex allegorical drama re-enacting the history of the Church witnessed by Dante in the Earthly Paradise, in which Church and State are represented by a chariot tied to a tree.

Finally, a wall of precious stones marks the domain of saints, among whom are four Irish bishops. Tundale sees an empty seat, which on enquiry he is told is reserved for a fifth bishop not yet dead:

Beside them stood another wondrously ornate throne, empty. Tundale asked 'whose is this seat, and why is it empty?' Malachias answered him, saying 'this seat is for one of our brothers, who has not left the body; when he does, he will sit here.' (p. 54)

Dante also sees an empty seat, in the eternal rose, which Beatrice explains is reserved for the emperor Henry VII, 'l'alto Arrigo':

> 'E 'n quel gran seggio a che tu li occhi tieni
> (. . .)
> sederà l'alma, che fia giú agosta,
> de l'alto Arrigo, ch'a drizzare Italia
> verrà in prima ch'ella sia disposta.'
>
> (Par xxx 133–8)

['And in that great seat on which you cast your gaze will sit the soul, which shall be emperor below, of the great Henry, who will come to set Italy straight before she is ready.']

Tundale also numbers the nine angelic orders in his Paradise, as does Dante in *Paradiso* XXVIII.

Tundale's representation of the elect within concentric circles, and Dante's description of them within concentric heavens, is not dissimilar to that adopted by the sculptors of the Gothic Last Judgment portals. At Paris (Plate 19) the blessed are contained within the concentric rows of the archivolts surrounding the portal. Closest to the centre, as in Tundale's Paradise, are two rows of angels; next comes a band of patriarchs, followed by one of prophets each seated on a throne and holding a book; the outer two rows are filled by ecclesiastics and finally by virgins.

The *Vision of the Monk of Eynsham* is perhaps the most original in its description of Paradise. The heavenly realm is divided into three areas, souls becoming progressively whiter as they pass from one stage of beatitude to another. In the first stage, the blessed rejoice in a flowery field before a vision of Christ on the Cross; this is the closest any of the popular texts comes to foreshadowing Dante's vision of Christ on the Cross in the Heaven of Mars (Par XIV 94–117). The second Paradise is a garden enclosed by a crystal wall in which steps are cut; from the summit of this wall, where the enthroned Christ is adored, the ascent may be made to a third area, the 'heaven of heavens where the just rejoice in the presence of God' (p. 315); this we are not shown. This vision is the only text to describe the eternal realm in three parts, thus foreshadowing Dante's representation of salvation in firstly the Earthly Paradise, secondly the celestial spheres, and thirdly the

Plate 19 Left archivolt, Last Judgment Portal, Notre Dame, Paris, 1220–30, showing the blessed in Paradise; angels (innermost), patriarchs and prophets, ecclesiastics, martyrs, virgins

Empyrean, in which the blessed enjoy the vision of the Trinity – except that the monk, unlike Dante, is not permitted to participate in the final vision.

The monk's two visions recapitulate the two phases identified by E. Mâle on the portals of the French cathedrals. He sees both Christ the King, enthroned as in the tradition of the Apocalypse, and Christ the Son of man, represented with the Cross as in the Last Judgment portals. Paradise is no longer conceived of as a golden city, but as firstly an Earthly Paradise with the characteristics of both Jerusalem and Eden, leading secondly to a celestial Paradise which no one is yet permitted to enter.

The evidence of the visual arts

It is not only in the visions but also in the visual arts that precedents can be found for Dante's representation of the blessed in eternity. The majority of the surviving visual representations of the blessed date from the thirteenth century, thus providing a continuous witness to the popular beliefs of a century from which there are few extant written representations of the other world.

Dante's final vision of Christ is foreshadowed to some degree, as we have seen, in the visions of Anskar, Adamnan and the Monk of Eynsham, who see a fiery mass of bright light surrounded, for Anskar, by a rainbow, and for Adamnan by three circles of colour. These characteristics are repeated in the paintings of the late thirteenth and early fourteenth centuries. Cavallini's fresco of the Last Judgment in the church of S. Cecilia in Trastevere (1289–93) shows Christ seated on a golden throne encrusted with gems, encircled by a glowing triple circle of gold, red and gold, 'tre giri/di tre colori' (Par XXXIII 116–17). A few years later in the Scrovegni Chapel (fresco finished 1305) Giotto depicts Christ seated within a mandorla of indigo, white, and the orange-red of leaping flames; 'e 'l terzo parea foco/che quinci e quindi igualmente si spiri' (XXXIII 119–20). The outer circle of this mandorla does indeed become a river of fire which flows down to engulf the damned. The mandorla is filled with golden light, the 'luce etterna' (l. 124), and in it Christ is 'painted' – 'pinta de la nostra effige' (l. 131). These descriptions are ultimately related to those of the Apocalypse: 'a throne stood in heaven, and one sat there enthroned. He who sat there bore the semblance of a jewel, jasper or sardius, and there was a rainbow about the throne, like a vision of emerald' (4.2–3).

Tundale records the presence of the angelic hierarchies in Paradise, numbering them idiosyncratically as follows:

and they saw the nine orders of blessed spirits, that is angels, archangels, virtues, principalities, powers, dominions, thrones, cherubim and seraphim.   (p. 52)

They are commonly depicted in frescoes of the Last Judgment; in the Scrovegni Chapel an angel of each order stands beside the mandorla of Christ. Their presence is most striking, however, in the mosaics of the Florentine baptistry (late thirteenth century), where they are arranged in the order defined by Dionysius and adopted by Dante in the *Paradiso*.[47] The first triad is as follows:

The representation of Paradise

> 'I cerchi primi
> t'hanno mostrato Serafi e Cherubi.
> (. . .)
> Quelli altri amori che 'ntorno li vonno,
> si chiaman Troni del divino aspetto,
> per che 'l primo ternaro terminonno.

['The first circles have shown you Seraphim and Cherubim. Those other loves which move around them are called Thrones of the divine aspect, and with them the first triad is completed'.]

The second and third:

> In essa gerarcia son l'altre dee:
> prima Dominazioni, e poi Virtudi;
> l'ordine terzo di Podestadi èe.
> Poscia ne' due penultimi tripudi
> Principati e Arcangeli si girano;
> l'ultimo è tutto d'Angelici ludi'.
> (Par xxviii 98–126)

[In this hierarchy are the other divine orders – first Dominions, then Virtues, and the third are Powers. Then in the two penultimate rejoicings wheel Principalities and Archangels, and the last dance is of Angels.]

In Florence the angels are depicted in the highest and most central circle of the golden mosaic. They are labelled alternately from right to left in the Dionysian order adopted in the *Paradiso*, and each order is distinguished from the others in appearance (see Plate 20).

In one respect, the visual representations of Paradise offer a closer precedent than the written texts for Dante's description of the blessed in the eternal rose. Dante describes the elect seated in rows as in an amphitheatre divided into two semicircles; on one side sit those who believed in the Messiah to come, and facing them are seated those who believed in Christ once he had come. Some of them he names:

> E come quinci il glorïoso scanno
> de la donna del cielo e li altri scanni
> di sotto lui cotanta cerna fanno,
> così di contra qual del gran Giovanni,
> che sempre santo 'l diserto e 'l martiro
> sofferse, e poi l'inferno da due anni;
> e sotto lui così cerner sortiro
> Francesco, Benedetto e Augustino
> e altri fin qua giú di giro in giro.
> (xxxii 28–36)

[And just as on this side the glorious seat of the lady of heaven and the other seats below it form the dividing line, so, opposite, does that of the great John, who, ever holy, suffered desert and martyrdom and then Hell for two years; and below him Francis, Benedict, Augustine and others have been allotted seats continuing the division from row to row right down to here.]

He includes Old Testament figures – Adam, Eve, Moses, Ruth, Judith, Sarah, Rachel; New Testament figures – Mary, John, Peter, Anne, John the Baptist; and more recent saints – Lucy, Benedict, Augustine, Francis. With these are assumed to be all the contemporary and historical characters met in the ascent through the celestial spheres, all seated in rows, each in his or her appointed place.

Dante is not alone in dividing the elect into rows in this way, although he is the first to use the imagery of an amphitheatre to describe the scene: all the previous visual representations of the Last Judgment, and most of the successive ones, depict the elect similarly seated in one or more rows; the earlier representations show only the twelve apostles, the later ones row upon row of figures from all periods of history. Often they are shown sitting on thrones as described in Apocalypse 4.4.

In the earlier representations, those which are most dependent on the Byzantine tradition, the rows are clearly defined; examples are the fresco at S. Angelo in Formis and the mosaic at Torcello, which show the twelve apostles seated on thrones with, at Torcello, rows of angels behind them. The Florentine baptistry and Cavallini's fresco in Rome also show the apostles seated on thrones, with John the Baptist and Mary standing (Cavallini) or sitting (Florence) beside them. Angels are seated behind the apostles in Florence. Giotto's Last Judgment in Padua is the least structured in this way of all the Last Judgment frescoes, but introduces more rows, this time with angels, apostles and the blessed flying, sitting and standing respectively, row upon row, in adoration of Christ. The apostles occupy, as in Cavallini's fresco, a special place; they sit on thrones to either side of the central mandorla.

As in Dante's amphitheatre, individual saints are often identifiable in these works. Giotto shows Mary, Gabriel, Anne, Elizabeth, Abraham, Isaac and Jacob beneath the throne of Christ; above is a company of the elect, crowded together in eight rows. Bellinati identifies Francis and Benedict, Dominic and Romuald, along with martyrs, confessors, virgins, early bishops and saints.[48] In the Last Judgment of S. Maria Donnaregina in Naples (first half of the fourteenth century), the company of the elect includes seven horizontal rows of figures identifiable by names and attributes, moving towards the gate of the celestial Jerusalem at which stand Christ and Mary with Abraham, Isaac and Jacob. They include rulers – Louis of France, Charles II and Mary of Hungary; saints – Silvester, Nicholas, Martin, Gennarus, Agrippinus, Severus, Agnellus, Anthony, Lucy and Bernard; founders of orders – Dominic, Francis and Benedict; and others such as Jerome and Ludovic bishop of Toulouse.[49] The arrangement of the seats in Dante's rose is paralleled most closely by an altarpiece now in the Pinacoteca at Bologna, but which almost certainly postdates the *Comedy* (Plate 20), in which the blessed are arranged as if in a theatre, divided into two lower and two upper companies, the lower ones seated on thrones, the upper ones standing, facing from the left or from the right towards a central area in which God, Christ and Mary are represented (above), with St Michael and his scales (below). The greatest number of rows of the blessed is shown by Nardo di Cione in his fresco of Paradise in S. Maria Novella, Florence (1357); his Last Judgment cycle is interesting in that it is based partly on the traditional iconography and partly on the *Comedy* itself.

The representation of Paradise

Plate 20 Last Judgment altarpiece, Bolognese school, fourteenth–fifteenth centuries,
showing the blessed in Paradise and the damned in Hell

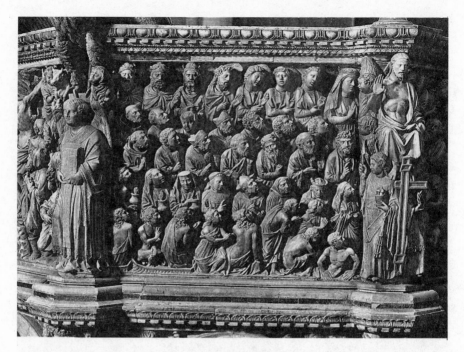

Plate 21 The elect in Paradise, panel from a pulpit by Nicola Pisano for Siena Cathedral, 1263–8

The practice of depicting the blessed standing or seated in rows is not restricted to representations of the Last Judgment; works from other traditions depict the blessed in the same way. The panel of Nicola Pisano's pulpit in Siena (1263–8) which shows the elect arranges them in five horizontal rows, all facing towards the enthroned Christ, who is depicted as in the Last Judgment portals, and as seen by the Monk of Eynsham, with the Cross and the instruments of the Passion (Plate 21). Duccio's *Maestà* (1308–11) shows the same arrangement around the enthroned Virgin and Child. Above them are the twelve apostles; to either side stand three rows of saints and angels. Carli identifies the saints as Ansanus, Savinus, Crescentius, Victor, Catherine, Paul, John the Evangelist, John the Baptist, Peter and Agnese.[50] Simone Martini (1315) and Lippo Memmi (*c.* 1318) show a similar crowd of saints.[51] And in the fresco of St Francis in glory in the lower basilica of Assisi by Giotto or his workshop (13th–14th century), the same iconography is observed.[52]

Of all the visual representations of Christ and the elect, however, there is one in particular which enables the onlooker to capture most closely the sensation described by Dante (Par XXXII–XXXIII) as he looks up from the middle of the golden rose of the elect, watching it spin gently around him, only to have that vision superseded by one of Christ himself. The ceiling of the Florentine baptistry (Plate 22) is covered by a vast golden mosaic, which can be fully observed by the

Plate 22 Ceiling mosaic, Florence Baptistry, thirteenth century, showing the nine angelic orders (central band), scenes from the Old and New Testaments (four outer bands), and Christ (lower centre) with angels and apostles (upper two registers) and scenes from Hell and Paradise (bottom register left and right)

beholder only as he stands in the centre of the building and looks upwards and rotates his gaze: figures from the Old and New Testaments meet his eyes, their stories represented in horizontal rows of narrative scenes; the angelic orders are there in the centre, the apostles are there, seated on thrones; and the whole is divided like the rose into a hierarchy of circular rows, decreasing in circumference as they near the centre. And then his eyes turn to the largest figure of all: Christ seated within a mandorla in human form, one hand stretched out to each side:

> Quella circulazion che sí concetta
> pareva in te come lume reflesso,
> da li occhi miei alquanto circunspetta,
> dentro da sé, del suo colore stesso,
> mi parve pinta de la nostra effige:
> per che 'l mio viso in lei tutto era messo.
>
> (Par XXXIII 127–32)

[The circle which, described in this way, appeared in you as reflected light, seemed to me, when my eyes dwelt on it for a time, to be painted with our human image within it and in its own colour, and so my sight was wholly given to it.]

At this point Dante's vision, like that of many others before him, comes to an end.

Notes

1 For the origin of the word and development of the concept see the relevant articles in *The Interpreter's Dictionary of the Bible*, edited by J. A. Buttrick and the *Dictionary of the Bible*, edited by J. Hastings.

2 The literary tradition of the Earthly Paradise has been analysed by A. B. Giammatti, *The Earthly Paradise and the Renaissance Epic*, 1966, and J. E. Duncan, *Milton's Earthly Paradise: A Historical Study of Eden*, 1972.

3 F. Cumont, *After Life in Roman Paganism*, deals with the entire history of the concept of celestial immortality. For the impact of Greek thought on Hebrew belief see N. De Lange, *Apocrypha: Jewish Literature of the Hellenistic Age*, 1978.

4 See W. Wetherbee, *Platonism and Poetry in the Twelfth Century: The Literary Influence of the School of Chartres*, 1972.

5 P. Rajna, 'La genesi della *Divina Commedia*', 1892, p. 175. The popular Paradise has been compared to Dante's *Paradiso* by Di Costanzo, 'Di un antico testo a penna della "Divina Commedia"', 1800, pp. 178–80, and by De Romanis, 'La Visione del Monaco Alberico riscontrata coi luoghi di Dante che le si avvicinano', 1822, chs. 22–45.

6 The Elysian Fields are described by Homer (*Odyssey* IV 561–8), and Virgil (*Aeneid* VI 628–901); the Isles of the Blessed by Hesiod (*Works and Days*, 167–9), Pindar (*Olympian* II), Horace (*Epode* XVI) and Plutarch (*Life of Sertorius* VIII–IX 571–2). See F. Cumont, *After Life in Roman Paganism*, and W. F. Jackson Knight, *Elysion*, 1970.

7 The garden in the East is treated most fully by Zosimus, Perpetua and Saturus, following the old version of Genesis 2.8 which translated 'ab oriente' instead of 'a principio'. See B. Nardi 'Intorno al sito del Purgatorio e al mito dantesco dell'Eden', 1930, pp. 356–7.

8 G. Ricciotti, *L'Apocalisse di Paolo siriaca*, 1932; L. Rosso Ubigli, 'Dalla "Nuova Gerusalemme" alla "Gerusalemme celeste"', 1981; E. Lamirande, 'Jérusalem céleste', 1974.

9 Notably those by Y. Christe, *L'Apocalypse de Jean: traditions exégétiques et iconographiques, III–XIIIe siècles*, 1979; and M. L. Gatti Perer, *La Gerusalemme celeste*, 1983.

10 I, cols. 1463–74; bibliographical references are given for the major commentaries. An updated bibliography is given by Mazzucco, in 'La Gerusalemme celeste dell'Apocalisse nei Padri', 1983.

11 It is striking that these periods correspond closely to the three chronological divisions in the popular representation of Paradise: until the fourth century the celestial city plays no part in descriptions of the realm of the blessed; from the fourth to the twelfth centuries, the period in which the allegorical tradition of the Ticonian commentaries is dominant, Jerusalem is the most common image for Paradise; after the change brought about by the spiritual commentaries of the twelfth century and finally by the prophetic interpretation of Joachim in the thirteenth, it disappears almost entirely from the vision literature.

12 The interpretation of the Apocalypse before the fourth century – the first of Mangenot's three periods – has been studied by Mazzucco in 'La Gerusalemme celeste'. Until that time, the authenticity of the work was under question; the majority of those who accepted it regarded it as an indivisible whole, interpreting it as a literal account of future events. These writers, principal among whom were Lactantius, Victorinus, Tertullian and Commodian, are known as the millenarists. Their interpretation was, however, overshadowed by that proposed in about 385 by Ticonius. His commentary, now lost, declared that the text should be interpreted symbolically, insisting that 'nihil est quod historicum sonat' (quoted by Y. Christe, *L'Apocalypse de Jean*, p. 130). The Apocalypse came to be regarded as an allegory of the sufferings and joys of the Church, coupled with a promise of eternal salvation. That salvation was represented in the account of the celestial Jerusalem.

13 The authoritative study on the *Vision of Paul* is that by T. Silverstein, *'Visio Sancti Pauli': The History of the Apocalypse in Latin*, 1935; see especially p. 61.

14 Paris manuscript, edited by M. R. James, p. 24. The quotation includes the editor's amendments; the text has been reproduced as given by the editor both here and in subsequent quotations.

15 There are no extant commentaries from the fifth century, although it is in this period that Cassian, in expounding the fourfold interpretation of Scripture, used Jerusalem as an example, thereby ensuring that the celestial city gained wide recognition as a symbol of eternal beatitude. See A. Colli, 'La tradizione figurativa della Gerusalemme celeste: linee di sviluppo dal sec. III al sec. XIV', 1983, p. 120; also H. de Lubac, *L'Exégèse médiévale*, II, ch. 10, 'Anagogie et eschatologie', 1959, pp. 621–81. The sixth century saw a renewed interest in the production of commentaries; the major ones are those of Primasius, Apringuis, Caesarius of Arles and Cassiodorus, all of which are based upon the exegesis of Ticonius. These are discussed by Christe, *L'Apocalypse de Jean*, pp. 112–13.

16 *Dialogues*, p. 289 *et passim*. The passage is discussed by C. Zaleski, *Otherworld Journeys*, 1987, p. 89.

17 The apocalyptic exegesis of the Carolingian era, in which the most influential allegorical commentaries were composed, is the subject of specific studies by Gousset and by Heitz, who identify as the main works those by Ambrose Autpertus, Beatus of Liebana, Alcuin, Haymon and Remi d'Auxerre; these together form the backbone of later works. They place great emphasis on the celestial Jerusalem as the eternal dwelling of the collectivity of the Church, but also as an allegory of the community of monks in their daily life of worship on earth (see A. Colli, 'La tradizione figurativa', p. 121). M-T. Gousset, 'La Représentation de la Jérusalem céleste à l'époque carolingienne', 1974; C. Heitz, 'Retentissement de l'Apocalypse dans l'art de l'époque carolingienne', 1979.

18 Heitz, pp. 220–1.

19 Accounts of the manuscript cycles are given by Gatti Perer, *La Gerusalemme celeste*, pp. 149–76; A. Colli, 'La Gerusalemme celeste nei cicli apocalittici altomedievali e l'affresco di san Pietro al Monte di Civate', 1982; and P. K. Klein, 'Les cycles de l'Apocalypse du Haut Moyen Age (IXe–XIIIe siècles)', 1979. Illustrations are given by Gatti Perer.

20 Nor are there any surviving commentaries on the Apocalypse.

21 There is evidence to suggest that the redactor had in mind not the Apocalypse itself but the commentaries: in contrast with the biblical text, which describes the city as square in shape, William's Jerusalem is circular, in defiance of the quoted stipulation that three gates face in each direction. The obvious precedent for this departure from scripture is to be found in two of the manuscript cycles of the commentaries, as defined by Klein 'Les Cycles de L'Apocalypse'. The first

comprises the Carolingian Valenciennes, Paris and Bamberg manuscripts, the second the twelfth-century illustrations of the *Liber Floridus* (see plates in Gatti Perer, *La Gerusalemme celeste*, pp. 156–60); both depict Jerusalem as a circular city with concentric walls. Gatti Perer, *La Gerusalemme celeste*, p. 157, suggests that this practice derives from a ninth-century guide to the historical Jerusalem which included a circular plan of the Holy Sepulchre. See also Heitz, 'Retentissement de l'Apocalypse', p. 228.

22 Christe's call for increased study in this fascinating area (*L'Apocalypse de Jean*, p. 115) has been answered in part by the catalogue edited with a number of essays by Gatti Perer in 1983 (*La Gerusalemme celeste*), which aims to provide an exhaustive account of the extant representations of the celestial Jerusalem.

23 Gatti Perer, *La Gerusalemme celeste*, pp. 201–11.

24 *Ibid.*, p. 185.

25 Examples survive at Ravenna in S. Vitale and S. Apollinare in Classe, and in Rome at SS. Cosma e Damiano and S Lorenzo fuori le mura; see Gatti Perer, *La Gerusalemme celeste*, pp. 186–7.

26 Of the four cycles defined by Klein, three are Carolingian: the Beatus cycle (Gatti Perer, *La Gerusalemme celeste*, pp. 149–55); the Valenciennes, Paris and Bamberg cycle (pp. 156–8); and the Treviri and Cambrai cycle (pp. 161–4). See Colli, 'La Gerusalemme celeste', p. 110.

27 Y. Christe, 'Traditions littéraires et iconographiques dans l'interprétation des images apocalyptiques', pp. 109–34, especially p. 119; Colli, 'La Gerusalemme celeste', p. 122.

28 Examples of mosaics are those in S. Maria in Trastevere and S. Clemente, Rome; see Gatti Perer, *La Gerusalemme celeste*, pp. 191–2. Examples of frescoes are those in St Gabriel's Chapel, Canterbury Cathedral; St Botolph, Hardham, Sussex; and St John the Baptist, Clayton, Sussex; see Gatti Perer, pp. 221, 248. For dates see Appendix 1.

29 The vision survives in two forms: accounts which represent the original text, and later medieval redactions. The relationship between the various manuscripts has been meticulously and thoroughly analysed by T. Silverstein, in his '*Visio Sancti Pauli*', and 'The Vision of St Paul: New Links and Patterns in the Western Tradition', 1959. Stemmae of the MSS are given on pp. 61 and 225 respectively. See also chapter 1, note 28.

30 Only four of the extant versions of the vision contain a description of the eternal city; these are the three manuscripts which transmit the archetype text, and the only redaction known to date from before the eleventh or twelfth centuries, surviving in a ninth-century manuscript. The account of the city in each case is similar to that quoted earlier. The three MSS transmitting versions of the archetype date from the fourth, ninth and at latest mid-twelfth centuries. For Redaction VI see Silverstein, '*Visio Sancti Pauli*', p. 58. There are ten further redactions, all extant in manuscripts dating from the twelfth century or later; these are united in completely omitting the description of Paradise in favour of concentration on Hell. Silverstein suggests dates for these redactions on pp. 6–10 and in 'The Vision of St Paul'.

31 Silverstein suggests that the change is due to a later preference for the graphic: 'The Latin Redactions (. . .) exhibit a strong preoccupation with the horrors of Hell-torment to the virtual exclusion of the less impressive joys of Paradise' ('*Visio Sancti Pauli*', p. 30). D. D. R. Owen is more speculative: 'Did they do it out of sheer masochism? (. . .) Or were they persuaded that their only hope of bringing their contemporaries to hell was by terrorising them through this grisly form of spiritual shock treatment?' (*The Vision of Hell*, 1970, p. 7).

32 The twelfth- and thirteenth-century commentaries are discussed by P. C. Spicq, *Esquisse d'une histoire de l'exégèse latine au Moyen Age*, 1944, and by B. Nolan, *The Gothic Visionary Perspective*, 1977. For Joachim see also Mangenot, 'Apocalypse', col. 1473–4; W. Kamlah, *Apokalypse und Geschichts-theologie: die mittelalterliche Auslegung der Apokalypse vor Joachim von Fiore*, 1935; and M. Reeves, *The Influence of Prophecy in the Later Middle Ages: A Study in Joachimism*, Oxford, 1969.

33 C. Morris, 'Individualism in Twelfth-Century Religion: Further Reflections', 1980, pp. 203–4.

34 *The Gothic Image: Religious Art in France of the Thirteenth Century*, translated 1968 from original edition of 1913; and *Religious Art in France: The Twelfth Century*, translated 1978 from original

edition of 1922. Mâle's studies have been updated by W. Sauerländer, *Gothic Sculpture in France 1140–1270*, translated 1972 from original edition of 1970; and by L. Réau, *Iconographie de l'art chrétien*, 3 vols., 1955–9.

35 Sauerländer, *Gothic Sculpture*, Plates 145–50 and pp. 450–3; Mâle, *The Gothic Image*, p. 366.

36 See Appendix 1 for examples.

37 *The Hour of Our Death*, translated 1983, pp. 97–101. See also, by the same author, *Western Attitudes toward Death*, 1974, pp. 29–33.

38 For authorities see note 3.

39 M. R. James, *The Lost Apocrypha of the Old Testament, their Titles and Fragments*, 1920, p. 72.

40 See C. H. Haskins, *The Renaissance of the Twelfth Century*, 1927, especially chapters 2, 'Intellectual centres', and 9, 'The translators from Greek and Arabic'; G. Leff, *Medieval Thought*, 1958, chapter 5, 'The renewal of letters and speculative thought in the eleventh and twelfth centuries'; and C. Morris, *The Discovery of the Individual*, chapter 3, 'New learning in a new society'.

41 Whether or not Dante knew the *Liber de Scalis* has been the subject of much debate. The principal studies are those by M. Palacios Asin, *Islam and the 'Divine Comedy'*, translated in 1926 from the original edition of 1919; E. Cerulli, *Il 'Libro della Scala' e la questione delle fonti arabo-spagnole della 'Divina Commedia'*, 1949; and T. Silverstein, 'Dante and the Legend of the Miraj: The Problem of Islamic Influence on the Christian Literature of the Other World', 1952.

42 *Ibid.*, pp. 96–100; also M. R. James, 'Irish Apocrypha' 1919; St J. D. Seymour, 'The Seven Heavens in Irish Literature', 1923; J. Stevenson, 'Ascent through the Heavens, from Egypt to Ireland', 1983; D. V. Dumville, 'Towards an Interpretation of Fís Adamnan', 1977–8.

43 See H. Bloch, 'Montecassino, Byzantium and the West in the Earlier Middle Ages', 1946; see also the discussion of Montecassino and S. Angelo in Formis in O. Demus, *Romanesque Mural Painting*, 1970, pp. 80–3.

44 L Russo, 'La letteratura religiosa del Duecento', p. 111.

45 Noted in connection with the *Comedy* by Zingarelli, *Dante*, pp. 469–70.

46 Carozzi suggests that Tundale's three walls allude to the three heavens mentioned by Paul in 1 Corinthians 3.10–12, and notes that in addition the vision devotes seven chapters to the description of Paradise: 'Structure et fonction de la vision de Tnugdal', 1981, p. 225.

47 Par xxviii 130–4. In the *Convivio* Dante had followed the order suggested by Gregory in the *Moralia*, xxxii, 48.

48 'La Cappella degli Scrovegni', 1975, pp. 265–6.

49 Figures identified by E. Bertaux, *Santa Maria di Donna Regina e l'arte senese a Napoli nel sec. XIV*, 1899, pp. 41–4; E. Carelli and S. Casiello, *S. Maria Donnaregina in Napoli*, 1975, pp. 38–9.

50 E. Carli, *Duccio a Siena*, 1983, p. 25.

51 Simone's *Maestà* is illustrated in many art histories; see for example G. C. Argan, *Storia dell'arte italiana*, iii, p. 24; and for Lippo R. Donati, *San Gimignano*, p. 22.

52 Reproduced in L. Bellosi, *Giotto*, p. 63.

APPENDIX 1

Chronological table of principal representations of the other world

PRINCIPAL WRITTEN REPRESENTATIONS

CENTURY

Classical texts

9 BC	Homer	*Odyssey*
8 BC	Hesiod	*Works and Days*
5 BC	Pindar	*Odes*
4 BC	Plato	*Gorgias*
		Phaedo
		The Republic (vision of Er)
		Phaedrus
1 BC	Lucretius	*De Rerum Natura*
	Cicero	*Somnium Scipionis*
		Tusculan Disputations
	Virgil	*Aeneid*
	Ovid	*Metamorphoses*
AD 1	Lucan	*Pharsalia*
	Statius	*Thebaid*
AD 1–2	Plutarch	*Moralia*
		– vision of Thespesius
		– vision of Timarchus

Old Testament apocrypha and pseudepigrapha

2 BC	*I Enoch*
BC	*Revelation of Moses*
AD 1	*II Enoch/Book of the Secrets of Enoch*
	II Baruch
	IV Esdras
AD 1–2	*Testament of Abraham*
AD 2	*III Baruch/Apocalypse of Baruch*
AD 3	*Apocalypse of Elijah*
AD 1–4	*Ascension of Isaiah*

Appendix

New Testament apocrypha and pseudepigrapha

1–2	*Apocalypse of Peter*
	Apocalypse of Zephaniah
	Acts of Thomas
2–3	*Sibylline Oracles*
	Shepherd of Hermas
3	*Apocalypse of Paul*
	Narrative of Zosimus
4–5	*Apocalypse of Thomas*
5	*Gospel of Nicodemus*
By 8	Seven Heavens apocryphon
8–9	Reichenau apocryphon
9	*Apocalypse of the Virgin*

Early Christian period

3	*Passio Perpetuae*
4–5	*Vision of Paul* (archetype of Latin text)
4–6	*Life of St Pachomius*
5	*Vision of Carpus*

Early medieval texts

6	Gregory of Tours: *Historia Francorum*
	– vision of Sunniulf
	– vision of Salvius
	– visions of Chilperic
	Gregory the Great: *Dialogi*
	– vision of Peter
	– vision of Stephen
	– vision of a soldier
7	Valerius: *Opuscula*
	– vision of Maximus
	– vision of Bonellus
	– vision of Baldarius
	Vision of Barontus
8	Bede the Venerable: *Historia Ecclesiastica gentis Anglorum*
	– vision of Furseus
	– vision of Drythelm
	– vision of a Thane
	– vision of a monk
	Boniface, saint: *Epistolae*
	– vision of a Monk of Wenlock

Lull, Bishop of Mentz: *Epistolae*
                  – vision of a woman
Vision of Josaphat
9   *Vision of Rotcharius*
Walafrid Strabo: *Visio Wettini*
Rimbert: *Vita Anskarii*
Vision of an English Presbyter
Hincmar: *Visio Bernoldi*
William of Malmesbury: *De gestis regum Anglorum*
                       – vision of Charles the Fat
Vision of a Poor Woman
Vision of Laisren
10   *Navigatio Sancti Brendani*
10–11 Ansellus Scholasticus: *Vision of a Monk*
Vision of Fulbert
Heriger: *Chanson sur les fausses visions*
Ordericus Vitalis: *Historia Ecclesiastica*
                  – vision of Walkelin
Othlo: *Liber visionum*
Hildebrand: vision of a German count
Fís Adamnaín

The twelfth century

Guibert de Nogent: *De Vita Sua*
Vision of Alberic
Vision of Orm
Hildegard of Bingen: *Scivias*
Vision of the Boy William
Vision of Tundale
Elizabeth of Schönau: *Vita*
Vision of Gunthelm
H. of Saltrey: *Tractatus de Purgatorio Sancti Patricii*
Vision of Godeschalc
Vision of a Monk of Eynsham
Innocent III: *De Contemptu Mundi*
Anon: Treatise on the journey of the soul

The thirteenth century

Ralph of Coggeshall: *Chronicum Anglicanum*
                      – vision of a monk of Streflur
Vision of Thurkill
Caesarius of Heisterbach: *Dialogus Miraculorum*
Etienne de Bourbon: *Tractatus de diversis materiis praedicabilibus*

Appendix

Giacomino da Verona: *De Babilonia civitate infernali*
De Jerusalem celesti
Bonvesin da Riva: *Il libro delle tre scritture*
Bongiovanni da Cavriana: *Anticerberus*
Liber de Scalis
Raoul de Houdenc: *Le Songe d'enfer*
La Voie de Paradis
Rutebeuf: *La Voie de Paradis*
Baudouin de Condé: *La Voye du Paradis*
Anon: *La Cour du Paradis*

PRINCIPAL MOSAICS, FRESCOES AND ALTARPIECES OF THE LAST JUDGMENT

CENTURY

6   S. Apollinare Nuovo, Ravenna

9   S. Johann, Munster, Graubunden (St Gall)

11   S. Angelo in Formis, near Capua (1072–87; Montecassino)
S. Michael, Burgfelden, Wurttemberg (Reichenau, late eleventh century)
Vatican Altarpiece (Nicolaus et Johannes pictores; Benedictine school, 1061–71)

12   St Michael's Chapel, St George, Oberzell auf der Reichenau, Baden (*c.* 1100)
Cathedral, Torcello, Venice (*c.* 1100)
Floor mosaic of Heaven and Hell, Otranto cathedral (1163–5)
S. Maria, Ronzano (1181; Montecassino)
S. Giovanni a Porta Latina, Rome
St Botolph, Hardham, Sussex
St Gabriel's Chapel, Canterbury Cathedral
Parish church, Clayton, Sussex
Parish church, Kempley, Gloucestershire

13   SS. Peter and Paul, Chaldon, Surrey (*c.* 1200)
S. Maria Maggiore, Pianella, Abruzzi (*c.* 1200; Montecassino)
Parish church, Stowell, Gloucestershire (1210–30)
S. Maria in Vescovio, Stimigliano (1246)
S. Pellegrino, Bominaco, Abruzzi (Montecassino, 1263)
S. Maria ad Cryptas, Fossa, Abruzzi (Montecassino, end thirteenth century)
S. Giovanni, Baptistry, Florence (Coppo di Marcovaldo, end thirteenth century)
S. Cecilia in Trastevere, Rome (Pietro Cavallini, 1289–93)
S. Maria in Piano, Loreto Aprutino (late thirteenth–early fourteenth century)

Appendix

Oratorio di S. Silvestro, SS. Quattro Coronati, Rome
Parish church, Kempley, Gloucestershire
St John's, Winchester

14   Scrovegni Chapel, Padua (Giotto; by 1305)
S. Maria Maggiore, Tuscania (Gregorio and Donato of Arezzo,
    first half fourteenth century)
S. Maria Donnaregina, Naples (1316–30)

Post-1321

Palazzo dell'Arengo, Rimini
Bologna altarpiece (fourteenth–fifteenth century)
S. Pietro, Viboldone, Milan (Giusto di Menabuoi, *c.* 1355)
Camposanto, Pisa (Maestro del Trionfo della Morte, 1360)
Basilica di S. Maria, Pomposa (1361–72)
Collegiata, S. Gimignano (Taddeo di Bartolo, 1396)
S. Maria Novella, Florence (Nardo di Cione, 1357 – modelled on
    the *Comedy*)
Cappella Bolognini, S. Petronio, Bologna (Giovanni da Modena
    1410–51)

PRINCIPAL SCULPTURES OF THE LAST JUDGMENT

12   St Pierre, Beaulieu (early twelfth century)
St Denis, Seine (1133–40)
Cathedral, Laon (1160)
St James, Compostela (1183)
Ste Foy, Conques
Cathedral, Mâcon
Cathedral, Autun
St Trophime, Arles

13   Cathedral, Chartres (1210–15)
Notre-Dame, Paris (1220–30)
Cathedral, Amiens (1225–35)
Cathedral, Rheims (*c.* 1230)
Cathedral, Bourges (1255–60)
Cathedral, Poitiers (*c.* 1250)
Cathedral, Bordeaux (*c.* 1260)
Notre Dame, Le Mans
St Urbain, Troyes
Cathedral, Dax (third quarter thirteenth century)
Cathedral, Bazas
Pulpit, Siena (Nicola Pisano, 1263–8)
Pulpit, Pisa (Giovanni Pisano, 1302–11)

14   Cathedral, Ferrara (*c.* 1300)

APPENDIX 2

Written representations of the other world – summaries with background and bibliographical information

Abraham, Testament of

A Jewish apocryphal work, composed probably in Egypt in the first or second century. The original language was Hebrew or Aramaic; there are only two extant recensions, both of later date and written in Greek; the longer contains approximately 1,500 words in translation. The work relates Abraham's visit, shortly before his death, to the gates in the East which lead to Heaven and Hell. Here souls are weighed and judged, in an episode which stems from Egyptian belief and recurs in the vision of Thurkill.

Bibliography: *The Testament of Abraham: the Greek Text now first edited with an Introduction and Notes*, M. R. James, Cambridge, 1892; 'The Testament of Abraham', translated by W. A. Craigie, *Ante-Nicene Christian Library, Additional Volume*, edited by A. Menzies, Edinburgh, 1897, pp. 183–201.

Baruch, Apocalypse of

Also known as *III Baruch*. Written during the second century in Greek, it also survives in various Slavonic translations. The redactor was a Christian working from Jewish material; the book bears similarities to *II Baruch*, and is related also to *II Enoch*. It relates the journey undertaken by Baruch through two heavens to a mountain, a lake and the gates of the remaining heavens. His angel-guide acts as his teacher. The apocalypse is approximately 3,000 words long in translation.

Bibliography: 'The Apocalpyse of Baruch', translated from the Slavonic by W. R. Morfill, *Apocrypha Anecdota*, second series, edited by M. R. James, Cambridge, 1897, pp. 96–102. The Greek text is translated by R. H. Charles in *The Apocrypha and Pseudepigrapha of the Old Testament*, II, London, 1913, pp. 527–41.

Appendix

II Baruch

A Jewish apocalypse written in the first century, partly in Greek, partly in Hebrew; it survives only in Syriac. It contains an account of the resurrection of the righteous and fate of the wicked. In translation it contains approximately 3,800 words.

Bibliography: A summary is given in *The Interpreter's Dictionary of the Bible*, edited by J. A. Buttrick, New York, 1962, I, p. 361–2; also in N. De Lange, *Apocrypha: Jewish Literature of the Hellenistic Age*, New York, 1978, p. 33. The work is translated by R. H. Charles, *The Apocrypha and Pseudepigrapha of the Old Testament*, II, London, 1913, pp. 470–526.

Carpus, vision of

The vision of Carpus, friend of St Paul, is recorded in the eighth letter of the Pseudo-Dionysus, and is therefore assumed to date from about the fifth century; it is approximately 550 words in length. Carpus relates to Dionysus how he saw the heavens open, revealing Christ, and the earth split, revealing the chasm of Hell; on the brink were two men who had turned away from Christianity and whom Carpus had wished God to destroy. Christ helps them and admonishes Carpus. This is one of the earliest of Christian visions.

Bibliography: The text is given in both Greek and Latin by Migne, *Patrologia Graeco-Latina*, III, cols. 1097–1100. See also *The Works of Dionysus the Areopagite, now first translated into English*, J. Parker, London, 1897, pp. 163–6.

Cicero

(a) *Somnium Scipionis*. A surviving part of the *De Republica*, modelled on Plato's myth of Er, and based upon Ptolemaic cosmology. It was transmitted to the Middle Ages along with the commentary of Macrobius. Scipio the Younger is told of his future by Scipio the Elder in a dream, during which he ascends through the heavenly spheres and looks down upon the Earth. The account is approximately 2,600 words long.

(b) *Tusculan Disputations*. Book I offers a discussion of the nature of death and of the soul, in the form of a survey of past beliefs. This is the first study of its kind, and important in transmitting Greek belief, in particular, to the Roman and thence the medieval world.

Bibliography: *Tusculan Disputations*, edited and translated by J. E. King, London and New York, 1927; 'Somnium Scipionis', *De Re Publica*, edited by K. Zeigler, Leipzig, 1969, pp. 126–36.

Elijah, Apocalypse of

A short Jewish apocalypse of the third century. It ends with a description of the new age which will follow the Day of Judgment; the wicked suffer in a fiery pit, and the blessed dwell in a celestial Jerusalem and the garden of Eden.

Appendix

Bibliography: 'Apocalypse of Elijah', *The Interpreter's Dictionary of the Bible*, edited by J. A. Buttrick, New York, 1962, II, p. 88. A summary is also given by M. Dods, *Forerunners of Dante*, Edinburgh, 1903, pp. 125–6.

I Enoch

I Enoch is based on Genesis 5.18–24, in much the same way as the Apocalypse of Paul has its origin in 2 Corinthians 12.1–5. It was written in the first or second century BC in Hebrew or Aramaic, and subsequently translated into Greek, Ethiopic and Latin; it was well known by the beginning of the Christian era, and influenced many writings, including *III Baruch*, *IV Esdras*, the *Assumption of Moses* and the *Testament of the 12 Patriarchs*. It is the oldest apocalypse in the Judaeo-Christian tradition. Enoch visits Sheol, where the souls of the dead are divided into four categories; he sees the area reserved for eternal torment after the Day of Judgment, and is taken to the garden of Righteousness. The work covers a multitude of other, related, subjects. It is approximately 40,000 words long.

Bibliography: *The Book of Enoch, translated with an introduction* by R. H. Charles, London, 1917.

II Enoch

Also known as the *Book of the Secrets of Enoch*. Written in the first century by a Hellenistic Jew in Egypt, it survives only in two Slavonic versions. It was influential on subsequent apocalypses, and is quoted in the *Apocalypse of Paul* and the *Sibylline Oracles*. In it Enoch is taken through ten heavens, in the third of which he sees the earthly Paradise and the place of torment, and in the last of which he is addressed by God. The book is about 20,000 words long.

Bibliography: *The Book of the Secrets of Enoch, translated from the Slavonic by W. R. Morfill and edited, with introduction, notes and indices, by R. H. Charles*, Oxford, 1896; also in R. H. Charles, *The Apocrypha and Pseudepigrapha of the Old Testament*, II, London, 1913, pp. 425–69.

Er the Pamphylian, vision of: see Plato: *The Republic*.

Esdras, Apocalypse of

IV Esdras, a pseudepigraph written in the first century in Hebrew or Greek and appended to the Vulgate, is the source of three apocalypses whose subject is the state of souls after death. The first of these is the Greek *Esdras Apocalypse*, of which a central section, about 1,250 words in length, is concerned with the afterlife; Esdras is taken down a series of steps to the bottom of Hell, and then transported to Paradise in the East. The second is the *Apocalypse of Sedrach*, similar but less varied; the third is the Latin *Visio Beati Esdrae*, which survives in two twelfth-century manuscripts. It is about 1,000 words long, and describes Esdras's journey through Hell, in which he sees various categories of sinner all of whom are first tested on the bridge of trial, to Paradise, and finally through the seven heavens to God. The text shows affinities to both the *Vision of Paul* and the *Vision of Tundale*.

Bibliography: O. Wahl, *Apocalypsis Esdrae, Apocalypsis Sedrach, Visio Beati Esdrae*, Leiden, 1977; 'Revelation of Esdras', translated by A. Walker, *Apocryphal Gospels, Acts and Revelations*, edited by A. Roberts and J. Donaldson, Edinburgh, 1870, pp. 468–76. The Latin vision was first edited by A. Mussafia as an appendix to his article 'Sulla Visione di Tundalo', *Sitzungsberichte der philosophisch-historischen Klasse der Kaiserlichen Akademie der Wissenschaften*, LXVII, Vienna 1871, pp. 202–6.

Hermas, Shepherd of

An apocryphal work of the second century, composed in Greek (probably in Rome) but translated almost immediately into Latin. It became widely accepted, and is cited as an authority in the vision of Wetti. It consists of a series of visions, mandates and similitudes, most of which act as vehicles for the ethical teaching given by the lady Rhoda, Ecclesia and the Shepherd. The ninth similitude takes the form of a vision of a number of mountains, each representing a different class of sinner. The work is approximately 30,000 words long.

Bibliography: 'The Shepherd of Hermas', *The Apostolic Fathers*, II, edited and translated from the Greek by K. Lake, London 1913; 'Sancti Hermae Pastor', Latin text edited by Migne, *Patrologia Graeco-Latina*, II, cols. 891–1011; see also the article in *The Interpreter's Dictionary of the Bible*, edited by J. A. Buttrick, II, pp. 583–4.

Homer

Book XI of the *Odyssey*, the 'Book of the Dead', relates Odysseus's encounter with the spirits of those in Hades. On the instructions of Circe he makes the appropriate sacrifices, and the spirits assemble. He speaks to many of them. He then sees Minos in judgment, and observes the torments of Tityus, Tantalus and Sisyphus. Many elements of the Homeric underworld recur throughout the subsequent tradition, transmitted mainly through the *Aeneid*. The account is approximately 6,800 words long.

Bibliography: *The Odyssey*, translated by E. V. Rieu, Harmondsworth, 1945, p. 175–93. See also C. Pascal, *Le credenze d'oltretomba nelle opere letterarie dell'antichità classica*, I, ch. 12, 'L'oltretomba omerico', Catania, 1912, reprinted Turin, 1924.

Isaiah, Ascension of

A composite text based on earlier sources, both Jewish and Christian, and thought to have been in circulation by about 400. It was probably written in Aramaic; only fragments survive, one of which is in Latin and recorded in a fifth-century manuscript. It describes part of Isaiah's ascent through the seven heavens to the abode of God.

Bibliography: C. Leonardi, 'Il testo dell'*Ascensio Isaiae* nel Vat. Lat. 5750', *Cristianesimo nella storia*, 1 (1980), pp. 59–74. See also the article in *The Interpreter's Dictionary of the Bible*, edited by J. A. Buttrick, New York, 1962, II, 744–6.

Lucan

Book VI of the *Pharsalia* contains the tale of the return to life at the summons of Erichtho of a soldier killed in battle. He relates the strife caused in Hades by the war, and promises Pompey will go to a bright, serene part of the underworld. Book IX gives an account of the ascent of Pompey's soul from the funeral pyre through the heavenly spheres to its place beside Brutus and Cato. The two accounts are approximately 1,550 and 100 words long.

Bibliography: Lucan: *The Civil War Books I–X, with an English translation by J. D. Duff*, London and New York, 1928.

Lucretius

Verses 830–1094 of Book III of the *De Rerum Natura* discusses belief in the afterlife, and in transmigration. Lucretius argues that the torments of Hell do not exist, but represent the torments of earthly life. He reinterprets the Homeric figures in this allegorical light.

Bibliography: *De Rerum Naturae*, edited by C. Bailey, London, 1900, second edition 1922; *On the Nature of the Universe*, translated by R. E. Latham, Harmondsworth, 1951, reprinted 1979.

Moses, Revelation of

Of unknown date, but thought by the editor to have been composed before the birth of Christ. Moses ascends through the seven heavens under the guidance of the angel Metatron, and is then taken by Gabriel to visit the seven regions of Hell. The journey ends in Eden. The longer of the two surviving versions contains about 4,700 words.

Bibliography: 'The Revelation of Moses' edited by M. Gaster, 'Hebrew Visions of Hell and Paradise', *Journal of the Royal Asiatic Society*, 1893, pp. 571–91.

Nicodemus, Gospel of

An apocryphal work widely known in the Middle Ages. It consists of two parts: the first recounts the Passion, the second describes Christ's descent into Hell. The two parts were united probably in the fifth century. The descent is related in the *Speculum historiale* of Vincent of Beauvais. There are two Latin versions and one Greek recension; numerous translations into the vernacular were made. The vision of Ansellus is based upon it. The account of Christ's descent into Hell contains about 13,000 words.

Bibliography: 'The Gospel of Nicodemus', *The Apocryphal New Testament*, Oxford, 1924, reprinted 1953, pp. 94–146.

Ovid

The fourth book of the *Metamorphoses* contains a brief account of the traditional classical underworld: Ovid describes the Styx and the city of Dis, Cerberus and the torments of Tantalus, Sisyphus, Ixion, Tityus and the Danaides. The account is approximately 400 words long.

Bibliography: *Metamorphoses, with an English translation by F. J. Miller*, 2 vols., London and Cambridge (Mass.) 1966, 1, pp. 208–11 (ll. 432–78).

Pachomius, Life of

Pachomius lived in the fourth century in Egypt, where he founded the first monastic community. The Latin account of his life, translated from an unknown Greek writer and subsequently included in the *Vitae Patrum*, contains a chapter which relates a vision experienced by a monk of the community. It is about 750 words long. The vision is also described by Ceasarius of Heisterbach. The monk sees a deep valley; in this valley are many monks suffering torment and attempting to climb up the sides towards the light. Pachomius, on hearing this, despairs; he himself then receives a vision of Christ, who tells him to correct the errors of the monks in order to ensure their salvation.

Bibliography: 'Vita Sancti Pachomii Abbatis Tabennensis', ch. 45, in Migne, *Patrologia Latina*, LVVIII, cols. 262–3.

Paul, Apocalypse of: see Part 2, *Vision of Paul*

Perpetua, Passion of

The third-century work known as the *Passio Perpetuae* is an account of the martyrdom of five early Christians in Carthage. It consists partly of first-hand accounts, partly of narrative; the redactor is thought to have been Tertullian. There are two manuscripts, both medieval, and a further account of the martyrdom is given in the *Legenda aurea*. Four visions are contained in the work, three by Perpetua and a further one by Saturus; they may have been influenced by

Appendix

an acquaintance with the *Shepherd of Hermas* and the *Apocalypse of Peter*. Perpetua's first vision is of a stairway to Heaven, bristling with sharp weapons; Saturus leads the ascent. They negotiate a dragon and reach a garden in which a white-haired man is seated. Perpetua's second vision is the first text in which the efficacy of prayer for the dead is stressed; she sees her dead brother Dinocrates suffering from thirst, prays, and sees him drinking freely. In her third vision Perpetua sees herself changed into a man and fighting with an Egyptian. She is victorious, and understands herself to have conquered the devil himself. For the vision of Saturus see separate entry. The *Passion* contains about 3,500 words.

Bibliography: *The Passion of S. Perpetua*, edited by J. A. Robinson, Cambridge, 1891; 'Passio Sanctarum Perpetuae e Felicitatis', edited by G. Lazzati, *Gli sviluppi della letteratura sui martiri nei primi quattro secoli*, Turin, 1956, p. 177–89. See also P. Dronke, *Women Writers of the Middle Ages: A Critical Study of Texts from Perpetua (†203) to Marguerite Porete (†1310)*, Cambridge, 1984, pp. 1–13.

Peter, Apocalypse of

An apocryphal work of great popularity composed in Greek in the first or second century. The original is not extant; there is a fragment in Greek and a version in Ethiopic. Its sources include the beliefs of classical Greece as expressed by Homer, Pindar and Plato, as well as the Orphic and Pythagorean accounts of the afterlife, the canonical Apocalypse, the Jewish tradition, and possibly also Egyptian and Persian beliefs. In the Ethiopic version, Peter is shown the fate of the damned, grouped like with like in Hell; he is then taken to Elysium and the Earthly Paradise. This text was of paramount importance for the formation of the Western tradition; it exerted a major influence on subsequent apocalypses, especially that of Paul, through which it was indirectly transmitted throughout medieval Europe. It is the earliest extant text in the Judaeo-Christian tradition, with the possible exception of the *Apocalypse of Esdras*, to offer a classification of sin, and to introduce the concept of the fitting of punishment to crime. The Greek fragment is approximately 1,000 words long, the Ethiopic version 5,000 words long.

Bibliography: 'The Revelation of Peter', translated by A. Rutherford, *Ante-Nicene Christian Library, Additional Volume*, edited by A. Menzies, Edinburgh, 1897, pp. 145–7 (Greek fragment); 'The Apocalypse of Peter', translated by M. R. James, *The Apocryphal New Testament*, Oxford, 1924, reprinted 1953, pp. 510–21 (Ethiopic version).

Plato

(i) *Gorgias*. The eschatological myth with which Plato concludes his *Gorgias* is the first of his four mythical representations of the other world. These exerted a profound influence on contemporary and subsequent thought. Here, Socrates explains the old Homeric system of judgment after death and outlines the new system decreed by Zeus. His account is about 2,200 words long.

Appendix

(ii) *Phaedo*. Written in 387 BC. Socrates, on the day of his execution, expounds the doctrine of the immortality of the soul and discusses the nature of the afterlife. He describes the otherworld rivers and seas, and outlines the fourfold division of souls. His account of the other world is approximately 2,500 words in length.

(iii) *The Republic*. Written in 375 BC. It closes with an account of the myth of Er, a Pamphylian; this is the most influential of the four eschatological myths. Er was killed in battle, but revived twelve days later and related his experiences. He saw the place of judgment of the dead and learned of the criteria applied; spirits are sent for a period of reward or punishment, and then required to select a new human life and sent back to earth. The account is about 3,000 words long.

(iv) *Phaedrus*. Thought to date from about 370 BC. It contains a description of the journey of the soul in a chariot pulled by winged horses towards the dwelling of the gods. The soul fails to reach this dwelling, and falls earthwards, where it is reincarnated. After a sufficient number of earthly lives, the soul may remain in the heavens. The myth contains about 2,250 words.

Bibliography: *Gorgias, translated with notes by T. Irwin*, Oxford, 1979; E. R. Dodds, *Plato: Gorgias: A Revised Text with Introduction and Commentary*, London, 1959; *Plato's Phaedo: Translated with Introduction and Commentary by R. Hackforth*, Cambridge, 1955; *Phaedo: Translated with notes by David Gallop*, London, 1975; *The Republic*, translated by D. Lee, Harmondsworth, 1955, second edition 1974; *Plato's Phaedrus. Translated with an Introduction and Commentary* by R. Hackforth, Cambridge, 1972.

Plutarch

Plutarch's *Moralia* contain two accounts of the afterlife. These are the earliest examples of the vision of the afterlife as related throughout the Middle Ages: a particular individual is taken on a journey through the other world, which he describes on his return. Plutarch was much influenced by Plato.

(a) *The Vision of Thespesius* is related in the essay 'De sera numinis vindicta', a discussion of the advantages and disadvantages of the late punishment of the wicked; Thespesius's experience is given as an illustration of the punishment of the soul after death. Thespesius undergoes his journey into the afterlife during a three-day concussion. He travels to the confines of the sublunary region, where he sees souls with various degrees of blemishing and meets the kinsman who becomes his guide. He is taken to the various regions of the other world, and the principles of punishment are explained to him. He lastly sees souls departing for reincarnation in animals. He returns to life and reforms his habits. The vision is about 3,000 words long in translation.

(b) *The vision of Timarchus* is related in the essay 'De genio Socratis'. Timarchus wishes to understand the nature of the communications received by Socrates from heaven. He descends into a cave to consult the oracle of Trophonius, returns three

Appendix

days later and relates his experiences. He had been carried into the heavens, seen the rotating spheres and looked down at the abyss below. The principles of life, birth, motion and decay were revealed to him, as was the role of the Fates. He had witnessed the departure of souls for reincarnation and learnt of the nature of the soul, after which he had been returned to the body. His account is approximately 1,600 words in length.

Bibliography: *Plutarch's Moralia, with an English translation by Phillip H. De Lacy and Benedict Einarson*, London and Cambridge (Mass.), 1959, pp. 269–99 and 459–77.

Reichenau Apocryphon

A fragment survives of this apocalypse in a manuscript dating from the eighth or ninth century. It describes the ascent of the soul through seven heavens in which it undergoes various torments.

Bibliography: D. De Bruyne, 'Fragments retrouvés d'apocryphes priscillianistes', *Revue Bénédictine*, 24 (1907), 318–35.

Saturus, vision of

Recorded in the *Passio Perpetuae* (see Perpetua). Saturus sees himself and his companions carried by four angels to a garden in the East, where they meet four more angels who conduct them into the presence of the blessed, who dwell in a place of waiting. They leave, and meet two contemporary clergy, who tell them to correct the errors of their people. The vision is about 600 words long.

Seven Heavens Apocryphon

An anonymous account of a journey through the seven heavens, the original text of which is no longer extant; composed before the eighth century, it seems to have been in use by the eleventh in Britain, influencing particularly the *Fís Adamnáin*. It is thought to have contained Gnostic elements and to have been Eastern in origin.

Bibliography: J. Stevenson, 'Ascent through the Heavens from Egypt to Ireland', *Cambridge Medieval Celtic Studies*, 5 (1983), pp. 21–35.

Sibylline Oracles

A collection of prophecies, combining classical, Jewish and Christian sources, and written in Greek hexameter verse. The first two books are Christian, composed in the second or third century. Book II gives a description of the Day of Judgment and the subsequent destiny of the blessed and the damned. Much of the material derives from the *Apocalypse of Peter*. The passage in Book II is about 1,500 words long.

Appendix

Bibliography: 'The Second Book of the Sibylline Oracles', *The Apocryphal New Testament*, translated by M. R. James, Oxford, 1924, reprinted 1953, pp. 521–4; see also *The Interpreter's Dictionary of the Bible*, edited by J. A. Buttrick, New York, 1962, IV, p. 343.

Statius

Book IV of the *Thebaid* relates the consultation of the seer Tiresias by Polynices and Tydeus, and the subsequent summoning of the inhabitants of Hades. Book VIII gives an account of the arrival in Hades of the prophet Amphiaraus. Pluto is in judgment, the infernal rivers are described, and reference is made to Elysium. The two accounts are respectively 750 and 1,500 words long.

Bibliography: *Statius, with an English translation by J. H. Mozley in 2 volumes*, London and New York, 1928, I, pp. 536–55; II, pp. 194–203.

Thomas, Acts of

A work of the first or second century, extant in Greek and Syriac; there are secondary versions in Latin, Armenian and Ethiopic. It relates the exploits of Thomas in India, and contains an account of a woman's vision of Hell. This account is based on the *Apocalypse of Peter*; it contains approximately 850 words in translation.

Bibliography: 'Acts of the Apostle Thomas', translated by A. Walker, *Apocryphal Gospels, Acts and Revelations*, edited by A. Roberts and J. Donaldson, Edinburgh, 1870, pp. 389–422; 'Acts of Thomas', *The Apocryphal New Testament*, translated by M. R. James, Oxford, 1924, reprinted 1953, pp. 365–438; see also the article in *The Interpreter's Dictionary of the Bible*, edited by J. A. Buttrick, New York, 1962, IV, pp. 633–4.

Virgil

Book VI of the *Aeneid* describes Aeneas's visit to Hades in order to speak with his father Anchises. He is ferried across the Acheron by Charon, visits firstly a neutral realm, secondly Tartarus, and lastly Elysium where he meets Anchises. He is guided by the Cumaean Sibyl. The influence of the *Aeneid* is felt throughout the medieval afterlife tradition. Book VI is approximately 6,000 words long.

Bibliography: *Virgil: Eclogues, Georgics, Aeneid I–VI, with an English translation by H. R. Fairclough*, London and Cambridge (Mass.), 1974.

Virgin, Apocalypse of the

A late compilation, perhaps of the ninth century; based on the Assumption legends and on the *Apocalypse of Paul*. It exists in a Greek and a shorter Ethiopic version; the former in translation is about 4,000 words long.

Appendix

Bibliography: 'The Apocalypse of the Holy Mother of God concerning the Chastisements', translated by A. Rutherford, *Ante-Nicene Library, Additional Volume*, edited by A. Menzies, Edinburgh, 1897, pp. 167–74; 'The Apocalypse of the Virgin', *The Apocryphal New Testament*, translated by M. R. James, Oxford, 1924, reprinted 1953, pp. 563–4; see also *The Interpreter's Dictionary of the Bible*, edited by J. A. Buttrick, New York, 1962, IV, pp. 788–9.

Zephaniah, Apocalypse of

An Egyptian work of the first or second century, of which the contents may be reconstructed from various fragmentary texts, and from quotations. It was probably influenced by the *Apocalypse of Peter*, and in turn acted as a source for the *Apocalypse of Paul*.

Bibliography: 'Apocalypse of Zephaniah', *The Lost Apocrypha of the Old Testament, their titles and fragments, collected, translated and discussed by M. R. James*, London and New York, 1920, pp. 72–4; see also the article in *The Interpreter's Dictionary of the Bible*, edited by J. A. Buttrick, New York, 1962, IV, pp. 950–1.

Zosimus, Narrative of

The *Narrative of Zosimus concerning the life of the Blessed* goes back to the third century, although in its present form it is more recent. It is an apocryphal work relating Zosimus's visit to the Earthly Paradise, of which it provides one of the earliest descriptions. The work exists in two Greek manuscripts; there are also versions in Slavonic, Syriac, Ethiopic and Arabic. It is about 3,000 words long.

Bibliography: 'The Narrative of Zosimus concerning the Life of the Blessed', translated by W. A. Craigie, *Ante-Nicene Christian Library, Additional Volume*, edited by J. A. Menzies, Edinburgh, 1897, pp. 219–24.

PART 2: MEDIEVAL TEXTS

Adamnan, Vision of

The *Fís Adamnáin* was composed in Irish, probably in the eleventh century, although Adamnan himself lived in the seventh and eighth, becoming abbot of Iona in 679. Its main sources were the Seven Heavens apocryphon, the *Vision of Paul*, and the writings of Gregory the Great. It is the most detailed of the visions in Irish, and is about 4,500 words long in translation. It survives in two manuscripts. On leaving the body Adamnan's soul is carried first to the land of the saints, and subsequently to the heavenly city, outside which the souls of the indifferently good await the Day of Judgment. Adamnan then ascends through the seven heavens, in which purgation occurs, to God. He witnesses the judgment of souls, and is sent to visit Hell. He is then returned to the body.

Appendix

Bibliography: C. S. Boswell, *An Irish Precursor of Dante: A Study of the Vision of Heaven and Hell ascribed to the Eighth-Century Irish saint Adamnan, with translation of the Irish text*, London, 1908.

Alberic, Vision of

Alberic, the nine-year-old son of a knight of the region of Campania, experienced a vision which prompted him to enter the Benedictine monastery of Montecassino as a novice. Here he related what he had seen; his account was recorded by the monk Guido on the instructions of the abbot, and corrected by Alberic himself with the aid of the deacon Peter at the instigation of a subsequent abbot. The vision, written in Latin, occurred in 1110, the final version being composed between 1127 and 1137. It bears traces of the influence of earlier works (the Perpetua, Wetti, Furseus and Brendan texts were all present in the monastery library), but cannot have been directly influential itself; the sole extant manuscript is the only one recorded. The text is about 7,000 words long; it is colloquial in tone, and recounted entirely in the first person. Alberic's guide is Peter, who interprets what is seen and acts as the mouthpiece for several discourses on the virtues and necessity of the monastic life. The vision falls into four main parts. Alberic visits first an upper Hell, from which he descends into lower Hell, where sinners are condemned without judgment; he is then led to an earthly Paradise, and finally travels up through the seven heavenly spheres and beyond them to a place about which he is forbidden to speak. The vision ends with a journey through the fifty-one regions of the earth.

Bibliography: The vision was first published with a translation in 1814 by F. Cancellieri, *Osservazioni intorno alla questione (. . .) sopra l'originalità della 'Divina Commedia' di Dante, appoggiata alla storia della visione del monaco casinese Alberico*, Rome, pp. 132–207. It was re-edited in 1932 by M. Inganuez, *Miscellanea Cassinese*, XI, pp. 83–103.

Ansellus Scholasticus, Vision of

Ansellus, a monk at Auxerre in the eleventh century, was the redactor of a vision which, like that of Wetti, exists in two versions, an earlier one in prose and a later one in verse. The visionary was a monk from Rheims, who related his experience personally to Ansellus. The vision occurred at Easter, while the monk was in church. He saw Christ descend from the Cross before him and lead the way through Hell. Both versions are about 2,000 words long; the verse account is in octosyllabic couplets. Both are in Latin. The vision is clearly influenced by the apocryphal *Gospel of Nicodemus*, in which the harrowing of Hell is related.

Bibliography: The verse text is given by Migne, *Patrologia Latina*, CLI, cols. 643–52, the prose text by J. Leclercq, 'Une Redaction en prose de la "Visio Anselli" dans un manuscrit de Subiaco', *Benedictina*, XVI (1969), 188–95.

Appendix

Anskar, Vision of – see Rimbert: *Vita Anskarii*

Baldarius, Vision of

The vision of Baldarius, a boy living with the hermit Fructuosus in the seventh century, is recorded by the Benedictine abbot Valerius in the year 656. It is about 450 words long. Baldarius's soul is carried by three doves to a beautiful mountain on which Christ is enthroned. At sunrise Baldarius sees a gigantic bird circling, and a vision of the whole world flashes into his mind. He opens his eyes and finds himself back on earth.

Bibliography: Sanctus Valerius Abbas, 'Dicta beati Valerii ad beatum Donadeum scripta', *Opuscula*, in Migne, *Patrologia Latina*, LXXXVII, cols. 433–5.

Barontus, Vision of

Barontus, a hermit of Pistoia, experienced a vision in the year 684, while living in a monastery in France. It is related, in Latin, in several manuscripts. The account is about 4,700 words long. Barontus's soul leaves the body, receiving a new one from the air, and is guided by Raphael through the four gates of Paradise; he meets many monks of his acquaintance. After an interview with Peter, Barontus is led by Framnoaldus, a recently deceased member of the monastery, through the torments of Hell. He returns to the body and exhorts his fellow monks to virtuous living.

Bibliography: 'Visio S. Baronti', *Acta Sanctorum Bolland. Mar.*, III, 567–74.

Baudouin de Condé

Baudouin, a *trouvère* of thirteenth-century France, composed an allegorical poem entitled *La Voye du Paradis*. It takes the form of a dream in which the poet finds himself at a fork in the road; he chooses the straight and narrow path, despite its thorns. Overcome by fear, he prays before a roadside cross; an old man appears and guides him, with much moral instruction, via the houses of Discipline, Abstinence and Silence, to Paradise. Here to overwhelming joy which he experiences interrupts his sleep. The poem is based on the one by Rutebeuf.

Bibliography: *Dits et Contes de Baudouin de Condé et de son fils Jean de Condé, publiés d'après les MSS de Bruxelles, Turin, Rome, Paris et Vienne et accompagnés de variantes et de notes explicatives par A. Scheler*, 3 vols., Brussels, 1866–7. The poem is also summarised by A. D'Ancona, *I Precursori di Dante*, Florence, 1874, p. 82.

Beggar, vision of a – see Othlo: *Liber visionum*

Appendix

Bernoldus, Vision of

The vision of the monk Bernoldus is recorded by Hincmar, archbishop of Rheims from 845 to his death in 882. The account is about 1,600 words long; reference is made to Gregory's *Dialogues*, to Bede, to Boniface's account of the vision of the Monk of Wenlock, and to the vision of Wetti. Bernoldus is conducted to a place of darkness and torment, and then to Paradise. In the former he meets 41 archbishops, Charles the Bald, and Jesse, who request prayer on their behalf; Bernoldus obtains this, and they are admitted to Paradise. A count, Otharius, makes the first attempt in the tradition to conceal himself from the visionary. Bernoldus is instructed to clothe the poor, and returned to the body.

Bibliography: Hincmar, 'De Visione Bernoldi presbyteri' in Migne, *Patrologia Latina*, CXXV, cols. 1115–20.

Bonellus, Vision of

Bonellus was a Spanish monk of the seventh century; his vision was recorded by the Benedictine abbot Valerius, and is about 700 words long. An angel leads Bonellus to a golden cell which it is promised will be his; he is then seized by an 'angelus malignus' and taken to Hell, where he finds a pauper he once tried to help. He is taken before the Devil, chained at the bottom of the abyss of Hell. He is conducted to a lake of fire, where arrows are shot at him by archers until he makes the sign of the cross. He is instantly returned to earth.

Bibliography: Sanctus Valerius Abbas, 'Dicta beati Valerii ad beatum Donadeum scripta', *Opuscula*, in Migne, *Patrologia Latina*, LXXXVII, cols. 433–5.

Bongiovanni da Cavriana

The fourth book of Bongiovanni's poem *Anticerberus* contains a description of Jerusalem and Babylon, in 117 verses. It is written in fifteen-syllable rhyming couplets. The author was a Franciscan from near Mantua, writing in the thirteenth century; his poem belongs to the tradition of the *De contemptu mundi*, and aims to guide the reader away from the dangers of Hell. It is influenced, as the title suggests, by the *Aeneid*.

Bibliography: F. Novati, 'Un poema francescano del dugento', *Attraverso il medioevo*, Bari, 1905, pp. 7–115. The description of Jerusalem and Babylon is given on pp. 103–12.

Bonvesin da Riva

Bonvesin, whose approximate dates are 1240–1314, was a Lombard, author of several works. Among these is the *Libro delle tre scritture*, written in about 1274. It is a poem of some 22,000 words (2,000 verses), composed according to a rigid structural scheme, and divided into monorhyming quatrains. It is tripartite: the 'Scriptura negra' describes the twelve torments of Hell; the 'Scriptura rossa' has as its subject not Purgatory but the Passion; and the 'Scriptura dorata' discusses the twelve joys of Paradise. The intention is didactic. The opening section of the poem on the misery of the human condition recalls the tradition of the *De contemptu mundi*, and particularly the work of that title by Innocent III.

Bibliography: *Il Libro delle tre scritture e il volgare delle vanità di Bonvesin da Riva*, edited by V. De Bartholomaeis, Rome, 1901; *Il Libro delle tre scritture e i volgari delle false scuse e della vanità di Bonvesin da la Riva*, edited by L. Biadene, Pisa, 1902. See also L. Russo, 'La letteratura religiosa del Duecento', *Ritratti e disegni storici, serie prima*, 1939, third edition, Florence, 1960, pp. 133–44.

Boy William, Vision of

The vision experienced by the fifteen-year-old William is recorded in Book XXVII of the *Speculum historiale* of Vincent of Beauvais, where it is assigned to the year 1146. It is short, being only 600 words long. It may have been influenced by the visions attributed to Paul and Drythelm, and refers explicitly to the canonical Apocalypse. William's journey takes place as he sleeps. He is led by a shining guide through an outer Hell to the pit of Tartarus, where Satan sits in flames; he is then taken to the heavenly city of the Apocalypse, to which it is promised that he may return. By virtue of its inclusion in the *Speculum historiale*, the vision must have become widely known.

Bibliography: Vincent of Beauvais, 'De revelatione inferni facta Guillelmo puero', *Bibliotheca mundi seu speculi maioris*, Book IV, *Speculum historiale*, XXVII, 84–5, Duaci, 1624, pp. 1125–6.

Brendan, the Voyage of

The *Navigatio sancti Brendani* is the most famous representative of an Irish literary genre, initially pagan and subsequently Christianised, consisting of accounts of marvellous sea voyages or imrama. Brendan lived in the sixth century; the oldest of the many manuscripts of the *Navigatio* dates from the tenth. It achieved immense popularity all over Europe; numerous manuscripts and translations exist, mostly dating from the twelfth century. Brendan's journey is a seven-year search for the Promised Land of the saints, the Earthly Paradise. It falls into three main parts: Brendan visits volcanic islands representing Hell, islands of choirs and neutral angels singing to God, and finally the island of Paradise itself. It is in this, its nature as a sea-voyage in search of an island Paradise, that the importance of the *Navigatio* resides.

Bibliography: *Navigatio Sancti Brendani abbatis*, edited by C. Selmer, Notre Dame, Indiana, 1959; *The Voyage of Saint Brendan: Journey to the Promised Land: 'Navigatio Sancti Brendani abbatis', translated with an introduction by J. J. O'Meara*, Dublin, 1976; 'La leggenda di S. Brandano', edited by P. Villari, *Antiche leggende e tradizioni che illustrano la 'Divina Commedia'*, Pisa, 1865, reprinted 1979, pp. 82–109.

Caesarius of Heisterbach

The *Dialogus miraculorum* was written between 1220 and 1235 for the instruction of novice monks. It is divided into twelve books, of which the fifth ('De demonibus') the eighth ('De diversibus visionibus') and the twelfth ('De praemio mortuorum') contain material relevant to the afterlife. Book XII is the most important; it is divided into chapters, each one relating the fate in the afterlife of a particular individual. An account of the legend of St Patrick's Purgatory is included. Chapters 2 to 23 and 40 to 42 deal with punishment in Hell, 24 to 39 with purgation, and 43 to 59 with the blessed in Paradise.

Bibliography: *Caesarii Heisterbachensis monachi ordinis cisterciensis Dialogus miraculorum*, edited by J. Strange, 2 vols., Cologne, Bonn and Brussels, 1851; *Caesarius of Heisterbach: The Dialogue on Miracles, translated by H. von E. Scott and C. C. Swinton Bland with an introduction by G. G. Coulton*, London, 1929, 2 vols.

Charles the Fat, Vision of

The emperor Charles the Fat experienced his vision, which is mainly political in content, between 885 and his death at Reichenau in 888. The vision gained wide currency; there are about twenty extant manuscripts. It is often recounted in the works of later writers, such as Hariulf, William of Malmesbury, Helinandus and Vincent of Beauvais. The vision is not long; William's account, given in Book II of his *De gestis regum Anglorum*, has about 1,500 words. Charles is taken first to Hell, where he sees various classes of sinner undergoing torment. He proceeds to a valley of purgation, where he meets his father Ludovic. Finally, in Paradise he is told that his nephew must succeed him; he gives the child the shining thread which has guided him through Hell.

Bibliography: *William of Malmesbury: De gestis regum Anglorum*, edited by W. Stubbs, London, 1887, pp. 112–16; *William of Malmesbury's Chronicle of the Kings of England, with notes and illustrations by J. A. Giles*, London, 1911, pp. 102–5.

Chilperic, Visions of

In Book VIII, chapter 4 of his *Historia francorum*, Gregory of Tours relates two visions, one experienced by himself, one by Guntram, in which Chilperic, a king of Neustria who was assassinated in 584, is seen undergoing torment in Hell. The account is about 200 words long; it is clearly intended to justify the assassination.

Bibliography: *Historia* VIII 4–5 (see entry for Salvius).

Appendix

Cour du Paradis, La

La Cour du Paradis, a short poem written by an unknown thirteenth-century *trouvère* in octosyllabic couplets, describes a feast held in heaven to celebrate All Saints' Day. Simon and Jude are sent through the various mansions of Paradise to issue invitations to all the elect, after which the poem is indistinguishable from an account of a purely secular, earthly banquet.

Bibliography: The poem is summarised by A. D'Ancona, *I Precursori di Dante*, Florence, 1874, pp. 83–4.

Drythelm, Vision of

The vision of Drythelm is first related in Bede's *Historia ecclesiastica*, Book v, ch. 12. Here we are told that Drythelm was a Northumbrian householder who died one night, was taken on a journey through the other world, and revived in the morning. This occurred during the reign of Aldfrid, who died in 705. Drythelm is guided through three regions: a valley of fire and snow where torment is purgative; Hell; and the Earthly Paradise. He is finally given a taste of heaven itself, after which he returns to the body and subsequently enters a monastery. Bede's account is 1,600 words long. The vision became influential in the later Middle Ages; accounts are given by Roger of Wendover, Othlo and Helinandus, and features of it recur in many subsequent visions. Its importance derives principally from the fact that it includes, for the first time, a separate place of purgation.

Bibliography: *Venerabilis Baedae 'Historiam ecclesiasticam gentis anglorum'*, edited by C. Plummer, 2 vols., Oxford, 1896; *Ecclesiastical History of the English Nation, based on the version of T. Stapleton, 1565*, translated by J. E. King, London and New York, 1930.

Elizabeth of Schönau

Elizabeth, a friend and contemporary of Hildegard of Bingen, began to experience visions in 1152, when she was 23. These are recorded in the account of her life written by her brother Eckbert, abbot of Schönau where she was a nun, partly at her dictation. The visions are many and varied; they include several specifically of the afterlife, and others related to the afterlife tradition. They are recounted in Latin. The work is about 35,000 words long. It was widely known in the Middle Ages.

Bibliography: Eckberti Abbatis Schonaugiensis 'Sanctae Elisabeth Vita', Migne, *Patrologia Latina*, CXCV, cols. 119–94.

English Presbyter, Vision of an

The vision experienced by an unnamed English presbyter in the year 839 is recounted in the continuation of the *Annali Bertiniani* by Prudentius of Troyes. His account is in colloquial Latin, and is about 350 words long. In his vision the presbyter is taken to a land full of magnificent buildings. In one of these he sees a large number of children, the souls of the saints, reading books in which are written the sins of men. The purpose of the account is didactic.

Bibliography: Prudentius of Troyes, *Annales sive Annalium Bertinianorum pars secunda: Ab anno 835 usque ad annum 861*, Migne, *Patrologia Latina*, CXV, col. 1385.

Etienne de Bourbon

Etienne's *Tractatus de diversis materiis praedicabilibus* is a collection of *exempla* for use in sermons, conceived in seven sections corresponding to the seven gifts of the Holy Spirit; only four and a half of these were completed, suggesting that the work was composed not long before Etienne's death in about 1261. A number of the anecdotes in the first section, that corresponding to the gift of fear, concern the afterlife. Of those grouped under the heading of Hell, two relate the fates of specific individuals; of those under the heading of Purgatory, one locates it in Etna, three concern particular individuals, and one, entitled 'De subvencione beatorum', is the account given to Etienne by Stephanus de Marusiaco of a vision experienced by his father. This man had been carried first to a house of torment, then to a wide fiery river full of fierce animals and crossed by a bridge; he is helped across by Mary, and returned to the body with a warning. The vision is about 700 words long. The *Tractatus* is in colloquial Latin.

Bibliography: *Anecdotes historiques, légendes et apologyes tirés du recueil inédit d'Étienne de Bourbon, dominicain du XIIIe siècle*, edited by A. Lecoy de la Marche, Paris, 1877.

Fulbert, Vision of

The vision of Fulbert of France is recorded in a Latin poem, probably of the eleventh century; it is about 200 words long, and written in quatrains. Each line contains thirteen syllables. A Fulbert was bishop of Chartres, where he died in 1028, although it is not clear that this is the Fulbert of the poem. Fulbert's soul leaves the body on death; a debate begins between the two, each accusing the other of responsibility for the soul's imminent damnation. Devils arrive, and the soul is carried off to Hell, where its torment begins. The debate between soul and body is a literary genre in its own right within the afterlife tradition. Fulbert's vision became fairly well known; there are several manuscripts, and the poem was translated into German. There are also versions in French, Italian, Spanish, Provençal, Dutch, Swedish, Danish and Greek.

Bibliography: 'La vision de Fulbert', edited by M. E. Du Méril, *Poésies populaires latines antérieures au douzieme siècle*, Paris, 1843, pp. 217–30.

Appendix

Furseus, Vision of

The two visions of Furseus are recounted in Book III, chapter 19 of Bede's *Historia ecclesiastica*. Furseus was an Irishman, living in the first half of the seventh century, who came to England and founded a monastery in East Anglia. Here he received visions initially of Heaven and subsequently of Hell. The first of these visions is reported briefly; the second is related in more detail. Furseus is carried into the heavens by three angels. From here he looks down towards earth, and sees the four fires of Hell burning below him. The angels lead him through the fires, explaining their purpose and allowing Furseus to return to Heaven, where he meets religious of his own country. On his journey back to the body he suffers burning from contact with a man from whom he had taken a garment; these burns remain with him throughout his life. Bede's account is 1,400 words in length; he cites a Latin life of Furseus and word of mouth as his sources. The fourfold division of Hell recalls that of the *Book of Enoch*. Furseus's vision became well known in the Middle Ages, due to its inclusion by Bede; it is related both in the *Legenda aurea* and by Vincent of Beauvais.

Bibliography: See entry for Drythelm above.

German count, Vision of a

In a sermon given in Arezzo by Hildebrand, before he became Pope Gregory VII in 1073, it is recounted how an anonymous visionary saw a certain German count who had died ten years previously suffering torment in Hell. The nature of the count's punishment recalls that of the popes in *Inferno* XIX: he is forced to stand on the upper rung of a ladder which descends through flames into a pit; his ancestors occupy the lower rungs, and all move down a step every time the present count dies. This torment is due to the first count, who unlawfully took possession of land belonging to the church of Metz. The sermon was recorded in a letter by Peter Damian.

Bibliography: See K. Vossler, *La fonte della 'Divina Commedia' studiata nella sua genesi e interpretata*, 1, pp. 186–7, second edition, Bari, 1927; F. D'Ovidio, *Studii sulla 'Divina Commedia'*, Caserta, 1931, p. 297.

Giacomino da Verona

Giacomino was a Franciscan living in Venice. Two works of his survive: the *De Babilonia civitate infernali* and the *De Jerusalem celesti*, thought to have been written in 1230 and 1260 respectively. Both are poems in the vernacular, composed in alexandrines and divided into monorhyming quatrains, written for a didactic purpose but popular rather than learned in nature; together they total about 5,500 words. The *De Babilonia* opens with a warning that it is an allegory; a description of the infernal city follows. Three separate episodes are then narrated: a cook named

Appendix

Bacabu roasts souls on a spit, devils chase and capture a sinner, and a father and son blame each other for their damnation. The *De Jerusalem* opens with a statement of the opposition between the two cities, and continues with a description of Jerusalem's walls, rivers, fountains and inhabitants; after a section devoted to the contemplation by the blessed of Christ and Mary, the poem closes with an exhortation to prayer.

Bibliography: The *'De Jerusalem celesti' and the 'De Babilonia infernali' of Fra Giacomino da Verona*, edited by E. I. May, London, 1930.

Godeschalc, Vision of

Godeschalc was a Holstein peasant, who in 1188 experienced a vision related subsequently in Latin by an anonymous redactor from the same village. The vision is, in the incomplete form in which it survives, 9,500 words long, and colloquial in style. It is unusual in the realism with which it introduces local characters and depicts life in the village. Godeschalc's vision occurs at Christmas. He is led by two angels over a thorny moor and across a river to a crossroads. To the left is Hell, to the right Paradise, ahead the third heaven. Godeschalc is taken first to Hell, then to the third heaven; in both places he meets many people of his acquaintance.

Bibliography: 'Visio Godeschalci', edited by R. Usinger, *Scriptores minores rerum Slesvico-Holtsatensium*, Kiel, 1875, pp. 89–126. A summary is given by K. Liestol, *Draumkvoede: a Norwegian Visionary Poem from the Middle Ages*, Oslo, 1946, pp. 91–3.

Guibert de Nogent

In his autobiographical *De Vita sua* Guibert, Benedictine abbot at Nogent-sous-Coucy, gives an account of a vision experienced by his mother. He was writing in about 1116, and the vision is described in approximately 850 words. Guibert's mother falls asleep one Sunday morning, and her soul is carried through a tunnel to Hell. She meets her husband, who tells her to speak to a certain Leodegardis, and an old woman with whom she had made a pact that the first of them to die would appear to the other. She sees a painting of a recently-deceased local knight, and of her son, still alive but preparing a place here for himself by indulging in blasphemy.

Bibliography: *Guiberti abbatis De Vita sua libri tres*, Migne, *Patrologia Latina*, CLVI, cols. 876–7; translated by J. Le Goff, *La Naissance du Purgatoire*, Paris, 1981, pp. 247–9.

Gunthelm, Vision of

Gunthelm, an English Cistercian, was still a novice when he received his vision in 1161. The account of the vision, in Latin, is possibly to be attributed to Peter the

Venerable. It is found in a number of manuscripts, and is also included in collections of legends of the Virgin and in the works of Helinand of Froidmont and Vincent of Beauvais; it is in these that the novice is named as Gunthelm. The style is colloquial, with frequent use of direct speech, but with a more formal introduction and conclusion. The account is 3,000 words long. Gunthelm's vision occurs one night as he lies prostrate after being subjected to temptation from a devil. He is led by Benedict to the chapel of Mary, and by Raphael to the Earthly Paradise and then to Hell. He is instructed not to reveal what he has seen, and is punished by Benedict when he disobeys.

Bibliography: 'The Vision of Gunthelm and other Visions attributed to Peter the Venerable', edited by G. Constable, *Revue Bénédictine*, 66 (1956), 92–114. Helinand's version is in *Helinandi frigidi montis monachi*, Migne, *Patrologia Latina*, CCXII, cols. 1060–4.

Heriger, Vision of

An unnamed man described a vision of the afterlife to Heriger, archbishop of Mainz from 912 to 926; this was subsequently made the subject of a brief satirical poem, in which the visionary tells Heriger that Hell is a place surrounded by dense woods, and Heaven the location of a feast served to the blessed by the saints. The poem is in Latin decasyllabic verse, and is about 150 words in length. It dates from the tenth or eleventh century, and constitutes the first example of satire in the afterlife tradition. The editor suggests that its aim is to remove pagan elements from Christian belief.

Bibliography: 'Chanson sur les fausses visions', edited by M. E. Du Méril, *Poésies populaires latines antérieures au douzieme siècle*, Paris, 1843, pp. 298–302.

Hildegard of Bingen

Hildegard's *Scivias* is an account of the twenty-six visions experienced by the author from 1141, her forty-third year, onwards. Each vision is followed by a discussion of the hidden meaning and doctrinal implications. Six visions in particular are concerned with the afterlife tradition. The work in its entirety is lengthy (about 160,000 words), and predominantly theological, rather than popular, in nature. It was written in Germany. There are ten manuscripts, all of N. European origin, eight of which date from the twelfth or thirteenth centuries.

Bibliography: 'Hildegardis *Scivias*', edited by A. Fuhrkotter and A. Carlevaris, *Corpus Christianorum continuatio medievalis*, XLIII, Turnholt, 1978.

Innocent III

Innocent III's treatise *De Contemptu mundi*, written in 1195 before his election to the Papacy, became the most influential work of its kind. Although it does not properly belong to the popular tradition, it contributed to the formation of that tradition: it exists in almost 500 separate manuscripts, and was widely translated into the vernacular. It includes a discussion of the various classes of sin, a description of Hell and an outline of the nine principal torments to be found there. It refers extensively to the Bible. The treatise is about 17,000 words in length.

Bibliography: *Lotharii cardinalis (Innocentii III) De Miseria humane conditionis*, edited by M. Maccarrone, Lugano, 1955.

Isaac, Vision of the monk – see Othlo: *Liber visionum*

Josaphat, Vision of

The legend of the saints Barlaam and Josaphat was written in the middle of the eighth century, possibly by St John of Damascus. Influenced by the legend of Buddha, and written in Greek, it was soon translated into several other languages. It is recorded in both the *Legenda aurea* and in the *Speculum historiale* of Vincent of Beauvais. The original account is about 600 words long. Josaphat is carried in sleep first to the abode of the righteous, a city of gold, jewels and light. He is then shown the place of the damned, of which the principal elements are fire and darkness, and returned to the body.

Bibliography: *John Damascene, Barlaam and Ioasaph*, translated by G. R. Woodward and H. Mattingley, London, 1914, pp. 469–73.

Liber de Scalis

The *Liber de Scalis* is a well-known Arab work whose subject is the otherworld journey of the prophet Mohammed. It was translated from a Castilian version into both Latin and French by Bonaventura da Siena in 1264. It is an important source for the diffusion in Europe of Eastern beliefs concerning the other world. There are three extant manuscripts; the legend is also mentioned in a number of other Western works of the thirteenth and fourteenth centuries. It is not cited in any of the European visions of the afterlife. The book gives an account of the ascent of Mohammed, under the guidance of Gabriel, through the heavens to Paradise and subsequently to the seven regions of Hell. In Hell he sees the damned grouped together according to their sin; the bridge of trial; and a beast with 30,000 mouths. In the course of his journey he receives the Koran from God, and is given much doctrinal teaching by Gabriel. The work is about 15,000 words long.

Bibliography: The text is edited by E. Cerulli, in *Il 'Libro della Scala' e la questione delle fonti arabo-spagnole della 'Divina Commedia'*, Vatican, 1949.

Appendix

Maximus, Vision of

The vision of Maximus, a Spanish monk of the seventh century, is related by the Benedictine abbot Valerius in a letter to a certain Donadeus, written in 656; Valerius's source is Maximus himself. The account is extremely colloquial; it is about 800 words long. Maximus is led by an angel to Paradise, where he is made to drink from the river he finds there; he is then shown the abyss of Hell. Throughout he is interrogated in a paternal fashion by his guide. He awakens just in time to prevent his own funeral.

Bibliography: Sanctus Valerius abbas, 'Dicta beati Valerii ad beatum Donadeum scripta', *Opuscula*, edited by Migne, *Patrologia Latina*, LXVII, cols. 431–3.

Monk, Vision of a

A short vision of about 400 words recorded in Book v, ch. 14 of Bede's *Historia ecclesiastica*. A sinful monk refuses to repent, and is rewarded firstly with a vision of Hell, where he sees a place reserved for himself along with such as Satan and Caiaphas, and subsequently with death. The story is told as a warning.

Bibliography: See entry under Drythelm.

Monk of Eynsham, Vision of the

The vision of the Monk of Eynsham occurred over Easter 1196; it was written down on the orders of the bishop of Lincoln by the subprior of the monastery, Adam. In the vision the monk is guided by Nicholas, with whom he visits the three areas of torment in Hell, meeting many people he knows. Nicholas accompanies him as far as the gate of Paradise, where he is forced to proceed alone. Here he sees the souls of the blessed begin their journey through the heavens to God. The vision lasts from Maundy Thursday to Easter Saturday. The account is written in a fairly straightforward Latin, with much use of direct speech; it is one of the most substantial, being 22,000 words long. It was possibly influenced by the vision of Drythelm. The vision became well known: there are seven extant manuscripts, and further accounts are given by Roger of Wendover, Matthew Paris and Ralph of Coggeshall. It is cited as an authority in the vision of Thurkill.

Bibliography: 'Visio monachi de Eynsham', edited by H. Thurston, *Analecta Bollandiana* 22 (1903), 225–319; E. Arber, *The Revelation to the Monk of Evesham, 1196, carefully edited from the unique copy, now in the British Museum, of the Edition printed by William de Machlinia about 1482*, Westminster, 1869.

Monk of Streflur, Vision of the

The vision of the Monk of Streflur is recorded under the year 1202 in the *Chronicum Anglicanum* of Ralph of Coggeshall. It is about 550 words long. The vision occurred in a Cistercian monastery in Wales. One night the monk sees an angel enter his room; the angel throws live coals at the monk, who feels fire spread throughout his body. This is the fire of Purgatory, and three days later he awakens purged of his sins.

Bibliography: The vision is edited by P. G. Schmidt, 'Visio monachi de Streflur in Gualiis', Appendix II, in *'Visio Thurkilli' relatore, ut videtur, Radulpho de Coggeshall*, Leipzig, 1978, pp. 39–41.

Monk of Wenlock, Vision of the

This vision is recounted by St Boniface in a letter to the Abbess of Thanet. It took place in about 717, in the monastery of Wenlock. Boniface's account is about 2,500 words long; his source is the monk himself. The monk dies one night; his soul is carried up beyond the fire which surrounds the earth, to a place where angels and devils dispute for its possession. He sees upper Hell, where torment is finite, and lower Hell, where it is eternal. He is then shown a garden Paradise, the temporary home of the blessed. A river of fire and pitch, crossed by a bridge, separates him from the heavenly city of Jerusalem, the final destiny of the blessed; in this river minor faults are cleansed. The monk's soul returns to its body, and he revives. The vision was perhaps influenced by the vision of Paul (immersion motif) and Gregory the Great (bridge motif). It exists in several manuscripts, including one in which it is immediately preceded by an account of the vision of Drythelm. Reference is made to it in the vision of Bernoldus, and it is included in Othlo's *Liber visionum*.

Bibliography: 'S. Bonifatii et Lulli epistolae', edited by E. Duemmler, *Epistolae merowingici et karolini aevi I, Monumenta Germaniae Historica Epistolarum*, III, Berlin, 1892, pp. 252–7; *The English Correspondence of Saint Boniface: Being for the most part Letters exchanged between the Apostle of the Germans and his English Friends*, translated by E. Kylie, London, 1911.

Orm, Vision of

The vision of Orm survives in a single twelfth-century manuscript, which also contains an account of the vision of Drythelm; it is about 1,000 words long. Orm experienced his vision at the age of thirteen; he died a few months later. The vision was recorded by Sigar, the parish priest, and sent to Symeon of Durham. On his journey through the other world Orm sees a walled Paradise, Hell, and an area outside Paradise.

Bibliography: 'The Vision of Orm', *Analecta Bollandiana*, 75 (1957), 72–82, edited by H. Farmer.

Appendix

Othlo: Liber visionum

Othlo, a Benedictine monk at Ratisbon in the eleventh century, composed a work entitled the *Liber visionum tum suarum, tum aliorum*. The book is about 20,000 words long. It contains twenty-three visions, of which seven are concerned with the afterlife. Of these, two relate the visions of Drythelm and the Monk of Wenlock as told by Bede and Boniface. The sixth vision is attributed to a servant woman who dies and returns to life with news of the state of the parents of the tribune Adalricus. It is about 450 words long. The eleventh vision was experienced by a local beggar, who is led first to a metal house containing the recently dead, secondly to an empty well surrounded by many unused paths, thirdly to a poorly kept monastery. Finally he is shown a tree, representing the bishop; it has begun to dry up. The vision is about 600 words in length. The fourteenth vision is attributed to a monk of Bohemia named Isaac, who is taken firstly to a beautiful place where he meets the hermit Gunther, secondly to a mountain on the slopes of which Hell is located, and thirdly to a place of judgment with seats of fire. Othlo laments the corruption of the clergy. The vision is 650 words long. The remaining two visions, the seventeenth and twenty-third, concern firstly the fate in Hell of the empress Theophanu, secondly the arrival of the devil at some wedding celebrations.

Bibliography: *Liber visionum tum suarum, tum aliorum*, edited by Migne, *Patrologia Latina*, CXLVI, cols. 341–88.

Paul, Vision of

The vision of Paul occupies a unique place in the afterlife tradition. Originally composed in the third century in Greek, probably by an Egyptian, and translated into Latin in the fourth or fifth, the vision spread gradually throughout Europe over the following thousand years. In this study the original work is referred to as the *Apocalypse of Paul*, the Latin translations and redactions as the *Vision of Paul*. The oldest and fullest Latin manuscript is of the eighth century, but the translation dates from the fourth to sixth. From this or a related manuscript some eleven medieval redactions developed, of which there are over fifty extant manuscripts. From these in turn, and particularly from that designated Redaction IV, many vernacular translations were made. The vision is also included and referred to in many other works; it exerted a great influence on medieval vision literature. It takes its starting point from the *raptus* of Paul recorded in 2 Corinthians 12.1–5; it is based initially on the apocalypses of Peter, Zephaniah and Elias, as well as on *II Enoch*, with borrowings from a variety of other sources. The main Latin version may be divided into four main sections. The first eighteen chapters relate the discovery of the text at Tarsus, and the judgment of men in life and after death. Chapters 19–30 recount Paul's visit to the heavenly city, which is surrounded by twelve gold walls and through which flow four rivers. Chapters 31–41 tell of the realm of torment; this became the most influential part of the work. The damned are seen suffering various degrees of immersion in a fiery river, plunged in ice and snow, pitch and brimstone, tormented like Tantalus, suspended by the hair, turned on spits, wearing rags of fire, or sealed sevenfold in a pit; their sins are always specified, like being grouped with like. Finally, chapters 42–45 relate Paul's intercessory prayer and his second visit to Paradise. The version is about 3,700 words long.

Bibliography: T. Silverstein, '*Visio Sancti Pauli': the History of the Apocalypse in Latin together with Nine Texts*, London, 1935; 'The Vision of Saint Paul: New Links and Patterns in the Western Tradition' in *Archives d'histoire doctrinale et littéraire du moyen âge*, 34 (1959), 199–248; H. Brandes, '*Visio S. Pauli': ein Beitrag zur Visionslitteratur, mit einem deutschen und zwei lateinischen Texten*, Halle, 1885, pp. 75–80 (Redaction IV); 'Visio Sancti Pauli', edited by M. R. James in *Apocrypha Anecdota*, I, *Texts and Studies* series, edited by J. A. Robinson, Cambridge, 1893, pp. 1–42 (Paris manuscript); 'The Apocalypse of Paul', translated by M. R. James in *The Apocryphal New Testament*, Oxford, 1924, pp. 526–55 (Paris manuscript), and also by A. Rutherford in the *Ante-Nicene Christian Library Additional Volume*, edited by A. Menzies, Edinburgh, 1897, pp. 151–66. Vernacular texts are edited by P. Meyer, 'La Descente de S. Paul en enfer: poème français composé en Angleterre', *Romania*, 24 (1895), 357–75 and 589–91; and P. Villari, 'La visione di S. Paolo', *Antiche leggende e tradizioni che illustrano la 'Divina Commedia'*, Pisa, 1865, reprinted 1979, pp. 77–81.

Peter, Vision of

The vision of the Spanish monk Peter is related in Book IV, chapter 37, of the *Dialogues* of Gregory the Great, which were written in 593–4. The vision is told in about 200 words. Peter is taken to Hell as a salutary warning; he is rescued from the torments awaiting him by a shining angel, who tells him to mend his ways and restores him to life. He becomes a hermit, and subsequently recounts his experiences to a monk of Illyria, who tells them in turn to Gregory.

Bibliography: See entry under *Vision of a Soldier*.

Poor woman, Vision of a

The redactor of the vision of a Poor Woman, who may have been the same Heito who recorded that of Wetti, gives a short (400 words) account with few details of circumstance. The vision is political in nature, and took place in Germany in the ninth century. The Poor Woman is guided by a monk through Hell, where she sees Charles the Fat, Picho and Irmingard in torment. She is then led to the Earthly Paradise, surrounded by a wall on which are engraved the names of those permitted to enter; she reads the names of Bernhart, in bright characters, and Ludovic, almost obliterated.

Bibliography: 'Visio cuiusdam pauperculae mulieris', edited by W. Wattenbach, *Deutschlands Geschichtsquellen im Mittelalter bis zur Mitte des Dreizehnten Jahrhunderts*, I, pp. 260–1, Berlin, 1885.

Appendix

Raoul de Houdenc

Raoul was the first among the French *trouvères* of the thirteenth century to compose an allegorical poem treating the afterlife. He wrote, in about 1225, a *Songe d'Enfer*, containing 682 octosyllabic verses; a corresponding *Voie de Paradis* was added by a *trouvère* also called Raoul, but probably to be distinguished from the first. Although purporting to describe journeys to Hell and Heaven, the poems in fact offer an allegory of the journey through life itself; the traveller passes through places named Convoitise and Foi-Mentie, meeting people called Envie and Tricherie or, conversely, visits the domain of Amour, meeting Discipline, Esperance and others. In the *Songe d'Enfer* he ends up participating in an infernal banquet, and in the *Voie de Paradis* eventually arrives, after a *psychomachia*, at the ladder of Jacob; he ascends, contemplates God, Mary and the blessed, returns to earth and wakes up. These poems are the first of a number with similar titles; they both satirise contemporary society and give some insight into the state of popular belief concerning the afterlife. They also provide a precedent for an allegorical treatment of the otherworld.

Bibliography: See D. D. R. Owen, *The Vision of Hell: Infernal Journeys in Medieval French Literature*, Edinburgh and London, 1970, pp. 158–60.

Rimbert, archbishop: Life of Anskar

Rimbert's *Vita Anskarii* is the biography of Anskar, who spent most of his life as a missionary in Denmark and Sweden. Anskar was born in 801, became archbishop first of Hamburg and then of Bremen, and died in 865. From an early age he received visions, including several relevant to the afterlife tradition; these were recorded in the account of his life written by Rimbert, who carried on his work. There are several manuscripts, three of which date from the twelfth century. Four of Anskar's visions are of particular interest. The first, experienced at the age of five, is of two paths, leading respectively to Heaven and Hell; it is about 250 words long. The second, twice the length, is of his own arrival in first the fire of purgation, subsequently in Paradise, where twenty-four seniors contemplate a vision of Christ. The seventh, of about 200 words, is of the Passion; and the eighth, of about the same length, is of the suffering on earth seen from the perspective of Heaven.

Bibliography: 'Vita Anskarii', edited by W. Trillmich, in *Quellen des 9 und 11 Jahrhunderts zur Geschichte der Hamburgischen Kirche und des Reiches*, edited by R. Buchner, Darmstadt, 1961, pp. 3–133; *Anskar, the Apostle of the North, 801–865*, translated by C. H. Robinson, 1921.

Rotcharius, Vision of

The vision of Rotcharius is a brief account of a visit to the mansions of Heaven, composed in the early ninth century. Rotcharius is shown three houses: that of God, that of the saints, and that of souls undergoing purgation.

Appendix

Bibliography: The vision is edited by W. Wattenbach in *Anzeiger für Kunde der deutschen Vorzeit*, XXII (1875), cols. 72–4; see also H. R. Patch, *The Other World, according to Descriptions in Medieval Literature*, Cambridge (Mass.), 1950, p. 104.

Rutebeuf

Rutebeuf, who spent most of his life in Paris, was one of the most prolific of the *trouvères*. The *Voie de Paradis* was composed probably in 1265. It is 902 verses long, and is written in octosyllabic couplets. It takes the form of a dream pilgrimage to Paradise; allegorical figures and cities, corresponding to secular vices and Christian virtues, are welcomed or avoided on the journey. The poem influenced Baudouin de Condé's composition of the same title.

Bibliography: *Oeuvres complètes de Rutebeuf*, I, edited by E. Faral and J. Bastin, Paris, 1959, pp. 336–70.

St Patrick's Purgatory

The legend of St Patrick's Purgatory is unique in being attached to a place rather than to a particular visionary. A cave on an island in Lough Derg was said to have been indicated to Patrick as an entrance to the other world; a tradition became established whereby whoever truly wished to pay penance for his sins could apply to spend, at his own peril, a night alone in the cave. During the reign of Stephen (d. 1154) a knight, Owen, survived this ordeal and emerged reformed. He related his experiences to a monk Gilbert, who related them in turn to Hugh (or possibly Henry) of Saltrey, who wrote the authoritative Latin version of the story, probably between 1179 and 1181. This version about 11,500 words long, and very much attached to previous tradition, gave the legend great popularity. Accounts of, and references to, it occur in the works of Roger of Wendover, Matthew Paris, Caesarius of Heisterbach, Jacopo de Vitriaco, Vincent of Beauvais, Etienne de Bourbon, Peter the Venerable, and in the *Legenda aurea*; it was known to Albert the Great and to Bonaventure. It was translated into French by Marie de France, six further versions in verse, others in prose, being soon composed; translations into Provençal and English followed, as did five Italian redactions. Owen's journey into the other world is the only one undertaken in the flesh and without the aid of a guide. He travels through the four fields of torment in Hell, and passes the entrance to its lower regions; he then crosses a bridge and comes to the Earthly Paradise, where he meets a procession of the elect and is given an assurance that one day he will reach the celestial Paradise. Next morning he leaves the cave and embarks upon a pilgrimage to Jerusalem. Other accounts of the Purgatory locate it on a mountain (Jocelin of Furness) or an island (Giraldus Cambrensis).

Bibliography: Henricus Salteriensis 'De Purgatorio S. Patricii', edited by Migne, *Patrologia Latina*, CLXXX, cols. 974–1003; R. Easting, 'Peter of Cornwall's Account of St. Patrick's Purgatory', *Analecta Bollandiana*, 97 (1979), 397–416; see also R. Easting, 'The Date and Dedication of the "'Tractatus de Purgatorio Sancti

Patricii"', *Speculum*, 53 (1978), 778–83. Other versions are given in S. Leslie, *Saint Patrick's Purgatory: A Record from History and Literature*, London, 1932, and in Ph. De Félice, *L'Autre monde, mythes et légendes: le Purgatoire de saint Patrice*, Paris, 1906. Italian versions are given by P. Villari, 'Il Purgatorio di S. Patrizio', *Antiche leggende e tradizioni che illustrano la Divina Commedia*, Pisa, 1865, reprinted 1979, pp. 51–76, and L. Bertolini, 'Per una delle leggende che illustrano la 'Divina Commedia': una redazione del "Purgatorio di San Patrizio"', *Studi Danteschi*, 53 (1981), 69–128.

Salvius, Vision of

The vision of the monk Salvius is recorded in Book VII, chapter 1 of the *Historia Francorum* of Gregory of Tours, where it is assigned to the year 584. It is about 950 words long; Gregory's source is Salvius himself. Salvius dies, undergoes a journey through the heavens, and revives the following morning. On his journey he ascends in the company of two angels through a place of light populated by a throng of spirits, and on to a luminous cloud, where dwell the martyrs and confessors. Here a voice tells him he must return to life, for the sake of the Church.

Bibliography: 'Gregorii episcopi Turonensis: Historiarium libri decem', edited by R. Buchner, *Gregori von Tours: Zehn Bucher Geschichten*, vols. 1–2. Berlin n.d.; see also *'The History of the Franks'*, by *Gregory of Tours*, edited by O. M. Dalton, Oxford, 1927.

Servant, Vision of a – see Othlo: *Liber visionum*

Soldier, Vision of a

The vision of a soldier is the longest and most influential of those recounted in Book IV of Gregory's *Dialogues;* together with the discussion which follows, it contains about 900 words. The soldier died of plague in Rome in about 590, returned to life and related his experiences. He is taken to a place where he sees a river, from which arises smoke and a strong stench, crossed by a bridge. On the opposite bank are a number of houses of gold, some infected by the fumes of the river, and a beautiful meadow. Saint and sinner alike must attempt the bridge; the sinful fall off into the river below. Stephen the blacksmith is among those who try. The vision is popular in nature, but is followed by a discussion in which Gregory explains that it is in fact to be understood symbolically: the houses represent good works, the fumes sins of the flesh.

Bibliography: Gregorii Magni: *'Dialogi', Libri* IV, edited by U. Moricca, Rome, 1924; *Saint Gregory the Great: 'Dialogues'*, translated by O. J. Zimmerman, New York, 1959.

Stephen, Vision of

The experience undergone by Stephen is related in Book IV, chapter 37 of the *Dialogues* of Gregory the Great. It is scarcely over 100 words long, and unique in the tradition. Stephen dies, and is summoned before the judge in Hell; the judge, however, declares that he had sent for Stephen the blacksmith, not this man. Stephen is restored to life, and the blacksmith duly dies.

Bibliography: See entry under the *Vision of a soldier*.

Sunniulf, Vision of

The vision of Sunniulf, abbot of Randau, is recorded in Book IV, chapter 33 of the *Historia Francorum* of Gregory of Tours, where it is assigned to the year 571. It is about 150 words long. Sunniulf is led to a river of flames in which sinners are immersed, as in the *Vision of Paul*, to varying degrees. A narrow bridge leads to a big white house on the far bank. Sunniulf is told that negligent clergy fail to cross the bridge.

Bibliography: See entry under *Vision of Salvius*.

Thane, Vision of a

This is a vision recorded in Book v, chapter 13 of Bede's *Historia ecclesiastica*. It is brief, being about 600 words in length, and is assigned to the period 704–9. In it an English thane receives on his sickbed a vision of certain men in white and of evil spirits, who bear books recording his good and evil deeds. The latter far outnumber the former, and his soul is claimed for Hell; the story is told as a warning.

Bibliography: See entry under Drythelm.

Thurkill, Vision of

The vision of Thurkill, an Essex peasant, occurred in 1206; it is the last of the series of major visions which reached a peak in the twelfth century. There are two complete manuscripts, and the vision is recounted in the *Flores historiarum* of Roger of Wendover and in the *Chronicus maioribus* of Matthew Paris. The redactor is thought to have been Ralph of Coggeshall; he is translating into Latin from Thurkill's oral account in English. In his preface he mentions the visions of Tundale, the Monk of Streflur, and especially the Monk of Eynsham; also *St Patrick's Purgatory* and Gregory's *Dialogues*. Parts of the account recall the vision of Gunthelm and the *Testament of Abraham*. The vision is about 8,500 words long. Thurkill's main guide is Julian the Hospitaler, who appears to him as he is working in the fields, and conducts him to a basilica, the assembly point for the recently dead. Souls, some white, some black, some spotted, congregate in the appropriate areas of the basilica. White ones are led by Michael to a mountain of joy; spotted ones by Peter into a purgatorial fire and an icy lake; black ones are weighed by Paul and a devil, and sent to Purgatory or Hell. Julian leads Thurkill through the fire and the lake, where he sees souls immersed to varying degrees, and then takes him to Hell, where he witnesses a devils' theatre in which souls are tormented in turn. A road leads on to the lower realms of Hell. They return to the basilica and proceed to the mountain of joy, on which there is a temple and the garden of Paradise. The mountain is linked to the purgatorial lake by a bridge. Thurkill meets people he knows, including his father; he is then returned to the body.

Bibliography: '*Visio Thurkilli' relatore, ut videtur, Radulpho de Coggeshall*, edited by P. G. Schmidt, Leipzig, 1978.

Treatise on the Journey of the Soul

There is one extant manuscript of an anonymous Latin treatise which proclaims its subject as the state of the soul after death, and which must have been written in the third quarter of the twelfth century, possibly in Catalonia. It bears witness to the conjunction between Arab Neoplatonism and the Western Christian tradition, is dependent on works and authors as disparate as the *Liber de Causis*, the Church Fathers and Servius, and is influenced in addition by Jewish and Gnostic sources. It is 2,600 words in length. After a preliminary discussion of its subject, the treatise describes the ascent of the soul through the ten degrees of beatitude, then through the angelic orders to God; there is a corresponding, alternative descent through the ten divisions of Hell, located in the planetary spheres which are governed by the angelic orders. A list of the ten prohibitions and commandments is then given, as communicated to man by Moses, Mohammed and Christ, and in terms of which the soul is judged. The treatise is of particular importance because, like the Seven Heavens apocryphon and the *Liber de Scalis*, it provides evidence for the intermingling fusion of Eastern and Western traditions concerning the afterlife.

Bibliography: M-T. D'Alverny, 'Les Pérégrinations de l'âme dans l'autre monde d'après un anonyme de la fin du XIIe siècle', *Archives d'histoire doctrinale et littéraire du Moyen âge*, 1940–2, pp. 239–99.

Tundale, Vision of

The vision of Tundale is one of the most important and influential in the entire tradition. Tundale, an Irish knight, is sent on a three-day journey under the guidance of his guardian angel, with the divinely ordained purpose of reforming his sinful soul. He travels firstly through upper Hell, participating in the torments for those sins of which he is guilty, until he reaches the pit of lower Hell where Satan is chained. He then visits a walled Paradise, where the journey ends. The importance of the vision lies in its detailed nature, in the breadth and depth with which it draws on the previous tradition (clear parallels can be drawn with the visions of Sunniulf, Paul, Drythelm and the Boy William, and with the Brendan legend; there are also classical and biblical allusions); in its literary merit; and finally in the wide diffusion it received. Tundale, a native of Cashel, experienced his vision in 1149 while in Cork. The redactor of the full Latin text is a monk named Marcus, who travelled probably in the same year to Ratisbon, where he translated what he had heard from Irish into Latin. This Latin text received a wide distribution; there are over 200 extant manuscripts scattered throughout Europe. The vision is related by other writers, including Helinandus and Vincent of Beauvais; it was eventually translated into German, Italian, French, Dutch, Gaelic, Norse and Icelandic. Marcus's version is about 10,500 words long.

Bibliography: '*Visio Tnugdali': lateinisch und altdeutsch*, edited by A. Wagner, Erlagen, 1882; 'La Visione di Tugdalo volgarizzata nel secolo xiv', edited by F. Corazzini, *Scelta di curiosità letterarie inedite o rare*, cxxviii, Bologna, 1872, reprinted 1968.

Walkelin, Vision of

The vision of Walkelin, a priest in the diocese of Lisieux, is recorded in Book viii, chapter 17 of the *Historia ecclesiastica* of Ordericus Vitalis, where it is assigned to the year 1091 and recounted in about 2,200 words. Walkelin is out one night visiting a sick man, when he is passed by the army of the dead. He recognises many people he has known, all undergoing various kinds of torment. The torment is, in some cases at least, purgative. The vision is unusual in that the visionary normally visits the land of the dead, rather than the other way round. The contents however are traditional.

Bibliography: *The 'Ecclesiastical History' of Orderic Vitalis*, iv, edited and translated by M. Chibnall, London, 1973.

Wetti, Vision of

Wetti, a monk of Reichenau, received a vision of the afterlife shortly before his death in 824. It was recorded immediately in 3,500 words of Latin prose by Heito, and turned into verse in 837 by Walafrid Strabo. This verse account, 7,000 words in length, written in an artificial, literary Latin, is of exceptional importance in the tradition. It is the first account of a vision in verse; previous accounts had been purely documentary. It contains the first mountain of purgation, and it enters into an unprecedented amount of social, political and religious polemic. It was influenced by the vision of Paul, the Apocalypse, and possibly the vision of Barontus; it cites Gregory's *Dialogues* and the *Shepherd of Hermas*. It is probable that the visionary or redactor was acquainted also with the visions of the Poor Woman and of Rotcharius. There are seven known manuscripts scattered in various parts of Europe, and Wetti is referred to in the vision of Bernoldus. Wetti is led by his guardian angel past a river of fire to the mountain on which purgation occurs, and thence to the heavenly city, where they beg the saints, martyrs and virgins to intercede on Wetti's behalf with God. The angel makes several speeches on the vices and errors of men, which Wetti is to relay, and the vision ends. Throughout his journey Wetti meets contemporary figures, including Charlemagne himself.

Appendix

Bibliography: D. A. Traill, *Walahfrid Strabo's 'Visio Wettini': Text, Translation and Commentary*, Frankfurt, 1974; 'Heitonis Visio Wettini', *Poetarum Latinorum medii aevi II: Poetae Latini aevi carolini*, edited by E. Duemmler, *Monumenta Germaniae Historica*, Berlin, 1884.

Woman, Vision of a

The vision of a Woman is recorded in a letter of Lull, bishop of Mentz; only a part of it survives. It is said to have occurred some time after 757. The woman sees the immersion of named sinners in [a river of] fire, the torment of others on a wheel, an earthly Paradise and three heavens. The fragment is about 700 words long.

Bibliography: 'Quidam monacho cuidam de visione feminae cuiusdam refert', 'S, Bonifatii et Lulli epistolae', *Epistolae merowingici et karolini aevi*, 1, edited by E. Duemmler, *Monumenta Germinae Historica*, III, Berlin, 1892.

Bibliography

This bibliography includes both those works cited in the text or notes and those to which I am indebted in ways which it is not always possible to acknowledge specifically.

Bibliographical details for the popular representations of the other world are given in the appendices, and are therefore not included here.

Abelard, Peter. *Peter Abelard's 'Ethics'*, ed. by D. E. Luscombe, Oxford, 1971.

Alan of Lille. *'Anticlaudianus': texte critique, avec une introduction et des tables*, ed. by R. Bossuat, Paris, 1955

　'Anticlaudianus'; or, The Good and Perfect Man: translation and commentary by J. J. Sheridan, Toronto, 1973

　'Liber Poenitentialis': texte inédit publié et annoté par Jean Longère, 2 vols., Louvain–Lille, 1965

Albert the Great. *De Resurrectione*, in *Opera Omnia*, XXVI, ed. by W. Kubel, Aschendorff, 1958

Alighieri, Dante. *Convivio*, ed. by E. G. Parodi and F. Pellegrini in *Le Opere di Dante: testo critico della Società Dantesca Italiana*, ed. by M. Barbi and others, 2nd edition, Florence, 1960, pp. 145–293.

　La 'Divina Commedia': testo critico stabilito da Giorgio Petrocchi, Turin, 1975

　La 'Divina Commedia', ed. by Natalino Sapegno, reprinted Florence, 1977–9

Alighieri, Jacopo. *Chiose alla Cantica dell'Inferno di Dante Allighieri attribuite a Jacopo suo figlio ora per la prima volta date in luce*, ed. by Lord Vernon, Florence, 1848

Anonimo fiorentino. *Commento alla Cantica dell'Inferno di Dante Allighieri di autore Anonimo ora per la prima volta dato in luce*, 1848

Anselm. *'Pourquoi Dieu s'est fait homme': texte latin, introduction, bibliographie, traduction et notes*, ed. by R. Roques, Paris, 1963

Aquinas, Thomas. *Summa Theologiae*, ed. by P. Caramello, 3 vols., Vatican, 1952

　Summa Theologiae, XXVII, *The Effects of Sin, Stain and Guilt: Latin text, English translation, Introduction, Notes, Appendices and Glossary*, ed. by T. C. O'Brien, Blackfriars, 1974

Bonaventure. 'Commentary on the *Sententiae* of Peter Lombard' in *Opera Omnia jussu et auctoritate P. Bernardini (Quaracchi)*, IV, 1882

Buti, Francesco da. *Commento di Francesco da Buti sopra la Divina Commedia di Dante Allighieri pubblicato per cura di Crescentino Giannini*, 3 vols., Pisa, 1858

Furnivall, F. J. (ed.) *Robert of Brunne's 'Handlyng Synne', AD 1303, with those parts of the Anglo-French Treatise on which it was founded, William of Wadington's 'Manuel des Pechiez', re-edited from manuscripts in the British Museum and Bodleian Libraries*, London, 1901

Geoffrey of Vinsauf. *Poetria Nova*, translated by M. F. Nims, Toronto, 1967

Gregory the Great. *Sancti Gregorii Magni Moralium Libri, sive expositio in librum B. Job*, in Migne, *Patrologia Latina*, LXXV, cols. 509–1162, and LXXVI, cols. 1–782.

Helinandus monachus. *Chronicon*, in Migne, *Patrologia Latina*, CCXII, cols. 771–1082 (*Vision*

Bibliography

of Tundale, cols. 1038–55; *Vision of Gunthelm*, cols. 1060–3)

Holy Bible, The: A Translation from the Latin Vulgate in the light of the Hebrew and Greek Originals (Knox Translation), London, 1945, one-volume edition 1961

Honorius of Autun, *Scala Coeli Major seu de ordine cognoscendi Deum in creaturis*, and *Scala Coeli Minor seu de gradibus charitatis opusculum*, in Migne, *Patrologia Latina*, CLXXII, 1229–42

Hugh of St Victor. *De Anima*, in Migne, *Patrologia Latina*, CLXXVII, cols. 165–90
De Fructibus carnis et spiritus, in Migne, *Patrologia Latina*, CLXXVI, cols. 997–1010

Jacobus de Voragine. *The 'Golden Legend' of Jacobus de Voragine, translated and adapted from the Latin by Granger Ryan and Helmut Ripperger*, London, New York and Toronto, 1941
Legenda Aurea vulgo historia Lombardica dicta, ed. by Th. Graesse, second edition, Leipzig, 1850

Michaud-Quantin, P. (ed.) 'Un manuel de confession archaïque dans le manuscrit Avranches 136', *Sacris Erudiri*, 17 (1966), 5–54

Migne, J. P. *Patrologiae cursus completus: series Graeco-Latina*, 161 vols., Paris, 1857–66
Patrologiae cursus completus, series Latina, 217 vols., Paris, 1844–1905

Penitential of Bede. ed. by H. J. Schmitz, *Die Bussbücher und die Bussdisziplin der Kirche*, Mainz, 1883, reprinted Graz, 1958, pp. 556–64.

Penitential of Theodore. ed. by H. J. Schmitz, *Die Bussbücher und die Bussdisziplin der Kirche*, Mainz, 1883, reprinted Graz, 1958, pp. 524–38

Peraldus, Guillielmus. *Summae virtutum ac vitiorum*, 2 vols., Moguntiae, 1618

'Poenitentiale Cummeani'. ed. by H. J. Schmitz, *Die Bussbücher und die Bussdisziplin der Kirche*, Mainz, 1883, reprinted Graz, 1958, 615–76

'Poenitentiale Romanum', in Halitgar, *De Poenitentia libri V* in Migne, *Patrologia Latina*, CV, cols. 693–710, and in H. J. Schmitz, *Die Bussbücher und die Bussdisziplin der Kirche*, Mainz, 1883, reprinted Graz, 1958, 465–89

Roger of Wendover. *Flores historiarum*, edited by H. G. Hewlett, Rolls Series 84, 3 vols., London, 1886–9
Roger of Wendover's Flowers of History, comprising the History of England, from the descent of the Saxons to AD 1235, formerly ascribed to Matthew Paris, translated from the Latin by J. A. Giles, 2 vols., London, 1849

II SECONDARY SOURCES

Alessandrini, S. *Saggio di studio comparativo fra i quattro inferni classici di Omero, Virgilio, Dante e Fenelon*, Fermo, 1926

Alger, W. R. *The Destiny of the Soul: A Critical History of the Doctrine of a Future Life*, 10th edition, Boston, 1880

Amat, J. *Songes et visions: l'au-delà dans la littérature latine tardive*, Paris, 1985

Anderson, W. *Dante the Maker*, London, 1980

Andriani, B. *La forma del Paradiso dantesco: il sistema del mondo secondo gli antichi e secondo Dante*, Padua, 1961

Argan, G. C. *Storia dell'arte italiana*, 3 vols., Florence, 1977

Ariès, P. *The Hour of Our Death*, translated by H. Weaver from the French edition of 1977, Harmondsworth, 1983
'Le Purgatoire et la cosmologie de l'au-delà, *Annales: Economies, Sociétés, Civilisations*, 38 (1983), 151–7
Western Attitudes toward Death: From the Middle Ages to the Present, translated by P. M. Ranum, Baltimore–London, 1974

Armour, P. 'Dante's Brunetto: the Paternal Paterine?', *Italian Studies*, 38 (1983), 1–38

Arnould, E. J. *Le 'Manuel des Péchés': Étude de littérature religieuse anglo-normande (XIIIme siècle)*, Paris, 1940

Asin Palacios, M. *Islam and the 'Divine Comedy', translated and abridged from the original edition of 1919* by H. Sunderland, London, 1926

Bibliography

Aubrun, M. 'Caractères et portée religieuse et sociale des "visiones" en Occident du VIe au XIe siècle', *Cahiers de civilisation médiévale*, 23 (1980), 109–30

Auerbach, E. *Dante, Poet of the Secular World*, translated by R. Manheim from the German edition of 1929, Chicago, 1961

'Farinata and Cavalcante', *Mimesis: The Representation of Reality in Western Literature*, translated by W. R. Trask, pp. 174–202, Princeton, 1953

'Figura' in *Scenes from the Drama of European Literature: Six Essays*, translated by R. Manheim and C. Garvin, New York, 1959

Literary Language and its Public in Late Latin Antiquity and in the Middle Ages, translated by R. Manheim from the German edition of 1958, London, 1965

Aurigemma, M. 'Paradiso', *Enciclopedia Dantesca*, IV, Rome, 1973, pp. 284–9

'Purgatorio', *Enciclopedia Dantesca*, IV, Rome, 1973, pp. 745–50

Bar, F. *Les Routes de l'autre monde: descentes aux enfers et voyages dans l'au-delà*, Paris, 1946

Bardy, G. *et al.* (eds.), *L'Inferno*, translated from the French by D. Tenderini, Brescia, 1953

'I Padri della Chiesa di fronte ai problemi posti dall'inferno' in *L'Inferno*, as above, pp. 105–68

Barral i Altet, X. 'L'Iconographie de caractère synthétique et monumental inspirée de l'Apocalypse dans l'art mediéval d'Occident (IXe–XIIIe siècles)' in *L'Apocalypse de Jean: Traditions exégétiques et iconographiques, IIIe–XIIIe siècles, Actes du colloque de la Fondation Hardt, 29 février–3 mars 1976*, ed. by Y. Christe, Geneva, 1979, pp. 187–216

Bataillon, L-J. 'Bulletin d'histoire des doctrines médiévales: généralitiés', *Revue de sciences philosophiques et théologiques*, 66 (1982), 244–65

Beauvois, E. 'L'Elysée transatlantique et l'Eden occidental', *Revue de l'histoire des religions*, 8 (1883), 273–318 and 673–727

Becker, E. J. *A Contribution to the Comparative Study of the Medieval Visions of Heaven and Hell, with special reference to Middle-English versions*, Baltimore, 1899

Beigbeder, O. *Lexique des symboles*, 1969

Bellinati, C. 'La Cappella degli Scrovegni' in *Padova: basiliche e chiese*, 2 vols., Vicenza, 1975, I, pp. 247–68

Bellosi, L. *Giotto*, Florence, 1981

Bergin, T. G. 'Hell: Topography and Demography', *Essays on Dante*, Bloomington, 1964, pp. 76–93

'On the *Personae* of the *Comedy*' in *American Critical Essays on the 'Divine Comedy'*, ed. by R. J. Clements, London–New York, 1967, pp. 117–24

Bertaux, E. *L'Art dans l'Italie méridionale de la fin de l'Empire romain à la conquête de Charles d'Anjou*, 3 vols., Paris, 1903, reprinted Paris–Rome, 1968

Santa Maria di Donna Regina e l'arte senese a Napoli nel sec. XIV, Naples, 1899

Bertolini, L. 'Per una delle leggende "che illustrano la *Divina Commedia*"', *Studi Danteschi*, 53 (1981), 69–128

'Una redazione italiana della "Leggenda del Purgatorio di San Patrizio"' (unpublished dissertation, University of Pisa, 1979)

Bindoni, G. 'Ubicazione e struttura del Paradiso terrestre' in *Indagini critiche sulla 'Divina Commedia'*, Milan–Rome–Naples, 1918, pp. 273–99

Bloch, H. 'Montecassino, Byzantium and the West in the Earlier Middle Ages', *Dumbarton Oaks Papers*, 3 (1946), 163–224

Boase, T. S. R. *Death in the Middle Ages: Mortality, Judgment and Remembrance*, London, 1972

Bogdanos, T. '"The Shepherd of Hermas" and the Development of Medieval Visionary Allegory', *Viator*, 8 (1977), 33–46

Bolgar, R. R. *The Classical Heritage and its Beneficiaries*, Cambridge, 1954

Boser, C. 'F. Novati: La "Navigatio Sancti Brendani" in antico veneziano, Bergamo 1892', *Romania*, 22 (1893), 581–90

Bibliography

Boswell, C. S. *An Irish Precursor of Dante: a Study on the Vision of Heaven and Hell ascribed to the Eighth-century Irish saint Adamnan, with translation of the Irish text*, London, 1908

Bottari, G. 'Lettera di un accademico della Crusca (Monsignore Gio. Bottari) scritta ad un altro accademico della medesima' (in 1753), in *Le Opere di Dante Alighieri*, I, 5 vols., ed. by L. Ciardetti, Florence, 1830, pp. 139–55

Botterill, S. N. 'A Study of the Influence of St Bernard of Clairvaux on the Works of Dante Alighieri', (unpublished PhD dissertation, University of Cambridge), 1984

Boyde, P. *Dante Philomythes and Philosopher: Man in the Cosmos*, Cambridge, 1981

Brandeis, I. *The Ladder of Vision: A Study of Images in Dante's 'Comedy'*, London, 1960

Brancon, S. G. F. *The Judgment of the Dead: An Historical and Comparative Study of the Idea of a Post-Mortem Judgment in the Major Religions*, London, 1967

Bredero, A. H. 'Jérusalem dans l'Occident médiéval' in *Mélanges offerts à René Crozet*, 2 vols., Poitiers, 1966, I, pp. 259–71

'Le Moyen Age et le Purgatoire', *Revue d'histoire ecclésiastique*, 78 (1983), 429–52

Brès, A-C, 'Jacques Le Goff, *La Naissance du Purgatoire*', *Revue philosophique de la France et de l'étranger*, 107 (1982), 540–1

Bullough, D. *The Age of Charlemagne*, 2nd edition, London, 1973 (1st edition 1965)

Busnelli, G. *Il concetto e l'ordine del "Paradiso" dantesco: indagini e studi*, 2 vols., Città di Castello, 1911–12

'L'"Etica Nicomachea" e l'ordinamento morale dell'"Inferno" di Dante', *Giornale Dantesco*, 13 (1905), 257–305

L'"Etica Nicomachea" e l'ordinamento morale dell'"Inferno" di Dante, Bologna, 1907

L'ordinamento morale del "Purgatorio" dantesco, 2nd edition, Rome, 1908

Bynum, C. W. 'Did the XIIth Century Discover the Individual?', *Journal of Ecclesiastical History*, 31 (1980), 1–17

Caliaro, I. *Dante*, Verona, 1981

Campbell, J. *The Mythic Image*, Princeton, 1974

Cancellieri, F. 'Lettera del sig. Ab. Cancellieri al sig. Cav. Gio. Gherardo De Rossi', (14.4.1815) in *La 'Divina Commedia' di Dante Alighieri, col commento del P. Baldassarre Lombardi M.C.*, ed. by G. Campi, F. Federici, G. Maffei, 5 vols., Padua, 1822, V, pp. 338–43

'Lettera del sig. Ab. Cancellieri al sig. Cav. Gio. Gherardo De Rossi' (16.4.1815), as above, pp. 347–8

Osservazioni intorno alla questione promossa dal Vannozzi, dal Mazzochi, dal Bottari, e especialmente dal P. Abate D. Giuseppe Giustino di Costanzo sopra l'originalità della 'Divina Commedia' di Dante, appoggiata alla storia della visione del monaco casinese Alberico, Rome, 1814

Carboni, C. *Tavole sinottiche e critiche di studio alla 'Divina Commedia'*, 3 vols., Rome [1963]

Carelli, E. and S. Casiello. *Santa Maria Donnaregina in Napoli*, Naples, 1975

Carli, E. *Duccio a Siena*, Novara, 1973

Carozzi, C. 'La Géographie de l'au-delà et sa signification pendant le haut moyen âge', *Settimane di studio del Centro italiano di studi sull'alto medioevo XXIX: Popoli e paesi nella cultura altomedievale (Spoleto, 23–29 aprile 1981)*, Spoleto, 1983

'Structure et fonction de la vision de Tnugdal' in *Faire Croie: Modalités de la diffusion et de la réception des messages religieux du XIIe au XVe siècle. Table ronde organisée par l'Ecole française de Rome en collaboration avec l'Institut d'histoire médiévale de l'Université de Padoue (Rome, 22–23 juin 1979)*, Rome, 1981, pp. 223–34

Carrouges, M. 'Immagini dell'inferno nella letteratura' in *L'Inferno*, ed. by G. Bardy *et al.*, translated by D. Tenderini, Brescia, 1953, pp. 11–61

Casella, M. *Le Guide di Dante nella 'Divina Commedia'*, Florence, 1944

Casey, R. P. 'The Apocalypse of Paul', *Journal of Theological Studies*, 34 (1933), 1–32

Bibliography

Castelfranchi, V. L., *L'Abbazia di Viboldone*, Milan, 1961

Castelli, U. and R. Gagetti. *Pisa e i suoi artisti*, Florence, 1977

Cavendish, R. *Visions of Heaven and Hell*, London, 1977

Cerulli, E. *Il 'Libro della Scala' e le questione delle fonti arabo-spagnole della 'Divina Commedia'*, Vatican, 1949

Charles, R. H. *The Apocrypha and Pseudepigrapha of the Old Testament*, 2 vols., London, 1913
  'Eschatology' in *Encyclopaedia Biblica*, ed. by T. K. Cheyne and J. S. Black, 4 vols., London, 1899–1903, II, (1901), cols. 1335–92

Chenu, M-D. *Nature, Man and Society in the Twelfth Century: Essays on New Theological Perspectives in the Latin West, selected, edited and translated from the original edition of 1957 by J. Taylor and L. K. Little*, Chicago, 1968

Chiappelli, A. 'Il Nuovo frammento dell'Apocalisse di Pietro', *Nuova Antologia*, Series III, 47 (1893), 112–22

Chiarini, E. 'Canto XXX, a cura di Eugenio Chiarini, Novembre 1963' in *Lectura Dantis Scaligera: Purgatorio*, ed. by M. Marcazzan and S. Pasquazi, Florence, 1971, pp. 1105–33

Chiffoleau, J. *La Comptabilité de l'au-delà: les hommes, la mort et la religion dans la région d'Avignon à la fin du moyen âge (vers 1320–vers 1480)*, Rome, 1980

Christe, Y. (ed.) *L'Apocalypse de Jean: traditions exégétiques et iconographiques, IIIe–XIIIe siècles, Actes du colloque de la Fondation Hardt, 29 février–3 mars 1976*, Geneva, 1979
  'Traditions littéraries et iconographiques dans l'interprétation des images apocalyptiques' in *L'Apocalypse de Jean* (as above), pp. 109–34

Ciccarese, M. P. 'Alle origini della letteratura delle visioni: il contributo di Gregorio di Tours', *Studi storico-religiosi*, V, fasc. 2 (1981), 251–66

Ciotti, A. 'Alano e Dante', *Convivium* 28 (1960), 257–88
  'Le guide di Dante nel suo viaggio, *Enciclopedia Dantesca*, III, Rome, 1971, pp. 315–17
  'Paradiso terrestre', *Enciclopedia Dantesca*, IV, Rome, 1973, pp. 289–91

Cirlot, J. E. *A Dictionary of Symbols*, translated from the Spanish by J. Sage, London, 1962

Cole, B. *Sienese Painting, from its Origins to the Fifteenth Century*, New York, 1980

Coli, E. *Il Paradiso terrestre dantesco*, Florence, 1897

Colli, A. 'La Gerusalemme celeste nei cicli apocalittici altomedievali e l'affresco di san Pietro al Monte di Civate', *Cahiers archéologiques*, 30 (1982), 107–24
  'La tradizione figurativa della Gerusalemme celeste: linee di sviluppo dal sec. III al sec. XIV' in *La Gerusalemme celeste: catalogo della mostra, Milano, Università Cattolica del S. Cuore, 20 maggio–5 giugno 1983*, ed. by M. L. Gatti Perer, Milan, 1983, pp. 119–44

Comparetti, D. *Virgilio nel medio evo*, Florence, 1872, new edition Florence, 1937–41, reprinted 1967

Consoli, D. 'Virgilio Marone, Publio', *Enciclopedia Dantesca*, V, Rome, 1976, pp. 1030–44

Constable, G. *Religious Life and Thought (11th–12th centuries)*, London, 1979
  'The Vision of Gunthelm and other "Visiones" attributed to Peter the Venerable', *Revue Bénédictine*, 66 (1956), 92–114

Cooke, G. A. 'The Earth from the Eighth Heaven: A Note on Dante, Paradiso XXII 133–54', *Journal of Theological Studies*, 34 (1933), 347–50

Cooper, J. C. *An Illustrated Encyclopaedia of Traditional Symbols*, London, 1978

Copleston, F. C. *A History of Medieval Philosophy*, London, 1972

Cosmo, U. 'Le prime ricerche intorno all'originalità dantesca e due letterati padovani del secolo passato', *Rassegna padovana di storia lettere ed arti*, I (1891), 33–43, 65–74

Courcelle, P. 'Les Pères de l'Eglise devant les enfers virgiliens', *Archives d'histoire doctrinale et littéraire du Moyen Age*, 22 (1955), 5–74
  'La Posterité chrétienne du "Songe de Scipion"', *Revue des études latines*, 36 (1958), 205–34

Culianu, I. P. '"Pons subtilis": storia e significato di un simbolo', *Aevum*, 53 (1979), 301–12

Cumont, F. *After Life in Roman Paganism*, New Haven, 1922

Bibliography

Curtius, E. R. 'Dante und Alanus ab Insulis', *Romanische Forschungen*, 62 (1950), 28–31
  European Literature and the Latin Middle Ages, translated by W. R. Trask from the original
  edition of 1948, London, 1953
D'Ancona, A. *I Precursori di Dante*, Florence, 1874, reprinted in *Scritti Danteschi*, Florence,
  1912–13, pp. 3–108
D'Ancona, P. and E. Aeschlimann, *The Art of Illumination: An Anthology of Manuscripts from
  the Sixth to the Sixteenth Century*, translated by A. M. Brown, London, 1969
De Antonellis, C. 'De' principi di diritto penale che si contengono nella *Divina Commedia*' in
  Collezione di opuscoli danteschi inediti o rari diretta da G. L. Passerini, VIII, Città di Castello,
  1894
Dauphiné, J. *Le Cosmos de Dante*, Paris, 1984
De Bruyne, D. 'Fragments retrouvés d'apocryphes priscillianistes', *Revue Bénédictine*, 24
  (1907), 318–35
De Champeaux, G. and S. Sterckx. *Introduction au monde des symboles*, 2nd edition, 1972
De Lange, N. *Apocrypha: Jewish Literature of the Hellenistic Age*, New York, 1978
Delmay, B. *I personaggi della 'Divina Commedia': classificazione e regesto*, Florence, 1986
De Lubac, H. *L'Exégèse médiévale: les quatre sens de l'Ecriture*, 3 vols., Lyons, 1959
Delumeau, J. *Le Péché et la peur: la culpibilisation en Occident, XIIIe–XVIIIe siècles*, Paris, 1983
Deman, Th. 'Péché' in *Dictionnaire de Théologie Catholique*, ed. by A. Vacant, E. Mangenot
  and E. Amann, 15 vols., Paris, 1909–50, XII, (1933), cols. 140–275
Demus, O. *Romanesque Mural Painting*, translated from the original edition of 1968 by M.
  Whittall, London, 1970
De Negri, E. 'Tema e iconografia del Purgatorio', *The Romanic Review*, 49 (1958), 81–104
De Romanis. 'La Visione del Monaco Alberico, riscontrata coi luoghi di Dante che le si
  avvicinano, seguita da alcune Lettere dei sigg. Cav. Gio. Gherardo De Rossi ed Ab.
  Cancellieri, e dalla Conclusione del sig. De Romanis' in *'La Divina Commedia' di Dante
  Alighieri, col comento del P. Baldassarre Lombardi M.C.*, 5 vols., ed. by G. Campi, F.
  Federici, and G. Maffei, Padua, 1822, V, pp. 281–368
De Rossi, G. G. 'Lettera del sig. Cav. Gio. Gherardo De Rossi al sig. Abate Cancellieri,
  Frascati 10.11.[1814] as above, pp. 331–7
  'Lettera dal sig. Cav. Gio. Gherardo De Rossi al sig. Ab. Cancellieri', 16.4.1815, as above,
  pp. 344–6
De Vivo, C. *La Visione di Alberico, ristampata, traddota e comparata con la 'Divina Commedia'*,
  Ariano, 1899
Di Costanzo, G. G. L. 'Di un antico testo a penna della "Divina Commedia" di Dante, con
  alcune annotazioni sulle varianti lezioni e sulle postille del medesimo: Lettera di
  Eustazio Dicearcheo (Il P. Ab. Di Costanzo) ad Angelo Sidicino', 15.7.1800 in *Le Opere
  di Dante*, ed. by L. Ciardetti, Florence, 1830, 5 vols., V, pp. 157–268
Dictionary of the Bible, ed. by J. Hastings, 5 vols., Edinburgh, 1898–1904
Dictionnaire de Théologie Catholique, ed. by A. Vacant, E. Mangenot and E. Amann, 15 vols.,
  Paris, 1909–50
Diels, H. 'Himmels- und Höllenfahrten von Homer bis Dante', *Neue Jahrbücher für das
  klassische Altertum Geschichte und deutsche Literatur*, 49 (1922), 239–53
Dinzelbacher, P. 'Die Visionen des Mittelalters: ein geschichtlicher Umriss', *Zeitschrift für
  Religions- und Geistesgeschichte*, 30 (1978), 116–26
  Die Jenseitsbrucke im Mittelalter, Vienna, 1973
Dionisotti, C. 'La scuola storica', *Lettere italiane*, 25 (1973), 339–55
Diringer, D. *The Illuminated Book: Its History and Production*, London, 1967 (1st edition, 1958)
Dods, M. *Forerunners of Dante: An Account of Some of the More Important Visions of the Unseen
  World, from the Earliest Times*, Edinburgh, 1903
Dodwell, C. R. *Painting in Europe: 800–1200*, Harmondsworth, 1971

Bibliography

Dolbeau, F. 'Une vision addressée à Heito de Reichenau dans la Chronique de Saint-Maixent', *Analecta Bollandiana*, 98 (1980), 404

Donati, R. *San Gimignano: Città delle belle torri*, Terni, 1980

Dorival, B. 'L'inferno nell'arte' in *L'Inferno*, ed. by G. Bardy *et al.*, Translated by D. Tenderini, Brescia, 1953, pp. 215–23

D'Ovidio, F. *Il Purgatorio, Nuovi Studii Danteschi*, III, Naples [1931]
    Studii sulla 'Divina Commedia', Milan–Palermo, 1901
    'La Visione di Alberico' in 'Tre Discussioni: Celestino V – la data della composizione e divulgazione della 'Commedia' – La Laurea di Dante – La Visione di Alberico', *Studii sulla 'Divina Commedia'*, Part II, Caserta, 1931

Dronke, P. 'Boethius, Alanus and Dante', *Romanische Forschungen*, 1966
    Dante and Medieval Latin Traditions, Cambridge, 1986
    Poetic Individuality in the Middle Ages: New Departures in Poetry 1000–1150, London, 1970
    'Purgatorio XXIX: The Procession' in *Cambridge Readings in Dante's 'Comedy'*, Cambridge, 1981, pp. 114–37
    Women Writers of the Middle Ages: A Critical Study of Texts from Perpetua (†203) to Marguerite Porete (†1310), Cambridge, 1984

Duby, G. *L'An mil*, Paris, 1967, reprinted 1980

Dumville, D. N. 'Towards an Interpretation of "Fís Adamnan"', *Studia Celtica*, 12–13 (1977–8), 62–77

Duncan, J. E. *Milton's Earthly Paradise: A Historical Study of Eden*, Minneapolis, 1972

Durand, G. *Les Structures anthropologiques de l'imaginaire: Introduction à l'archéo-typologie générale*, Paris, 1969

Easting, R. 'The Date and Dedication of the "Tractatus de Purgatorio Sancti Patricii"', *Speculum*, 53 (1978), 778–83
    'Peter of Cornwall's Account of St Patrick's Purgatory', *Analecta Bollandiana*, 97 (1979), 397–416

Eliade, M. *The Myth of the Eternal Return*, translated by W. R. Trask from the original edition of 1949, New York, 1954, reprinted London, 1955
    Myths, Rites, Symbols: A Mircea Eliade Reader, ed. by W. C. Beane and W. G. Doty, 2 vols., New York, 1975
    Patterns in Comparative Religion, translated from the French by R. Sheed, London–New York, 1958
    Shamanism: Archaic Techniques of Ecstasy, translated by W. R. Trask from the original edition of 1951, London, 1964

Ellis Davidson, H. R. (ed.) *The Journey to the Other World*, Cambridge, 1975

Emiliani, A. *La Pinacoteca Nazionale di Bologna*, Bologna, 1979

Enciclopedia Cattolica, ed. by P. Paschini, 12 vols., Vatican, 1949–54

Enciclopedia Dantesca, ed. by U. Bosco, 6 vols., Rome, 1970–9

Encyclopaedia Biblica, ed. by T. K. Cheyne and J. S. Black, 5 vols., London, 1901

Erikson, C. *The Medieval Vision: Essays in History and Perception*, New York, 1976

Ermini, F. 'La "Visio Anselli" e l'imitazione nella "Divina Commedia"', in *Medio Evo latino: studii e ricerche*, Modena, 1938, 309–15

Esposito, M. 'Sur la Navigatio Sancti Brendani et sur ses versions italiennes', *Romania*, 64 (1938), 328–46

Evans, J. (ed.) *The Flowering of the Middle Ages*, London, 1966

Every, G. *Christian Mythology*, London, 1970

Fallani, G. *Dante e la cultura figurativa medievale*, Bergamo, 1971
    L'esperienza teologica di Dante, Lecce, 1976

Fanti, M. *La Basilica di San Petronio*, Bologna, 1967

Fedi, R. *Visioni d'oltretomba antiche e moderne*, Rome–Milan, 1954

Bibliography

Félice, Ph. De, *L'Autre monde, mythes et légendes: le Purgatoire de saint Patrice*, Paris, 1906

Foratti, A. 'Il Giudizio Universale di Giotto in Padova', *Bollettino d'arte del Ministero della Pubblica Istruzione*, 1 (1921), 49–66

Foscolo, U. 'Discorso sul testo e su le opinioni diverse prevalenti intorno alla storia e alla emendazione critica della "Commedia" di Dante' in *Prose Letterarie*, Opere, III, Florence, 1850, pp. 85–484

'Osservazioni intorno alla "Questione sopra la Originalità del Poema di Dante", di F. Cancellieri, Roma 1814', *Edinburgh Review*, September 1818, 317–51

Foster, K. *The Two Dantes and Other Essays*, London, 1977

Fox, J. *A Literary History of France: The Middle Ages*, London–New York, 1974

Frati, L. 'Tradizioni storiche del Pozzo di S. Patrizio', *Giornale storico della letteratura italiana*, 17 (1891), 46–79

Friedel, V. H. and K. Meyer. *La Vision de Tondale (Tnudgal): textes français, anglo-normand et irlandais*, Paris, 1907

Fritzsche, C. 'Die lateinischen Visionen des Mittelalters bis zur Mitte des 12 Jahrhunderts', *Romanische Forschungen*, 2 (1886), 247–79 and 3 (1887), 331–69

Gardiner, E. (ed.) *Visions of Heaven and Hell before Dante*, New York, 1989

Garnier, F. *Le Langage de l'image au Moyen Age: signification et symbolique*, Paris, 1982

Gaster, M. 'Hebrew Visions of Hell and Paradise', *Journal of the Royal Asiatic Society, New Series*, 25 (1893), 571–611

Gatti Perer, M. L. (ed) *La Gerusalemme celeste: catalogo della mostra*, Milano, Università Cattolica del S. Cuore, 20 maggio–5 giugno 1983, Milan, 1983

Gatto, G. 'Le Voyage au Paradis: la christianisation des traditions folkloriques au Moyen Age', *Annales: Economies, Sociétés, Civilisations*, 34 (1979), 929–42

Gendronneau, P. *De l'Influence du Bouddhisme sur la figuration des enfers médiévaux*, Nîmes, 1922

Genicot, L. 'Mélanges: l'Occident du xe au xiie siècle, *Revue d'histoire ecclésiastique* 78 (1983), 397–429

Giamatti, A. B. *The Earthly Paradise and the Renaissance Epic*, Princeton, 1966

Gianfreda, G. *La Cattedrale di Otranto*, Galatina, 1975

Gilson, E. *Dante et la philosophie*, 2nd edition, Paris, 1953

Giontella, G. *Tuscania attraverso i secoli*, Tuscania, 1980

Gmelin, H. 'L'ispirazione iconografica nella "Divina Commedia"', *Il Veltro*, 3 (1959), 13–16

Gousset, M-T. 'La Représentation de la Jérusalem céleste à l'époque carolingienne, *Cahiers archéologiques*, 23 (1974), 47–60

Grabar, A. *Christian Iconography: A Study of its Origins*, London, 1969

'L'Iconographie du ciel dans l'art chrétien de l'Antiquité et du haut Moyen Age', *Cahiers archéologiques*, 30 (1982), 5–24

Grabar, A. and C. Nordenfalk. *Romanesque Painting from the Eleventh to the Thirteenth Century*, translated by S. Gilbert, 1958

Graf, A. *Miti, leggende e superstizioni del Medio Evo*, 2 vols., Turin, 1892–3

'A proposito della "Visio Pauli"', *Giornale storico della letteratura italiana*, 11 (1888), 344–62

Grana, G. 'Canto xxxii: l'Apocalisse di Dante' in *Lettura critica della 'Divina Commedia'*, II: *Purgatorio*, ed. by T. Di Salvo, Florence, 1969, p. 286–94

Grimm, R. R. *Paradisus coelestis, Paradisus terrestris: zur Auslegungsgeschichte des Paradieses im Abendland bis zum 1200*, Munich, 1977

Grof, S. and C. *Beyond Death: The Gates of Consciousness*, London, 1980

Grossi, G. B. B. 'Di Alberico e della sua visione', *Bibliografia Cassinese*, quoted in full by T. Vitti in 'Le Origini della "Divina Commedia"', *L'Alighieri*, 1 (1890), pp. 37–9

Guercio, L. *Di alcuni rapporti tra le visioni medievali e la 'Divina Commedia'*, Rome, 1909

Bibliography

Guiral, J. 'Le Goff (Jacques): "La Naissance du Purgatoire"', *Archives de sciences sociales des religions*, 53 (1982), 318–19

Gurevič, A. J. 'Au Moyen Age: conscience individuelle et image de l'au-delà', *Annales: Economies, Societés, Civilisations*, 37 (1982), 255–75

'Per un'antropologia delle visioni ultraterrene nella cultura occidentale del Medioevo' in *La semiotica nei paesi slavi: programmi, problemi, analisi*, ed. by C. Prevignano, Milan, 1977, pp. 443–62

'Popular and Scholarly Medieval Cultural Traditions: Notes in the Margin of Jacques Le Goff's Book', *Journal of Medieval History*, 9 (1983), 71–90

Hall, J. *Dictionary of Subjects and Symbols in Art*, London, 1974, revised edition, 1979

Harvey, P. (ed.) *The Oxford Companion to Classical Literature*, London, 1937, reprinted 1974

Haskins, C. H. *The Renaissance of the Twelfth Century*, Cambridge (Mass.), and London, 2nd edition 1955 (1st edition 1927)

Hazeltine, H. D. 'Roman and Canon Law in the Middle Ages' in *The Cambridge Medieval History*, v, *Contest of Empire and Papacy*, 1929, pp. 697–764

Heitz, C. 'Retentissement de l'Apocalypse dans l'art de l'époque carolingienne' in *L'Apocalypse de Jean: traditions exégétiques et iconographiques, IIIe–XIIIe siècles, Actes du colloque de la Fondation Hardt, 29 févier–3 mars 1976*, ed. Y. Christe, Geneva, 1979, pp. 217–43

Hetherington, P. *Pietro Cavallini: A Study in the Art of Late Medieval Rome*, London, 1979

Holdsworth, C. J. 'Eleven Visions Connected with the Cistercian Monastery of Stratford Langthorne', *Commentarii Cistercienses*, 13 (1962), 185–204

'Visions and Visionaries in the Middle Ages', *History*, 48 (1963), 141–53

Hughes, R. *Heaven and Hell in Western Art*, London, 1968

Huxley, A. *Heaven and Hell*, London, 1956

Interpreter's Dictionary of the Bible, The, ed. by J. A. Buttrick, 4 vols., New York, 1962; supplementary vol. 1976

Jaconizzi, G. *Il Precursore immediato della 'Divina Commedia'*, Udine, 1911

James, M. R. *Apocrypha Anecdota*, 2 vols., *Texts and Studies*, ed. by J. A. Robinson, Cambridge, 1893 and 1897

The Apocryphal New Testament, London, 1924, reprinted 1953

'Irish Apocrypha', *Journal of Theological Studies*, 20 (1919), 9–16

The Lost Apocrypha of the Old Testament, their Titles and Fragments, London, 1920

James, M. R. and J. A. Robinson. *The Gospel according to Peter and the Revelation of Peter: two lectures on the newly recovered fragments together with the Greek texts*, London, 1892

Jeauneau, E. *La Philosophie médiévale*, Paris, 1963, 3rd edition, Paris, 1975

Jung, C. G. *The Archetypes and the Collective Unconscious*, translated by R. F. C. Hull, New York, 1959

(ed.) *Man and his Symbols*, London, 1964

Kamlah, W. *Apokalypse und Geschichtstheologie: die mittelalterliche Auslegung der Apokalypse vor Joachim von Fiore, Historisches Studien*, 285, Berlin, 1935

Klein, P. K. 'Les Cycles de l'Apocalypse du haut Moyen Age (ixe–xiiie siècles) in *L'Apocalypse de Jean: traditions exégétiques et iconographiques, IIIe–XIIIe siècles, Actes du colloque de la Fondation Hardt, 29 février–3 mars 1976*, ed. Y. Christe, Geneva, 1979, pp. 135–86

Knight, W. F. Jackson. *Elysion: On Ancient Greek and Roman Beliefs concerning a Life after Death: with an introduction by G. Wilson Knight*, London, 1970

Krapp, G. P. *The Legend of Saint Patrick's Purgatory: Its Later Literary History*, Baltimore, 1900

Kretzenbacher, L. *Die Seelenwaage*, Klagenfurt, 1958

Bibliography

Labitte, C. 'La "Divine Comédie" avant Dante', *Revue des Deux Mondes*, 31 (1842), 704–42

Ladner, G. B. *The Idea of Reform: Its Impact on Christian Thought and Action in the Age of the Fathers*, Cambridge (Mass.), 1959

'Medieval and Modern Understanding of Symbolism: A Comparison', *Speculum*, 54 (1979), 223–56; also in *Images and Ideas in the Middle Ages*, Rome, 1983, pp. 239–82

Lamborn Wilson, P. *Angels*, London, 1980

Lamirande, E. 'Jérusalem céleste', *Dictionnaire de Spiritualité*, 8 vols., Paris, 1932–72, VIII, 1974, pp. 944–58

Larousse Encyclopedia of Byzantine and Medieval Art, ed. by R. Huyghe, London, 1958

Le Bras, G. 'Notes pour servir à l'histoire des collections canoniques: v – "Judicia Theodori"', *Revue historique de droit français et étranger*, Series 4, 10 (1931), 95–115

'Pénitentiels', *Dictionnaire de Théologie Catholique*, ed. by A. Vacant, E. Mangenot and E. Amann, Paris, 1909–50, XII, 1933, cols. 1160–79

Le Don, G. 'Structures et significations de l'imagerie médiévale de l'enfer', *Cahiers de civilisation médiévale*, 22 (1979), 363–72

Leff, G. A. *Medieval Thought*, London, 1958

Le Goff, J. 'Dreams in the Culture and Collective Psychology of the Medieval West' in *Time, Work and Culture in the Middle Ages*, translated by A. Goldhammer from the original edition of 1977, Chicago, 1980, pp. 201–4

La Naissance du Purgatoire, Paris, 1981

'Le Purgatoire entre l'enfer et le paradis', *La Maison-Dieu*, 144 (1980), 103–38

Lentini, A. 'Alberico di Montecassino' in *Dizionario biografico degli italiani*, 1, pp. 645–66, Rome, 1960

Leonardi, A. M. Chiavacci. 'Le beatitudini e la struttura poetica del "Purgatorio"', *Giornale storico della letteratura italiana*, 161 (1984), 1–29

Lerner, R. 'Jacques Le Goff: "La Naissance du Purgatoire"', *American Historical Review*, 87 (1982), 1374–5

Leslie, S. *Saint Patrick's Purgatory: A Record from History and Literature, compiled by S. Leslie*, London, 1932

Lewis, C. S. *The Discarded Image: An Introduction to Medieval and Renaissance Literature*, Cambridge, 1964

Lewis, R. E. 'More New Manuscripts of Pope Innocent III's "De Miseria humanae conditionis" (concluded)', *Manuscripta*, 19 (1975), 119–22

Liestol, K. *Draumkvoede: A Norwegian Visionary Poem from the Middle Ages, Studia Norvegica*, 3, Oslo, 1946

Lightfoot, J. B. *et al.* (eds.), *Excluded Books of the Old Testament, translated by J. B. Lightfoot, M. R. James, H. B. Swete and others, with an introduction by J. Armitage Robinson*, London [1927]

Lodolo, G. 'Il tema simbolico del Paradiso nella tradizione monastica dell'Occidente latino (secoli VI–XII): lo spazio del simbolo', *Aevum*, 51 (1977), 252–88

'Il tema simbolico del Paradiso nella tradizione monastica dell'Occidente latino (secoli VI–XII): lo svelamento del simbolo', *Aevum*, 52 (1978), 177–94

Louandre, C. 'Le Diable: sa vie et son intervention dans les choses humaines', *Revue des deux mondes*, 31 (1842), 568–95

Lovejoy, A. O. *The Great Chain of Being: A Study in the History of an Idea*, Cambridge (Mass.), 1936

Luzzatto, G. *Storia economica d'Italia*, 1, *L'antichità e il Medio Evo*, Rome, 1949

MacCulloch, J. A. *Early Christian Visions of the Other-World*, Edinburgh, 1912

McDannell, C. and B. Lang. *Heaven: A History*, New Haven and London, 1988

McGinn, B. *Visions of the End: Apocalyptic Traditions in the Middle Ages*, New York, 1979

Bibliography

McNeill, J. T. and H. M. Gamer. *Medieval Handbooks of Penance*, New York, 1938

Mâle, E. *The Gothic Image: Religious Art in France of the Thirteenth Century*, translated by D. Nussey from the French edition of 1913, New York, 1958, reprinted 1972

Religious Art in France. The Twelfth Century: A Study of the Origins of Medieval Iconography, ed. by H. Bober and translated by M. Matthews from the French edition of 1922, Princeton, 1978

Mancini, F. 'Un *auctoritas* di Dante', *Studi Danteschi*, 45 (1968), pp. 95–119

Mangenot, E. 'Apocalypse', *Dictionnaire de Théologie Catholique*, ed. by A. Vacant, E. Mangenot and E. Amann, Paris, 1909–50, 1, cols. 1463–79

'Apocalypses apocryphes', *Dictionnaire de Théologie Catholique* (see above), 1, cols. 1479–98

Mango, F. 'Due visioni predantesche' in *Note Letterarie*, Palermo, 1894, pp. 110–22

Manselli, R. 'Bernardo di Chiaravalle, santo', *Enciclopedia Dantesca*, 1, Rome, 1970, pp. 601–5

La Religion populaire au moyen âge: problèmes de méthode et d'histoire, Montreal, 1975

Mariani, V. 'Dante e Giotto' in 'Dante e Giotto: Atti del Convegno di studi promosso dalla Casa di Dante in Roma e dalla Società Dante Alighieri, Roma, 9–10 novembre 1967', *Il Veltro*, 7 (1968), 5–18

Marshall, J. C. D. 'Three Problems in the "Vision of Tundal"', *Medium Aevum*, 44 (1975), 14–22

Matalon, S. and F. Mazzini. *Affreschi del Tre e Quattrocento in Lombardia*, Milan, 1958

Mauro, G. 'Conobbe Dante il "De Republica" di Cicerone?', *Giornale italiano di filologia*, 11 (1958), 232–5

Mazal, O. *Buchkunst der Romanik*, Graz, 1978

Mazzoni, F. 'Canto XXXI, a cura di Francesco Mazzoni' in *Lectura Dantis Scaligera: Purgatorio*, ed. by M. Marcazzan and S. Pasquazi, Florence, 1971, pp. 1141–88

Mazzucco, C. 'La Gerusalemme celeste dell'"Apocalisse" nei Padri' in *La Gerusalemme celeste*, ed. by M. L. Gatti Perer, Milan, 1983, pp. 49–75

Menzies, A. (ed.) *Ante-Nicene Christian Library, Additional Volume, containing early Christian works discovered since the completion of the Series, and Selections from the Commentaries of Origen*, Edinburgh, 1897

Michaud-Quantin, P. 'A propos des premières "Summae confessorum"', *Recherches de théologie ancienne médiévale*, 26 (1959), 264–306

Sommes de casuistique et manuels de confession au moyen âge (XII–XVI siècles), Louvain, 1962

Michel, A. 'Purgatoire', *Dictionnaire de Théologie Catholique*, ed. by A. Vacant, E. Mangenot and E. Amann, vol. XIII, Paris, 1936, cols. 1163–326

Migliorini Fissi, R. *Dante*, Florence, 1979

Mila y Fontanals, M. 'Antecedentes de la "Divina Commedia"', in *Obras completas*, ed. by D. Marcelino Menéndez y Pelayo, Barcelona, 1892, IV, pp. 481–6

Miller, M. *Chartres Cathedral: The Medieval Stained Glass and Sculpture*, London, 1980

Milosevic, D. *The Last Judgment*, translated from the German by G. H. Genzel and H. H. Rosenwald, Pictorial Library of Eastern Church Art 3, Recklinghausen, 1967

Mirra, A. 'La Visione di Alberico', *Miscellanea Cassinese*, 11 (1932), 33–79

Monnier, J. *La Descente aux enfers: étude de pensée religieuse d'art et de littérature, thèse présentée à la faculté de théologie protestante de Paris*, Paris, 1904

Moore, E. 'The Classification of the Sins in the *Inferno* and *Purgatorio*' in *Studies in Dante*, II, Oxford, 1899, reprinted 1968, pp. 152–209

'The Date assumed by Dante for the Vision of the "Divina Commedia"', *Studies in Dante*, III, Oxford, 1903, reprinted 1968, pp. 144–77

'The Reproaches of Beatrice', *Studies in Dante*, III, as above, pp. 221–52

'Sta Lucia in the "Divina Commedia"', *Studies in Dante*, IV, Oxford, 1917, reprinted 1968, pp. 235–55

Studies in Dante, 4 vols., Oxford, 1896–1917, reprinted London, 1968

Bibliography

Moraldi, L. *L'aldilà dell'uomo nelle civilità babilonese, egizia, greca, latina, ebraica, cristiana e musulmana*, Milan, 1985

Morgan, N. *Early Gothic Manuscripts 1190–1250*, London, 1982

Morisani, O. *Gli affreschi di Sant'Angelo in Formis*, Naples, 1962

Mormone, R. *La Chiesa trecentesca di Donnaregina*, Naples, 1977

Morris, C. *The Discovery of the Individual: 1050–1200*, New York–London, 1972

'Individualism in Twelfth-Century Religion: Further Reflections', *Journal of Ecclesiastical History*, 31 (1980), 195–206

Mulhall, M. 'The Celtic Sources of the "Divina Commedia"', *Dublin Review*, 119 (1896), 343–52

Murray, Sister C. *Rebirth and Afterlife: A Study of the Transmutation of some Pagan Imagery in early Christian Funerary Art*, BAR International Series 100, Oxford, 1981

Murray, J. 'Dante and Medieval Irish Visions' in *An Irish Tribute to Dante on the Seventh Centenary of his Birth*, Dublin, 1965, pp. 57–95

Musca, G. 'Dante e Beda' in *Studi storici in onore di Ottorino Bertolini*, II, 1972, pp. 497–524

Mussafia, A. 'Sulla visione di Tundalo', *Sitzungsberichte der philosophisch-historischen Klasse der Kaiserlichen Akademie der Wissenschaften*, 67 (1871), 157–206

Nardi, B. *Dante e la cultura medievale*, Bari, 1942

'Intorno al sito del Purgatorio e al mito dantesco dell'Eden', *Giornale Dantesco*, 25 (1922), 289–300; also in *Saggi di filosofia dantesca*, Milan, 1930, pp. 347–74

'Pretesi fonti della "Divina Commedia"' in *Nuova Antologia*, 464 (1955), 383–98

Neveux, H. 'Les Lendemains de la mort dans les croyances occidentales (vers 1250–vers 1300)', *Annales: Economies, Sociétés, Civilisations*, 34 (1979), 245–63

Niemann, T. C. 'Pearl and the Christian Otherworld', *Genre*, 7 (1974), 213–32

Nocke, F-J. *Escatologia*, translated by E. Gatti from the German edition of 1982, Brescia, 1984

Nolan, B. *The Gothic Visionary Perspective*, Princeton, 1977

Novati, F. 'Un poema francescano del Dugento' in *Attraverso il Medioevo*, Bari, 1905, pp. 7–115

Ntedika, J. *L'Evocation de l'au-delà dans les prières pour les morts: Etude de patristique et de liturgie latine, IVe, VIIIe s.*, Louvain, 1971

Nutt, A. 'The Happy Otherworld in the Mythico-Romantic Literature of the Irish: The Celtic Doctrine of Rebirth – An Essay in Two Sections', vol. II of *The Voyage of Bran Son of Febal to the Land of the Living*, ed. by K. Meyer, 2 vols., London, 1905

Olivar, A. '"Liber infernalis" o "Visio Pauli"', *Sacris Erudiri*, 18 (1967–8), 550–4

Ombres, R. 'The Doctrine of Purgatory according to St Thomas Aquinas', *The Downside Review*, 99 (1981), 279–87

'Images of Healing: The Making of the Traditions concerning Purgatory', *Eastern Churches Review*, 8 (1976), 128–38

'Latins and Greeks in Debate over Purgatory, 1230–1439', *Journal of Ecclesiastical History*, 35 (1984), 1–14

The Theology of Purgatory, Theology Today Series 24, Cork, 1978

Owen, D. D. R. *The Vision of Hell: Infernal Journeys in Medieval French Literature*, Edinburgh–London, 1970

Ozanam, A-F. 'Du cycle poétique et légendaire auquel appartient la "Divine Comédie"' in *Dante et la philosophie catholique au treizieme siècle*, Paris, 1839, pp. 325–42

'Des sources poétiques de la "Divine Comédie"' in *Les Poètes franciscains en Italie au treizieme siècle*, 7th edition Paris [1913], pp. 307–416

Palgen, R. *Mittelalterliche Eschatologie in Dantes 'Komodie'*, Graz, 1975

Das mittelalterliche Gesicht der Gottlichen Komodie: Quellenstudien zu 'Inferno' und 'Purgatorio', Heidelberg, 1935

Bibliography

'La "Visione di Tundalo" nella "Commedia" di Dante', *Convivium*, 37 (1969), 129–47

Parodi, E. G. 'F. Novati: "La 'Navigatio Sancti Brendani' in antico veneziano", Bergamo 1892', *Romania*, 22 (1893), 304–10

'Il primo viaggio di Virgilio attraverso l'Inferno' in *Fanfulla della Domenica*, 37 (1915), 1–2

Parrinder, G. (ed.) *An Illustrated History of the World's Religions*, Feltham, 1983

Pascal, C. *Le credenze d'oltretomba nelle opere letterarie dell'antichità classica*, 2 vols., original edition Catania, 1912, 2nd edition Turin, 1924

Pascoli, G. *Minerva oscura*, Livorno, 1898

Pasquazi, S. 'Antinferno', *Enciclopedia Dantesca*, 1, Rome, 1970, pp. 300–2

'Antipurgatorio', *Enciclopedia Dantesca*, 1, Rome, 1970, pp. 304–6

Patch, H. R. *The Other World, According to Descriptions in Medieval Literature*, Cambridge (Mass.), 1950

Paul, J. 'Jacques Le Goff: "La Naissance du Purgatoire"', *Revue de l'histoire de l'église de France*, 68 (1982), 284–6

Payne, R. 'Pearl: A Revelation of its Relationship to the "Divina Commedia"' (unpublished dissertation, University of Denver) 1984

Pelleri, M. A. *La Pittura a Firenze nei secoli XIII–XVI*, Florence, 1978

Peri, H. 'The Original Plan of the "Divine Comedy"', *Journal of the Warburg and Courtauld Institutes*, 18 (1955), 189–210

Perry, M. P. 'On the Psychostasis in Christian Art', *Burlington Magazine*, 22 (1912–13), pp. 94–104 and 208–18

Petrocchi, G. *L'Inferno di Dante*, Milan, 1978

Il Paradiso di Dante, Milan, 1978

Pietrobono, L. *Dal centro al cerchio: la struttura morale della 'Divina Commedia'*, Turin [1923]

Piolanti, A. 'Il dogma del Purgatorio', *Euntes Docete*, 6 (1953), 287–311

Porter, J. R. 'Muhammed's Journey to Heaven' in *The Journey to the Other World*, ed. by H. R. Ellis Davidson, Cambridge, 1975, pp. 1–26

Proto, E. *L'Apocalisse nella "Divina Commedia"*, Naples, 1905

Puppo, M. 'Beatrice', *Cultura e Scuola: volume speciale sotto gli auspici del comitato nazionale per le celebrazioni del VII centenario della nascita di Dante*, 13–14 (1965), 356–61

Purce, J. *The Mystic Spiral: Journey of the Soul*, London, 1974

Rajna, P. 'La genesi della "Divina Commedia"' in *Vita italiana nel Trecento II: Conferenze tenute a Firenze nel 1891*, Florence, 1892, pp. 225–68, reprinted Milan, 1908, pp. 152–82

Reau, L. 'Escatologia: il mondo cristiano' in *Enciclopedia Universale dell'Arte*, 16 vols., Rome–Venice, 1958–67, IV (1960), cols. 843–50

Iconographie de l'art chrétien, 3 vols., Paris 1955–9

Ricciotti, G. *L'Apocalisse di Paolo siriaca*, 2 vols., Brescia, 1932

Rizzatti, M. L. *Dante*, Florence, 1976

Robbe-Grillet, A. *Pour un nouveau roman*, Paris, 1963

Roberts, A. and J. Donaldson (eds.) *Apocryphal Gospels, Acts and Revelations*, translated by A. Walker, Ante-Nicene Library XVI, Edinburgh, 1870

Robinson, J. A. *Barnabas, Hermas and the Didache*, London, 1920

Rosso Ubigli, L. 'Dalla "Nuova Gerusalemme" alla "Gerusalemme celeste": contributo per la comprensione dell'Apocalittica', *Henoch*, 3 (1981), 69–80

Rüegg, A. *Die Jenseitsvorstellungen vor Dante und die übringen literarischen Voraussetzungen der 'Divina Commedia'*, 2 vols., Einsiedeln–Cologne, 1945

Russo, L. 'Genesi e unità della "Commedia"' in *Problemi di metodo critico*, Bari, 1929, pp. 39–79, reprinted in *Ritratti e disegni storici* (see below), pp. 209–43

'La letteratura religiosa del Duecento' in *Ritratti e disegni storici* (see below), p. 75–150

Ritratti e disegni storici, serie prima: studii sul Due e Trecento, Genoa, 1946, 3rd edition, Florence, 1960

Russo, V. *Il romanzo teologico: sondaggi sulla 'Comedia' di Dante*, Naples, 1984

Bibliography

Salinari, G. 'Il comico nella "Divina Commedia" ', *Belfagor: Rassegna di varia umanità*, 10 (1955), 623–41

Salmi, M. *L'Abbazia di Pomposa*, Rome, 1936, 2nd edition Milan, 1966
Italian Miniatures, translated by E. Borghese-Mann from the Italian edition of 1954, London, 1957

Sanminiatelli, B. 'Le Leggende celtiche e la "Divina Commedia" ', *Il Veltro*, 1 (1957), 43–50; also in *Maestro Dante*, Milan, 1962, pp. 12–32

Santoro, M. 'Virgilio personaggio della "Divina Commedia" ' in *Cultura e Scuola: volume speciale sotto gli auspici del comitato nazionale per le celebrazioni del VII centenario della nascita di Dante*, 13–14 (1965), 342–55

Sauerländer, W. *Gothic Sculpture in France 1140–1270*, with photographs by M. Hirmer, translated by J. Sondheimer from the German edition of 1970, London, 1972

Sayers, D. *Further Papers on Dante*, London, 1957

Scarano, N. *Prolegomeni al poema sacro*, Campobasso, 1918

Schmidt, P. G. 'The Vision of Thurkill', *Journal of the Warburg and Courtauld Institutes*, 41 (1978), 50–64

Schmitz, H. J. *Die Bussbücher und die Bussdisziplin der Kirche*, Mainz, 1883, reprinted Graz, 1958
Die Bussbücher und das Kanonische Bussverfahren, Dusseldorf, 1898, reprinted Graz, 1958

Segre, C. 'L'invenzione dell'altro mondo', *Autografo: Quadrimestale del Centro di Ricerca sulla tradizione manoscritta di autori contemporanei*, Università di Pavia, 1 (1984), 7–14
'L'*itinerarium animae* nel Duecento e Dante', *Letture Classensi*, 13 (1984), 9–32

Selmer, C. 'The Beginnings of the St Brendan Legend on the Continent', *The Catholic Historical Review*, 29 (1943), 169–76

Severin, T. *The Brendan Voyage*, London, 1978

Seymour, St John D. 'Irish Versions of the Vision of Paul', *The Journal of Theological Studies*, 24 (1922), 54–9
Irish Visions of the Other-World: A Contribution to the Study of Mediaeval Visions, London, 1930
'The Seven Heavens in Irish Literature', *Zeitschrift für Keltische Philologie*, 14 (1932), 18–30

Silverstein, T. 'Dante and the Legend of the "Mi'raj": The Problem of Islamic Influence on the Christian Literature of the Otherworld', *Journal of Near Eastern Studies*, 11 (1952), 89–110 and 187–97
'Dante and the "Visio Pauli" ', *Modern Language Notes*, 47 (1932), 397–9.
' "Inferno", XII, 100–26, and the "Visio Karoli Crassi" ', *Modern Language Notes*, 51 (1936), 449–52
'The Vision of Saint Paul: New Links and Patterns in the Western Tradition', *Archives d'histoire doctrinale et littéraire du moyen âge*, 34 (1959), 199–248

Simon, U. *Heaven in the Christian Tradition*, London, 1958

Sims-Williams, P. 'The Visionary Celt: the Construction of an Ethnic Preconception', *Cambridge Medieval Celtic Studies*, 11 (1986), pp. 71–96

Singleton, C. S. *The Divine Comedy, translated with a commentary by C. S. Singleton*, 6 vols., London, 1971–5
Journey to Beatrice, Dante Studies, 11, Cambridge (Mass.), 1958, Part 11, pp. 141–287

Sivo, V. 'Popoli e paesi nell'Alto medioevo: Spoleto 23–9 aprile 1981', *Quaderni medievali*, 12 (1981), 199–211

Smalley, B. *The Study of the Bible in the Middle Ages*, London, 1941

Smart, A. *The Dawn of Italian Painting 1250–1400*, Oxford, 1978

Southern, R. W. 'Between Heaven and Hell', *The Times Literary Supplement*, 18 July 1982, pp. 651–2
The Making of the Middle Ages, London, 1953, reprinted 1967

Spicq, P. C. *Esquisse d'une histoire de l'exégèse latine au Moyen Age*, Paris, 1944

Bibliography

Stevenson, J. 'Ascent through the Heavens, from Egypt to Ireland', *Cambridge Medieval Celtic Studies*, 5 (1983), 21–35

Stone, M. E. 'The Metamorphoses of Ezra: Jewish Apocalypse and Medieval Vision', *Journal of Theological Studies, New Series*, 33 (1982), 1–18

Stubblevine, J. H. *Giotto: The Arena Chapel Frescoes*, London, 1969

Thérive, A. 'L'Ancêtre de la "Divine Comédie"', *Revue Politique et Littéraire*, 59 (1921), 671–3 and 700–4

Thorlby, A. 'The Individual in the Mediaeval World: Dante's "Divina Commedia"' in *Literature and Western Civilisation*, ed. by D. Daiches and A. Thorlby, 3 vols., London, 1972–4, II (1973), pp. 601–42

Thurlow, G. *Biblical Myths and Mysteries*, London, 1974

Torraca, F. 'I Precursori della "Divina Commedia": lettura fatta nella sala di Dante in Orsanmichele il 6 aprile 1905' in *V Lectura Dantis: le opere minori di Dante Alighieri*, Florence, 1906, and in *Nuovi studi danteschi nel VI centenario della morte di Dante*, Naples, 1921, pp. 269–307

Torri, A. 'Su l'inedito comento di Francesco da Buti alla "Divina Commedia": lettera del Dott. Alessandro Torri al chiarissimo signore il Cavaliere Giuseppe Bernardoni a Milano', Pisa, 15.10.1845 in *Studii inediti su Dante*, ed. by S. Centofanti, A. Torri, Visc. Colomb de Batines *et al.*, Florence, 1846

Toynbee, P. *A Dictionary of Proper Names and Notable Matters in the Works of Dante*, revised by C. S. Singleton, London, 1968

Tristram, E. W. *English Medieval Wall Painting: the Thirteenth Century*, 2 vols., London, 1950
English Medieval Wall Painting: the Twelfth Century, London, 1944
English Wall Painting of the Fourteenth Century, London, 1955

Ullmann, W. *The Individual and Society in the Middle Ages*, Baltimore, 1966

Ursino, G. *La struttura del poema di Dante*, Rome, 1959

Valli, L. 'La struttura morale dell'universo dantesco' in *La struttura morale dell'universo dantesco*, Rome, 1935, pp. 151–69

Vallone, A. 'Beatrice', *Enciclopedia Dantesca*, I, Rome, 1970, pp. 542–51

Van Der Meer, F. *Apocalypse: Visions from the Book of Revelation in Western Art*, London, 1978

Van Os, A. B. *Religious Visions: the Development of the Eshatological Elements in Mediaeval English Religious Literature*, Amsterdam, 1932

Vantaggi, R. *Siena, città d'arte*, Terni, 1977

Vasoli, C. 'Alano de Lilla', *Enciclopedia Dantesca*, I, Rome, 1970, pp. 89–91

Villari, P. *Antiche leggende e tradizioni che illustrano la 'Divina Commedia', precedute da alcune osservazioni di P. Villari*, Pisa, 1865, reprinted [Bologna] 1979

Vinton, F. 'St. Patrick's Purgatory, and the "Inferno" of Dante', *Bibliotheca Sacra*, 30 (1873), 275–86

Vitti, T. 'Le origini della "Divina Commedia"', *L'Alighieri*, I (1890), 33–45

Vogel, C. 'Les "Libri Paenitentiales"', *Typologie des sources du Moyen Age occidental*, 27, Turnhout, 1978

Volpe, C. 'La pittura gotica da Lippo di Dalmasio a Giovanni da Modena', *La Basilica di San Petronio*, I, ed. M. Fanti *et al.*, Bologna, 1983, pp. 213–94

Vossler, K. *La fonte della 'Divina Commedia' studiata nella sua genesi e interpretata*, 2 vols., 2nd edition, Bari, 1927

Ward, H. L. D. *Catalogue of Romances in the Department of Manuscripts in the British Museum*, 3 vols, vol. 2, London, 1893
'The Vision of Thurkill', *Journal of the British Archeological Association*, 31 (1875), 420–59

Watmough, J. R. *Orphism*, Cambridge, 1934

Weitzmann, K. *Art in the Medieval West and its Contacts with Byzantium*, London, 1982

Bibliography

Wetherbee, W. *Platonism and Poetry in the Twelfth Century: The Literary Influence of the School of Chartres*, Princeton, 1972

Wettstein, J. *Sant'Angelo in Formis et la peinture médiévale en Campanie*, Geneva, 1960

White, J. *Duccio: Tuscan Art and the Medieval Workshop*, London, 1977

Wilkins, E. H. 'Dante and the Mosaics of his Bel San Giovanni', *Dante in America: The First Two Centuries*, ed. A. B. Giammatti, New York, 1983, pp. 144–59

Wright, T. *St Patrick's Purgatory: An Essay on the Legends of Purgatory, Hell, and Paradise, Current during the Middle Ages*, London, 1844

Zabughin, V. *Dante e l'iconografia dell'oltretomba: arte bizantina-romanica-gotica, Codices e Vaticanis selecti: i Codici Istoriati di Dante nella biblioteca Vaticana*, Milan–Rome, 1921

L'oltretomba classico, medievale, dantesco nel Rinascimento, Florence–Rome, 1922

'Quattro "geroglifici" danteschi', *Giornale storico della letteratura italiana*, Supplement, 1921, 505–63

Zaleski, C. *Otherworld Journeys: Accounts of Near-Death Experience in Medieval and Modern Times*, New York, 1987

Zanfrognini, P. *Di due innavvertite fonti apocalittiche della 'Divina Commedia'*, Modena, 1911

Zingarelli, N. *Dante*, Milan, no date

'Il viaggio di un diplomatico al Purgatorio', *Fanfulla della Domenica*, 19 July 1903

Index

Index

infernal rivers, 29
living character in, 55
other rulers, 67
political nature of, 3
prayer for dead stressed, 152
sins, 113, 116
as source for the *Comedy*, 6
Chilperic, Visions of, 17, 52, 197, **216**
Christian tradition, popular, 1–3
chroniclers of visions, 4
Cicero
  Somnium Scipionis, 85, 176, 196, **202**
  Tusculan Disputations, 196, **202**
Comedy, the
  choice of characters, 53–4, 59–60, 67
  classification of sins, 129–34
  as climax to the visions, 6
  episodes reminiscent of visions, 14
  final vision foreshadowed, 178–84
  guides, 84–5
  iconography of Purgatory, 156–60
  influence of intellectual developments on, 8
  inhabitants of other world, 78–82
  precedent for presentation of earthly and
    celestial Paradises, 177–8
  presentation of character, 71–2
  purpose, 5
  reference to vision literature, 5
  relationship to popular tradition, 7–9
  sources for, 5–7
  treatment of barratry, 21
  use of motifs of other world, 46–7
confession manuals
  classification of sins, 128–9, 131
  expansion in production, 126
  law and theology reflected, 112
  purpose, 110
  relationship between punishment and
    penance, 119
  relationship with visions, 119, 127
  scheme of capital vices, 122, 127
  as source for classification of sins, 110
Cormachus, King, 62–3
Cour du Paradis, La, 199, **217**
critical approaches, 5–8, 11–13
Cummean, Penitential of, 115
Curtius, E. R., 7, 51, 66
custody of a soul, contest for, 11, 47, 70

Delumeau, J., 112, 122
Drythelm, Vision of, 197, **217**
  guide, 90, 103
  Hell in, 14
  Paradise in, 170
  purgation in, 150
  as source for the *Comedy*, 6

Ecclesia, 87
Elijah, Apocalypse of, 196, **202**
Elizabeth of Schönau, 162, 198, **217**
English noble, an, 63
English Presbyter, Vision of an, 198, **217**
I Enoch, 28, 160, 196, **203**
II Enoch, 114, 175, 196, **203**
IV Esdras, 52, 168, 175, 196
  Apocalypse of Esdras, **203**
  Apocalypse of Sedrach, **203**
  Visio Beati Esdrae, 21, **204**
Etienne de Bourbon, 17, 158, 198, **218**

Fire motif, 156–7
Fulbert, Vision of, 198, **218**
Furseus, Vision of, 6, 197, **219**

Geoffrey of Vinsauf, 69
German count, Vision of a, 198, **219**
Giacomino da Verona, 20, 58, 180, 199, **219**
Godeschalc, Vision of, 198, **220**
  biblically defined sins, 113
  guides, 64, 93, 96, 98, 100, 102
  historical characters, 59
  immersion motif, 33
  infernal river, 29
  number of characters in, 56
  Paradise in, 173
  parallel to traitors in Cocytus, 120
  presentation of character, 54, 63–4
  principle of punishment, 120
  wheel motif, 121
Godeschalcus Dasonide, 63–4
goldsmith, the, 69–70, 93–4
Gregory the Great, 197, 226, 229
  account of bridge motif, 33
  allegorical description of Paradise, 169
  contribution to doctrine of purgatory, 150
  definition of capital vices, 122
  papal authority conferred on visions, 2
Gregory of Tours, 197, 216, 229, 230
Grosseteste, Robert, 126–7
Guibert de Nogent, 198, **220**
guides, 87–107
  abandonment by, 86, 90, 97–100, 102, 105
  choice of, 93–4, 104
  in the *Comedy*, foreshadowed, 85, 94 104–5
  instruction and intervention, 87, 90–2, 95–6,
    104
  as interpreters, 86, 90, 91, 100–1, 104
  as leaders, 86, 90, 96–7, 102, 104
  relationship with visionaries, 87–8, 91, 102–5
  role of: in apocrypha, 86–7; in early
    Christian tradition; 87–9; in classical
    tradition, 85–6; in eighth to eleventh
    centuries, 90–3
  successive, 87–9, 101–2, 104, 105

Index

Index

reflecting moments in the narrative, 11
selection of, 13
see also entries under individual motifs
Moutain of Purgatory, the, 144–62
  precedents for Dante's mountain, 157–8

Nicholas, St, 59, 94, 102
Nicodemus, Gospel of, 197, **205**

Ordericus Vitalis, 198, 232
Orm, Vision of, 198, **224**
Othlo, 3, 59, 198
  vision of the monk Isaac, **225**; guide, 93; fire of
    purgatory in, 153; precedent for Dante,
    158
  vision of a beggar, **225**; Paradise in, 161; places
    for the living in, 55
  vision of a servant, **225**
Ovid, 196, 206
Owen, D. D. R., 12

Pachomius, Life of Saint, 197, **206**
Paradise, Celestial, 58, 177–8, 178–86
Paradise, Earthly, 58, 144, 160–2, 166, 177–8
Paradise, representation of, 166–95
  in the Apocalypse, 167, 173
  before the 4th century, 167
  as celestial spheres, 173, 174–7
  Dante's, foreshadowed in vision, 178–86
  in early visions, 169–72
  history of concept, 166–7
  iconography used for, 172–3
  in late visions, 172–3
  models for, 166
  relation between Earthly and Celestial,
    177–8
  in visual arts, 172, 173, 184, 186–92
Paraldus, Guglielmus, 131, 132
Paul, Apocalypse of, 2, 114, 175, 197, **225**
Paul, Vision of, 197, **225**
  biblical characters, 58
  choice of characters, 52
  motifs in: bridge, 33; cauldron, 18;
    immersion, 31; infernal river, 28–9;
    ladder, 38
  Paradise in, 47, 169
  presentation of characters, 54
  purgatorial area in, 153
  relationship between versions, 48
  Satan in, 22
  sins, 114, 130, 135
penitential books, 115, 116, 117
Penitential, the Roman, 116
Perpetua, Passion of, 41, 150, 197, **206**
Peter, Apocalypse of, 114, 161, 197, **207**
Peter, St, 68, 69, 89, 99, 100
Peter, Vision of, 87, 197, **226**
Pindar, 196

Plato, 28, 113, 125, 149, 175, 196, **207–8**
Plutarch
  Thespesius, Vision of, 85, 125, 149, 176, 196,
    208
  Timarchus, Vision of, 196, **208**
Poor Woman, Vision of a, 52, 198, **226**
Prior, a, 65–6
Punishment, 116–20
Purgatory
  Dante's classification of sin, 132–3
  development of concept, in visions, 149–55
  development of doctrine, 28, 122–3, 128,
    132, 145–9
  iconography of: fire, 156–7; bridge, 157;
    mountain, 157–60
  precedents for Dante's mountain of, 157–8

Rajna, P. 167
Ralph of Coggeshall, 198, 223, 230
Raoul de Houdenc, 38, 199, **227**
Raphael, Archangel, 89, 101, 103
Raymond de Penyafort, 128–9
Reichenau Apocryphon, 197, **209**
Representations of the other world
  law and confession manuals reflected in,
    118–19
  relationship with the *Comedy*, 7–9, 11, 46
  as sources for the *Comedy*, 5–7
  visual, 4–5
  written, 1–4, 201–33
Rhoda, 87
Rimbert, Archbishop
  Life of Anskar, 198, **227**; biblical characters,
    58; descriptions of individuals, 68, 92;
    guides, 92; precedent for Dante's final
    vision, 182; purgation in, 152
Robbe-Grillet, A., 71
Rotcharius, Vision of, 52, 198, **227**
Rüegg, A., 8
Rutebeuf, 199, **228**

St Patrick's Purgatory, 198, **228**
  motifs in: bridge, 35; cauldron, 18; fire, 156;
    immersion, 32; infernal river, 29; wheel,
    154, 156
  parallel to Dante's Purgatory, 159
  Purgatory in, 154–5, 172
  relationship, earthly and celestial Paradise,
    178
  as source for the *Comedy*, 6
Salvius, Vision of, 87, 170, 197, **229**
Satan, presentation of, 21–3
Saturus, Vision of, 52, 87, **209**
Sedrach, Apocalypse of, see under IV Esdras
Servant, Vision of, see under Othlo
Seven Heavens Apocryphon, 197, **209**
Sheol, 2, 14, 167
Sibyl, the, 86

Index

Index

Index of longer quotations from the *Comedy*